DANGER →

Life and Death Stories from the US Navy's *Approach* Magazine

Derek Nelson and Dave Parsons

Motorbooks International
Publishers & Wholesalers ®

First published in 1991 by Motorbooks International
Publishers & Wholesalers, P O Box 2, 729 Prospect Avenue,
Osceola, WI 54020 USA

Motorbooks International books are also available at
discounts in bulk quantity for industrial or sales-promotional
use. For details write to Special Sales Manager at the
Publisher's address

Library of Congress Cataloging-in-Publication Data
Parsons, Dave.
   Danger :   life and death stories from US Navy pilots /
Dave Parsons, Derek Nelson.
    p. cm.
  ISBN 0-87938-517-0
   1. United States. Navy—Aviation—Biography. 2. Fighter
pilots—United States—Biography. I. Nelson, Derek. II. Title.
VG93.P374 1991
358.4′14′092273—dc20
[B]   90–24881

On the front cover: An F-14 Tomcat from VF-101, the "Grim
Reapers," about to touch down. *Michael O'Leary*

Printed and bound in the United States of America

Contents

Acknowledgments	4
Introduction	5
Anymouse's Anniversary	20
Anymouse and His Hairy Tales	22
It Finally Happened	23
—And Then There Were None . . .	24
The Return of Walter Smitty	27
Crank It Right!	29
Time Zero!	30
Only Thunderstorms	32
Over, Under, and Out!	33
Saga of a Sea Squatter	34
In the Beginning	36
Search Discontinued	38
O-Club Saturday Night	40
"Only the BuNo Has Changed . . ."	41
NavCad's Diary	44
. . . Then the Fun Began	45
Wild Ride	46
You Wrote the Caption	48
Remember How Much Fun Flying Used to Be?	48
No Connection	49
First Time	51
No Secret: "I Ejected Underwater"	52
"Here I Go!"	52
. . . No Place to Go but Down!	53
Night Fright	55
Anymouse Special: Divert or Disaster	56
Proficiency Pros?	58
Through a Sheet of Flame	59
Pastry Twist	60
Pucker Factor	61
Bad Day at Black Rock	62
Will to Survive	63
In Extremis	66
Over and Out	69
A Night in the Jungle	69
Wind, Waves and CVs	73
A Collection of Midairs	74
Fire Flight	76
Crusader Crisis	77
Monday, Monday	79
A Most Regrettable Decision	82
Carnival Ride	83
Can of Worms	84
The Case for More and Better Hangar Flying	86
A Wing and a Prayer	88
"I've Got Trouble"	90
Bronco Bustin'	91
Eject! Eject!	93
Home Free	94
Out of Control	95
Nightmare	96
Sixty Seconds to Doomsday	98
We Just Spun It	99
Routine Cross Country	100
Putting Yourself on Report	101
The "Scapegoat"	101
Midair	102
King of the Road	103
Low, Low Approach	105
Phantom Phlameout	106
The Night the World Died	107
Nugget Nightmare	108
Nighttime Eye-Opener	108
Not Just Another Sea Story	109
How Not to Do It!	111
Touch-and-Go with the Grim Reaper	113
Oh What a Night!	114
A Terrible Trip	115
Experience by Proxy	117
Look Out! Midair Collision in the CV Pattern	119
Nightmare	120
The Disappearance	121
Real Aviators Don't Read NATOPS	123
Into the Island: An NFO's Eye View	125
Feast or Famine	127
Hard Knocks	128
Censored-mice Arise!	129
A Look Back: Forty Years of Reminiscing	129
The Marble Theory	134
Living an Approach Article; or, All Is Well and Pressing On	135
My Time	137
A Cold, Rainy December Night	139
Squeaking by a Sandstorm	140
Skiing Lessons from an A-4	142
Night Skimmer	143
"That Was Barbed Wire We Just Flew By!"	144
Somebody Out There Is Trying to Kill Me	146
Needed: A Bigger and Better Anymouse	148
Fuelishness	150
A Night to Remember	151
More than Just a Single-Engine Landing!	153
Wint. '86 Transoceanic Ordeal	156
A Day to Remember	158
The World's Greatest Attack Pilot	159

Acknowledgments

This book is the work of hundreds of mostly anonymous naval aviators, people who had the strength and courage to earn their wings, the skill and luck to live through mishaps and in-flight emergencies, and who cared enough to write about the lessons they learned. The book also reflects the efforts of the editors and staff writers of *Approach* through the years, whose names appeared on the masthead of the magazine but rarely on the articles they wrote or edited.

We owe a debt of gratitude to several Navy aviators who helped explain the significance of stories and the meaning of technical terms. Capt. Ken Craig, an A–6 pilot and former skipper of Attack Squadron 95, communicated the depth of his respect for (and knowledge of) the lessons of aviation history. Lt. Ward Carroll, an F–14 radar intercept officer who edited *Approach* in 1989 and 1990, displayed an encyclopedic knowledge of the alphabet-soup acronyms and initializations of his profession.

Thanks also to the staff at Motorbooks International, notably Greg Field, for perceiving the value of these old magazine yarns, and for helping them escape the shelves of obscure reference libraries by giving the stories new life and a new audience. Thanks to copy editor Cheryl Drivdahl, for skillfully adding a level of standardization and clarity to the stories that is superior to the original.

And, as always, thanks to my wife Mary, the source of honesty and the trigger of exploration in my life, and my son Nate, who says he wants to fly Tomcats.

If this book helps explain the intensely demanding nature of the job of flying military aircraft, and if it helps pass on some hard-earned knowledge to new generations of aviators, then producing this book will have been worthwhile.

Introduction

There are plenty of reasons why since the mid–1950s nearly every Navy and Marine aviator has read *Approach* magazine, remembers it and may have written an article for it. Why Air Force pilots respond to reader surveys that they like *Approach* better than their own service's magazines. Why a moderately sophisticated magazine published by an obscure Navy command sells a couple thousand paid subscriptions without advertising or making any concession to its nontarget audience. Why, as they find themselves running out of options in the cockpit or considering a foolhardy airborne move, Navy and Marine pilots sometimes report that they check themselves by asking, "How would this read in *Approach?*" And why, when everything goes wrong and they pull it out and manage to walk away, they're glad to tell the yarn to their peers in print.

One reason is that aviators love to tell stories, and—thanks to the adventuresome nature of their profession—the stories they tell in the pages of *Approach* are varied and exciting. They make good reading. In 1955, eight aircraft take off on a routine cross-country; none make it (see "—And Then There Were None..."). An F–4 climbing away from a carrier smashes into an A–7 waiting to recover; the F–4 spins in, killing the aircrew (see "Look Out! Midair Collision in the CV Pattern"). A helicopter pilot warily accepts a Sea Stallion that has an ominous recent history of mechanical problems; coming back to the ship, he loses control, puts the helo in the drink and is almost overcome by the water suction as he tries to escape the sinking cabin (see "My Time").

Hundreds such stories—generically and colorfully known as "there I was" stories—have been published in *Approach* through the decades. They contain occasional chunks of aviation jargon and a fair amount of technical information, but—even if you aren't an aviator—those things add flavor and credibility to the narratives. If you distilled the aviationese out of these stories, what you'd be left with would be pure, edge-of-the-seat, white-knuckled adventure yarns.

On the whole, the stories teach the guys in the cockpits useful lessons about what to do if they're ever in similar situations. Even more often, they convince the pilots that they never want to get in those situations to begin with. Which brings up another reason for the popularity of *Approach*: the readers feel that the magazine just might save their lives some day.

No organization, no matter how tightknit and colorful, just sits down and says, "Let's create a popular, meaningful magazine that the readers will support and that is full of great, true stories written by nonprofessional writers." Producing a journal that meets those criteria takes certain conditions, shared perceptions and problems that need to be solved. In the case of the Navy and *Approach*, those problems were called aircraft accidents. Specifically, after World War II and during the early fifties, way too many of them occurred, and most of them were

As the Weekly Aviation Safety Bulletin *matured, its graphics improved dramatically, and its focus shifted from data and platitudes to gripping stories.*

preventable. In order to emphasize the fact that people could prevent them, in the mid-1970s the Navy phased in the word "mishap" as a substitute for "accident" (which seemed to imply a fatalistic helplessness).

To appreciate the panorama of stories in the pages of this book, some background is in order. You'll need to glance at the precursors of *Approach*—the newsletters and bulletins that paved the way for it. You'll need a side order of statistics—a brief survey of safety problems and hazards that have plagued military aviation since its inception, and a report card on how the Navy and Marine Corps have done in terms of safety during the life of the magazine. You'll need an introduction to some members of the staff, especially during the early years, and to two recurrent features—"Anymouse" and the "there I was" stories—that have appeared in the magazine's pages. Finally, you'll need a snapshot of the command that has produced the magazine.

After those brief introductions, let the yarns begin. We chose them for a variety of reasons, primarily because they were exciting, humorous or thrilling, and made vivid points about the hazards of flying. They appear in the order they were written and published, and all (with one exception) are from *Approach*.

The Precursors of *Approach*

The roots of the modern Navy's safety consciousness were put down back in the wreckage-strewn early fifties, which also engendered the precursors of *Approach*. The magazine's earliest ancestor was a small newsletter called the *Weekly Aviation Safety Bulletin* (*WASB*), which gradually grew into an increasingly magazinelike publication called the *Naval Aviation Safety Bulletin*.

An index for the *Weekly Aviation Safety Bulletin* goes back to 1951. However, copies are rare and only one citation (1–51) is given for that year and few for early 1952. In those years, the newsletter may have been published irregularly.

WASB 1–54 is typewritten and includes a few half-tone pictures. More significantly, it includes the character Anymouse, who would become a mainstay in the long publishing life of *Approach* magazine. *WASB* 1–54 also summarizes the accidents of 1953: 2,036 major accidents, 225 fatal accidents and 422 fatalities. Today, we wouldn't call those totals accidents—we'd call them carnage. But back then, 1953 was an improvement over 1952.

For those who keep track of the Navy's current accident rates, it is an exercise in head shaking to review the mishaps back in the early fifties. You are confounded that aviators could have accepted that mayhem as the cost of doing business. As reported in *WASB* 2–54, January 3–9, 1954, for example, the Navy had already tallied fifty-five major accidents, and twenty-one fatalities from seven mishaps. *WASB* 14–54 reported a rate of 3.9 aircraft carrier (CV) landing accidents per 1,000 landings.

One narrative says "the cause of the accident is unknown," a statement that wasn't too unusual back then but is extremely rare these days, when the Navy spends millions of dollars investigating and analyzing mishaps, even salvaging aircraft from the ocean floor to look for causes. Keep in mind also that acceptable explanations of mishaps were much more vague in the early fifties than today.

Reading the old bulletins is also an exercise in nostalgia for the old-timers among us. *WASB* 22–54 lists an aircraft carrier "box score" for such US ships as, among the CVAs (attack carriers), the *Lake Champlain, Kearsarge, Leyte, Wasp* and *Boxer;* among the CVLs (light carriers), the *Cabot, Bataan* and *Wright;* and among the CVEs (escort carriers), the *Mindoro, Siboney, Kula Gulf* and *Bairoko.*

It was in the pages of the *Weekly Aviation Safety Bulletin* that the crucial interconnection was made between Anymouse's hairy tales and the "there I was" story that became a virtual trademark of *Approach*. Anymouse was a

Early Ted Wilbur illustration from the Naval Aviation Safety Bulletin, *April 1955, just months away from the birth of* Approach.

Feature from the Weekly Aviation Safety Bulletin *18–54. Lt. (j.g.) Will Riskit, one of Wilbur's comic masterpieces, had a great career as a bad example. In this episode, he illustrates an actual mishap.*

sort of first person free-for-all column, ostensibly written by readers, aimed at highlighting hazards and sharing "lessons learned" by personal error. An editorial in *WASB* 2–54 says, "The important thing to remember is the fact that *you* can contribute to this effort by sending in a description of *your* hairy experiences. . . . After all, *second hand experience is the only cheap kind.*" The basic truth of this statement wasn't lost on the generations of aviators who were to come.

WASB 25–54 has a first person narrative about ditching a P2V; the editor calls it a letter rather than a story, for some reason. That issue also contains an item in its "Anymouse" feature headlined "There I Was! . . ."

The newsletter gradually picked up the trappings of a more professional publication. *WASB* 18–54 has display headlines, regular departments and cartoons. The arrival of Lt. Ted Wilbur gave the staff a cartoonist who combined extraordinary talent, a vivid sense of humor and the credibility of having been there himself. Along with Wilbur's cartoons, dramatic halftones of crashed or sinking aircraft began to appear in the pages of the bulletin. The publication also grew larger.

One of Wilbur's minor comic masterpieces was an enduring character called Lt. (j.g.) Will Riskit, a prototypical Navy pilot—cigar chewing, salty beyond belief, a true kick-the-tires type of aviator. Riskit started out as a character in cartoon illustrations for narratives of actual mishaps. In *WASB* 18–54, for example, he is described and pictured as he "dribbled off the bow when his engine quit on take-off" in an AF-2S. By the June 1955 issue of the *Aviation Safety Bulletin*, Riskit had been promoted to lieutenant. A small subtitle in the first panel of the cartoon says that it is "adapted from an Anymouse report."

In January 1955, the bulletin changed to a monthly magazine-style publication. It was printed on uncoated paper, but it featured a true masthead and was twenty-

Feature from the Naval Aviation Safety Bulletin, *June 1955. Riskit gets a promotion. Note Anymouse in the third panel.*

Cover of the Naval Aviation Safety Bulletin, *April 1955.*
*Wilbur's dramatic lighting and perspective combine to produce a
striking view of carrier ops. Note that the barricade has been
rigged. Lieutenant Wilbur stayed on the* Approach *masthead
through the February 1958 issue.*

Cover of the first issue of Approach *magazine, July 1955. This
issue had a foreword from the deputy chief of naval operations
(air). The early issues were thirty-two pages, but the magazine
soon grew to a forty-eight pager. The word* the *was quickly
dropped from the magazine's title.*

**"THE DATE: JUNE 17TH, 1955. THE
PLACE: 25,000 FEET OVER ST.
LOUIS. THE EVENT: A JET ENGINE FLAME-
OUT UNDER IFR CONDITIONS — AND**

"The date: June 17th, 1955.
The place: 25,000 feet over St.
Louis. The event: A jet engine
flameout under IFR conditions

the pattern of the past, which is
unlikely, there will be an
occasional "live" show with just
such a plot featuring an all-star

to do at the right time. He will
also tell you, for free, that his
seeming ability to ad lib out of a
tight situation is merely the

Article from the final issue of the Naval Aviation Safety Bulletin, *June 1955. This article works hard to get the reader into*

*the middle of the action. Stories in the second person also became
a standard tactic in the decades to follow.*

four pages long. Already, the kind of story that would become a mainstay was prominent, as if the staff was beginning to fully explore the medium. In the June 1955 issue, one department was titled "You Are There." The lead was a classic:

The date: June 17th, 1955. The place: 25,000 feet over St. Louis. The event: a jet engine flameout under IFR [instrument flight rules] conditions— and YOU are there!

The article was written in present tense, a technique that added drama and immediacy to an already exciting narrative. During the coming years, some of the best stories—many included in this book—would also put the reader in the cockpit.

The first issue of the bulletin's next incarnation appeared in July 1955. It was called *The Approach*.

A Box Score Written in Blood

Mishap statistics offer a peculiar sort of box score, one that is written in blood, as the Navy cliché goes. At least, it is written in twisted metal, blown tires and shattered canopies. The stats don't tell you about the mishaps that were prevented. And the most important mishap is the one that is just about to happen, because that is the only one you can do anything about.

The oldest statistics available reach all the way back to 1922, when the Navy tabulated all mishaps without breaking them down into levels of severity. The all-accident rate ranged from twenty-three to thirty-one mishaps per 10,000 flight hours for the years 1922 to 1926. It steadily declined from 1924 to 1928, and it zigzagged between ten and eighteen mishaps per 10,000 flight hours from 1929 to 1936. By themselves, those numbers seem random, without context. One fact is already clear to those familiar with the Navy mishap rate: the Navy no longer measures by accidents per 10,000 flight hours but by accidents per 100,000 flight hours. The reason may become clear as you trace the rate through the years.

The Navy began measuring "major accidents" in 1936, defining these mishaps as destruction of any major component of the aircraft, such as a broken wing or sheared landing gear. The old classification of "major" mishap doesn't correspond to the modern classification of "Class A mishap." The best way to compare the postwar years and today is by gauges such as destroyed aircraft or fatalities.

The rate steadily declined until the outbreak of World War II, when it jumped from four mishaps per 10,000 flight hours to almost double that amount in 1945. That total doesn't include aircraft lost or damaged in combat; as Vietnam would also show, the accident rate goes up during high-stress periods. The rate gradually began tailing off again in 1947, settling down to the prewar level by 1956.

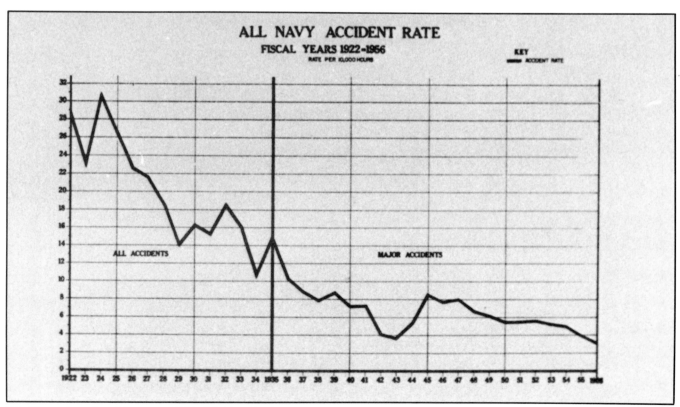

The Navy aircraft accident rate, 1922–56. Note the sharp climb during World War II.

The gradually declining rate of mishaps in the early fifties was no cause for celebration. Navy pilots were still crashing more than fifty airplanes for every 100,000 hours of flight time. More than 700 aircraft per year were ending up in smoking holes, killing 200 pilots and aircrew members. Anyone with a glancing familiarity with the specifics of these mishaps knew that many of them simply didn't have to happen.

Furthermore, the cost of those accidents continued to climb, from just more than $50 million in 1948 to more than $225 million in 1956, in part because the newer jet aircraft were much more expensive than prop aircraft. Another cause for increased concern was that although the rate of "major damage accidents" declined in the late forties and early fifties, the rate of fatal aircraft accidents stayed level from 1950 to 1956. The same number of pilots died, and the costs of training them continued to rise— steadily and then, like the costs of aircraft, meteorically.

In the early years of Navy aviation, flying was a new and dangerous thing. Plenty of people accepted accidents as "the cost of doing business." Flying was just plain dangerous, they figured, and luck was the major determinant in whether you pranged an airplane or not. Maintenance was often hit-or-miss. Wartime combat masked some of this needless carnage, and many pilots accepted any sort of disaster with a shrug. Attitudes that today seem ludicrous—"Hell, it flew in, it'll fly out," "If it isn't leaking, it isn't a real [fill in the blank with an aircraft type]" or the classic, skip-the-brief-and-preflight "Let's kick the tires and light the fire"—were commonplace, indeed expected. Safety was for sissies. It was like the modern motorcycle bumper sticker: "If you're afraid, say you're afraid."

Those weren't the attitudes that the American taxpayer liked to hear about. Nor were they welcomed by the squadron skipper who was left with half as many aircraft as he needed for a mission because the others were wrecked and letters to write to the dead pilots' next of kin.

The problems were intensified by the transition from the prop-driven aircraft of World War II to jet aircraft, which began in the late forties. "From aircraft accident statistics it became unmistakably clear that modern high-performance aircraft are mercilessly unforgiving of the mistakes of the pilot or aircrew, of inadequate facilities, of faulty design or material, of poor maintenance, and of deficiencies in supervision," wrote Lt. Cmdr. R. A. Eldridge in a July 1961 *Approach* article entitled "The Carrier Landing Story." When airplanes were light and slow, you had a better chance of plowing into something and walking away from it. Those chances were diminishing. Your chances of surviving an engine failure in a Spad were much higher than in a jet. The Spad had a better glide ratio. Jets were going much faster and their fuselages were more fragile.

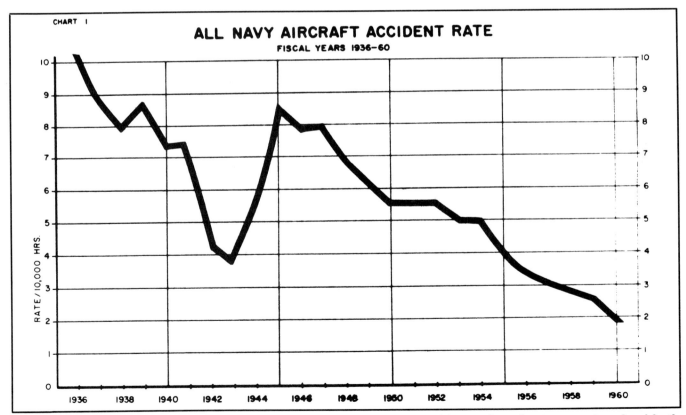

CHART I

ALL NAVY AIRCRAFT ACCIDENT RATE
FISCAL YEARS 1936-60

Another look at the aircraft accident rate, 1936–60. The steadily descending rate starting with 1952 is a tribute to the effectiveness of the new and innovative safety programs introduced by the Navy.

Other problems awaited solutions. For example, the night accident rate ranged from three to six times as severe as the day rate. But the dedication to recognizing and solving problems would gain momentum.

Major changes in attitude, in programs and in the rules were clearly in order and became top priorities. Success came steadily and convincingly. In contrast to the carnage of the late forties and early fifties, a precipitous drop in the accident rate has marked the modern era. The rate was halved between 1955 and 1959, and halved again by the midsixties. In fiscal 1950, the carrier landing rate was 36.7 per 10,000 landings; ten years later, it was 3.9.

Time and time again, the Navy racked up the safest year in its history. From 1955 to 1956, for example, the overall accident rate declined twelve percent and the accident rate for carrier landings was reduced twenty-eight percent. Soon the Navy stopped even measuring an accident rate for carrier landings—it simply didn't have enough data.

Major innovations in equipment and training spurred the improvements. British inventors deserve credit for major breakthroughs, including the angled-deck aircraft carrier and the Fresnel lens and meatball system of giving visual cues to pilots. The installation of angled decks on carriers in 1955 vastly improved the ease and safety of carrier landings. When the Navy had both the new angled and the old axial decks in use—in fiscal 1956, for example—the accident rate of angled decks was 1.24 mishaps per 1,000 landings, against a rate of 1.95 for the axial decks. Pilots quickly made up their mind which deck they preferred.

"Prior to the advent of jet aircraft and the angled deck into the fleet, two of the cardinal mistakes associated with the technique of landing aboard were **diving for the deck** and **holding off**," Lieutenant Commander Eldridge wrote. "In either case the result was usually the same—a damaged aircraft entwined in the barrier cables or ingloriously arrested, with broken wheels, struts or buckled fuselage." In the old days, the pilot was committed to getting down, either in an arrested landing or in a barrier crash. The angled deck and the chance for a bolter (missing the wires and going around for another try) were a breakthrough, once pilots figured out that they needed to approach the landing deck at a higher angle and with more power than they did in prop planes. "When the angled deck carriers became a reality, pilots who held off on a landing merely chalked up a bolter instead of winding up in the fence under the scrutiny of the C.O., the air boss, and the remaining ghouls in vultures' row," Eldridge pointed out. (Incidentally, Eldridge later joined the *Approach* staff as a civilian writer.)

The establishment of the Naval Aviation Maintenance Program (NAMP) in 1959 was of far-reaching importance. It standardized and tightened the procedures that mechanics used for inspecting and repairing Navy aircraft. In the old days, if you lost a screwdriver while working on an aircraft, you just bought another at the hardware store and stuck it in your toolbox. The NAMP paved the way for such things as strict tool-control

WEEKLY SUMMARY

FROM MESSAGE REPORTS	THIS WEEK	TOTAL 1954	TOTAL THIS WEEK LAST YEAR
Major accidents	51	55	31
Fatal accidents	7	7	7
Fatalities	21	21	7
Strike damage	17	17	14
Overhaul damage	13	15	4

THE WEEK OF
3 - 9 January 1954

AIRLANT (15)

AIRCRAFT	DAMAGE	INJURY	DESCRIPTION
F2H-2	Overhaul	None	Undershot normal landing
F2H-2P	Strike	None	Hard CV landing, rough seas
F2H-3	Overhaul	None	Hard CV landing, dive for deck
F9F-5	Overhaul	None	Hard CV landing, rough seas
F9F-5	Overhaul	None	Hard CV landing, rough seas
F9F-5	Substantial	None	Hard CV landing, rough seas
F9F-6	Strike	FATAL	See Note 1
F9F-6	Overhaul	None	Cooling air manifold weldment failure
F9F-6	Overhaul	None	Hard CV landing
F9F-6	Strike	Serious	Flameout, crashed on forced landing
AD-4L	Substantial	None	Scar rocket exploded on rocket run
AF-3S	Substantial	None	Hit birds on rocket dive pullout
UF-1	Undetermined	Serious 2 Minor	Groundlooped, aborted take-off, wet snow on wings
JRB-4	Substantial	None	Landing gear collapsed on take-off

AIRPAC (13)

AIRCRAFT	DAMAGE	INJURY	DESCRIPTION
F2H-3	Strike	None	Brake failure, taxied over side of CV
F2H-3	Overhaul	None	Hard CV landing, dive for deck
F2H-3	Strike	2 Minor	Swerved off runway during rollout and collided with F9F-6 on taxiway
F9F-6	Overhaul	None	
F9F-2	Strike	FATAL	See Note 2
F9F-5	Substantial	None	Hard CV landing
F9F-6	Overhaul	None	CV landing, barrier crash
F9F-6	Overhaul	None	Hard CV landing, dive for deck
TV-2	Strike	None	Flameout, overshot runway
AD-4B	Substantial	None	CV landing, barrier crash
AF-3S	Substantial	None	Night CV landing, barrier crash
AF-3S	Strike	FATAL	Engine failure, CV night take-off
P4Y-1P	Strike	6 FATAL 7 Serious Minor	See Note 3
P2V-5	Strike	10 Missing	See Note 4

MARINES (7)

AIRCRAFT	DAMAGE	INJURY	DESCRIPTION
F9F-2	Substantial	None	Swerved into embankment on rollout
F9F-5	Overhaul	None	Flameout at 38,000 feet, ditched
AD-4D	Strike	FATAL	See Note 5
AD-4	Substantial	None	Wheels-up landing, material failure
HRS-1	Substantial	None	Lost power, settled into ground
HRS-2	Overhaul	None	Engine failure, CV deck crash
SNB-5	Overhaul	None	Landing gear collapsed on take-off

A page from the Weekly Summary of Aircraft Mishaps, *a newsletter still published by the Naval Safety Center. The numbers are sky high compared with those in 1990. Most of the reasons for the mishaps—in the Description column—are obsolete.*

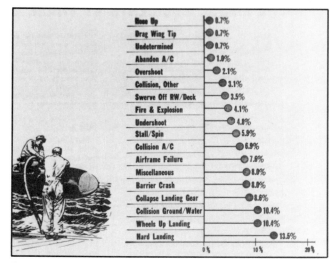

Reasons for aircraft mishaps. Wheels-up landings—the second item from the bottom—were a recurrent problem. This chart is from a Naval Aviation Safety Center research report from the midfifties.

programs that would down an aircraft until a missing tool was found. It improved and standardized technical manuals, giving much more exact and complete directions for maintenance tasks. The NAMP also established mandatory training for technicians.

The initiation of the Replacement Air Group (RAG) concept, also in 1959, dramatically improved the training of new pilots entering fleet squadrons. In 1961, the establishment of the Naval Air Training and Operating Procedures Standardization (NATOPS) program produced, among other things, easy-to-use, technically accurate manuals for all types of aircraft. Before NATOPS, squadrons had their own training programs, standard operating procedures (SOP) and even tactical rules, all of which tended to be short and not very complex. When pilots moved from one squadron to another, they found radically different methods. The NATOPS manuals earned respect as sources of knowledge and guidance while airborne and especially during emergencies. Through the years, aircraft manufacturers consistently improved the technical safety features of aircraft as well. Improved backup systems, ejection seats and instruments, to name just a few features, made the days when the Cutlass was called the "ensign eater" seem nightmarish.

Other milestones were the start of squadron safety programs in 1975 and a major revision to the governing instructions for safety in 1980.

It is ironic to look back at the 1956 rate of 3.33 accidents per 10,000 flight hours and to read official descriptions of that rate as "outstanding" and a "gratifying achievement"; by the late eighties, the mishap rate was one tenth of that.

The Staff

These days, in the early nineties, *Approach* is a twenty-four-to-thirty-two page monthly magazine, known extremely well by a small community of current and former naval aviators and military aviation insiders, and known hardly at all by anyone else. It has thrived for nearly four decades because it has had consistently powerful support from the Naval Safety Center, which publishes it and which devotes nearly twenty percent of its budget to publications. And it has enjoyed the support of generations of Navy and Marine Corps aviators, who send in stories by the hundreds, as well as powerful support from the Assistant Chief of Naval Operations for Air Warfare (known as OP–05) and an occasional Secretary of the Navy.

Cover of the February 1956 issue. This illustrates a main reason for the continuing popularity of Approach—*stories that put the reader airborne, and stories written by guys who have been there. "The Many Behind The Man At The Wheel—that's the aircrewman of today's naval aviation," the original caption read.*

Cover of the December 1958 issue. Flying during the late fifties was unpredictable enough, but winter weather only made it worse.

The Navy distributes some 18,000 copies of the magazine to a primary target audience of about 90,000 Navy and Marine Corps aviators, defense contractors and US allies around the world. The distribution totals would almost certainly be much higher, but the command's budget won't permit one copy for everyone who wants or requests the magazine. The ostensible reader ratio is about one copy per eight or ten readers. The Government Printing Office sells nearly 2,000 commercial subscriptions to the magazine—an astonishing number for a government publication, leading the subscription totals for all other military magazines by a wide margin.

A small part of the magazine's success is due to the famous names that have appeared in it: fighter aces such as John Bolt of the Black Sheep; Marion Carl, a Marine Corps ace; James Flatley, the first commander of the Naval Safety Center and later an admiral; and Donald Engen, later an astronaut. Their no-nonsense reputations added to the magazine's credibility.

In recent years, Tom Wolfe wrote an editorial about the relationship of safety and the "right stuff," and best-selling author Stephen Coonts contributed an article about a near miss that he actually had in Vietnam but featuring his characters from *Flight of the Intruder*.

Ted Wilbur, the skillful cartoonist who was on active duty and on the staff at the birth of the magazine, went on to join the first rank of aviation artists. Wilbur was unusual in that he was a naval aviator as well as an artist of merit. He played a significant part in shaping the direction and tone of the magazine, and contributed to the magazine even after his tour at the safety center.

In the late eighties, the magazine featured illustrations by a string of nationally known artists, including Blake Morrison, Keith Ferris, Mike Machat and Jeff MacNelly. R. G. Smith has contributed top-of-the-line covers throughout the magazine's life.

Approach has been edited by active-duty Navy officers and staffed with civilian writers. Several members of the staff have had considerable success as editors of commercial magazines, as authors of books and as free-lance writers.

The editor in 1990, F–14 radar intercept officer Ward Carroll, would have been right at home on the first staff of the magazine. Lieutenant Carroll is a cartoonist, creator of "Brownshoes in Action Comix," starring a character ironically named Dangerboy. The cartoon strip is a popular item in the magazine, with a devoted following in ready rooms throughout the Navy.

Cover of the June 1965 issue. The goal of Approach *articles has always been to prevent the situation shown here: a pilot in the drink, and the search-and-rescue (SAR) helo launched. This UH–2B was painted by C. McDonough of Kaman Aircraft Corporation.*

Cover of the July 1969 issue. Well-known illustrator R. G. Smith of McDonnell-Douglas has contributed outstanding illustrations to Approach *since the midsixties. In this one, SBDs "sweep out of the past for another curtain call," the original caption said.*

13

Since he was a naval aviator before moving into the White House, it was only natural that George Bush would join John Glenn, James Stockdale and others in a series of interviews in the April-May 1990 issue of *Approach*. Nevertheless, the key to the success of the magazine has always been in-the-cockpit stories from junior officers, stories that tell of unvarnished adventures in the day-to-day life of Navy aviation. To understand why there were so many of these adventures to describe in the pages of the magazine, we have to turn back the clock to the late forties and early fifties, back to the days when you needed an altimeter to track the mishap rate and when, unlike today, wrecked airplanes weren't news, they were par for the course.

Recurrent Features

Anymouse

Approach's style and tone have changed through its three decades of publication. One regular column, however, has remained stable; it is called Anymouse. Legend has it that the name Anymouse started out as a simple typo; someone somewhere didn't know how to spell *anonymous* and didn't have a dictionary. Whatever the origins, by the time the Naval Safety Center began publishing the *Weekly Aviation Safety Bulletin* in the early fifties, Anymouse was already recounting his hairy tales. His column served as a fertile breeding ground for the hair-raising "there I was" stories to follow.

In *WASB* 2–54, a column from W. E. Scarborough, the command's officer-in-charge, reported, "For the three month period ending 31 December 1952, 90 ANYMOUSE reports were received from pilots who had unusual experiences in flight.... [These reports] proved valuable in preventing aircraft accidents, improving operating procedures, and aiding in improvement in design of aircraft." The article urged readers to send in their own stories, in order to share the lessons learned.

In mid-1954, the bulletin ran an item in "Anymouse" headlined "There I Was! ..." As used by hangar flyers and taletellers around the fleet, however, the phrase didn't necessarily start a story that was true. Although many feature articles through the years would contain elements of humor, Anymouse wasn't interested in malarkey, practical jokes or hot air. He was a serious fellow at heart.

The column was intended as an alternative to existing hazard-alert and mishap-report systems. According to a 1956 study issued by the Naval Safety Center, Anymouse

Cover of the September 1970 issue. A loaded-up A–7 launches, no doubt into some Vietnam action. The painting is by Steve Anderson, then a third-class petty officer in the Navy.

was "originally intended as a means of encouraging flight personnel to make voluntary and anonymous reports of near-accidents and incidents which they might not report through established channels and formal reporting systems." Why wouldn't something be reported? Well, because of what people in the Navy call the hammer—punitive action that might be taken, given circumstances and the personality of the commanding officer in question. "Any aviator desiring to report a situation merely takes a form and envelope from one of the attractive suggestion-type boxes available in all operating units," the report continued. "Anonymity is the heart of the system."

No official directive established or continued Anymouse. This lack of marching orders is unusual and a testimony to Anymouse's effectiveness and popularity. Most Navy programs are usually awash in multilayered and pompous directives, full of bloated language and either nitpicked or rubber-stamped by numerous echelons. Navy aviators probably enjoyed doing something they didn't have to. They certainly took an altruistic interest in keeping their fellow aviators from learning the hard way. The job of flying was difficult and dangerous

enough without everyone making the same mistakes. At any rate, the yarns poured in, from pilots who had been at all sorts of altitudes.

July 1955: "At about 3000 feet I suddenly noticed my altimeter starting to unwind very rapidly. My first impulse was to haul back on the stick, but I forced myself to check the needle-ball . . ."

August 1955: "My next look at the instruments brought a chill of horror. The needle was against the left peg, the gyro horizon was showing an eight ball and the needle was plummeting downward!"

November 1955: "About 30 minutes east of my destination I ran into a solid cloud deck extending from about 1500 feet up to 12,000 feet. . . . I was not instrument qualified in jets and couldn't continue IFR on top and didn't believe I had enough fuel to turn back and reach an air station . . ."

January 1956: "There we were at about 75 feet, gear coming up, both engines cut with about 115 knots of airspeed . . ."

These yarns were short, punchy and fun to read. The vicarious fear was almost addictive.

The September 1957 issue of *Approach* announced Anymouse's tenth anniversary. That issue featured a meeting between Anymouse and another cartoon character who happened to be in the safety business: Gram-

Cover of the August 1976 issue. Staff artist Blake Rader painted these F6Fs as they would have appeared in combat, circa 1943. Back then, the accident rate was astronomical. Rader painted thousands of illustrations for the magazine during his career as staff artist.

Cover of the October 1980 issue. Another R. G. Smith cover, this one shows AV–8B Harriers when they were new.

paw Pettibone, who was apparently kidnapped from his parent publication, *Naval Aviation News,* for the occasion. Whether the meeting was sanctioned by Pettibone's guardians at *Naval Aviation News* is questionable. At any rate, the safety center was hospitable, and Gramps seemed to be in a good mood. "By tarnation boy, it's time we got better acquainted!" he told the mouse. "I'm interested in hearing some more of those 'hairy tales' of yours and how you've been doing in this rat race... Uh, I mean business." In the ensuing years, Anymouse was often overshadowed by his flamboyant, acerbic competitor. Still, a tenure of forty-plus years isn't bad, and Anymouse may outlive Grampaw yet.

Some Navy planners apparently thought Anymouse and Grampaw Pettibone should have been roommates all along. Back in the early fifties, an influential Navy report had triggered the dramatic improvement and growth in the Naval Safety Center. This report made numerous recommendations. One was that the command should

start a monthly safety magazine, "printed on quality stock" and "well illustrated." The report said the magazine should include ten things, number one of which was Grampaw Pettibone. A great idea, except that the already popular and well-known Pettibone belonged to another Navy magazine, which was if not an actual competitor of the safety center's publication-to-be, nevertheless aimed at the same target audience. That magazine, *Naval Aviation News,* wasn't about to let the character go.

Grampaw Pettibone had made his first appearance in the January 15, 1943, issue of the Bureau of Aeronautics *News Letter.* "The idea took off because things were so volatile in those days that you could put anything like this right into print and in two weeks get it going," longtime artist Robert Osborn said in an interview that appeared in the January 1983 issue of *Naval Aviation News.* The idea was to have "this old aviator who has survived with his wisdom trying to speak, rather sharply, to these young pilots."

Pettibone was the brain child of Lt. Cmdr. Seth Warner, who later recalled that the character was "conceived in desperation, the offspring of frustration and despair" that came from reading accident reports. Cartoonist Osborn described Pettibone as "a cantankerous old codger with a low boiling point and uninhibited with official language" who was simply "turned... loose, [in the hope] that his pithy remarks and sardonic humor would hold their [the readers'] attention long enough to stab with a vital safety factor."

Osborn himself had firsthand experience with aviation and with safety, and was an inspired choice as car-

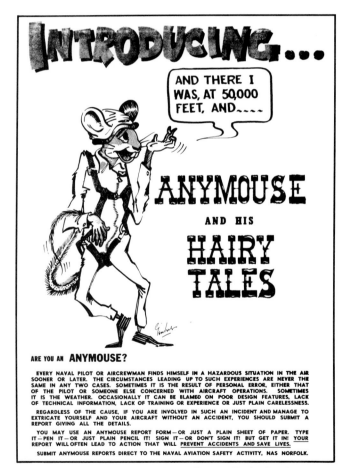

Anymouse poster ad, drawn by staff artist R. A. Genders, some time before the Naval Aviation Safety Activity became the Naval Aviation Safety Center. The height at which the adventures occurred seems to keep increasing—now we're at 50,000 feet, instead of the usual 30,000. Genders became art director in February 1956.

Article in the September 1957 issue of Approach. *Grampaw Pettibone, right center, with his arm around Anymouse, gets shanghaied by the* Approach *staff for an impromptu visit and bull session. Pettibone was—and is—a resident of* Naval Aviation News *magazine, and a jealously guarded one at that.*

toonist. In one interview, he described the difference between the aircraft of World War II and aircraft of the seventies. "I once saw a pilot at Corpus Christi slam his F4F off a barracks wall," Osborn said, "demolishing the wall as well as his aircraft[,] and then skid down the street. He walked away from the crash . . . he was flying the next day." Would that modern jets were so forgiving.

Pettibone himself was—and is—never forgiving of bonehead ploys by aviators. In a typical early installment of the series, he describes the "antics" of a reserve ensign who racked up seven flight violations in less than two hours, including buzzing a farmer's car and missing it by 10 feet, flying down a gully at below treetop level, severing two power lines, and then landing and claiming he'd hit a duck or some sort of bird. "Ah, for the good old days of public hangings," Grampaw mused. "We could have all gone and taken a picnic lunch."

The Pettibone character continues to this day as a popular feature of *Naval Aviation News;* the text has been written by a succession of incognito naval aviators. A surprising and—given Pettibone's roots—ironic number of aviators still associate the character with *Approach.* Sometimes the staff at *Approach* gets articles addressed to him.

The "there I was" stories

Pilots love to tell stories, especially the kind that start, "There I was, inverted, out of gas and out of ideas, when . . ." The telling and the listening are called "hangar flying." The stories describe adventures, near-misses, the cutting of corners, the facing of bad luck and worse weather and pulling it out through nerve and skill. Especially in the demanding world of aircraft carriers, these events have always been the daily, verbal fare in ready room discussions and happy hours at the club.

Some of the stories are the unvarnished truth. Others . . . if you put them between two slices of bread, you'd have a passable baloney sandwich. They take on the dimension of the tall tales once told about Paul Bunyan and Babe, the Blue Ox. That's why the members of the fighter squadron nicknamed the Red Rippers explain that the item below the boar's head on their squadron insignia isn't just decorative, it is a "line of baloney" that the squadron members are adept at feeding unsuspecting listeners. Storytelling aviators are rarely known for their modesty, and the protagonist (the storyteller) tends to cast himself or herself in the role of hero. Other storytellers are humorists, making light of their own misadventures.

When and where the "there I was" story first began to be published is open for debate. Just after World War II, *Naval Aviation News* launched a feature called "And There I Was . . .," but it didn't deal with safety. The feature was a forum for sea stories from the war years. Most of the items recounted practical jokes, gags and other humor-in-uniform tidbits. "Any stories concerning activities above 30,000 feet in positions other than horizontal must be accompanied by photographs," the introduction to the feature said.

In the safety business, however, the point was not to merely entertain or to excite vicarious adrenaline. Jour-

The "Anymouse" column, which is still a regular feature in the magazine, was clearly the genesis for the classic "there I was" story that Approach *raised to an aviation art form.*

nalists had long known that first person accounts were an effective technique for relating human experience. *Approach* magazine would publish thousands such stories. Its predecessor—the *Weekly Aviation Safety Bulletin*—had experimented with the form. Issue 20–54 had an article called "The Man with the Banjo," which the editor called an "outstanding example of articulate reporting." It was a first person narrative, something that was quite unusual back then.

A 1954 *WASB* article was headlined "There I Was! . . ." In this case, the editor adapted the classic format for his own purposes. "There has been many a joke about the pilot who explained his World War II heroics by starting with the phrase 'and there I was at 30,000 feet,'" the article said. "ANYMOUSE was at 30,000 feet when he ran into trouble but there were no heroics, just plain common sense. You can't breathe up there without oxygen."

The September 1955 issue of *Approach* celebrated the second anniversary of Anymouse as a safety center character, although Anymouse had been created in 1945 by a squadron safety officer. By late 1955, the safety center had received more than 400 "candid confessions," an article titled "Anymouse's Anniversary" in the September issue reported. "[The yarns] usually begin with 'There I was . . .' and . . . invariably close with a fervent 'never agin!' note of wisdom," the article pointed out.

Many early "Anymouse" features—in *Approach* and its precursors—appear to be the actual words of the people who submitted them. Later, some were probably written by the staff or ghosted from other sources during periods when the flow of Anymouse submissions ebbed temporarily, or when the staff wanted to include a particularly telling or juicy episode.

The "there I was" story—in which an aviator confesses her or his own mistakes, or tells about his or her own experience—offers a direct contrast to the Grampaw Pettibone approach. In a first person story, the author invites the reader to share as an equal. The author drops pretenses and defenses; if she or he admits to cutting a corner or making a bonehead decision, it cements the bond with the reader, who certainly remembers doing the same things. Grampaw Pettibone, however, holds the errant aviator up to ridicule and scolding.

Both approaches seem to work, as their continuing popularity attests. Part of Pettibone's popularity depends on the basic human trait of enjoying someone else's misfortune, a sort of combination of "misery loves company" and ambulance watching.

The *Approach* stories remain readable and attractive because they have always seemed to be the truth. No official party line, no mincing around the facts, no pompous policy, no barrage of platitudes from up the totem pole. The "there I was" tale in *Approach* acknowledges the general agreement among pilots—no matter how well hidden by bravado—that you have to learn as much as you can about flying airplanes or you will sooner or later end up in a smoking hole.

The Publisher

In the fall of 1953, those smoking holes were many and close between. As a result, what proved to be an influential Navy study—the Flatley Report—was issued to review the methods then used in the effort to prevent accidents in naval aviation. The study began by discussing the recent crash of a Navy transport at an air station in Florida; forty-four people were killed in the mishap. The accident report about the crash had listed the cause as "undetermined," a finding that was clearly unsatisfactory from the perspective of preventing accidents. In fact, the pilots of the transport lacked night-flying experience; it was questionable whether they should have been assigned the mission at all.

The 1953 study painted a bleak picture of the state of Navy aviation safety, in spite of gradually decreasing mishap rates. In fiscal 1953, one out of every 4.4 aircraft was involved in an accident, and one out of every six suffered major damage. Five percent of all the aircraft then in the Navy inventory were destroyed, and 423 Navy aviation personnel were killed in mishaps. The cost of repairing or replacing aircraft was $500 million.

The study analyzed some "typical" mishaps of the time. A pilot misjudged his altitude and flew into water while making an unauthorized low pass. Another pilot led a flight of five aircraft into thick clouds instead of turning around, and crashed into a mountain. Yet another pilot, and an extremely experienced one at that, ran out of fuel at night, over water, with no life jacket or raft aboard his aircraft.

What brought matters home to the Navy brass was the experts' belief that of the 2,266 major accidents in fiscal 1953, twenty-two percent were avoidable. In retrospect, it appears that belief was almost ridiculously conservative. Of the more than 1,400 accidents that had been attributed to pilot errors, three quarters were "errors in judgment and technique" that, according to the thinking of the times, were *not* considered "avoidable." Once the Navy acquired professional accident investigators and safety specialists, and those people gained experience and knowledge, the definition of *avoidable* would tighten considerably.

Although none of the findings of the 1953 study were surprising, together they made a convincing case for sweeping renovations and improvements in the way the Navy worked to prevent aviation accidents. Too many avoidable accidents were occurring, because of a litany of problems or errors: Pilots were careless or even negligent, or didn't have enough technical knowledge. Some aircraft equipment was poorly designed. Potentially costly errors were scattered through the process of designing, maintaining and operating aircraft and aviation equipment.

Furthermore, the system that should have prevented these accidents or hazards was unwieldy. In one case, a three-month delay occurred in getting out official information about air starting the F9F after a flameout, even after it became clear that the pilot's handbook contained incorrect information. The system was ineffective and suffered from a lack of innovation. The study also cited inadequate procedures for inspections and crash investigations, and said that squadrons lacked experienced supervisors.

One of the study's findings was near the bottom of the list but central to our interests in this book. The study recommended an increase in the quantity and quality of aviation safety print media, to increase the effectiveness of getting useful information to the squadrons. Although the Navy was then getting some publications from the Air Force, Navy squadrons needed and deserved their own publication that dealt with the problems they faced every day. The recommendation was that the Navy start a high-quality, well-illustrated monthly safety magazine. Like the other proposals, this one was acted on with dispatch and with success.

Responsibility for Navy aviation safety was distributed throughout the aviation headquarters. A small, field branch, the Naval Aviation Safety Activity, which had been established in 1951, had eleven officers, four civilians and thirteen enlisted men. In 1953, the assistant secretary of the Navy (air) and the deputy chief of naval operations (air) acted to increase emphasis on aviation safety. The Naval Aviation Safety Activity was made a division in the latter's organization, and its staff was expanded to twenty-seven people. It grew to fifty-six people a year later, then to eighty-eight in 1955, when it traded the word *Activity* for *Center.*

Other improvements in the midfifties included establishing primary billets for aviation safety officers on all major staffs and in each operating squadron. The Navy increased the emphasis on the flow of information to and from the field, the safety center and the Washington, DC, bureaucracy. It also mandated better investigations of mishaps, and more meaningful analyses of causes and recognition of trends.

By 1956, the Naval Aviation Safety Center (NASC) had seven departments, including literature, crash investigation (then conducting a small number of independent investigations), maintenance and material, records and stats, aeromedical, and analysis and research. The US Navy Aviation Safety Program Report, issued in November 1956, said that the literature department "provides the major 'voice' of the Navy's aviation safety program" and that *Approach* magazine was the "primary Navy-wide published media" for aviation safety. "[*Approach*] is written in an easy reading style in order to present technical information and official directives in a manner that will interest as well as educate the reader," the command report said.

The expertise and purview of the safety center grew steadily during the ensuing decades. The center gradually added responsibility for surface ship and submarine safety programs, dropping the word *Aviation* from its title. In 1990, it employed a staff of nearly 300 people, roughly half military and half civilian, and had vastly increased its data-gathering and data analysis techniques. It had expanded into such areas as motor vehicles, off-duty and recreation activities, system safety and Navy-wide training. The aviation departments—both operations and maintenance—still constituted about half the command's resources and programs.

Approach magazine is thriving. The stories that follow explain why.

Poster from the January 1982 issue. This piece sums up the philosophy and the spark of Approach *and of the Navy's aviation safety programs in general.*

SEPTEMBER 1955

the Approach

THE NAVAL AVIATION SAFETY REVIEW

Anymouse's Anniversary

The theme of this [Anymouse] is to induce "all hands" to report incidents by submitting Anymouse Reports. This is one answer to getting the word out on safety.

September 1955

With this issue Anymouse celebrates his second anniversary of duty with the Aviation Safety Center. Born some eight years ago in VR–31, the original idea of submitting anonymous reports is credited to *LCDR Trygve A. Holl*, USN [US Navy], safety officer of that squadron.

Since reporting to the Aviation Safety Center in 1953, Anymouse and his many cousins scattered throughout naval aviation have busied themselves most encouragingly.

Officially, the word Anymouse designates a form available to Navy and Marine Corps personnel for reporting, anonymously, near-accidents or incidents which might have led to aircraft accidents of a more serious nature. These hairy tales, submitted by nameless airmen, provided a means for pilots and crewmen to gain valuable knowledge from the experience of others.

Many Reports Received

How has Anymouse prospered? "Any" can grin proudly over just a few statistics: To date there have been over 400 of these candid confessions which usually begin with "There I was . . . ," and which invariably close with a fervent "never agin!" note of wisdom. Involved in the accounts have been some 36 different model aircraft; an impressive number of air stations and facilities, not to overlook a generous coverage of carriers.

In particular aircraft, the F9F leads in the number of reports (59) with the F2H *Banshee* a close second with 40 reports. In close order thereafter are represented the SNB and the AD.

Some of the reports gripe about inadequacies of certain components or procedures. Others blushingly admit personal mistakes and analyze their actions in close situations. Many reported maintenance discrepancies which caused hair-raising moments. All displayed individual initiative and professional consideration in taking time to submit an Anymouse Report. The value in lives saved and damage to property prevented can only be guessed from the occasional reports received of positive saves resulting from Anymouse information.

One pilot expressed it this way. "This Anymouse business is all right as never before could a man admit he had a close one, yet not hurt his career and at the same time help to save lives and aircraft. Long live Anymouse!"

Anymouse in Action

In troubleshooting Anymouse reports have proved their worth. Because of the nature of the reports, many saves are not credited to the Anymouse system. But some of his work has been acknowledged specifically. For instance an omission of certain instructions in the pilot's flight handbook of a jet fighter was noted. The report got official attention and action was promptly taken to correct the deficiency.

One Anymouse reported an undesirable feature of the control stick in a particular model aircraft. This was also given official attention for consideration in redesigning the stick. Then came an Anymouse report on a hazardous runup condition existing at a naval air station. The CO of the station was advised and immediate action eliminated the hazard.

In another instance, a report of a small flash explosion in an oxygen mask interested an officer in BuAer and through his efforts a thorough investigation was made. The incident had happened before and was being blamed on poor maintenance. The real trouble was discovered in the cockpit microphone receptacle. It had been modified by the contractor and allowed the plug and receptacle to be connected wrong. A field change was issued as an interim to the contractor's engineering change.

All reports received have not been printed as yet, though many have been published in *The Approach* and other reports issued by NASC. However all reports received are analyzed for use in research studies and many requiring action are handled through personal phone calls, letters or become the subject of an article or research project. Tentative plans have been made to publish the majority of the Anymouse reports in a series of digests beginning in the near future.

Others Use System

The value of Anymouse reporting has been recognized by both the United States Air Force and several of its commands, as well as certain commercial airlines who have adopted similar systems of incident reporting.

Anymouse blanks are available on every carrier and air station. Reports can be submitted by personal letter or memorandum as well. If the supply of forms in your squadron or base is running low, send a formal or informal request for more copies to the Naval Aviation Safety Center, NAS, Norfolk, Virginia.

As one poetic Anymouse said:
"Cut the 'axe' out of accident with the 'in' it's an incident.
The difference is an Anymouse
Send us yours. It's worth your life."

To Anymouse, that sage of the skyways whose hard-earned wisdom has been a positive contribution to safety in naval aviation, birthday greetings, Well Done, and happy landings without incident!

But if you should have an Anymouse type experience, just take a pencil and SUBMIT AN ANYMOUSE, and save a life!

Anymouse reports have been received covering a great variety of situations. Some of these, and the number of each type incident, are:

Turbulent weather and thunderstorms 25
Material failure and maintenance 59
Inadvertent operation of cockpit controls 30
Takeoff situations 47
Near wheels-up landings 11
Near mid-air collisions 18
Communication difficulties 31
Taxiing 17
Flameouts, airstarts and dead-stick landings ... 13
Oxygen experience and systems 17
Preflight laxity 21
Carrier takeoffs and landings 16

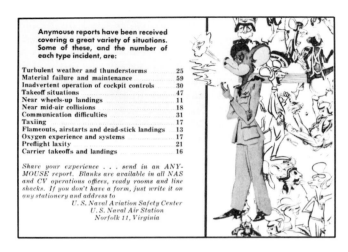

Anymouse and His Hairy Tales

September 1955
It's the Little Things

Anymouse was cavorting amongst the thunderheads on a night intercept hop in a *Banshee* which had seen better days. However, despite some low visibility and occasional rain squalls no particular difficulty was anticipated during recovery.

About 20 minutes before Charlie Time, Anymouse experienced aileron boost failure when the circuit breaker popped, popped again on being reset, and thereafter was left discretely out. No sweat there, for though Anymouse hadn't made a no-boost landing before, it wasn't uncommon and involved little more than a long final. So with the time remaining, Anymouse busied himself with checking the feel of the airplane at lower speeds, assuring himself that even his stringy muscles were adequate for the task.

About this time he observed his left corner instrument panel lights go out. No reason, they just stopped working. And of course the emergency floods proved inoperative. This left Anymouse somewhat in the dark as to what his airspeed, altimeter and RPM might be. Then he discovered that the control rheostat knob to his other instrument lights had disappeared, leaving an unmovable shaft. Ah, well, just have to use the ol' flashlight a little more often.

Anymouse called home to the carrier, which was poking its way through an area of scattered showers, eased on down, tooled by the ship and dropped his hook handle—and squinted in considerable dismay as the light in the hook handle remained on. It focused a rather brilliant beam into his eye, advising that a possible no hook situation existed. Up hook, down hook, same result, same light. Coulda sworn he felt the hook chunk down properly, but have to make a hook check pass to be sure. Nothing to get excited over.

Upwind, an easy instrument turn, gear down (*that* item did work!) roll back out on the straightway—and the darn airplane tried to roll right over on its back. Frantic muscling of the stick to slop back level, thumb jabbing the aileron trim knob—oops! No knob! Trim had run completely right wing-down and the ever-loving knob had fallen off . . . Glove off, finger probing urgently to activate the tab—no dice, too far recessed in the stick.

Anymouse continued downwind, with knee pressure assisting both hands on stick, and taking occasional hasty stabs of flashlight at airspeed, altimeter and RPM—each glimpse revealing either too much or too little of something.

WOW! That was the reflection of the wing lights on the water! Vrooooom, go the engines. Whew, must look like a porpoise on a pogo stick. Abeam now. Not *too* low—probably higher'n a kite, and I *like* it! Begin easy turn in—oops, not too much, stupid. Chug up the wake for a hook check, boy.

What in the . . . ! Another plane cutting me out on a normal approach. Left hand off stick momentarily for a fast transmission: "Getthatdamplaneouttamywayeican't-ridehisslipstream!"

A cheerful voice came from the ship: "Roger, he's just making a hook pass." The other pilot, bless him, elects to go around. Anymouse wobbles by the LSO platform. "Hook is down." Back up ahead of ship for a very, *very* gentle turn . . . Now down the stretch; deep approach, chugging up the wake with rain streaking canopy.

Well, I'm a sad cookie . . . *Another* plane cutting me out! Go around again.

Upwind, tuuurrn, down wind. Leg muscles jumping and arms aching in every bony joint. Oh, to have been a preflight product! Approach groove, long. Getting slants from LSO, but can't take 'em—blasted airplane is just aching to join the sub service . . . Crabbing to come out lined up with ramp. T'aint orthodox and if I don't answer a slant, ol' Paddle's gonna wave me off but quick. Try one itsy bitsy one. Yipe! Brace and pull the wing up.

At the ramp—lined up—there was the cut—I think. Cut, schmut, here I go. Took a mad stab to whack off the throttles, and get my hand back to stick. Whoops! Darn near rolled again, haul her up, now we're lined up and down we go. Come on, dadburnit! Forgot the book—this time you gotta flare! Brace yourself, we'll probably drive this one into the wardroom.

Ka-wump! Whatta you know! I've hit harder during daylight!

Whooie. Taxi forward. Down number one. Now the reaction—the slow burn really begins to sizzle. Then the payoff: the plane captain bustles up innocently to inquire "Is the plane Up?"

Mike Failure

On climbout in an F9F–5 Anymouse's oxygen mask mike failed, leaving him with a decision as to whether or not to continue his 500–mile cross-country, using boom mike for transmissions, or return to base.

Weather and cockpit pressurization were good and he decided to continue, descending to a lower altitude if flight safety was endangered. From previous low pressure chamber experience Anymouse believed his reaction to hypoxia was panic first, without the usual hail and hearty drunk stage.

"Nearing the final part of the climbout," he said, "several extra transmissions were necessary in order to clear up a miscalculation by ground personnel. I had to fly with my knees of course, while transmitting, holding my mask away from my face with my left hand and shoving the boom mike in place with my right. As I ascended and control became more sloppy I proceeded to do mild acrobatics when using my knees.

"Due to the rarefied air at altitude my transmissions became very weak and I lost radio communication about one-third of my way along. Also the cloud layers built up below me making me doubtful about any unauthorized change of altitude. I gave up trying to communicate anymore until very near my destination when I raised

another facility somewhere north of my path. All this time I was on 100 percent and used safety pressure after each unmasking, but I noticed also that the total amount of oxygen used was only 150 pounds. No wonder I felt slightly lousy near the end of the one hour and 20-minute hop.

"The big realization came however, only after I landed safely just how Anymouse I was with neither my brain nor my oxygen regulator working properly.

"It became apparent too, that old hypoxia had me from my climbout (or should I say takeoff) or I would have taken one of several recourses:

1. Turned back and aborted the hop.
2. Request a low altitude immediately upon mike failure.
3. Jeopardized my no-flight-violation record instead of my life and descended anyhow, authorization or no.

It Finally Happened

November 1955

"He nearly put one into the spud locker!" is a traditional comment of naval aviation which refers to a low

carrier pass that puts the plane in danger of hitting the stern of the ship. The odds against successful accomplishment of this feat are astronomical, and there have been no reports of pilots surviving a trip through the fantail. But there's always a first time. . . .

Following a night flight, the pilot of an F2H-3 began a carrier approach which was normal until he neared the groove. At this time the LSO [landing signal officer] observed an uncorrected rate of descent which necessitated a wave-off. Although the pilot added power, the plane did not respond in time to clear.

The airplane crashed into the starboard side of the fantail, just below the ramp, and exploded on impact, but the right wing and aft fuselage broke away and fell into the sea, carrying the fire away.

The pilot was able to scramble, unassisted, from the cockpit section which was wedged in the fantail. He sustained no serious injuries. The effective use of shoulder harness, safety belt, protective helmet and oxygen mask undoubtedly enabled the pilot to survive this most unusual accident.

"Arrangements were made with a nearby air station for repairs."

"When the airplane was again ready for flight . . ."

". . . it was pushed to the highway by local citizens."

As the aircraft took off down the highway everyone in town came out to take pictures of the unusual event.

—And Then There Were None . . .

Again, the Naval Aviation Safety Center has obtained a factual account of a flight situation of such impact as to warrant special treatment. And again, as in the presentation of the "Man With the Banjo" (Aviation Safety Bulletin No. 20–54) the report is offered without editorial comment and with only a brief introduction.

It began as a routine cross-country. En route these five pilots encountered unexpected weather. Faced with this emergency and others, each handled the situation differently. Here's a blow by blow account.

November 1955

It was a "routine" flight by members of a reserve squadron—eight pilots were scheduled; seven got airborne; five continued the flight to its unscheduled conclusion; one pilot died.

Concerning the five pilots, it is believed that their individual experience and backgrounds provide a fairly typical cross-section of reserve aviation. The list, which might well be repeated in any of a hundred similar activities, includes a manager of an electrical supply firm, the director of industrial relations for an oil refinery, a member of a construction company, an associate of a farmers' cooperative supply organization, and the director of a local chamber of commerce.

Married, family men almost without exception, these pilots drive or are flown to their base once each month to engage in three or four flights and to log an average of about 10 flight hours per month.

This is their story.

Eight reserve pilots were scheduled for a VFR cross-country navigation flight to provide cruise control training in F9F–7s prior to engaging in forthcoming maneuvers. Originally projected several months before, the flight received final approval and pilots were designated about 1030 one Saturday morning.

Because of the relatively short notice on which the flight was finally undertaken, the squadron found it necessary to obtain two replacement pilots from a local companion squadron. One of the replacements was designated flight leader because he had the necessary instrument qualification required for such flights.

Of the eight pilots scheduled, three had flown a hop previously during the day; only four had made cross-country flights in the F9F–7. As finally organized, the flight appeared something like this:

Number 1: (flight leader) received checkout in F9F–7 two months before and had logged 10.7 hours in model.

Number 2: Checked out in model a year previously and had about 60 hours in model.

Number 3: Checked out in model previous year and had about 30 hours in model.

Number 4: Checked out in model a year before; had about 29 hours in model.

Number 5: Checked out about two months before and had approximately 20 hours in model.

Number 6: Checked out a year before; had 20 hours in model.

Number 7: Checked out about three months before; had about five hours in model.

Number 8: Checked out a year before; had some 40 hours in model.

Distance of the flight was 555 miles over a route which approached mountainous terrain near the destination. Weather briefing noted a tornado well to the southwest of the route and scattered thunderstorms predicted en route. Time en route was one hour 30 minutes, with the flight to arrive over destination with an estimated 1840 pounds of fuel remaining.

Preflight planning was accomplished with most of the pilots working out their own flight plans, and with the flight leader completing a briefing "as thorough as any flight I ever briefed."

Starting, departure from the line and preliminary radio check was according to normal procedure. One aircraft was delayed on starting and was left at the line. Radio communications check proved difficult, with considerable shifting of frequency required to establish a common tactical channel.

On reaching the head of the runway there was an initial delay of several minutes while a number of aircraft landed. Takeoff was at 1705. Joinup after takeoff was quickly accomplished and the leader then circled the field at a low altitude to check the status of the delayed aircraft, which failed to leave the line. Flight members figured that some 800 pounds of fuel had been expended during delays.

Then There Were *Seven*

Departure and climb to 36,000 feet on a northwest course was uneventful, but approximately 110 miles out on course the No. 5 and No. 6 men returned to base after reporting excessive fuel consumption. No. 7 then moved up into the No. 5 position astern.

Then There Were *Five*

About 200 miles on course the flight encountered the first thunderstorm, an anvil head at about 32,000–34,000 feet, which they were able to drop under without difficulty. Thereafter several small thunderheads were flown over. Weather to the north and east of course appeared relatively clear.

About 250 miles out the canopy of No. 5, formerly No. 7, began icing over despite constant use of manual control, and in a short time he was looking out "through a dollar-sized hole." In a few minutes, however, the icing abruptly disappeared.

A radio check netted the report that destination weather was a comfortable 15,000 feet, scattered, with thunderstorms to the southeast.

Noting what appeared to be a sizable thunderstorm ahead, the flight began climbing to top it. At this time No. 5 began to lag behind. When the flight had attained 38,000–40,000 feet, and was nearing the thunderstorm, the flight leader advised he was reducing power to 87 percent to allow No. 5 to catch up. No. 5 gave a count for a DF [direction finder] steer from the planes ahead, which he could no longer see. On reduction of power by the leader, Nos. 3 and 4 overran and used their excess speed to pull up slightly higher than the rest of the flight.

Now No. 3 called in that he was encountering stall in his airplane and No. 5 noted the same condition. At this time a pilot, possibly No. 3, suggested reversal of course, but No. 4, higher than the others, reported he could see over the top of the thunderstorm.

Just short of the thunderstorm the leader began a left turn which immediately aggravated the stall of the aircraft. Mushing considerably, the flight entered the cloud, No. 2 entering first, followed by No. 1, No. 4 held course and altitude. No. 3's actions from this point are not known, but possibly he elected to go down through the clouds. No. 5 attempted a 180 but stalled through the tops of the thunderhead at about 39,000 feet.

From this point, the integrity of the flight disappeared as each of the remaining pilots found himself in a situation requiring a separate solution. The account of how each pilot attempted to solve his individual problem follows.

Lose Leader

Completing his turn away from the cloud and circling in the clear at about 34,000–36,000, No. 1 began calling the flight, but was unable to establish satisfactory communications. He then began a descent in the trough paralleling the near side of the cloud, throttle at idle, and leveled at 17,000 feet to go around the edge of the thunderhead and to resume base course.

It was then apparent that the 1500 pounds of fuel remaining would be insufficient to make destination, and No. 1 began looking for a place to land. Following a highway he descended to 5000 feet to select a stretch on which to set down. After dragging the road for obstructions he made an approach over a pickup truck and touched down, blowing a tire as brakes were applied. On landing runout he noted a slight hill over which he might expect to see a car come at any time, so he turned off the highway at a side road intersection to clear. A car immediately came over the hill to investigate the low flying airplane.

Driven into a nearby town the pilot obtained the services of a tractor and a hired hand to tow the plane into town. This was accomplished after a few mishaps involved in being towed off the pavement onto the soft shoulder.

Thereafter No. 1 was advised of the crash of another aircraft some 40 miles away and was driven to the scene to assist in its identification.

There There Were *Four*

On entering the cloud, No. 2 elected to descend through what he assumed to be only a layer, to bust out under, and remain contact to go on to destination. He extended speed brakes, reduced throttle and began a 5000–6000 fpm rate of descent, holding base course. The descent was considerably prolonged. He first encountered lightning and then severe turbulence, and meanwhile he attempted to hold a nose-down attitude to prevent stalling.

After the first period of turbulence No. 2 became concerned about his altitude with reference to surrounding terrain, believing that below 15,000 feet he would be dangerously near to the mountains ahead. He turned north, and got into more violent turbulence, lost control of the airplane a couple of times and at 15,000 feet decided to eject. Still in turbulence, still in a dive, he jettisoned his canopy (he lost his helmet but does not recall when this occurred), and releasing the controls, pulled the curtain. Nothing happened, but he had been told that he might reasonably expect a two or three-second delay in the firing of the seat, so he was not particularly upset over the delay.

Curtain over his chin, he waited—then decided to peek around the curtain to see if he were still in the airplane. He was. He released the curtain, waited, still diving, considered re-safetying the curtain, discarded the idea and went back to driving the airplane.

While considering his next move he saw the ground materializing below to show that he still had a safe altitude. Breaking out beneath the clouds at about 5500 feet he retracted speed brakes and took up an easterly heading, unable to get much speed because of the absence of the canopy. After searching for a time for a place to land, he selected a stretch of highway near a town. He was down to 500 pounds of fuel now. Checking the wind from the local trash dump he made an approach over an automobile at about 150 feet, leveled at 10 feet, cut the throttle and landed. Slowing to taxi, he folded the wings to cross a bridge and continued into town where he turned off to park on a side street.

After his report was made, arrangements were made for a nearby air station to send a crew with another canopy, fuel, a starter unit, and to disarm the hot seat. Faced with the problem of what to do with the seat cartridge, the pilot considered throwing it into a lake, burying it, and then obtained a shotgun from a patrolman and shot the side of the shell open, rupturing it so the powder could be removed. The shell case was turned over to investigating personnel for further check.

When the airplane was ready for flight, it was pushed by local citizens back to the highway, which was blocked off. A clear stretch of road about a mile in length was then available before the highway crossed a low bridge. Thereafter, another mile of open highway was usable. There was no fuel in the wing tanks; elevation of the "field" was 2200 feet.

The airplane was almost airborne at the first bridge, and in accordance with his preplanning, the pilot was able to lift the plane up on the oleos to clear the bridge safely. Thereafter he was airborne on the second stretch of "runway."

"After I got off," said the pilot, "I came back and made a pass by the town to do a roll of appreciation for their help."

Then There Were *Three*

Because No. 3 was not observed from the time the flight entered the top of the cloud, nor were any radio transmissions heard, his actions may only be guessed. The airplane crashed some 40 miles away from the point at which No. 1 landed. The plane hit in a near-vertical angle on the corner of a cement foundation of a farm structure, digging a large hole and being demolished by the impact.

After the initial inspection the investigating party concluded that the ejection seat was not in the wreckage. Shortly thereafter, because of the inconvenience caused the property owners by the crowds of spectators and souvenir hunters attracted to the scene, it was decided to bulldoze the wreckage into the hole and to cover it up. The pilot was later found, dead of injuries which possibly resulted from hitting some part of the plane on bailout. Questions then raised concerning the absence of the ejection seat prompted the re-opening of the crash hole to re-examine the wreckage. Parts of the ejection seat were then found in the wreckage.

Then There Were *Two*

The No. 4 man stated that from his position 1000–2000 feet above the rest of the flight, he could see over the top of the cloud, and recommended going over.

However, when the leader reduced power to allow No. 5 to catch up, No. 4 encountered stall and began to lose altitude. He increased power to 100 percent but still lost some 1000 feet more. A tentative turn with the rest of the flight increased the stall and he returned to base course and was in the cloud. He too, thought he would be able to penetrate quickly.

Within the cloud, he reports that his fuel consumption appeared to have increased, and he decided to get down in order to have some fuel remaining for landing. At this time he had about 1500 pounds. Knowing that a range of mountains was directly ahead on course he turned to parallel the mountains and continued his descent at about 4000 fpm. He too encountered violent turbulence but the airplane handled very well and he never lost control. He attempted to raise CAA and Navy towers without success and then called "Mayday." His only answer was from an Air Force B–25 which gave him some idea of weather conditions beyond the storm area.

At 15,000 feet he heard No. 2 call he was in the clear. At 12,000 feet the fuel warning light came on (he had not retarded throttle during his descent). At 11,000 feet he broke out beneath the thunderstorm and turned to intercept base course. After attempting to locate himself by landmarks and down to 700 pounds of fuel remaining he circled a reservoir with the intention of a water ditching.

Noting the length of the reservoir dam, about 9300 feet, and its width, some 25 feet, he elected to try and land on the dam itself. To one side, the water level was about 15 feet below the top of the dam. On the other side was a drop of about 250 feet. A guard rail, about three feet high ran along either edge of the dam.

On touchdown, he avoided use of brakes and, flaps clattering on the tops of the guardrail pipes, completed the rollout and added power to taxi off the far end of the dam. Taxiing down to some buildings he was met by an irate reclamation official who advised him that "Son, you're in *trouble!* You can't go landing on government property like this!"

Shortly thereafter, arrangements were made to report the landing and for the removal of the airplane.

Then There Was *One*

At the time the formation approached the cloud, No. 5 was at about 39,000 feet at about 170 knots, stalling through the tops of the clouds. On trying to make a 180, he stalled and mushed into the clouds. Attempting to fly out of the clouds on instruments, he also hit violent turbulence, being flipped on his back and getting into other unusual attitudes.

At times he was gaining 6000 fpm and at other times he was descending 4000 fpm. He came out below the clouds at 17,000 feet in a slight nosedown turn, but a low airspeed brought on a stall. He nosed over to pick up speed and lost altitude down to 6000 feet. He then climbed back to 15,000, having about 1900 pounds of fuel left.

Taking up an easterly course away from the storm area he was unable to establish his position, and spotting an abandoned airstrip, with only 700 pounds of fuel indicated, he elected to land. The strip was about 5800 feet long, and landing was without incident. No. 5 then "took a chance and started walking." He was later informed that he was quite fortunate in his choice of direction, for had he taken the opposite direction he would have found no houses, just a long stretch of open country.

He found a house and was able to report his landing and arrange for fuel to be brought to the airstrip. Then, he reports, "I got my biggest shock when I saw a spectator smoking near the airplane as it was being fueled!" The plane was returned to base.

—*And Then There Were None.*

The Aviation Safety Center is indebted to the pilots who voluntarily provided this candid account for the benefit of other pilots.

The Return of Walter Smitty

Herewith, in response to the number of requests (two by actual count), the Approach *chronicles another episode in the fabulous career of LTJG Walter Smitty, Scourge of the Skies. Smitty's initial appearance was in the August 1955 issue. With proper apologies to James Thurber, creator of the original character, the reader is invited to participate in another "incident," the details of which are based on two actual Anymouse reports.*

July 1980; from March 1956

LTJG Walter Smitty, aviator extraordinary, pilot's pilot, air adventurer, lounged against the coffee mess bar and listened indifferently to the readyroom chatter about him. As always, his lean, hawklike face was inscrutable, masklike. Idly his tapered fingers drummed in time with music from the radio nearby. Rocka-rolla-rocka.

Across the readyroom, elbows nudged into ribs and furtive, respectful whispers marked the presence of Smitty the Sky Scourge.

"That's Walter Smitty," a lieutenant whispered to a newly reported ensign, "The one and *only* Walter Smitty. And believe me, one . . . " The rest of the sentence faded as Smitty's steely glance flicked about the room.

"Who's Walter Smitty?" The newcomer, Ensign Peavey, was plainly unaware of the reputation of the Sky Scourge.

"Gad, man!" His companion regarded him with pity as he sought to correct this educational deficiency.

"Well," he began carefully, "You know who Lindbergh was, don't you? Did you ever hear of Rickenbacker?

Well, now forget them and just try to imagine Jesse James playing Captain Video, and . . . " The lieutenant found the task too great and got down to cases.

"Do you know that Smitty once shot off a tow banner?"

"So what's so amazing about that?" Peavey was still dubious.

"Nothing, stupid, except Smitty happened to be flying the tow plane at the time!"

Peavey gaped and stared with unabashed wonder at this marvel of military aviation. At the snack bar, Walter Smitty permitted the faintest of smiles to drift across his face. Abruptly he wheeled toward the door.

"Okay, you tigers!" his voice cracked vibrantly in the stirring language of airmen, "Launch 'em! Let's get that 'ol *Beechcraft* into the blue!"

The other pilots flinched slightly and, eyes averted, chewed vigorously on their hamburgers.

Chompa-choppa-chomp.

"Well?" Smitty demanded. "Ain't nobody gonna go with me on this hop to pick up them spare parts at Jax?" The answering silence was mute tribute to the awe in which the Sky Scourge was held. Then the new ensign, Peavey, leaped to his feet.

"Sir, *I'd* like to go with you." And the young man was suddenly red-faced under the keenly appraising eyes that swept him. The ensign shuffled nervously under the penetrating glance that seemed to ferret out his innermost secrets.

"You a pilot?" With characteristic directness, Smitty's question drove straight to the heart of the matter.

"Yessir, designated 3 months past, sir."

Again the cool, hard look—weighing, testing, searching.

"Okay, let's go, son. A night cross-country'll do you real good."

And the two, master airman and apprentice pilot, strode into the night. In the readyroom, a long sigh from the other pilots marked their departure.

When airborne, Smitty turned the *Beechcraft* to a southerly heading and, as ENS Peavey watched in appreciative bewilderment, his hands moved knowingly over radio controls tuning in JAX omni. Clicka-screecha-squawk. Under Smitty's sure touch the little twin-engined plane bracketed easily between the Atlantic coastline and the Appalachian mountains. Bracka-brackayaw. Nearing Jax, Smitty disclosed further evidence of his legendary prowess as he bird-dogged in on NAS Jax's low frequency range.

Over the range station, the Great Pilot graciously allowed the delighted Peavey to assist.

"Which way's the field from here, son?"

The copilot gulped slightly but was ready with the answer.

"East, sir," and Peavey's heart quailed at the quick frown on Smitty's face. Then the Sky Scourge permitted another of [his] rare smiles to be visible as his hawklike vision spied a field with a well-lighted runway dead ahead.

"Never mind, son. Course inbound is 269 degrees. There's the field straight ahead." The copilot wagged his head, amazed. Egad! The man's skill confounded even the Radio Fac Charts! The RFC showed the inbound bearing to NAS Jax to be 089 degrees from their position!

Peavey's heart swelled at the knowledge that he was flying with True Greatness.

On standard tower channel, Smitty requested landing instructions of Navy Jax and the acknowledgement came promptly. Landing Runway 27. Smitty descended into the pattern and began his normal approach, Vrooma-zooma-vroom.

Below, on Runway 27 at Navy Cecil Field, members of the crash crew glanced up from their task of removing a crippled Banshee fighter from where it had engaged the field arresting gear following a landing gear malfunction. The unidentified aircraft on downwind continued its approach, and Cecil tower began to call frantically to warn the airplane of men and equipment on the runway. UHF, VHF, and Guard frequencies gained no response. Two signal lights then speared their red warning beams at the Beech. The crash crew scrambled to clear the runway.

In the *Beech*, Smitty unfolded another bit of flying lore to the admiring Peavey.

"Ya see lotsa diffrunt kinds of lighting on these fields. That cluster of lights up there at the other end of the runway fr'instance. Some new kinda threshold or boundary markers, I reckon." The copilot bobbed his head in agreement, marveling anew at the uncanny depth perception of the Master Pilot.

The *Beech* touched down neatly, with lots of room to spare, and Smitty allowed the plane to roll out easily with deft touches of braking—Scruncha-screecha-scrunch. Nearing the end of the runway, the *Beech* jolted over the arresting gear anchor chain and Smitty spat a blistering remark about fouled-up air stations which permitted such a threat to runway operations. Peavey attempted unsuccessfully to imitate the deep growl of the Sky Scourge and, failing, curled his lip scornfully at this sad-sack air station.

Now, as the *Beech* threaded its way towards the turn-off, shadowy figures on either side scurried madly for cover. Pat-a-patta-pat. Smitty's contempt increased.

"Wish they'd knock off that blasted red light blinking over there by the tower—danged thing might confuse an inexperienced pilot. Wait'll I get into operations, I'll tell those characters off."

Peavey nodded firmly, resolving to make a few remarks of his own, say to a line crewman, or even a chief, maybe. He glanced approvingly at Smitty and tried to compress his lips into the same bitter line that creased the mouth of the Great Man.

At Navy Jax, a tower operator peered again into the darkness around the field, and seeing nothing, continued to call the Beechcraft. Some 12 miles west, the Cecil Field operations officer strode the floor in purple-faced wrath as he awaited the arrival of the pilot of the airplane which, unannounced, had just narrowly missed piling into the runway crash equipment.

The operations office door swung open, and a lean, hawkfaced pilot strolled in, cigarette drooping from the corner of his mouth, and flicked a negligent glance about the room. Tossing a flight plan towards the duty officer, Smitty yawned broadly and draped himself with unconscious grace over the counter, smoke curling lazily past half-lidded eyes.

"How ya, pal," the Sky Scourge's steely stare was only half-veiled, "Crummy sort of a outfit you folks run here . . ."

Across the field, the crash crew paused in their task as a sudden outburst of sound erupted from the vicinity of the operations building. Powa-powa-yeow.

The driver of the cherry picker squinted towards the source of uproar, flinching as the noise increased in volume.

"Cheeze," he exclaimed wonderingly, "I think the hangar roof just blew off!"

Crank It Right!

April 1956

So there you are, pretty well settled in your seven-man liferaft as you paddle away, a little reluctantly, from the sinking P2V.

All of you, pilot, copilot, aircrewmen and you, the passenger who just came along for the ride, are probably still surprised at the ease with which the crippled P2V was ditched. Now, with the preliminary counting of noses and injury check complete, you look expectantly at the pilot for the word.

Naturally, the first thing he directs is a check of the survival gear available for this unscheduled sea voyage. Then you go about the highly interesting business of unwrapping a remarkable number of ingenious devices and vitamin-loaded victuals all calculated to cover, comfort and conserve you during your enforced cruise. Now your little group leans forward to consider the last item to be unwrapped.

There it sits, atop a pyramid of assorted equipment—a squarish yellow-painted metal dingus which you regard with considerable puzzlement. Now, there's an impressive gadget—and you just wish you could recognize it.

Your initial guesses at identification don't contribute much either, as they range from "automatic canasta dealer" to "charcoal-fired rotisserie." Then some imaginative soul suggests reading the multi-form labels. Verrry interesting!

Yessir, lads, it's a CRT–3, which you now recognize to be the well known "Gibson Girl." Hurrah! Men! We've got it made! With this magical mechanism we can now tell the world of our plight and we're practically home! Whereupon there is general rejoicing and much toasting of electronics engineers with succulent fish juices—until some killjoy mumbles, "How do we work it?"

Loud hoots and jeers from the little assemblage. Why, it's simple, you just rig the thing according to the directions, turn these knobs and things and wind this crank.

All very heartening, until the Gibson Girl is rigged up in all her aerial splendor, and you find that there are just a few details which prevent your competing with John Cameron Swayze on the kilocycles. Things like knowing when to key it.

Well here's the ungarbled word on how to put out the ungarbled word to the folks who can write a happy ending to your lifeboat cruise.

Time Zero!

. . . The pilot of the F9F-6 walked directly to his aircraft, and the final part of the pattern fell into place—the hands of the unseen clock moved closer together. Time was running out. Bu[n]o 123456 was a TIME BOMB!

May 1956

There was nothing unusual about Sunday morning's activities at the reserve air station. It was cold—a 9–knot north wind put a cutting chill into the near zero temperature—but December in the Middle West was expected to be cold. A high overcast with good visibility promised favorable flying conditions and the station prepared for a busy day.

On the flight line of a reserve fighter squadron, crewmen worked at removing snow and ice from the squadron's *Cougars*. Two pilots had been scheduled for a 0900 launch but because of the ice removal takeoff time was delayed.

Shortly after 0900 the two pilots checked through the clearance desk and proceeded to the line shack where they signed out their aircraft. Leaving the line shack the pilot of Buno 123456 (a fictitious number) walked directly to his aircraft.

Ice and snow up to an inch covered the ramp with streaks of grey showing behind the parked airplanes where prop and jet blast had uncovered the concrete. Operations had inspected the area and declared braking action to be good. No sweat there.

As he walked up to his aircraft the pilot noted several crewmen finishing up the ice removal. Buckets and swabs lay off to one side and an NC–5 starting unit was in position. There was nothing to indicate that Buno 456 was different from any of her half-dozen sisters on the flight line and after a brief glance into the nosewheel well the pilot climbed into the cockpit.

But there was a difference this morning. Two weeks earlier there had been established a pattern of events which now moved to a climax. An unseen clock had been set in motion and time was running out. Buno 456 was a time bomb . . .

The chain of events had begun innocently enough. On the first Saturday in December Buno 456 was written up for a hydraulic leak in the nosewheel well area. A dropcheck showed no trouble but a hydraulic leak was found in the canopy selector valve which caused fluid to leak onto the pilot's oxygen system bottles.

No further work was attempted by hydraulic shop personnel as the bottles had to be removed for cleaning and work on the canopy selector valve would then be easier.

In the F9F-6 the oxygen bottles are just behind the pilot and are reached through a hinged access door on the left side of the fuselage. Two control systems, the elevator control cable and the throttle linkage, obstruct any work in the area of the bottles and must be disconnected. The elevator cable is broken by quick-disconnect fittings at blow-in doors on top of the fuselage with the resulting slack allowing the cable to be pushed clear of the oxygen bottles up forward. The throttle linkage is disconnected in a prominent spot right at the access door.

The oxygen shop was notified of the need to clean the oxygen bottles. Another work order was now issued to clean and reinstall the bottles. Fifteen days to time zero.

Sunday was a busy day and no time could be spared for Buno 456. Monday and Tuesday were non-working days and not until Wednesday morning did two men from the oxygen shop begin to remove the oxygen bottles. **A man from the airframes shop was asked to disconnect the elevator control cable. One of the oxygen shop men disconnected the throttle linkage.** Eleven days to time zero.

With this routine and uncomplicated act the breakdown of the maintenance system began. The hands of the unseen clock moved steadily on.

How does a maintenance system break down? Where and when does the initial flaw appear in a system which had been in successful operation over a span of several years? Inadequacies of the work order system existed—the vital problem of dual responsibility of shops in completing a joint operation had not been completely resolved—yet, there is no known system or safety device which can remove responsibility from the individual connected with aircraft maintenance.

After the elevator control cable and throttle linkage had been disconnected **the oxygen bottles were removed** and cleaned. Two hydraulics men **removed the leaking canopy selector valve** and repacked it.

Next day a different hydraulics man bench-tested the valve, reinstalled it, and checked the aircraft hydraulic system for satisfactory operation. He then signed off the maintenance department work order on the hydraulics discrepancy and returned it to the maintenance department planning office. He also notified both the planning office and the oxygen shop that Buno 456 was ready for the installation of the pilot's oxygen system bottles.

The planning office changed its status board to show that the aircraft was **down for oxygen equipment** rather than for hydraulics and two men from the oxygen shop began the work of replacing the bottles.

Though two men had been assigned to this job, only one of them worked on Buno 456 until the task was completed. After installing the bottles and hooking up the oxygen system the oxygen shop man called to a few mechanics working on a plane next to Buno 456. His words were to the effect that **Buno 456 was ready to have the throttle linkage connected.**

As this man walked away the unseen clock began ticking in deadly earnest. **He had neither observed nor received any indication that anyone heard him.**

Going to the airframes shop the oxygen man requested an AM [airframe man] to connect the elevator cable on Bruno 456. After this he went to the maintenance department planning office where he signed off the oxygen shop work order. In the meantime two airframe men connected the elevator control cable. **They checked the control stick for proper operation and then went on to another job.**

Ten days to time zero.

During the time Buno 456 was down a leak had developed in the left brake assembly. On Friday the brake was repacked but it failed to hold under pressure. A new assembly was ordered but as there were none in the local supply the plane was grounded.

The new brake did not arrive so on the following Wednesday a brake from an ACOG aircraft was installed. **On Friday hydraulics personnel changed the canopy.** Two days to time zero.

By Saturday morning Buno 456 had been an armed lethal package for more than a week, the disconnected throttle poised like a firing pin as the hours moved past.

Now it appeared that her fatal ailment would be diagnosed—a mechanic began a preflight inspection in the hangar. However, in the course of his inspection he noted that the left fire warning light was inoperative. **He stopped his uncompleted inspection** and reported the discrepancy to his crew leader who reported it to the electric shop.

The electric squawk was soon corrected and then another mech was assigned to finish preflighting the aircraft. During his inspection he noted that the plane needed fuel and after having it towed to the flight line he went to the line shack where he reported this fact. While he was in the line shack it started snowing and word was passed that flying had been secured.

The mech never did return to finish the inspection he had started.

The number of hours remaining for Buno 456 could now be counted on your fingers. But there was one more good chance that she could be de-armed. Early Sunday morning an airman began another preflight inspection.

This time a small hydraulic leak was found on the nose strut and upon completion of his preflight the airman returned to the line shack and reported the leak. No mention was made of the condition of the throttle linkage.

One more small chance remained although only minutes were left now. As the airman departed for the line shack the oxygen cart was making its way up the flight line toward Buno 456. The airman had observed that oxygen pressure had been down to 700 psi and it was oxygen shop practice to replenish any system which was below 1000 psi. **If the system were filled the fuselage access door would have to be opened.** Just inside that door was the throttle linkage.

The airman and a mechanic returned to the plane to check the hydraulic leak and it was decided it did not warrant grounding the plane. Thereupon both men returned to the line shack and **the plane was made available for flight.**

Oxygen shop personnel had not kept a log and they were unable to recall whether Buno 456 had been serviced.

After putting his plane "Up," the airman left the line shack and returned to the flight line where he began working with a group of men removing ice and snow from the parked *Cougars*. The group moved down the line, swabbing the icy aircraft surfaces with frost spray and they were just finishing Buno 456 as the pilot walked up to his plane.

Buckets and swabs lay off to one side and an NC–5 starting unit was in position. There was nothing to indicate that Buno 456 was different from any of her half-dozen sisters on the flight line, and after a brief glance into the nosewheel well the pilot climbed into the cockpit.

But there was a difference. For Buno 456, time had run out. The engine starter whined against the inertia of the compressor and with the usual "bloomph" of igniting fuel the lightoff was completed. The last link in the chain of events fell into place—Buno 456 became an instrument of destruction.

After a normal start the engine did not level off at idle speed but roared into 100 percent power. In a runaway engine resulting from a disconnected throttle linkage, the high pressure shut-off valve would be free to move between the positions of *CUTOFF* and full *OPEN*.

Buno 456 slid forward on the icy ramp, jumped the chocks and headed for a P2V parked 200 feet in front. Picking up speed to 40 knots it struck the P2V's nosewheel and prop blade and began a skidding starboard turn which ended 240 degrees from the original starting direction. Part of the *Cougar's* right wing was torn off upon impact with the P2V.

Engine still roaring at high power, Buno 456 again picked up speed and raced 200 yards into the side of another P2V at 60 knots. Emerging from the other side of the *Neptune*, minus a port wing, windscreen and other small parts, the *Cougar* ripped off the tail of an SNB, ran between two fueling trucks then penetrated the side of a hangar at 85 knots.

The time was zero plus 30 seconds.

An intense fire broke out immediately and swept through the hangar, destroying the hangar and three planes parked inside. The pilot and two men in the hangar were killed.

After the fire the throttle linkage was recovered. It provided unmistakable evidence that it had remained disconnected in the oxygen compartment.

Only Thunderstorms

Over, Under, and Out!

The Navy's first example of a successful underwater ejection occurred in March of this year. Anticipating the high degree of interest in this unusual accident, Approach *presents a special account of the instance, obtained from the advance Aircraft Accident Report and from a telephone conversation with the pilot involved.*

June 1957

Following his fourth (mirror) carqual landing in an F4D–1, the pilot experienced an apparent brake failure as he taxied forward. Unable to answer the plane director's signals, the pilot could not correct a veer to the starboard side, where the plane fell into the catwalk. The aircraft hesitated for a few seconds (during which the pilot rechecked the oxygen to be on 100%) and then fell into the water inverted.

The impact was "extremely hard" and the pilot was momentarily stunned. The glass canopy of the F4D shattered upon impact and water immediately filled the cockpit. The pilot's first action ("just to be doing *something*") was to unlock the manual canopy release, after which he reached the face curtain with no difficulty and fired the ejection seat.

The pilot does not recall any excessive force of the ejection, and is confident that the automatic lap belt release functioned normally with no effort on his part. He first attempted to get rid of his seat "as if I were sitting in it," but being unsuccessful, was then able to roll out of the seat. In the total darkness, he wondered which way to swim, but "nature took care of this," and he was carried to the surface by the buoyancy of his parachute pack. During his underwater journey, the pilot passed through the turbulence of the ship's wake to emerge approximately 1000 feet astern, where he was promptly picked up by the helicopter.

The helicopter pilot observed the large bubble made by the ejection charge, and timed the ensuing period until the pilot's appearance as being of 45 seconds duration. (Pilot's estimate: "About three weeks"). The pilot's injuries included bruises and small skin abrasions, the latter probably caused by the shattering glass of the canopy. He has since returned to normal flying status.

The rapid pickup by the helicopter made it unnecessary for the pilot to inflate his mae west, and although he found his water-logged gloves (correct size not available for issue to him) an impediment to releasing his parachute harness, he was retrieved with harness and parachute intact.

(In the light of other accident information, it is considered that the possible deployment and fouling of the chute during retrieving makes this procedure undesirable.—Ed.)

The pilot's helmet and mask (with a MC–3 connector) remained on and the pilot recalls no difficulty in breathing prior to ejection, or in holding his breath after ejection. He was conscious of some ear pressure, which he relieved on surfacing.

Queried about his previously stated conviction to eject in just such a situation, the pilot observed that this idea resulted partially from his misconception that the manufacturer had tested both canopy and ejection seat to a depth of 50 feet. (*Approach* is informed by Douglas that the canopy was successfully tested to a depth of 15 feet. DAC [Douglas Aircraft] adds the opinion that the fact that the canopy glass broke on impact or that the cockpit was punctured apparently was the reason the canopy separated from the aircraft and pulled the safety firing pin of the Type I catapult.)

Saga of a Sea Squatter

Scene: aboard a submarine shortly after it had picked up the crew of a P2V which had ditched about four hours earlier. The P2V, with a crew of 10, had been on a routine night antisub searchlight exercise and had been airborne about seven hours when it experienced an uncontrollable fire in the starboard reciprocating engine. The pilot had a little over 2000 total hours, of which 1250 were in P2V.

November 1957

"Everything worked real fine except this lighter I've been carrying for years[,]" the wet but unhurt pilot was telling the skipper of the sub. "Soon as I get into these dry clothes I'll tell you 'bout it."

"Sure, take your time, we've got several hours yet. I'm glad to see all 10 of you got out in good shape—you must have had your crew well trained and ready."

"I'd say we were all pretty lucky too, getting out with just two of us getting slight bruises. Sure glad you people came along when you did though—I was really beginning to cuss this lighter, 20 good, dry weeds and nothing to light 'em with. Gimme a light, would you skipper?"

"Sure, here—you should get yourself one of these, we all use them cause they work *under water*—heh! Now, tell me how this iron bird of yours came to rest in our ocean."

"It came upon us without much warning—we were tooling along with 160 BMEP [brake mean effective pres-

sure], 34 inches and 1950 turns when suddenly the starboard recip backfired real violent-like. We riched up the mixtures and reduced MP [manual proportional] some, and watched 'er pretty closely. The BMEP was 10 pounds low and fluctuating. Well, we were in the midst of a small conference on the subject when she went POW! again. Kinda muffled this time, and immediately started to burn."

"Fire in the air, that's a real hair-raiser for you guys isn't it?"

"Well, it sure isn't any tea party, but it's an emergency which normally should give you enough time to think and act—if you think and act quickly. The fire generally takes a certain amount of time before it can burn through vital structural members. During that time the plane is, most always, controllable. In our case, for example, we had about 2000 feet so we tried to dive the fire out. Soon as we saw we couldn't, I decided to ditch. By that time we were shedding wheelwell doors and the oil coolers off the starboard engine."

"Did you have much time to prepare?"

"We had about 10 minutes between the first backfire and the time we actually joined the surface Navy. Soon as No. 2 caught fire I shut it down, the copilot secured the gas, oil and hydraulic fluid, and started the jets. We switched to emergency IFF [identification, friend or foe] and I had the radioman send an SOS. Right after that we lost all radio and ICS [intercockpit communication system] too."

"Do you have an alarm bell or something like our horns to signal for ditching?"

"No we don't, and by gosh that's one thing I'm gonna recommend back on the beach. We shouted the word back to the flight deck, and everyone got ready in time. The men heaved all loose gear down into the tunnel. Boy, it's important to get that stuff out of the way—I hate to look back at the nav table and see a pair of dividers lying there, pointing right ahead. Anyway, everyone was in his ditching station before we splashed. Radioman popped his hatch open and strapped in facing aft.

One of the boys decided the Mk IV raft on the wing center section should be made ready, so he propped it in the radio compartment. I think that's probably why we lost the raft, it must have been washed aft by the inrush of water. They should have left it in place, it's secured for ditching there and can still be jerked loose in a hurry."

"So that's why you were all in one raft—you were crowded in there like a Sheepshead Bay fishing boat. You didn't step right into the raft did you? Like those people did when that commercial plane went in out here recently?"

"No, we weren't quite that stylish. We went into the water and had two men climb in on opposite sides to keep it from tipping. You know, we're all eligible for membership in the Sea Squatter's Club."

"Mmmmm, I've heard of that. Some outfit that makes raft inflation gear started it, didn't they?"

"Yep, I know several guys who belong. They send you a lapel emblem and a card that other Sea Squatters can autograph. Sorta like the Short Snorters only more exclusive. I heard of one guy who became a member when he overshot the *Wolverine* in Lake Michigan—as they were trying to haul him aboard he was still trying to inflate his raft to become eligible!"

"With this fairly calm sea I'd guess you didn't have time to travel very far, did you?

"Did you use all of the equipment they put on those things?"

"We didn't try to go anywhere except to pull away from the plane before it sank. It stayed up for about 20 minutes, I guess that's because it didn't break up. Well anyway, we used everything except the emergency rations, and by gosh, like I said, everything worked except this stinkin' lighter. Got another light? Mpfff, thanks. We broke out the radar reflector right away, and the oars. Got kinda worried when my first seagoing command began to ship water and no bailing bucket or sponge in sight. One of the boys contributed his Wellington boots for bailing buckets.

"We cranked up the Gibson Girl, and inflated the balloon with the hydrogen generator. Kinda hard holding that generator under water[;] I wish they'd weight it more.

"Someone had brought along a flashlight, so we were able to read the instructions. All our life jackets lights worked too[;] I had everyone turn 'em on when you got near. About two hours after we began sailing we saw a plane coming right for us and we lit off two flares. I guess he saw us right away, cause he began circling, so we quit cranking the Gibson Girl and began combing our hair so we'd look real presentable to whoever picked us up."

"Were you able to talk with the plane that sighted you?"

"No, we didn't find our walkie-talkie right away. Funny, we found it when one of the boys went hunting among the survival gear for cigarets. Soon as we came up on the air we were answered by an Air Force plane and we talked pretty steadily with them until you fished us out. You know, that li'l rig sure is good for the old morale—I could see everyone in the raft sort of light up inside soon as we were answered, like when the travelogue is over and Jayne Mansfield comes on."

"Say, tell me, I'd been told that your P2V breaks off somewhere near the tail when you ditch—you say it stayed afloat for 20 minutes and didn't break up?"

"This is one time the bird didn't break apart, Skipper. Most likely because our ditching was somewhat unorthodox. I'm gonna write in to APPROACH about it, although I'm sure they'll say 'it's interesting, but let's look further into the possibilities before recommending any changes in ditching SOP [standard operating procedure].' We ditched with gear down and no flaps.

"We had dropped the gear to prevent the starboard tire from exploding in the wheelwell. It was burning when it came down, but the airstream blew it out. I decided not to use flaps because things looked pretty well under control and I thought of the possibility of getting unbalanced flaps with all that fire out there. We retarded the good recip and the jets, turned parallel to the swells, and set up 200 feet per minute at about 125 knots.—

"Biggest thing I noticed on touchdown was we didn't do that bump-skipitty-BUMP that I was anticipating. We just hit once and stuck, and the deceleration wasn't nearly as much of a jolt as I'd expected.

"We began shipping water pretty quickly though. I went out my overhead hatch and the copilot pulled the raft release before climbing out."

"You think everyone did all he could then, to make your ditching successful?"

"Generally yes, I think everyone aboard contributed something, and no one got panicky or helpless. One of the men, in his eagerness to get out, got a bit shook when he found he couldn't get up, but he calmed down soon as he realized he just hadn't unbuckled his safety belt. I learned later, on the raft, that one of the men had loosened the water breaker just before the ditching—he said he wanted to be sure it would come loose when he went to remove it later. Luckily, it didn't come loose by itself, but I convinced him it wasn't the thing to do. He admitted he was wrong, and I think he did it just because he had no specific duty assigned and felt he *had* to do *something*—you know, same as the guy who runs around getting hot water while his wife is having a baby?—

"Well anyway skipper, I'm now a firm believer in survival equipment—and in submarines!—

"Here skipper, you keep this lighter, even though it doesn't work, it's got my name engraved on it so maybe you can put it in a trophy case or something. This is the first time it let me down, I used to win bets on it lighting the first time, just one spin and—HEY, looky skipper— it WORKS!"

In the Beginning

Lt. Cmdr. R. P. Brewer, assistant air operations officer, USS Intrepid; August 1958

People and pilots being what they are, when two or more generations of airplane drivers get together to talk shop—shop-talk still takes precedence over the Number Two Subject by a narrow margin—seems as if the tales the old boys spin just naturally dominate the conversation. Young bucks discover, after a few unrewarding efforts to depict the zest of sonic flight and stratospheric heights, that *their* petty world of afterburners and electronics pales into insignificance beside the soaring exploits of the Elder Pilot. How can the kerosene contrail of a thousand-knot magnesium monster compare with the heady perfume of airplane dope and burnt castor oil?

Yessiree, when the old boy begins to weave a yarn there's a certain magic glow about the Past that makes "way back when" the golden era which the rest of us unfortunates missed.

There is, however, some considerable evidence to show that the good old days were not without their pitfalls and prattfalls—the very same kind of troubles we still urge you to avoid. Matter of fact, there's a surprising similarity in the pattern of bang and prang down through the years. The principal difference between Then and Now seems to be that when spruce and glue and linen were replaced by titanium and flush riveting, the prangs merely became noisier, the repairs got awfully expensive, and bodily damage was not limited to bruises incurred in climbing down out of trees and haystacks.

Prompted by a curiosity as to just what was the accident picture in the stick-and-wire era, we poked into the dusty files of the Safety Center and came up with a portrait which is perhaps a bit more candid than that painted by the nostalgic brush of the greybeard yarn spinners. Mind you, the exploits and achievements of this magnificent group of pioneers can never be belittled by the likes of us Johnnie-come-lately throttle benders. But if, amidst the constant nagging of folks who insist that you fly in a manner calculated to keep you a regular member of bull sessions, you can derive some comfort from the facts that the old folks had their share of troubles too, well, pull up a chair.

The official recording of accident data appears not to have gone back beyond 1920—although it's pretty well established that there were numerous clouds of dust generated around the sod fields of yore—and we're pretty certain the lusty clatter of the OX–5 and its predecessors was often interrupted by the crunch of spruce and bamboo. As to the accident *rate*—well, it must have been pretty terrific during the fabled era when One Flight usually equalled One Crackup.

The first known AAR [aircraft accident report], as recorded on one side of a modest 5 x 6 card, is noted to have occurred on January 2, 1920. The name of the individual who thus achieved this dubious distinction was charitably unrecorded. The airplane involved was a something called a HS-3L—no relation to the helicopter family of more recent designation.

The crash chroniclers of that early day were usually terse to the point of secretiveness concerning the details of flying fiascos, and this first one observes only that there were no injuries, and the aircraft suffered damage only to the "keel fittings." A neat package, uncluttered by tiresome conclusions as to cause factors, and completely free of the reproachful recommendations which give great pain to the makers of doctrine and airframes alike.

Accident Number Two of the official record accounts briefly for a vaguely untoward event involving a JN-6B, the revered *Jenny*. This also happened on January 2—1920 was off with a bang.

Some four days later there is noted the first forced landing, made "in a heavy sea as a result of a gas line failure." Additional details, which must have been dramatic, if not tragic, are missing. The fundamental flight safety philosophy of passing along the experiences of others was yet to attain any formal status.

The next day, January 7, 1920, there occurred the first ground accident, when an N–9 was destroyed "due to handling and storage." From which fragment of intelligence one can only conclude that here was new evidence that there was indeed an era of iron men and wooden ships.

Moving along, and at quite a clip too, on January 13, the first Navy dirigible accident, so recorded, occurred as a result of a "rent in envelope." The uncertainties of test flying next are revealed when, on January 15, a Loening "Kitten" monoplane encountered difficulties which are sketchily recorded in an account chiefly notable for the wryly puzzled comment: "A peculiar airplane."

"Carrier" aviation enters the accident picture with an equally un-illuminating entry which notes merely that a *Sopwith Strutter* came a cropper in operations off the U.S.S. *Pennsylvania*. This on January 29, 1920.

Interspersed through the record are numerous, exasperating notes which create vivid images of aerial drama—cryptic accounts of happenings the complete story of which can only be guessed. For example there is recurrently mentioned the thought provoking term "Kite balloon," which offers all kinds of mental pictures of pre-Vanguard experiments.

The first naval aviation fatality recorded in the card system happened on March 19, 1920 in a Pensacola accident. Cause: "Lack of judgment on part of the pilot."

Then there was the one which seemed to fall, literally, in a class by itself. A slightly heavier-than-air product called a T-5-L met with misfortune due to "failure of glue," and incidentally became the first recorded material failure. Seems the "failure" caused a strut to spring out of line, with unhappy results.

The names of the airplanes appearing on the accident cards read like a recognition journal of the day, had there been such a thing—Sopwith One-and-a-Half Strutter, HS-3L, HS-2, MF Boat, Martin, VE-7—all names to swear by or at, as the situation indicated.

Another "Kite balloon," there's that thing again, was struck by lightning in May, 1920 at San Pedro, California. Injuries, if any, to pilot, if any, unrecorded. The first fatal midair collision is listed as having occurred between an N-9 and an HS-2 at Pensacola. The pilot of the HS-2 was killed. Even then, it seems, there were times when things could move "faster than you think."

Some accidents appear to have resulted from certain occupational hazards peculiar to the times. Case in point is that of the JN-6D on June 19, 1920. This *Jenny* was taking off closely behind another airplane (no tower/radio control then, junior) which left a billowing cloud of dust (no runways either, Lieutenant) which obscured the view somewhat for the *Jenny* pilot. Midway in his takeoff run, the latter individual suddenly beheld a large stack of baled hay dead ahead. The pilot "jerked" the airplane around (no brakes, buster) to miss the haystack, and "slipped" on the left wing and nose. Damage to flier, flying machine and fodder, not known.

Free balloons drift occasionally through the picture, as on June 25, 1920, when some unknown aeronaut provided an early, if definitely not the last[,] argument against "improper landing in a high wind."

All throughout this record of bamboo boo-boos, the startling similarity of cause factors, when compared to almost identical accidents down through the years, repeats itself with a regularity which speaks poorly for man's ability to profit from past experience. Take a look at some of these, partly classified by present day criteria—and lest you're prone to chuckle smugly at our ancestors' antics, try substituting current aircraft models and present day situations for these relatively ancient happenings.

Judgment: A Nieuport 28, on June 28, 1920, equipped with detachable wheels, managed to "retract" same permanently when the airplane struck the ground with exceptional force on landing, causing the wheels to part company with the airframe. This at a place called Hampton Roads, Virginia.

Facilities: A JN-6 hit a rut on landing, swerved and hit a tractor.

Pilot technique/Judgement: An early Boeing pilot tried a loop, with too little airspeed, at 200 feet altitude. The plane fell off on the right wing. Survey damage, no injuries.

Proficiency: A Burgess-Curtiss N-9 accident was concluded to have resulted from "lack of practice on part of pilot, who had been recalled from inactive duty for 15 days . . ."

Maintenance/Material: The first passenger fatality is recorded on August 9, 1920, when a DH-4B (referred to as a "flaming coffin," if our War-Birds background serves us correctly) had an engine failure at low altitude due to gas line stoppage.

Pilot Error: The first recorded use of *this* familiar phrase is found in the account of an August 20, 1920 DH-4B accident. Airplane rolled off the field into the mud and flipped over on its back.

Planning/Weather Damage: On September 17, 1920, at Pensacola, a pilot was drowned and eight seaplanes were overturned and lost in a storm.

Supervision: First student fatality reported in November, 1921, in a VE-7.

Flight Planning/Fuel Management: A sergeant, "not a graduate of Great Lakes nor an aviation man . . ." consequently not drawing flight pay, crashed a JN-6HG-1 on empty tanks. However, "in view of his previous excellent performance, no disciplinary action taken."

Disposition Board: Another, if unpleasant first, is noted on June 30, 1923, when there was recorded the first recommendation to examine a pilot for fitness for flying.

Maintenance/Personnel Error: On 1 August 1923, a VO-1 got a premature catapult shot from the U.S.S. *Richmond.* Probable reason for no injury: No personnel on board the aircraft at the time.

Aero-Medical: On 24 April 1924, following a fatal N-9 accident, there is reported the first instance of an autopsy. Results of the autopsy revealed that the pilot was "subject to fainting spells."

Technique: In 1925, during a carrier landing aboard the *Langley*, a VE-9 hit the ramp, knocked the wheels off, was sent to a nearby NAS [naval air station] and landed with no injuries.

Judgment: September, 1924: Pilot of an HS-2L "flew up a small creek with insufficient altitude" (and doubtless without a paddle).

Experimental Test: During an experimental flight a TS-1 made a CV landing on the *Langley*, which happened to be tied up at the dock at the time. Pilot settled at the ramp, but was "stopped by arresting gear."

There, at least in part, is the first chapter of what was naval aviation's most colorful era. If certain aspects of this thumbnail sketch of the accident picture of 1920 seem vaguely familiar, perhaps it is because the total picture is a sort of daguerreotype of the same subject which has been reproduced all too often in naval aviation of 1958. Only the more recent addition of cinemascope-quality accident coverage and 3-D investigative methods have served to bring the background causes into clearer focus. The record is emphatically consistent on one point: people and hardware can mean trouble.

Knowing this, you can arrange to stay out of the accident picture simply by developing a professional appreciation of the lessons to be learned from the past. And that, the Old Pro will probably tell you, is what is known as avoiding over-exposure to trouble—by recognizing both capabilities *and* limitations of yourself and your airplane.

Search Discontinued

January 1959

Flight operations above the carrier were proceeding routinely on a day in June in the Mediterranean.

A two-plane combat air patrol was taking part in a NATO exercise involving foreign aircraft. Vectored for an intercept of two friendlies, the section leader in an F9F-8B observed a pair of F9F-8's close ahead at about 28,000 feet. He began a steep right turn to come around behind them. Suddenly a NATO fighter appeared in his path . . .

Mid-air collision.

"A ball of fire," one witness described it. Another said it was "exactly like a 5-inch shellburst."

Immediately following the explosion, a parachute with alternating red and white panels was seen opening.

As it descended to the water, the NATO pilot showed no signs of life. No one saw the American pilot.

Although three eyewitnesses of the mid-air collision were positive there could have been no survivors, the American pilot did survive.

As the two aircraft collided, the American pilot was jolted by the crash which ripped his cockpit canopy away. The next thing he was aware of was the sky in his face as his oxygen mask and helmet and his life vest flashlight were torn off by the blast. Above him he saw the face curtain handle, reached for it and pulled it. He was immediately ejected.

During his five-mile descent to the water, he breathed oxygen by mouth from the tube on his bailout bottle.

The pilot was equipped with an automatic lap belt release but did not have an automatic parachute opener. He free-fell for almost 27,000 feet in a head-down position. At an altitude of 1500 feet, he finally pulled his chute ripcord. The chute opened at 1200 feet and he was swung feet down under the canopy. As the investigating flight surgeon later wryly commented in his report on the accident, to freefall to such a low altitude before actuating your chute is "not the way to live to be 90."

Releasing his leg and chest snaps and retaining his chute by crossing his arms to hold the harness in the descent, the pilot hit the water head up, feet first, opened his arms and fell free of the chute. The chute pack was still attached by the lanyard to his Mk II life vest.

A strong wind billowed the chute, dragging the pilot through the water by the liferaft lanyard. He went under several times before he was able to spill the air from the canopy by pulling on the top shrouds. As the chute suddenly collapsed, his feet became entangled in the shroud lines.

After inflating his mae west, the pilot broke out his pararaft and inflated it. He was still unable to free his legs from the shroud lines.

At this point, the pilot committed what he later realized was an "almost fatal error." In his desperation to get into the raft, he pulled his sheath knife from its scabbard on the left leg of his summer flight suit and cut through the tangled shroud lines. He then climbed into the raft.

About a half-hour later, he realized that along with the snarled shroud lines he had cut loose his PK-2 survival kit containing both seawater desalting chemicals and solar still. Among the other items in the kit were two packets of dye marker, a signalling mirror, a poncho, one can of rations, a corner reflector and two distress flares.

All that he had left was his knife, the equipment on his Mk II life vest minus the flashlight, and his two-piece personal survival kit, the PSK–2.

Meanwhile, although witnesses felt that no one could have survived the mid-air collision, an extensive search of the collision area had begun. AD aircraft began to search upwind from the point at which the NATO parachute had landed, through the area where the collision had occurred. Shortly afterwards, a squadron of destroyers began a line-abreast sweep of the same area. The wind at this time was 30 to 35 knots and the sea condition was rough with whitecaps.

The mid-air collision had taken place in the late afternoon. That evening, the pilot saw two AD's flying at about 1500 feet in a good position to see him on his life raft. He fired one of his day-smoke signals; it functioned well but did not attract attention. The night portion of this flare did not work.

When he saw two more searching aircraft, he fired the night portion of his second and last flare. It was brilliant but went unseen. The day portion of this flare did not work.

Several times he used his dye marker but with no success.

That same night, the pilot saw the lights of several merchant ships. Later, he spotted about 10 mast-top lights and realized that this was a destroyer line searching for him. Passing close to two of the destroyers, he blew wildly on his whistle—his only means of signalling left—but was unable to attract attention.

Around dawn the next morning, the pilot saw the destroyers returning. This time he passed outboard of the flanking destroyers so close that from the crests of the waves he could make out figures on the deck. Again he blew his whistle, waved frantically and released dye marker but he could not attract their attention.

He saw more planes later in the morning—two AJ's headed east, a P2V in the distance and a NATO twin-float seaplane. The seaplane turned from its course directly toward him and for a few joyful minutes he thought he had been spotted. However, the plane flew right over him and continued in a westerly direction. It became smaller and smaller until finally it disappeared into the distance.

That afternoon, the aircraft and destroyer search was called off as hopeless.

During the day, the winds and seas increased. Although the sea and air were warm, the wind blowing on the pilot's wet clothes kept him constantly chilled. Shivering continuously, he pulled the raft's covers up like a tent and huddled beneath them.

The wind was high and the sea was rough on his second night on the raft. During that night and the following day, the raft overturned five times. Each time, the pilot had to unsnap the PK–2 retaining lanyard to get back into the raft, then resnap it.

On the afternoon of the third day, the pilot sighted a flight of ADs going from south to north at a low altitude. He put dye marker in the water but again was not seen.

Desperately thirsty by this time, he thought first of the solar still and desalting chemicals in the survival kit he had cut loose and then of the bottle of ice water his wife always kept in the refrigerator back home in the States.

During the day he managed to fish a bottle of liquid out of the sea but it turned out to contain vinegar. Except for the two chocolate bars in his personal survival kit, the closest he came to food was when he passed a few rotten apples bobbing in the water.

The raft overturned several times that day but by night the seas and winds had calmed considerably.

By this time, the pilot had given up all hope of being picked up and began to wonder what he could do to help himself. Getting to land, he decided, was his only chance but which way was land?

The morning of the fourth day, shortly after light, two peaks of an island appeared on the southern horizon. A bit later he saw an island to the east which he could identify as Stromboli.

Referring to his wet but still legible WAC [world aeronautical chart], the pilot identified the southern island as Salina; he estimated its distance as about 15 miles. Knowing his survival depended on his getting to this island, he determined to paddle to it if it took him all day and all night.

Paddling steadily as possible for an hour at a time without measuring his progress, he managed to make headway by the day's end. At sunset, he could make out what looked like houses on the hillside. After dark, village lights were visible although dim. Using the lights for direction, he paddled toward the island.

At about 0200, he was within 100 yards of the shore but was so exhausted that he could not continue. He passed out in the raft. When he regained consciousness, with great effort he climbed up onto a breakwater and pulled the raft behind him. The time was approximately 0300.

When he tried to stand, his legs were too weak to support him and he fell on his face. Stumbling and falling, he struggled to the foot of the hill only to find all the houses empty. With great difficulty, he climbed the hill until he found an occupied house. He pounded on the door and called for water, then collapsed in the courtyard. The people in the cottage thought he was drunk and, at first, would not open the door to help him.

After a short time, the householders' suspicions quieted and they came out to investigate. They brought the exhausted pilot some water, then took him inside the house. After giving him dry clothes, they put him to bed and summoned the village doctor. The pilot later stated that, in spite of the time of year, this was the first time he had been warm in three-and-a-half days.

. . . Three-and-a-half days.

What had been happening during this time at the pilot's home back in the States?

After the unsuccessful search had been called off and a memorial service conducted aboard the carrier, a second memorial service was scheduled at the pilot's home base. Relatives, former Naval Academy classmates and friends gathered from all over the country to be with the pilot's "widow" and her two young daughters.

On Salina, the village doctor had notified local authorities who in turn sent word of the pilot's survival to Naples and the U.S. Navy. A destroyer picked him up at the island the next day and returned him to the carrier. Meanwhile, the miraculous news had been speeded to the States in time to cancel the memorial service.

O-Club Saturday Night

April 1959

In the main dining room, the scraping sounds of chairs being pushed back from tables mingled with the rattle of dishes and silver and the strains of the Saturday night dance band tuning up. In the adjoining bar, a white-jacketed attendant wiped circles of moisture off the counter as two aviators approached.

"What'll it be, gentlemen?"

"Couple of beers. Okay, Bob?"

"Right, Jim. Match you for it."

A few minutes later, the two pilots were settled in a corner, glasses in hand.

"Now, my friend, let's have the whole story, or as the Madison Avenue types say, the Big Picture," Jim said as he lit a cigaret and stretched back for an ashtray from the next table.

"Okay," Bob said with a grin, "but remember, as the television types say, YOU asked for it!

"First, just to relieve your anxious little mind, I came out of this whole thing all in one piece. What really hurt, though, was that my accident was the first one in the squadron in almost two-and-a-half years—nearly 44,000 hours of flying. I couldn't have done anything to prevent the accident—it was cylinder failure—but, man, I sure hated to be the guy to shoot down that squadron record. And another thing that killed my soul was that I was so damn careless when I strapped in. But I'll get to that later.

"There I was cruising along in my AD-4B... beautiful day... IFR [instrument flight rules]... clearance on Green Six... ceiling unlimited, visibility 15 miles. I'd been up about four-and-a-quarter hours. Dusk was just coming on.

"All of a sudden there was a surge in the engine and it began to run rough; flames started coming out from the lower right side, then along the right side of the canopy. I decided to bail out. I was afraid flames might come into the cockpit when I opened the canopy so I reached back for the fuel selector handle and turned off the gas. A few seconds later, the fire went out but smoke continued to come from the right side of the engine and into the cockpit through the crack between the canopy and the fuselage.

"As I said, I had made up my mind to bail out so I broadcast a Mayday on channel 4. Couldn't get through the traffic for other aircraft making position reports so I went to guard. Some guy was yakking on guard so all I could do was push the mike button and broadcast in the blind. Then I went back to channel 4 and broadcast in the blind again. I found out later that somebody heard me, but as it worked out, it didn't make any difference because I didn't bail out."

"You didn't bail out?" Jim interrupted.

"I didn't bail out. But it wasn't because I didn't try. First, I disconnected my radio cords and oxygen hose. When I couldn't breathe through the mask—excitement, I guess—I unhooked my mask from my helmet which, by the way, is NOT the thing to do before a bailout. I unlocked my seat belt, opened the canopy, stood up and started to bail out. Then, I say in a masterpiece of understatement, I began to have trouble.

"The first thing that happened was I lost my APH-5 helmet. And don't think I enjoyed telling this bit at the green table—(1) my visor was up; (2) I didn't have a nape strap; and (3) my chin strap was loose because I'd been using my oxygen mask to hold my helmet on. The AAR described my performance as 'violating several rules of survival,' I believe."

"So what happens next?" Jim asked.

"Well, there I am... trying to bail out... the aircraft is descending 2000 feet a minute and—get this—something is holding me fast in the cockpit. I tugged and I pulled and I yanked but I couldn't break loose. Then I looked for whatever it was that was holding me.

"Now let's go back for a minute to when I was strapping myself in before takeoff. You know that small canvas bag we're issued on a cross-country for the let-down charts, RadFacs, gas chits—all that stuff?

"Normally I carry this between the seat and the right console where it won't be in the way. When I strapped in, I inadvertently (that's a word that covers a multitude of sins)... I inadvertently looped my right leg strap through the handle of the map bag. When I did this, the seat was in an up position. After takeoff I bottomed the seat to get low enough to see the instrument panel. When I bottomed the seat, the map bag got caught under it. So there I was, held fast to the map bag by my leg strap and the map bag held fast to the aircraft by the seat."

"What did you do?"

"Did the only thing I could," Bob replied. "Sat back down, unhooked my leg strap, freed it from the map bag handle and restrapped it. My altimeter was registering between 4000 and 5000 feet. I knew the terrain in this area was about 1000 feet, higher in some places. I felt I might be too low to bail out safely so I decided to ride the aircraft down. Naturally, in this event, I wanted the protection of my shoulder harness. Remember I had unfastened my lap belt when I was getting ready to bail out? My shoulder harness was now hanging out the left side of the cockpit in the slipstream. I hauled it back in, put it on, secured my belt and cinched up tight. Fortunately, the aircraft stayed trimmed and I was able to hold it level with my knees while I strapped in.

"I started looking around for a good place to belly the plane in. There was a highway below but that was out because of the cars. Nearby there was a plowed field but I saw houses at the far end which I might hit if I overshot. Time was getting short. All that was left was this small dirt road going through some woods. There were other better roads and fields around, but by this time I was too late and too low to pick any other spot but the one I was headed for. I lined up on the road, flaps down, wheels up, canopy open, airspeed 130. I thought I had it made."

"This is the end?"

"Not quite. Right where I was going to touch down I saw an old stone chimney about 30 feet high where some house had been. I was sure I was going to hit it. I banked the aircraft to the right around the chimney and back to the left onto the road. I sheared the tops off of some trees before I hit the ground nose high and wings level. With no helmet I was worried about knocking myself out on the gunsight so I put my head down and my arms over my head. I guess my shoulder harness was tight enough because I didn't hit the gunsight. The impact felt something like an arrested landing aboard ship. The plane slid down the road about 150 feet, kind of sideways, and came to an abrupt stop against a six-foot bank.

"I unlocked my lap belt. There were flames all around me. I figured the fuel cell had ruptured when I saw gas burning on the ground. I didn't take time to get rid of my chute pack. I stood up, stepped out onto the left wing, went out to about the tip and jumped to the ground. Then I started running.

"When I was about 30 feet away, I felt a big blast of hot air and heard a big 'Whoosh.' I turned around and saw what was apparently the fuel tank blowing up. I kept on running until I was well clear of the aircraft; then I took off my chute and started up the road to look for a farmhouse.

"My only injuries were what the docs call 'minor' bruises and one small cut on my chin from the parachute chest buckle."

"You sure almost had it that time," Jim said shaking his head.

"I sure did—talk about lucking out. You know, you really don't take all that safety and survival stuff to heart until something like this happens to you. From Pensacola on, I've heard about checking personal equipment before each flight and taking time to strap in carefully and correctly. I didn't pay a whole lot of attention to it—I got careless—and the lesson really came home!"

"Only the BuNo Has Changed . . ."

Only the BuNo and the date, and the group of letters and numbers that tell what kind of an airplane it is. Everything else reads right up to date in this "old but new" true narrative of events aboard the Navy's first real flat-top. ". . . he hauled back on the stick . . . and floated," "he was coming in too slow and was being given a 'comeon' . . . ," ". . . just as he got to the stern he got cocked a little . . ."—doesn't read like history, does it? Reads like last week's AAR. And yet the events in these vividly descriptive letters from aboard the USS Langley *occurred back when your leading chief first joined the Navy—and now he's going out on thirty.*

Yes, we make mistakes and we learn from them, and we pass our learning on to the youngsters fresh out of flight training and they listen to our wise words as they filter through our beard, and they nod knowingly and condescendingly. And then they go right out to learn the hard way from the only teacher who doesn't overlook or forgive mistakes—experience. So they still "haul back on the stick," come in too slow, and get cocked a little, more or less, and someone writes a letter to a friend about the day's events. Thirty years or so from now it'll make interesting historical reading—someone who's joining the Navy today will be getting out on thirty, and he might

observe, "doggone, they're still doing it—only the BuNo has changed . . ."

September 1959

UNITED STATES FLEET AIRCRAFT SQUADRONS, BATTLE FLEET U.S.S. LANGLEY

Dear S——,

We have had four major casualties in 738 landings since we first took off the fore and aft wires. The first egg was laid by a Chief A.P. [aviation pilot] in one of our FUs. He hauled back on the stick when he got the "cut gun" and floated over the entire gear, finally crashing into the barrier. The principal damage was done by the prop cutting the top barrier wire so that a taut whip end of it came back & broke the spars of the right tip & lower wings, broke the left V-strut, broke two engine cylinders & ripped the fuselage. Also he blew his right tire & broke the tail skag. Fore and aft wires could never have saved him.

The second egg was laid by Ens. J. in an O2U2. He came over the stern OK. Then he started to haul back & float. He floated to the starboard side of the deck and landed somewhere between #3 & #4 wire, almost at the outboard limit of the gear. Even then he would have been OK except for a peculiar accident which, it was discovered later, must have happened as he passed over #4 wire. The aluminum fairing piece which the O2Us carry underneath the fuselage right at the tail skid, and on which the leather tail skid boot is mounted, had apparently come loose at the forward edge. It was caught by some obstruction & pulled back slightly and simultaneously the hook bounced up against the fuselage. As this happened the plate snapped forward & caught the hook against the fuselage, preventing it from engaging #4 or #5 wire. The plane therefore rolled into the barrier, binding the prop, crashing the landing gear, and ripping the fabric in various places.

All squadrons with O2Us out here have been warned to secure these plates by means of clips and bolts to the tubular members of the fuselage directly above the plate instead of by means of the wood screws now used at the forward edge to a false wooden crosspiece put there merely for securing purposes. The accident probably won't happen again in a hundred years because of all the peculiar accidents which had to take place almost simultaneously for this to occur.

The third crash which hardly damaged the plane at all was the T4M flown by Ens. S. He came aboard with his tail hook not released, first because he forgot it and second because no one on deck saw it. He ran normally down the centerline and into the barrier. Little damage was done to the plane because the top barrier wire hit the extremely heavy oleo cylinders of the landing gear merely tearing the light streamline plate. The lower wire of the barrier apparently was rolled over by the large wheels just as they roll over crosswires. Except for a damaged lower right aileron which couldn't clear the starboard barrier standard he could have continued flying. The report that he ran almost to the bow is in error as he stopped about 110 feet from it, at least. It just seemed far to observers back aft. Also no unusual damage was done to the barrier. If his right wing could have cleared the starboard standard we would have had only one broken wire. As it was, this standard was bent forward, tearing the gusset plate at the deck and cracking the

diagonal angle. It was easily replaced, the old one was straightened & welded and is now actually back in place again. To avoid recurrence of this we have had large cards printed with HOOK on them with a string attached which we hand to any pilot who is slow about lowering his hook & tell him to hang it around his neck. It is large enough so that it is inconvenient & he is constantly reminded. Also we have placed an extra man behind Billings with a pair of flags to give the OK when the hook is lowered or to notify Bill in case it isn't. This man has no other duties.

The latest crash, also a T4M, was flown by an AP just out of Pensacola. He was coming in too slow & was consistently being given a "come-on" by Bill. At the last come-on he went haywire and completely cut his gun, just barely connecting with the deck. The mark of his tail skid was left on the ramp. He landed about 10 feet inboard from the port edge of the deck, plane heading for the stacks. His hook mark on the deck shows that it passed about a foot outboard of the sheave of #1 wire so that it couldn't engage anything. He continued his course, passed over the stacks & port operating platform with right wheel still on the deck. Just after passing the stacks, his right wheel rolled off the deck and he went into the net with his landing gear. This obstruction caused him to make a half outside loop so that he landed on his back in the water, nose toward the ship. After what seemed 5 minutes he came up from underneath & found a ring buoy which had been tossed there for him and almost immediately thereafter the plane sank. He was picked up by the Aroostook unhurt. The next day he came out again in a T4M, made fine landings & was qualified. What can be done to avoid stage fright & failure to follow signals on first landing, I don't know, especially when a man shows up excellent in field training and gives no cause for suspicion.

As you can see, not a single one of these crashes would have been averted by fore and aft wires. On the other hand several of the successful landings which have been made would have been certain crashes with the old gear because of the jazzy way in which some of them have landed.

Of minor crashes we have had 29. Thirteen of these have been merely broken tail skid or tail skid shoe casting. Seven have been blown tire or broken wheel. Five have been breakage of a landing gear strut, some involving bending or pulling out spreader tube, 1 caught aileron horn in wire, 1 tore wing fabric on a pie, 1 bent axle on a pie, 1 pulled spreader out after a bounce. Worst of these have happened in FUs, with weak landing gear and tendency to bounce due to rubber shock absorber. None of these would have been avoided with fore and aft wires. Get rid of wooden tail skids and brittle tail skid shoe castings and most of the minor crashes will be avoided. There is no question in anybody's mind but that the simplified gear is a great improvement and is here to stay.

Regarding ——'s crash all I know is what I have heard, viz that he is inexperienced in carrier landings even though an old timer and every landing of his was a potential crash. Yet he goes to work & makes landings at night right after cracking up at day.

I have just completed a thorough analysis of the characteristics of the Langley gear, which I will forward to you as soon as blue printed. I think similar studies should be made of each type of gear we now have and I was surprised to find nothing about ours in our files.

Will write you soon again about some experimental work.

P——

15 August 1929

Dear S——,

When I wrote the account of crashes which you received this week I thought I would have a rest for a while before another account would be due. But this week's operation of three days has added three more—two major and one minor. The two majors happened Monday on successive landings and I suppose you got the headlines on them by dispatch. Here are the details: An AP had the first one in an F3B. He was making his 6th or 7th qualification landing in apparently normal style till he reached the stern. All preceding landings had been fine as was his work at the field. This time, however, when he got the cut gun signal he failed to do so completely. Then to make matters worse he hauled back on the stick and floated over the entire gear at about 6 feet off the deck until he had passed #5 wire. By that time his wheels had just about reached the deck and it looked like just a plain barrier crash. But he still had a surprise in store, for just before getting to the barrier (forward one) he gave her full gun and flew right through it cutting both wires without much retardation—instead he ground looped to the right and went over the side landing right side up in the water. In going through the barrier he practically cut off his nose and badly sliced his face, presumably from broken goggles, so he landed in the water bleeding like a stuck pig and looking worse. But the signals on deck were missed until it was all over when a pair of spare fingers were found lying on the port side of the deck. It appears that one of the gasmen was standing in the nets right next to port barrier standard. His story is that he pushed the man next to him out of the way when he saw the crash impending and in so doing lost his balance and grabbed something which we found later must have been one of the anchor wires where the barrier wires are secured to the deck at the waterway. As he grabbed it, the wire snapped down and yanked off his third and fourth fingers, right hand at the first joint against the waterway. On the starboard side, things were happening too, for a whip end of one of the parted barrier wires came singing back and laid open the scalp of another bystander in the starboard nets. Well, needless to say, there was much excitement. The plane in the water sank and the pilot grabbed a ring buoy tossed to him, the Aroostook meantime sending out her life boat to pick him up. The wounded on deck were taken to sick bay and we were proceeding to fix up the barriers—that is replace the barrier wires, when the decision was made to land the three planes in the air and park them. Looking back I saw

an F2B approaching in the groove, Ens. R. as pilot. Just as he got to the stern he got cocked a little and as a consequence was heading for the port side. To make matters worse he dove for the gear, and held on plenty of left rudder. This was his first landing and whether that fact plus what he had just seen take place put him all haywire or not I don't know. However, he hooked #2 wire just about 4 or 5 inches inboard of the sheave and it promptly parted because of his speed, the angle of approach, and no span on the wire. He continued then to port, left wheel over the side, right wheel crashing a little further on. Just as he passed the port brake handle, his right lower wing then being practically on deck, he picked up a man on the deck and rolled him between his wing and the deck as you would roll a cigaret with the palm of your hand on the table. The man he caught was the regular brakeman for that side, but he had been up the barrier helping to fix it when the plane started to come in. Seeing his brake unmanned he dashed down the deck to get to it and then got caught like a man between third base and home not knowing which way to turn. Meantime another man in the net had hopped on the brake handle so it was actually operated. However, plane, pilot, and man on deck all went over the side. I felt sure that the man on deck had had his body severed as the plane's wing squeezed him over the edge of the deck and never expected to see him come up to the surface. However he landed flat on his side in the water and almost instantly appeared threshing around with blood spouting from a long gash in his head. Pilot & plane landed right side up and we all yelled to the pilot to grab this man which he did and both hung on to a life buoy tossed to them. Our life boat by then was in the water and coming around to pick them up. Again a pair of spectators on deck were hurt and discovered later. One man was cut on the head by the whip end of #2 wire snapping around and another man was very lightly side swiped by it and in excitement or otherwise stepped over the side from the nets without being observed by anyone. However, as the air cleared we finally found the following conditions: two planes already sunk, one pilot just being picked up by the Aroostook's life boat, one pilot and man on the port side about to be picked up by our own life boat, and this other man not far from them. He was also picked up by our boat. The injured were brought aboard from both lifeboats and we all turned to on deck and started to put it back into condition to operate. #2 wire had to be renewed, the first barrier still was unfixed and two sections of netting and supporting stanchions on the port side had to be repaired. By 12:45, or about one hour after the second crash, we had the deck ready again & at 1:15 we held flight quarters continuing training operations with two T4Ms without further incident. All injured persons are now coming along nicely as all head wounds were severely cut without fractures of the skull. The man rolled over the side is in the worst shape with unknown internal chest damage. However, the doctors say that if pneumonia does not set in he will come out of it all O.K.

In carefully going over both of these there is nothing that I can lay my finger on and say if this were corrected they would not have happened or could be avoided in the future. And certainly the absence of fore-&-aft wires did not have one iota to do with these crashes. They would have crashed just as certainly & in the same way if they had been in place. How does it appear to you from longer range, not only from the details I have given you of these crashes but also those I gave in the last letter?

The minor crash occurred in today's operations with our squadron VS–1, out for training for the tactical exercises which start next week. K. came in for the first landing with the O2U amphibian and sat down a little hard on the deck. As a result the port axle broke and the threaded member inside the sleeve under the pontoon pulled out about 5 inches. No damage was done to the main float except a small dent on the port wing tip float was also dented a little. He might have avoided it only by carrying a little throttle after getting the cut gun signal as the amphibians drop like a stone from a slow or normal approach.

As to the queries raised in Nick's letter I don't think lowering of the hook is at all necessary, nor do I think that lowering the height of the wires has anything to do with the crashes we have had. We only have two low wires, #1 and #3. The others are still kept at the same height as they are coupled wires and have no tension on them from the weight system. The reason we have not lowered them is that in normal operations some stretch is induced in them and having no tension on them we can't afford to lower them for fear they might sag to the deck from a lower pie. Having some high and some low wires and no crashes being due to the height of either kind eliminates that factor. As to maintenance of arresting gear in planes, there is no doubt but what some of our minor crashes have been due to improper condition of maintenance by the squadron. As a consequence, we have made up a new carrier plane check off list, which I am enclosing. Copies of these have been furnished each squadron with directions to make sure that their planes comply in every detail before coming aboard, so that the planes will be in proper condition & the pilot can truthfully sign to that effect.

If you want any more dope in addition to what I have sent in this and the last letter, let me know.

Best regards,
P———

These letters courtesy of Mr. Lee M. Pearson, BuAer scientific historian.

NavCad's Diary

The purpose of Anymouse (anonymous) Reports is to help prevent or overcome dangerous situations. They are submitted by Naval and Marine Corps aviation personnel who have had hazardous or unsafe aviation experiences. As the name indicates these reports need not be signed. Forms for writing Anymouse Reports and mailing envelopes are available in readyrooms and line shacks. All reports are considered for appropriate action.
—REPORT AN INCIDENT, PREVENT AN ACCIDENT—

November 1959

Being a NavCad [Navy cadet], I am in the lower ranks of the flight students and along with this status go various duties that are not required of the officer students. We can usually be found in some remote corner of the ready-room, feeling more at home with our own contemporaries.

But it never fails when the most interesting subject arises, up strolls the squadron duty officer and casually remarks how untidy everything appears to him and it ought to be cleaned up. Now a NavCad's second duty to his country is to keep the area clean and neat. With cheery smiles, we all launch our brooms and commence to sweep down fore and aft.

On the day in which my story takes place there was a loud silence on the flight line. All the yellow birds were tied neatly in rows and the forecaster said they'd probably stay that way all day and night. Yes, it was another of those days when I would wade back to my room, splashing through several inches of Florida sunshine.

While waiting for the hours to pass my attention was suddenly caught by the bulkheads decorated with the latest bulletins and flight posters. The safety officer had done a good job. There are book racks full of all the safety magazines and pamphlets that relive all the "hairy tales" of this year and last. Each work of literature contains at least several articles which pertain to every individual who comes in contact with an aircraft.

This was the thought that suddenly blazed in my NavCad skull: It was a type of day which encourages students to bone up on their flight and safety procedures! After all, no one can truthfully say he knows everything about his aircraft's structural limitation or emergency procedures.

As I pondered this, the duty officer wandered in, made his gloomy observation about the need for a little cleanliness so forthwith I preflighted my broom. I didn't mind. This was a wonderful opportunity to check my theory and remain incognito at the same time. As I swept from desk to table, I observed with veiled eyes what particular subject each potential naval aviator chose to study this fine rainy day—procedures or safety.

My first victim was Ensign Rodney Hoarth, a graduate of Harvard Business School. I maneuvered my broom behind his soft sunken chair, casually glancing at the book he grasped.

He was totally engrossed in a volume of Carter Brown's "The Lover." Appalled as I was, I controlled the twitch in my cheek and managed to sweep on without apparent detection.

I did not realize it then, but this was only the beginning. Next I chose Lt.(jg) Orville Crumpton who came to the Training Command from an LST [landing ship, tank] based in Uturoa, a small island in the Tuamotu Archipelago. He looked very happy to be here and was content with a volume of James Emmey's immortal "Lisbon After Dark." Startled, I lost control of my broom and it bounced off the chair. He never even looked up.

A group of four I ignored. They were carelessly throwing cards about a table and billowing gargantuan quantities of cigaret smoke into the air. They had been flying for five months now so I assumed they knew everything there was to know about flying.

My hopes revived as I swept toward a grim-faced individual. He presented a true picture of a professional military man. He had that "Go-Get-'Em" attitude of every true warrior.

Maneuvering closer I saw that with his emergency flip pad he was avidly crushing flies and keeping count of his kills on his knee pad. At any rate he was making use of his emergency procedures I thought sadly. Next to him, Ensign Loyd Lubeck and friend Elrod Jader were arguing whether or not the P2V could successfully be launched from a Sherman class destroyer.

By now I had accumulated a great pile of dust and was in the process of picking it up when Second Lt. Antonio Domiono stumbled across my broom handle. He was returning from the gedunk with an armful of goodies and now these were scattered about the readyroom. I helped him retrieve his vast fortune of fig newtons, sardines, anchovies, egg omelet and a heaping bowl of ravioli. Then he wallowed to his private chair in the far corner, pulled out a book entitled "Aerial Cropdusting After Dark in Formation," and began to consume vast amounts of food and knowledge.

Two can play at this game was my thought. I banged the dust pan loudly against the GI can, clearing off the last shreds of candy wrappings, and turned back towards the group. Much wiser now, I felt humble in the presence of greatness. NavCad Wulfgang Fudernic was thumbing idly through a copy of "Naval Officer's Guide" as I walked over and began discussing the prospects of the Modern Jazz Quartet with him. We quickly and seriously got down to business with the semantics of their latest LP entitled "Progressive Inclinations Toward Bach." . . .

. . . Then the Fun Began

March 1960

The arrestment and runout appeared normal. Then the fun began . . . "

The A3D with a crew of three had been launched from the carrier at approximatley 2000 for CCA [carrier controlled approach] practice. Recovery was scheduled at 2030. The weather was clear above with scattered low clouds. Visibility was 10 miles. The air temperature was 50° F., water temperature 78°. Five-foot waves rolled across the ocean surface.

Under positive control of CCA, the pilot made three CCA penetrations to a waveoff before being cleared for a CCA penetration to a landing. On the fourth pass for a landing aboard, the aircraft appeared to be in good shape, on speed, on glide slope and lined up on center line until just prior to touchdown. (The LSO was handicapped in determining wing position because the aircraft's port wing light was out.) The mirror was working properly. The pilot experienced no difficulty with the brilliance of the deck runway lights.

At this point, the pilot, detecting a left drift, attempted to correct the situation. Before his corrections could become effective, however, the aircraft engaged the No. 4 cross-deck pendant.

As the pilot said later, "The arrestment and runout appeared normal. Then the fun began . . . "

On runout, the aircraft tracked from starboard to port. At completion of the runout, the plane hesitated momentarily, then slowly went over the port side . . . paused . . . then became inverted . . . and paused again. The arresting wire parted. Dislodging several life rafts stowed in bins, the A3D dropped into the water inverted and in a slightly nose-down attitude.

Water rushed through the open upper escape hatch into the dark cockpit. The pilot released his safety belt and discarded his APH–5 helmet and oxygen mask. He rose to the floor of the aircraft to take several deep breaths of the trapped air he knew would be there, then submerged to search for the bombardier-navigator and gunner-navigator. He found no one. After returning to the air space for a few more breaths, he dived down and out through the open hatch. He surfaced alongside the fuselage on the starboard side.

Meanwhile, the gunner-navigator had escaped through the canopy above his seat where the plexiglass had broken out on impact. He surfaced near the wing tip, inflated his life vest and looked around to see if anyone else had gotten out. Moments later, the pilot surfaced nearby.

Pilot Inflates Life Vest

When the pilot inflated his Mark 2 life vest, tears in the outer flotation cell allowed some of the CO_2 to escape. Holding on to the gunner-navigator, he inflated the center flotation cell orally. The men then crawled onto the wing to rest and plan their next move. They shouted the bombardier-navigator's name several times but there was no answer.

Although they could see two plane guard destroyers lying dead in the water with their searchlights working the area, the survivors did not fire signal flares because of the strong smell of fuel around the crash area. They decided to get away from the aircraft and to swim toward the closer destroyer. After blowing some more air in their life vests, they jumped off the aft edge of the wing and swam toward the ship. The gunner-navigator blew his whistle and the pilot waved a life vest flash-light. A few minutes later, they were picked up 100 yards from the wreckage by a motor whaleboat from the destroyer. They had been in the water 14 minutes.

Whaleboat Circles Wreckage

Following the pick-up, the whaleboat circled the aircraft wreckage twice in a search for the third crewman. As the boat headed away from the plane, in the distance the occupants saw a small light intermittently some 1,000 yards from the wreckage. Drawing nearer, they heard a whistle, then were able to make out the figure of the bombardier-navigator from the light reflected off his orange summer flight suit. As they got closer they saw he was sitting in the middle of an inflated life raft—one of the rafts the A3D had knocked off the carrier as it went over the side.

At approximately 2335, the bombardier-navigator was pulled aboard the whaleboat. The signalman signaled the plane guard destroyer that all survivors had been rescued and 10 minutes later, the whaleboat was hoisted aboard.

The gunner-navigator and the bombardier-navigator suffered only minor bruises and cuts in the crash. The pilot sustained a moderately severe injury of the right hand requiring several months' grounding.

Wild Ride

An F8U on a two-plane VFR [visual flight rules] flight from Massachusetts to South Carolina flamed out at 47,000 feet over North Carolina.

The pilot noted engine rumble and thumps. The fire warning light came on, the pilot reduced power and the light went out; however, the RPM dropped to zero and the EGT [exhaust gas temperature] fluctuated to a high of 800° then decreased to zero. The emergency power package was extended and the emergency generator switch placed in the ON position, with no response. Realizing that he was without radio, instruments and power controls and the stick freezing in the neutral position, the pilot decided to eject before descending in uncontrolled flight into the top of a thunderstorm. The pilot ejected directly over an extensive thunderhead estimated to have been 100 miles in diameter. The speed at the time of ejection was Mach .82 or approximately 210 knots IAS [indicated air speed].

His dramatic 40-minute, nine-mile descent through a violent thunderstorm was widely and somewhat inaccurately covered in the nation's press. However, because of its great interest to Approach readers, here is a more detailed account of the pilot's experiences after ejection compiled from his statements during the accident investigation:

May 1960

"My first sensation was one of severe cold and extreme expansion as if I were about to explode. The cold

46

rapidly changed to a burning, tingling sensation. I felt as if millions of hot pins were sticking in me. I sensed that I was tumbling and spinning like a pinwheel. My arms and legs were out and I could not get them in.

"In a matter of seconds I realized I had retained my helmet and mask but no longer had my visor although I had been flying with it down because of the bright sunlight and reflection from the top of the clouds. I believe it was torn away on ejection.

"I opened my eyes and saw I was entering wispy clouds. I was going into the tops of the fleecy overcast that I had flown through just a few minutes before. I seem to remember saying to myself, 'Well, you're entering it and it's about 44,000 feet.' About this time I managed to get my arms in to my body.

"I looked down and noticed that I was absolutely forcing my torso harness. It looked like it was going to burst. My stomach popped out under my life vest as though I were pregnant.

"I had the feeling that I fell and fell and fell and fell for an eternity. My oxygen mask was beating against my face. I held my mask with my right hand. I put my left hand on my helmet which was pulling on the chin strap as if it was going to go off. My left hand was very cold and numb—it felt like somebody else's hand, not mine.

"Sometime during the free fall, my right glove got in my way. It was inflated like a balloon so I let it go—just jettisoned it. I remember seeing it go off and I thought 'Why did I throw the glove away?'

"During the free fall I had the feeling of not being able to exhale; in fact, I seemed to have to work very hard to be able to exhale, but all I had to do was open my mouth and in-rushing air just seemed to fill my lungs. At this time it was getting a bit darker in the cloud.

"I had an urge to open the parachute but I told myself I was still far too high and if I did I would either freeze to death or die from lack of oxygen. I still had this tingling sensation but I sort of had the feeling that I was slowing down and falling into denser atmosphere and I seemed to be getting a little warmer.

"I was still in the free fall and thinking about opening the chute. It was quite dark but I don't recall any great moisture or any great violence. It seems like while I was thinking about opening the chute, all of a sudden there was a terrific jolt and I knew the chute had opened. I looked up but by this time I was in such a dense, dark cloud that I couldn't even see my canopy. I reached up and got hold of the risers and gave them tugs on both sides; it felt like I had a good chute.

"From here on, my memory of what happened seems much better. I now clearly recall running out of oxygen, having the mask collapse against my face, and I believe I disconnected it from the right side as I always do. At about this time I thought I definitely had it made and was going to survive. However, I noticed I was still bleeding from the nose, my right hand was cut, and my left hand was frozen numb, but the pressure was going and I was much more comfortable. Then the turbulence started and I realized I was entering the thunderstorm.

"As the turbulence started, I was pelted all over by hail. Then I fell a little bit more and I seemed to be caught in a violent up-draft. I had the feeling that I was being tossed around . . . that I was actually going around in a loop and I was looping over my canopy like being on the end of a centrifuge. I got sick in the turbulence and heaved.

"Sometimes I could see the canopy and sometimes I couldn't. The tossing and turbulence was so violent it is difficult to describe. I went up and down . . . I was buffeted about in all directions . . . at times I felt like I was going sideways. One time I hit a very rough blast of air—I went soaring back up and got in a very severe hailstorm. I remember the hail beating on my helmet. I had the feeling it would tear my canopy up. The next thing I knew I was in rain so heavy I felt like I was standing under a waterfall. I had my mask loose and the water was so great that when I tried to inhale I got water with the air like I was swimming. It seems to me that some time in the storm I noticed my watch and was surprised that it had stayed with me. I'm not sure but I think I was able to tell the time by the luminous dial . . . I believe it was around 1815.

"At one time during an up or down draft, the parachute canopy collapsed and came down over me like a big sheet. I could see my legs in the shroudlines. This gave me some concern—I thought maybe the chute wouldn't blossom again properly and since the hail seemed to be larger now I was afraid it might damage the canopy and put holes in it. I fell and the canopy blossomed again. I felt the risers and everything seemed all right.

"At this time, I looked down and saw what appeared to be a big black elevator shaft. Then I felt like I had been hit by a blast of compressed air and I went soaring back up again—up and down—sideways. How much of this soaring went on I don't know. I had the feeling that if it went on much longer I was not going to maintain consciousness. I was being tossed around and beaten around and I wasn't quite sure how much more I could take.

"The violence was so great that I thought that if it doesn't stop soon, my gear will come apart . . . my chute will come apart . . . and my straps will break . . . I will come apart. Stretching . . . twisting . . . slamming . . . the turbulence of this thunderstorm was so violent I have nothing to compare it with. I became quite airsick and I had considerable vertigo. Again I had the feeling that I couldn't take much more of this but if I could only hold out a little while longer, I would be falling out of the roughest part of the storm.

"The lightning was so severe that I kept my eyes closed most of the time. Even with my eyelids closed, there was a blinding reddish-white light when the lightning flashed. I felt rather than heard the thunder; it just about burst my eardrums. As I recall, I had the feeling that I was in the upper part of the storm because the lightning seemed to be just flashes. As I descended, I seemed to see big streaks headed towards the earth. All of a sudden I realized that it was getting a little calmer and I was probably descending below the storm. The turbulence grew less, then ceased and I realized I was below the storm. The rain continued, the air was smooth and I started thinking about my landing.

"By now my shoulders and legs hurt pretty badly. I checked myself over again and thought I was O.K. I kept looking down and said to myself 'Under the storm you probably won't have more than 300 feet.' It was just like breaking out when you're making a GCA [ground controlled approach]. First thing I saw was green and then I was able to see trees and then I knew I was very close to the deck.

"I remember seeing a field off in the distance and I thought there must be people nearby. As I got close to the trees I suddenly realized that there was a surface wind and I was being carried horizontally over the ground quite rapidly maybe 25 knots. I oscillated about three times, then went into the trees. It seemed that my chute fouled in two pine trees and I continued in a horizontal position with the wind, then swung back to the left. I came crashing back through the trees like a pendulum and hit a large tree with my left side. My head, face and shoulder took most of the blow. My helmet was knocked crooked but I think it did a great deal to save me here. The blow was so violent that it twisted my helmet back on the right side and pulled the chinstrap so tight over my Adam's apple under my chin that I had to loosen it when I got on the ground. Anyway I came down with a crash. I slid down and landed on my side. I was cold and stunned but still conscious. At first I thought I had broken something and was paralyzed. Pretty soon, however, I was able to move my head and then my arms. I checked the time; it was between 1840 and 1845."

The pilot got up shakily, freed himself from his chute and started to make his way out of the woods. He panicked momentarily, then recovered. Although it was quite dim in the woods, he observed a sawed-off tree stump nearby. He looked around; there were several others. Reasoning that if men had been logging, there must be a logging road in the vicinity, he set up a square search. On the third leg, he hit the road. Following the road, he came to a clearing and a cornfield. Beyond the cornfield he saw automobile headlights. Making his way to the two-lane highway, he stood on the edge of the pavement and tried without success to wave down a car. Some 15 drivers went by without stopping.

"I must have looked like something real unusual—all wet and bleeding and standing out there in my flight suit in the dark and rain," he states. "I guess they figured I was drunk. Then after all these other cars had kept on going, a car came by and I thought I heard a boy say, 'There's a pilot, daddy.' "

The car went on down the road, turned around and came back. The pilot's ordeal was over.

You Wrote the Caption

Remember How Much Fun Flying Used to Be?

Cmdr. R. P. Brewer, staff, postgraduate school, Monterey, California; May 1961

The current spate of nicotinic nostalgia offered in TV commercials ("Remember how good cigarets *used* to taste?") moves us to note briefly the recurrent, similar flashbacks in flying, in which we elder pilots are prone to indulge.

Such harkenings back to yesteryear usually are prompted by the appearance of new instructions and procedures which seem to be fiendishly designed to remove the last vestiges of enjoyment from the aviating business. Whereupon there is loud lament concerning the state of aviation nowadays, and considerable listener sympathy is aroused on hearing . . .

"Why, bub, when *I* was an ensign, fresh out of Pensacola . . ." and thereafter you're regaled with heart-stirring tales of how they used to leap into the blue—the near deserted blue it was then, unmarred by the flicker of anti-collision lights, uninhibited by the insidious influence of IFR and the prying eye of radar surveillance.

Then, the "famming" pilot of, say a F6F, might roam the high (2 to 10,000′) sky in search of new transports (NATS) [Naval Air Transport Service], questing the dimly defined air trails for kindred spirits, perchance to scissor them into satisfying two-turn spins over Old Smoky (Pittsburgh).

Or to stalk, gleefully, an unwary "wrappie" (Army Air Corps) citizen. Or, remember the high spirited antics that greeted you in your first squadron, when you swelled with pride to be invited along on a "freeze-out" tailchase under the Old Bridge—how the lowly earthbound peasants shrieked with awe, or something, as you buzzed down the highway—the beauty of the perfect man-machine team marred only occasionally by encounters with high tension wires. Yessiree, those were the days, ehh? None of your fancy dan flight planning for that hardy breed—"Gimme an Esso map and a city directory, buster, and I'll get you there!" A rolling takeoff, tuck up the Goodyears (or was it Firestones), and a neat roll before passing the end of the runway. "Meet me over the field."

Man, that was living. Now? Hah? Why even the carefree chatter of the past has been replaced by your stodgy, uninspired radio discipline. Remember the way we used to pull the hilarious "Who dat? Who dat say who dat?" routine that used to sizzle CAG [the commander of a carrier air wing] when he was trying to rendezvous the group grope?

No sir, things just aren't the same. The sublime satisfaction of sneaking in under the overcast . . . "Cheeze! I got a hatful of pine cones outta my oil scoop!" They've taken the individuality out of the business . . . A good LSO could recognize every pilot by the peculiarities of his pass; all different—but no more. CCA and the mirror approach changed all that, along with the heady joy of the high speed break.

Navigation? Just get out and go, we did, into the chute-pinching thrill of a low-frequency range orientation, without a chart. Tacan and OMNI and radar and UHF do the job for you now, but then, no tiresome requirements of position reports and altitude assignments and nagging safety officers—Dilbert cartoons were good enough for us.

Yessir, they'll say, give me the plain, simple life, uncluttered with checkoff lists and Vg diagrams [which measure the stress limits of aircraft] and FURs [failure and unsatisfactory report] and computers and such. Shoulder straps? Who wants to fly in a straight jacket? Crash helmets? Sonny, we were a real hard-headed group, when the measure of a pilot was his ability to sideslip off a buggered-up overshoot; to horse a reluctant bird off the runway in jig time; to interpret a 200 mag drop as a transient bit of water, and let's get the show on the road!

Those were the days, indeed. It was a great life, the likes of which we'll never see again, those of us who are still around. And there were giants in those days too, who can still spin a wonderful yarn of a lusty era—yarns that glow more warmly with each passing year and each fond retelling. So, you youngsters, listen and learn—you can filter out a great deal of satisfying information. But there's one thing . . .

Just don't ask him what the accident rate was that year!

No Connection

August 1961

After briefing for an instrument hop with my wingman, we went to our A4D's. Preflight, strapping in, all went as it normally does. I make it a practice to check my oxygen system by fastening my mask and trying to breathe, then turning on the oxygen switch. I performed this check and the mask was airtight. After a normal start we proceeded to the duty runway. We had to wait for landing traffic for several minutes.

Takeoff clearance was received and takeoff and climbout was uneventful. I made the call to TACC [tactical air coordinator] and got a radio check on tactical with my wingman. I had planned to fly to Miramar, Yuma and El Toro, flying on the gages and getting to El Toro with enough fuel to make three approaches. In the briefing, my wingman had asked questions concerning the use of the autopilot, particularly engaging the altitude hold mode. I called him and said we'd level at 29M on the autopilot to demonstrate how the aircraft reacted. I had planned to write down the exact altimeter readings for future reference. For some reason, I didn't look at the altimeter to make sure of these readings. I knew I should be at 30M so I climbed and continued to Miramar and turned for Yuma, tracked out of Miramar and switched to Yuma TACAN [tactical air navigation] . . . After a TACAN check, I had trouble writing the number "8" and took several tries to do it legibly . . . my writing didn't look right.

I decided to turn for El Toro early for fuel economy and thought I'd better check visually my area for the TACAN confusion and to make sure we could pass between the restricted areas. I looked for Yuma but couldn't find the field though I could find Pilots Knob. Having operated from Yuma, I knew I should be able to find the field and thought it was odd that I should be confused.

For some reason, I looked down into the cockpit towards the AFCS [automatic flight control system] panel and saw my mask mounted Firewel regulator swinging free. This was odd also. At no time did I think I had any trouble up to this moment.

I grasped the hose and felt the oxygen blowing in my face. I knew I had to descend to 10M. I tried twice to tell my wingman but couldn't get an answer. I decided I couldn't wait any longer so I rocked my wings, turned inverted, speedbrake out, and pulled through. I thought that having flown ADs, my wingman would understand the wing rock and follow. We had had difficulty with communications when he was not in close. I don't remember retarding the throttle. As I saw the ground move under me I thought this is the target area and it will be a good run. I had planned to go to ram air passing 17M and pull out at 10M. I knew I was diving but there was nothing wrong with that. I tried to gage my pullout so as not to overstress the bird at 10M. My gages said I bottomed out at 10M and climbed to 11M. My wingman now went by me over running 200–300 feet. He couldn't fly formation and that was funny. I'd really have a good time when we got home. But I thought, he's got 500 hours in type and is a good pilot—I must be doing something wrong.

—Wingman:

As the lead pilot rolled out on a westerly heading at 30M he suddenly rocked his wings real fast, then split "S" straight down. I rolled over after him in a vertical dive, power at idle, brakes out and was going .86 mach with a 300-gallon centerline store. I still could not catch him. I finally caught him at 1000 feet straight and level. When I got in transmission range, he mumbled that his mask had separated and that he thought he had hypoxia and that he wanted to go home. I then advised him to go to 10M, level off on autopilot to clear the mountains, and go to ram air so he would not get oil fumes from the 13th stage compressed air . . . I kept up a small chatter to keep him on his toes and let him know that I was right with him.

So I checked my cockpit . . . speed brakes were in, no light, power was at idle. I added power and pulled my Hardman fitting open on the right side. I put the regulator in my mouth and turned the oxygen back on. I had shut it off when I was diving to save what I had left. I don't remember looking at the gage. I thought that everything was okay now. My wingman was talking to me and seemed to understand what was wrong. I shut off the oxygen and told him I was okay and wanted to go to El Toro although El Centro was right off the port wing. He told me to go to ram air and hit the altitude hold. I thought I had gone to ram air already. I looked down but am not sure if I did or not. I tried to write on my kneeboard what had happened. I couldn't read what I had written very well so I went to the oxygen again.

By now I could see my way home—Palomar, George AFB and Saddleback. Everything was fine, my fuel was good, too good. I wanted to be lighter on landing so I told my wingman I'd orbit the field and I was okay. While breathing from the regulator, my mouth would get dry and I'd stop for a while. I probably did this at least 6 or 8 times before we went in to land. I tried reading my gages to my wingman and he nodded. Each one cross-checked so I felt I was okay now. I didn't want to break my habit pattern so I asked him to tell El [Toro] I would make a circling approach. I asked him to fly my wing to check my gear and flaps as I felt I could still use the help and asked for the crash crew to be out. I now began to orbit the field at 8000 to burn down.

Wingman:

We arrived over El Toro after erratic altitude flying at 8M and commenced a left orbit in a 60-degree bank. When transmission could be read by him I told him to shallow out of his steep bank. He finally shallowed out after 3 turns around the field at 350 knots. I then decided that he better get on the deck as soon as possible since his flying was not getting any better. By the looks of things I thought that he might be going to the other extreme—hyperventilation. I informed him of these things and finally got him to agree to go in and land.

I remember I was relaxed and thought it was no problem now. My wingman said I was not doing any good and we were going in to land. I told him to tell the tower I'd make no transmissions and I went to channel 4. The tower gave clearance and I headed up the duty at 2000′, a slow, shallow break, 200 knots, gear down, flaps down and set 80 percent on the throttle. I tried to keep the doughnut in the AAI [angle of approach indicator] lit but couldn't. My wingman said I was slow so I lowered my nose and added power. He said I was too low so I added more power and thought I was doing just fine but he said power so I added it.

As I came up to the ramp, I heard someone say shut down but I thought they're crazy so I put the speedbrake out just prior to touchdown, landed, pulled the throttle to idle, pulled up the flaps, held the nose up, saw the 6000-foot mark and shut the throttle off. The aircraft began to slow down. I was going so slow I didn't need to brake. I thought I had to clear the runway so I rolled off and stopped. I was almost at a dead stop now and clear of the duty runway. Very, very little brake was needed. I was moving much slower than I can walk. I now began to shake all over and decided to relax on the oxygen so I turned it on and began sucking on the regulator. The crash crew was there and climbed up to me. The corpsman said to keep breathing the oxygen. I wasn't nervous nor did I feel as though I had been in any trouble. I thought I had done everything perfectly and had made a good approach and landing. Somebody took my mask and I went with the flight surgeon to the hospital. I felt okay but had trouble remembering exactly when each thing had occurred . . . I could reason but now I question if I did what I reasoned I should do.

According to the Flight Hazard Report, the pilot's oxygen mask and regulator were not connected securely. He did not check the connection before flight.

50

First Time

Following an emergency on a high altitude flight, the pilot of an F8U–2N ejected. The fact that he was wearing a full pressure suit turned an otherwise "routine" ejection into a unique experience—the understatement of the month. Here are excerpt from his narrative:

October 1961

"The indicated airspeed was approximately 250 knots. The aircraft was in a wings-level attitude approximately 10 miles north of Chincoteague. I positioned myself erect with my feet resting on the cockpit deck just aft of the rudder pedals, grasped the face curtain handle and gave a hard pull. Immediately I was aware of a loud explosion and blast of air and knew that at least the initial part of the ejection had been successful. I had the distinct impression of doing a somersault before the face curtain came loose in my hands. Immediately thereafter I was pulled sharply by the main parachute and simultaneously my head was slammed down and into my left shoulder with a terrific jolt. My face was pushed down and to the left and the face seal was pulled diagonally across my mouth and nose, right side high.

"I could see very little of what was going on from this position but did see the seat and other objects falling away from me. The emergency bailout oxygen system was actuated automatically and supplied sufficient oxygen for me to breathe comfortably. I then attempted to get my head free. I felt as though my entire weight was being supported by the pressure suit helmet oxygen hose. I was unable to remove any of the pressure which kept forcing my head into my left shoulder. Since I knew I was at an altitude at which oxygen was not required, I tried to get my pressure suit face plate open but was unsuccessful. After what I estimated to be about two minutes, my bailout oxygen supply ran out and immediately my face plate fogged over. I knew I had to get some air quickly or I would suffocate. Since I had been unable to get the face plate open, I attempted to reach my survival knife, a switch blade model, and cut a hole in my pressure suit. Because of the strain on the pressure suit material which effectively sealed the knife in its pocket on the left upper leg, I couldn't get the knife.

"By this time I realized I was in extremis and numerous uncomplimentary remarks concerning the design of the pressure suit helmet were passing through my mind. I decided my only chance was in getting a glove off and attempting to introduce some air into the pressure suit through the sleeve. I felt along my left arm with my right hand until I located the zipper tab, unzipped it and removed the glove. By holding the sleeve out with my right hand I was able to breathe again.

"After a few breaths I started to work on the helmet again as I expected to hit the water at any instant. I found the neck release ring, unlocked it with my left hand and, placing one hand in front of the helmet and the other behind, began rocking it with all my strength. The neck ring finally separated and I was able to get the helmet off my head and breathe again. I was completely exhausted at this point and relaxed for a few minutes.

"Now that my helmet was off, I could see that I was going to land in Chesapeake Bay and I released the left hip rocket jet fitting to allow my seat pan to hang free. It became apparent at this time that I was drifting fairly rapidly in a northwesterly direction and that I would hit the water facing backwards to the direction of drift. I removed my right glove and dropped it to get some idea of how high I was above the water but I lost sight of it as it passed my feet. I attempted to cross my arms and grab the parachute risers to turn myself around but didn't have the strength. I decided to conserve my energy in order to free myself from the parachute after I hit the water. I remember thinking that at the rate things were going wrong I would undoubtedly be involved in another flail shortly.

"I placed my hands around the rocket jet fittings on each shoulder and waited to hit the water. I hit with a force much greater than I had anticipated while moving backwards. I was flipped over backwards with my feet coming up over my head and ended up facing the parachute when I came to the surface of the water. My right foot had gone into the center of the parachute shroud-lines and was thoroughly entangled in the lines. The chute was half collapsed. I immediately spilled the other half and released the parachute rocket jet fittings. Then I inflated my mae west and attempted to free my right leg from the shroudlines. I soon realized that this would not be possible as the more I attempted to get free, the more entangled I became. I pulled the seat pan over to me, released the rocket jet fitting on my right leg and inflated my life raft. My pressure suit had filled with water at this time through both sleeves and the neck; however, my mae west supported me satisfactorily.

"Climbing into my life raft, I began to untangle the parachute shroudlines from around my right foot. I had almost freed myself when I heard an aircraft. I began to unpack my survival equipment in order to get a smoke flare to attract the attention of the aircraft when I heard a boat approaching.

"A young man had observed my parachute descending while he was sitting in front of a store in Greenback-ville, Va., and had run down to his boat and started out after the parachute. As he pulled alongside my life raft, the first thing I saw was a large brown Chesapeake Bay retriever staring at me from the boat. I thought this most appropriate at the time. . . .

No Secret: "I Ejected Underwater"

This, in the pilot's own words, is the story of the Navy's second successful underwater ejection and subsequent rescue. (Ed. Note: The U. S. Navy's first successful underwater ejection occurred in March '57 when the pilot of an F4D successfully ejected from an inverted position while underwater). It shows that the ejection seat has a capability of emergency egress below the water as well as above. However, it should be remembered that as an automatic mechanical device the parachute deployment process will function "as advertised" in the water as well as in the air.

May 1962

"I was the eighth aircraft launched from the starboard catapult. I was launched five to six seconds after another FJ. I noticed that he went straight ahead and did not climb . . . I encountered slip-stream as the gear came up and the right wing started down. I went in with full left rudder and aileron. The aircraft continued to roll and turn to right. Although the idea to eject was strong[,] I ruled it out because of the poor attitude of the aircraft. I felt the wings go almost level and thought I might make it when I received a tremendous sideways g-load which felt like a small nuclear war commencing.

"Things are a little hazy, but to the best of my recollections after the initial realization that I wasn't dead, I also realized that I wasn't flying—rather, in fact, underwater and going down. I don't remember pulling the emergency canopy release handle, but may have done so. I pulled at the face curtain left handed and the seat worked as advertised. I either saw or felt the chute deploy underwater and then I was free of the seat.

"I pulled the bottle on my C–3 vest and released the right rocket fitting on my canopy harness. By this time the mask and helmet [were] full of water. After trying to release the Hardman fitting one time to no avail, I raised the visor and grabbed the back of the helmet, rolling it forward and down off my head. This done, I took a big gulp of air, congratulated myself on being alive and tried to get rid of my parachute by the left rocket release. I couldn't release it. By this time I'd tried it with my gloves off. My knife and hip holster (both worn on my right side) were torn off sometime in the melee.

"The chopper dropped the horse collar and I was hoisted aboard. Since my chute was still attached the chopper driver had a real rough job on his hands. He did a magnificent job while his crewman tried to cut away the canopy shrouds. Needless to say I had a death grip on the chopper. The chute billowed out and to the dismay of both the crewman and myself, I fell back into the water. The sling was dropped again; I hooked an elbow through it and pointed to a motor whale boat arriving on the scene from the carrier. The chopper dragged me toward it and the rescue was finalized." . . .

"Here I Go!"

October 1962

The ensign's second flight of the day was to be a simulated instrument hop in an F4D. The thorough briefing covered everything on the flight including GCA and emergency procedures.

After checking the yellow sheets and preflighting the aircraft, he started the engine and began the normal checks with the plane captain. When the chase pilot's aircraft went down because of radio difficulties, the ensign shut down his engine until a replacement was available. When he started up a second time, all checks were again normal.

Takeoff was uneventful. Climbout was straight ahead from duty runway 13 to the southeast operating area, the ensign first and the chase pilot following. At 3,000 to 4,000 feet, the chase pilot cleared the ensign to go hooded.

The ascent continued on climb schedule and straight ahead until they reached 14,000 when, because of a broken cloud haze layer at 18,000, the chase pilot directed the ensign to turn port to a heading of north. As the ensign turned, he heard two loud bangs and the stick became extremely stiff. He reported this to the chase pilot who told him if he was still hooded to go visual and stow the hood out of the way.

In spite of all the pilot's attempts to remedy the situation, the stick became increasingly more difficult to move and finally froze in neutral.

The two F4Ds flew around in the vicinity of the field to burn down. When the external tanks were empty, the ensign put the speed brakes out and went into burner. He could fly it "fairly well" using trim and rudder. When he had burned down to about 2900 pounds, he put the landing gear down to check the slow flight characteristics, pulling the power back to about 80% and using speed brakes. When the plane started descending, he used the emergency trim to get it level. As he lowered the landing gear, the aircraft commenced a violent yaw back and forth and then flipped upside down. Although the chase pilot told him to get out, the ensign decided since he was at 14,000 feet to try to get the aircraft righted. He managed to get it straight and level and in a climb when the yawing started once again.

Fearing the aircraft would enter a spin before he could eject, the ensign decided he'd better leave it then and there. He positioned himself back in the seat and took off his knee board. The chase pilot heard him say, "Here I go," and suck in an audible breath as he pulled the face curtain.

Here are excerpts from the ensign's narrative:

"When the drogue chute opened, it put me face down toward the ocean. The main chute opened without much of a jolt which surprised me. After the main chute opened, I felt my limbs and moved them. Only my neck hurt—it felt as if it were broken or pretty badly sprained. I had to hold my head up with my hands in order to keep it from hurting. (Medical personnel later attributed the pilot's spinal injury to possible improper positioning before ejection or force applied to his head by the uncontrollable yawing movements of the aircraft at the time the seat fired.)

"The parachute descent seemed to take an awfully long time. There was no sensation of falling until about the last 500 feet or so. Then I noticed I was falling pretty fast and drifting backwards, so I put my hands on the quick release fittings. As soon as my feet hit the water, I released the parachute. While still under water, I pulled both CO_2 toggles of my life vest and quickly bobbed to the surface.

"Before hitting the water I had taken off my oxygen mask and let it drop. I had tried to remove my helmet but this was so painful that I left it on. I was still holding my head in an upright position with my hands.

"After coming to the surface, I unbuckled the two quick release fasteners on my seat pack and got it out in front of me to inflate the raft. It floated well but I didn't know how to get the life raft out of the pack. I had been shown where the raft was and how to inflate it but I had never been shown how to get it out of the pack or somewhere along the line I had missed it.

"I unzipped the seat cushion and finally found the D-ring and pulled it. Finally I got it to come out and got hold of the CO_2 bottle and pulled the little cord but nothing happened. I pulled the toggle again until the lever came up 180° to the stowed position and still nothing happened. I thought of blowing the raft up orally but then I decided that I couldn't climb into it anyway. Because my head was hurting so much I abandoned the raft. (Although the raft was not recovered, it is thought that the valve lever was broken or a leak had developed in the valve assembly allowing the CO_2 to vent to the atmosphere so that at the time of actuation there was no pressure in the cylinder.)

"By this time I could hear the chopper although I couldn't see it. I couldn't raise my head but I knew he was there. I tried to signal him that I had a bad neck. The helicopter pilot and crewmen were extremely good and brought the seat right under me. I didn't have to move an inch. All I had to do was put my arms around the shank of the seat and I was hoisted up into the chopper. Throughout the whole situation everyone helped out as much as possible." . . .

. . . No Place to Go but Down!

December 1962

It was early December as we filed for El Paso from the West Coast. The weather was supposed to be ideal for the flight and we anticipated being at our scheduled RON [remain overnight] point, NAS Dallas, for dinner.

Upon preflighting, several discrepancies were uncovered that I felt needed attention prior to takeoff for this transcontinental haul. Six hours later, we refiled and manned our *Stoof*, which now had windshield anti-icing fluid, operating alternate air doors, a heater, and good prop de-icers.

In the meantime, out over Harrington Ranch, the elements were stacking up awaiting our arrival in the area of El Paso. As we leveled off at 9000 feet and took stock of the situation, we found everything normal except we hadn't been topped off and were short about 300 pounds of fuel. But since El Paso weather, though deteriorating, was still forecast to remain good enough that no alternate was required, we droned eastward not overly concerned.

We passed Tucson just at sunset, on schedule according to the flight plan, with 1700 pounds of fuel aboard, climbing to 13,000 assigned. We nursed our bird upward into the rarified air far above its natural habitat and donned oxygen masks in a rather regulation-like manner. Twelve minutes beyond Tucson, the first indication that this was not to be a routine flight was recognized as our DME [distance-measuring equipment] showed us 42 miles past Tucson, ripping along at 205 knots ground speed with a 50-knot tailwind component. My heartbeat increased about 10 BPMs as I pondered the thrill of flying at such an exciting speed. A few deep breaths accompanied my thoughts and suddenly I realized that I was hyperventilating. I became nauseated and removed my oxygen mask just as we entered the clouds.

Pitot heat was ON, and that wonderful alternate air that we had waited on back at the base was now warming the icicles in the carburetors. It was snowing now as we reasoned it would be for we were passing Hilltop, the highest point in the mountains along our route between the Atlantic and the Pacific. I wondered if the Sheriff of Cochise was wearing his snowshoes down there. A glance at the prop dome showed a slight accumulation of rime ice. The rocket sight confirmed this. The propeller deicers were performing their function.

As we approached Columbus we were cleared to contact El Paso Center and they picked us up with an immediate descent to 11,000. I was wearing my oxygen mask again and as I read back the clearance I thought how I probably sounded like a jet pilot. But my opportunity to reflect further was cut short as Center came back with weather. El Paso International was 500 overcast 2 miles in moderate snow.

A quick glance at the fuel gages, now summing 1350 pounds, and a few mental calculations and I came up with a computer-like solution: *Once approach is commenced, Tucson out as alternate.* The fuel we took off without haunted me as I broke the news to Smilin' Jack, my copilot, flying in the left seat.

I asked Center for the Walker AFB forecast for the next two hours. As if anticipating my request, Center came right back with the information. Walker was a legal alternate with nothing to spare.

By this time we were approaching El Paso Vortac at a ground speed of 190 knots. We were shifted to Approach Control just in time to hear a transport announce that he had missed an approach to International. He was switched to center for clearance to his alternate. Knowing we were in a hole, I immediately called approach for clearance to Walker, but as I called, Control said, "Standby Navy S2F. Navy Jet 999, you are cleared for a GCA into Biggs. Contact Biggs GCA this frequency now."

And we listened as Navy Jet 999 flew through a GCA to a missed approach.

The picture was clear to Smilin' Jack and me. When the opportunity came Control would tell us Biggs was below minimums and ask us what our intentions were. "Navy S2F, El Paso Approach. Biggs weather 200 overcast ¼ mile in heavy snow. What are your intentions?" "Roger, Approach, what is the Walker weather?" "Walker is reporting below minimums now. What are your intentions, sir?"

Everything east of Guadalupe below minimums in fog. Walker down. Holloman will be below minimums in 30 minutes and we were 40 minutes away. Columbus and Deming were at minimums in blowing sand and snow. It was a dirty night out on that desert. Douglas was up but only omni was available for an approach and we didn't have it. My mind measured the situation in a second and I glanced at Jack, his features exposed by the faint red glow from the instrument panel as he held us in a perfect race track high above the Vortac, and wondered where he got the name Smilin' Jack. I gestured a downward signal and said over the intercom, "Let's spend the next two hours practicing GCA's." Jack, his face grimaced in concentration, nodded in approval.

"Approach, Navy S2F, request GCA to Biggs." Now came the test—a precise GCA. No margin for error. As we started down, the turbulence became severe and then abated to a smooth air situation. We were below the mountains now. It was difficult to slow down with ⅔'s flaps. Full flaps were dropped. On airspeed, 210 degree was the heading, on glide path. The windshield anti-icing fluid was flowing freely. The heater was providing maximum defroster action. We were at GCA minimums. I saw the approach lights—not clearly, but we were between them. "Stay on instruments, Jack, you're O.K." We were over the threshold lights, barely visible, but the high intensity runway lights were clearly visible now. "Go visual, Jack. Hold what you've got." We touched down gently in six inches of fresh snow and rolled out.

After we arrived at the ramp, the airdrome officer advised that Navy Jet 999 had made it into Holloman AFB with 50 gallons on board just before that field went below minimums. "You fellows are just in time for the Christmas party at the club," said the AO. "It's a perfect night for a Christmas party." I looked at Jack. He was smiling.

Night Fright

Night carrier operations account for a good share of our aircraft accidents. This episode is typical of most of them.

Lt. G. W. Lubbers; June 1963

2102.1 This is Tiger One, speed brakes now.

2102.3 Tiger One departing marshall with two. Tiger Two has no TACAN.

2102.7 This is Tiger One, what is the final bearing?

2102.8 (Controller) Expected final approach bearing is 010, over.

2102.9 Tiger One roger 010.

2103.4 Tiger One and Tiger Two this is control, squawk 3–62. Correction, squawk 2 in your descent.

2103.5 Tiger One squawking 2.

2103.6 Tiger Two squawking 2.

2105.4 (Controller) Tiger One I hold you at twenty-one miles.

2105.5 Tiger One concur.

2105.7 This is control, final approach bearing now 007.

2107.0 This is Tiger One; Platform.

2107.1 (Controller) Roger Tiger One. Come right 20.

2107.2 (Tiger One) Roger right 20.

2109.3 Tiger One is at Gate One. Brakes in, Two.

2110.4 Tiger One, Gate Two, heading 020, state 24.

2110.5 (Controller) Roger Tiger One. Right thirty.

2110.8 (Controller) Tiger One and Two right thirty more for separation. I'll carry you across the centerline then back to it.

2110.9 (Tiger One very questioningly) Understand right thirty?

2111.0 (Controller) That is affirmative.

2111.2 (Tiger Two) How about adding a few knots, Tiger One? I'm indicating 120.

2111.3 (Tiger One) Right. I've got 130.

2111.9 Tiger One this is control, descend to and maintain 600 feet.

2112.0 Roger, descend to 600 feet.

2112.2 (Controller) Tiger One what heading?

2112.3 Tiger One 010/600′.

2112.4 (Controller) Tiger One left to 355.

2112.5 (Tiger One) Left 355.

2112.9 (Controller) Tiger Flight check your gear, hook, and flaps.

2113.0 Tiger Two Roger. I have the ship in sight now.

2113.5 (Tiger One) Do you have the meatball yet, Tiger Two?

2113.6 (Tiger Two) I have the ship in sight but I miss— (Sounded as though he started to say something then changed his mind). Have I been detached?

2113.7 (Tiger One) A little bit high now.

2113.8 (Controller) Tiger Two you are lined up right.

2114.0 (The following transmissions were broadcast simultaneously by the two aircraft). Tiger One in the groove, no meatball.
This is Tiger Two, am I cleared to make an approach, over?

2114.1 (LSO) PULL UP, PULL UP, WAVE OFF, WAVE OFF, PULL UP!!

2114.2 (Controller) Tiger One and Two wave off, climb to 1500 feet, enter the wave off pattern.

2114.7 (Controller) Tiger One radio check.

2114.7 Tiger One loud and clear.

2114.8 (Controller) Tiger Two radio check.

2114.9 Tiger Two this is Tiger One radio check.

2115.4 (Controller) Tiger One cleared downwind heading 190.

2115.7 Tiger Two, Tiger One radio check.

2115.8 This is Tiger One, unable to read Tiger Two.

2116.0 (Controller) Tiger One report abeam.

2116.1 This is Tiger One abeam. Do you have contact with Tiger Two, over?

2117.2 (Controller) Tiger One, left to final bearing 007.

2119.1 Tiger One, Control; I have an aircraft off your right wing at one-half mile, easy right, distance is opening.

2121.1 (Controller) Tiger One, what is your position?

2121.3 Tiger One Control, What is your position?

2121.6 (Controller) Tiger One radio check.

2121.8 Tiger One Control—

Most people would describe that fatal night as a dark but good night. Experienced and currently qualified night carrier pilots would describe it as a "Blackie," meaning that it was a night when they were more susceptible to vertigo, and one that required meticulous attention and concentration on instrument flying. Certainly not the roughest night of their careers but one of those black nights in which professional attention to detail, particularly during the transition phase from instruments to visual reference, was mandatory.

This accident, though a double tragedy, is typical of most night carrier accidents. The approach was perfectly normal until fairly close in (within Gate One). From this point on the lead pilot began to question the directions of CCA and an element of doubt entered his mind as to whether or not he would be able to lead his wingman to the proper position to pick up the meatball. With this thought pressing, he shifted from instruments to visual flight while still considerably off final bearing. This deviation greatly multiplied the problem of making the approach. Not only must he establish a glide slope but he must also obtain line-up. At this point disorientation and possibly optical illusions occurred and thinking he was high the leader started a descent without having the meatball in sight.

It might be said that these two pilots made fatal mistakes in deviating from SOP, but for two of the most experienced pilots in the squadron to do this leaves a question that must be answered as soon as possible in order to prevent possible recurrence of similar accidents.

Night carrier operations are, have been, and probably will account for an alarmingly high percent of the Navy's aircraft accidents unless immediate steps are taken to remedy existing conditions. In these days of technological advances, we are rapidly approaching that sought after stage in aviation when "look Ma, no hands," is the byword for carrier approaches and landings. But meanwhile, "back at the ranch" or perhaps we should say, "back at the carrier," we are still operating multimillion dollar, supersonic iron birds with antique procedures and equipment.

Statistics for fiscal years 59–62 show that approximately one-third of all Navy fixed wing aircraft accidents occur while embarked. Of this percent, 37.4% occur at night. Offhand this may not appear to be an alarming percentage but if related to hours of training the figures take on a different meaning. Approximately 1900 day embarked hours are flown per accident as compared to 775 night embarked hours per accident. If these percentages had been expressed in yankee dollars the figures would take on astronomical proportions. Even though strenuous efforts have been and are being made to reduce this percentage, the rate still remains fairly constant.

All too frequently accident reports and endorsements have noted and discussed the fact that pilots do not get an adequate amount of night flying time. Most of the flying prior to deployment and all shore based flying while deployed is usually controlled and scheduled by the squadron and air group commanders. In many instances the amount of time devoted to night flying is alarmingly small and usually consists of several night bounce periods prior to deployment. . . .

Anymouse Special: Divert or Disaster

July 1963

During a recent Mediterranean deployment in A–4s (A4Ds), I was launched one evening on what I thought would be a routine instrument and practice inflight refueling hop. The hop was proceeding as planned and briefed until I called the meatball on my approach to the ship.

Pri-Fly waved me off for priority and approach instructed me to enter the bolter pattern and call abeam with my state. My fuel state was okay so I was not worried about being waved off. On the next pass I encountered a great deal of trouble controlling the meatball and as a result boltered. My fuel state was still 2000 lbs. plus, so the thought of bingoing never entered my mind. My next pass resulted in a waveoff for poor ball control technique and was followed by a bolter, a waveoff, and another bolter.

On the third bolter my fuel was 1300 lbs. Approach control gave my downwind information. When I called the 180 with my state of 1200 lbs., I was instructed to clean up and that my signal was bingo. I requested one more pass which was turned down with, "Negative, your signal is bingo, steer 358 degrees-65 miles to the —— Airport." I immediately cleaned up and turned to the bingo heading commencing a climb to 20,000 feet.

I was not tanked inbound as the tanker had gone down prior to launch. The primary divert field had no tacan or homer so I found myself tracking outbound on the ship's tacan. The divert field was equipped with omni, UHF, and VHF. Attempts were made to contact the field tower but I was unsuccessful. I later found out their UHF receiver was out. The ship gave me the divert field weather as 3000 scattered which later turned out to be varying from 200 overcast to 1500 broken.

An airborne A–3 (A3D) which was in the area of the divert field at the time, was told that I was inbound. He made several attempts to contact the tower both on UHF and VHF but had no success. The area over the field was overcast. Since the A–3 (A3D) was equipped with omni he began making omni approaches to the field in an attempt to locate it for me and lead me in utilizing the buddy system. His approaches were unsuccessful as the runway lights were not on and with the marginal weather conditions the field could not be sighted.

The A–3 (A3D) pilot orbited the area of the field and spotted a commercial aircraft making an approach. He tailed in behind it and about 2 miles from the field the runway lights were turned on and left on after the commercial jet had landed.

In the meantime I had arrived overhead with 800 lbs. and had no field in sight since I was above the overcast. I could see lights up and down the coast through the overcast but could not recognize any of the towns.

I turned to the southwest and started down in hopes of finding a hole to get through to take a look around. I leveled off before entering the overcast as I could not find a hole. I went to the Mayday squawk on the IFF and Guard channel on the UHF as the ship was having trouble picking me up. The CCA officer on the ship picked up my squawk and told me he was going to penetrate me out to sea through the overcast and bring me back inbound to the field. I was beginning to get nervous due to my fuel state. The CCA officer sensed this from the tremor in my voice and said "I'm going to bring you in boy, I'm going to bring you in." His voice and words of reassurance calmed me down immediately and gave me a feeling of security. I penetrated through the overcast and turned inbound at half my altitude.

The overcast along the coastline was about 500 feet so I was just skimming along the bottom of it watching my altimeter very closely so as not to fly into the water. As I approached the coastline I noticed several ships rigged with in-port lighting anchored in the bay. I informed the CCA officer of this and he told me that his radar was land locked and he had me at the wrong town. He said to follow the coastline and I couldn't miss the airport about 15 miles away. I started up the coastline but went IFR and missed a right turn at the coastline. I began a shallow climb as I knew there were mountains in the areas and I didn't care to leave an airplane and myself splattered on one.

A few seconds later I popped into VFR conditions and found myself in a valley with mountains sticking up into the soup on both sides. I thought to myself how lucky I was not to have hit anything and for about the tenth time checked the location of the face curtain ejection handle and proper positioning of the seat. A quick look and the fuel gage revealed 400 lbs.

The CCA officer was still in radio contact with me but had lost radar contact since I was in the valley. He told me to stay close to lights so I wouldn't hit anything. Proceeding up the valley which paralleled the coastline I suddenly went over the roof of a building which was sitting on a ridge running across the valley. I hadn't seen the ridge and for a brief instant as my lights lit up the roof I was petrified. I am certain I hadn't missed it by more than 10 feet. I again checked the face curtain with both hands but again decided against ejecting.

The CCA officer asked me what my fuel state was. I replied that my state was 300 lbs. and asked for a Charlie time overhead for the next day. This request seems rather ridiculous now since at the time ejection was imminent. He gave me several Charlies times which I wrote down on my kneeboard. On the ship my squadron commander

was making the decision to have me head to sea and eject since he felt my chances of survival would be much better ejecting over the water than over mountainous terrain at night. He got out the first word to tell me to eject when the A–3 (A3D) overload spotted my rotating beacon through a hole and turned me right 90 degrees. He brought me down through another valley and out over the city. He asked me if I had the runway in sight. I answered with a negative. Then thinking I had spotted the airfield at 11 o'clock said, "Roger, I have it at 11 o'clock." He told me it was at my 3 o'clock and when I looked I found myself looking down a runway.

The A–3 (A3D) pilot told me the wind direction and to enter downwind for a right-hand approach to the field. My fuel state at the time was 150 lbs. I left the gear and flaps up, the speedbrakes in, and turned off the 180 with 100 lbs. indicated. I was high and fast so reduced the power to IDLE, still climbing into the soup but keeping the runway lights in sight through the overcast. As I rolled wings-level on final about a quarter of a mile from the end of the runway I lowered the gear, flaps and speedbrakes with the throttle still at IDLE. I was high and fast intentionally in case I experienced a flameout.

I was sure at that instant I could have made the runway if I did flameout. I never noticed the blinking approach index light since the hook was up nor do I recall looking at the gear indicators. This pass had to get me on the deck since there wasn't going to be another.

I commenced a flare as I passed the threshold lights and touched down about ⅓ of the way down the 6800 foot runway with the throttle still at IDLE. As I turned off the end of the runway and started up the taxi way I heard the engine die, then catch again. I looked at the fuel flow gage just in time to see it come up to idle fuel flow, then drop to 0. The fuel gage said 50 lbs. The sound that followed sounded to me at the time like death.

It wasn't until then that I actually realized how close I had come to losing an airplane. Many thoughts went through my mind for the next few hours as I was wondering how I was so lucky to still be around. I definitely owe my life or at least an airplane to the quick thinking and reassuring words of the CCA officer and the keen eyeballs and help of the A–3 (A3D) pilot and his crew for spotting me.

Next morning a starter probe arrived from the ship and I was started, using a *Caravelle* jet starter. My return to the ship was very heartwarming after having spent the last 20 hours in an anti-exposure suit.

Proficiency Pros?

February 1964

Ol' Walt, you know Walt Smitty, I'm sure, and yours truly, Will Riskit, had been ok'd for a bug-smashin' T–28B ride from NAS Boondock to the east coast to build up our already impressive flight time totals. First, perhaps I should explain that through some typical assignment foul-up Walt and I (both hot, special-card, experienced aviators) had been erroneously assigned to shore duty staff billets. We were sure that the big men up there in D.C., as soon as they realized their mistake, would send us (hot, special card, experienced aviators) back to the tailhook Navy. But in the meantime, to get a breather from the paper mill, we had condescended to help out NAS Maintenance by putting some time on their bird.

As was our habit from long experience in this flying game, Walt and I allowed a full 15 minutes for getting into flight gear, making a steely-eyed check of the weather, filing our flight plan, having a cup of joe, and preflighting the aircraft. The weather was VFR to the moon, which wasn't much of a challenge to our talents, but we filed IFR anyway and headed for the line. After a thorough pre-flight of our little training bird (we're both of the tire-kicking school of preflight) we fired up the old R–1820 and headed for the runway. I was in the front and Walt had condescended to do the backseat "book work" of the first leg. At the end of the runway I kept getting bodacious mag drops. However, reaching into my vast grab-bag of flight experience, I decided to try the mag check again—this time with the mixture rich. This solved the mag drop problem, and I commented to old Walt about how they're not makin' em like they used to.

Just about the time I was ready to call for clearance, Walt allowed as how I'd better pass back the FLIP charts as sort of back-up to his highly developed navigational acumen. Well sir, right then and there I realized we had been duped by these clods in Operations. They'd forgotten to put a nav-kit in the bird. I called the tower, informed them of their boo-boo, and much to the tower operator's embarrassment, we taxiied back to the Ops building. I also informed the tower people as nicely as possible to minimize any further chagrin on their parts, that they might as well toss in a couple of fuel chits as well. Walt and I were as forgiving as possible about this foul-up too. After all, such are the inconveniences we (hot, special-card, experienced aviators) must face when inadvertently assigned to CRT billets.

Well sir, back to the runway we went. After completing my personal checkoff-list (cigarettes, lighter, handkerchief, candy bar) we were off into the blue. Immediately I could tell that "Center" had a trainee controller on the air, since he was really confused, screaming a lot of nonsense about frequencies, radar identification, and such. Obviously he wasn't listening either, since Walt was amicably chatting with him. Walt later pointed out that those maintenance clods must have crossed the mike and intercom button wiring. Just to be on the safe side I hit the switch to take radio control in the front cockpit. A couple of my calls to Center were answered by NAS Tower (boy, do these air control personnel get confused) so, with the lightning-like decisions for which I am known, I switched over to Center Frequency. From then on Walt and I got everybody squared-away in short order. When those FAA [Federal Aviation Administration] boys realized who they were dealing with, the rest of the first leg was relatively uneventful.

About halfway to our destination Walt and I (with our combined technical competence and knowledge of aircraft systems) were quick to note that the right wing tank was being emptied only half as fast as was the left wing tank. What to do? Naturally, we decided to land somewhere, since we couldn't make it on the left tank alone, and we knew the 1820 was a little fussy about running smoothly without fuel.

Because of the poor quality of printing on current FLIP charts, the poor quality of ground maintenance on some of these FAA omni stations, and the fact that in-flight visibility was restricted to about 50 miles, we weren't too sure of our exact location. After 10 or 15 minutes of moderate activity in the rear cockpit (Walt's banjo kept getting in his way as he tried to tune the radio gear with a cigarette in his hand), Walt managed to pinpoint our position as somewhere over western North Carolina. I, of course, could have done the task with much greater dispatch if I had had some nav pubs in the front seat.

We finally found an omni station that wasn't broadcasting bogus ID signals and selected for our landing spot a civilian field with contract fuel. After 15–20 minutes of fruitless scanning and selective orbiting, (during which we remembered to cancel our IFR and inform Podunk Radio we were changing our destination—cool thinking, eh?) a couple of lesser aviators might have concluded that they were lost. But ol' Walt and I finally solved the problem. After turning his confusing FLIP chart 90 degrees, Walt determined the field was *north* not west of the omni station, and from there on it was a piece of cake.

To make a long story a little shorter, we removed a little ol' mud clod from the starboard fuel tank ram/static vent (terrible maintenance at Boondock NAS—the plane captain missed that little jewel on his preflight inspection). We refueled, refiled, and hopped on to the east coast for a short chin with our old fleet buddies. Not wanting to air dirty laundry, however, we were discreet enough to refrain from any comment on our difficulties which might unfavorably reflect on the shore establishment.

To this day, however, ol' Walt and I wonder what embarrassment and heartache might have resulted had these trying circumstances been faced by a couple of birdmen with less aviation savvy than we. After all, we're a couple of hot, special-card, experienced aviators. . . .

Through a Sheet of Flame

March 1964

During a trans-Pacific flight aerial refueling, an F8E's main fuel cell ruptured causing a fire. The pilot ejected . . .

Even through the canopy, the heat from the fire was intense. I reached up with both hands and pulled the handles. Ejection forces were surprisingly slight and when I opened my eyes it seemed as though I was still in the fire. I felt a hot searing pain on both knees and on my left arm. Finally, ever so slowly, the burning spinning *Crusader* gradually dropped away. I smelled burned hair and found out later it was my eyelashes. My visor, locked down tightly, undoubtedly saved my eyes.

The seat started to corkscrew rapidly so I threw out one arm and then a foot. This stopped the oscillations. The bailout bottle worked fine and my mask was still on. Just as I located the emergency seat release, the automatic barostat functioned and the chute opened with a surprising shock. I took off my oxygen mask and leg straps and dropped them. An F–8E flew by. I waved to let him know everything was as good as could be expected. I stopped the chute's oscillations by pulling the risers.

Preparing for the water landing coming up, I undid my left seat pack rocket fitting, allowing the seat pack to drop to my right side. I tried to connect the pararaft lanyard to my torso harness but the lanyard was buried inside the pack. I opened the pack, found the lanyard and attached it to the lower left torso harness rocket jet fitting (*Lower right is recommended.—Ed.*), and pulled out the raft and clutched it firmly under my left arm.

I entered the lower cloud deck and a few seconds later spotted the whitecaps. Fairly high swells and a wind of 12 to 15 knots meant that it was imperative to get out of the chute immediately on touchdown. I put my hands on the upper rocket jet fittings and as my feet hit, I released both. The chute took off at a rapid rate. I inflated my Mk3C life preserver and then inflated and boarded the pararaft.

In crawling aboard, I somehow ripped a small hole in the raft—probably with my survival knife. This didn't do much to ease the situation. I inventoried my survival gear, counted arms and legs and mentally prepared myself for at least an overnight water voyage such as we had been briefed for back in the ready room. The raft was pitching pretty strongly and the possibility of being turned over was apparent. So was the possibility of sea-sickness. I deployed the sea anchor and seat pan for drag.

I loaded my .38 revolver with tracers (*Preloading is a good idea.—Ed.*) and got out a distress signal flare and a dye marker packet and tied them to my helmet strap. In about 20 minutes I spotted a destroyer less than a mile away. Incredulously, though I knew a vessel was stationed just abeam of ARCP [air refueling control point] No. 1, and still not really believing my eyes, I got out the signal equipment. With dye marker I immediately turned the entire general area a bright emerald green. I lit up a daysmoke distress signal and even fired off five tracer rounds. I blew my whistle for my own psychological benefit.

As the destroyer pulled slowly closer, a KC–130F tanker flew by. Later an SAR amphibian also flew by. I believe both aircraft were able to spot the life raft.

The seas were such that a whaleboat was lowered to recover me. In all I was in the water about 20 minutes and in the raft 20 minutes before being rescued. (Water temperature was reported to be about 64° F.)

Everything in my survival equipment functioned perfectly. The helmet visor, as I've said before, certainly saved my eyes and face, and the leather gloves and flight suit sleeves greatly reduced the severity of the burns as I pulled and held the face curtain. I had third degree skin burns under my flight suit but the suit didn't even scorch. It had never been laundered. The backs of my gloves were deeply burned when I pulled the face curtain but my hands were all right. My only injuries were minor burns: a burned neck where I wasn't protected by my oxygen mask, flight suit or scarf, and burned kneecaps and left forearm. My APH-5 helmet was cracked above the left Sierra fitting—damage probably sustained during the aircraft spin. The silk scarf which I was wearing around my neck was extensively burned and probably provided some protection.

As a postscript, from talking with the ship's crew that rescued me, I learned that they saw and heard an explosion, then saw black smoke just at the base of the overcast. This was apparently the *Crusader* blowing up. The ship steamed by the debris on downwind where they found me less than 1000 yards away.

Pastry Twist

*Manual bailout, from a Crusader? Sounds impossible—
but it actually happened. To make it worse—that wasn't all
of his troubles . . .*

May 1964

During aerial refueling of an F–8E on a trans-Pac flight, continued flow was indicated aboard the tanker after the aircraft had received a capacity load. There was a 3 to 4 foot fuel stream from the jet's tail. The pilot heard a loud pop. Observers saw the tail section enveloped in a cloud of raw fuel. Fuel poured from the left rear fin and out around the lip of the intake duct. Streaming a curtain of fuel, the F–8E lost power and began to drop back out of formation. "You are on fire," the wingman transmitted, "Eject!"

As the pilot got ready, his burning, barely controllable aircraft had descended to approximately 15,000 feet. Stick control was becoming less and less effective but there was no smoke, fumes or heat in the cockpit and no evidence of decompression.

Grasping the face curtain loops firmly, the pilot forcibly pulled until he could see the yellow flannel backing of the curtain and the loops were at the level of his chin. Nothing happened . . . the canopy did not jettison. He brushed the extended curtain back behind his helmet and pulled the alternate firing handle three times, extending the cable 4 to 5 inches . . . canopy still did not jettison. Grasping the emergency canopy release with his left hand, he pulled it to its full extent. Still the canopy would not jettison.

Leaving the handle dangling on its extended cable, he took hold of the canopy handle and manually unlocked the canopy which then jettisoned into the airstream. (*The pilot did not pull his canopy interruptor handle because he felt that the face curtain had been fully extended and thus was extended beyond the interruptor stop. He felt that pulling it again would be a waste of time.*) Still above 5000 ft, the pilot abandoned any attempt to eject after canopy removal and broadcast his decision to bail out manually. With his right hand he pulled the guillotine handle and began to position himself for bailout. The slipstream sucked out his left arm but he was able to forcibly retrieve it without injury. He did not disconnect his oxygen lines, leg restraints or any connections, but after the guillotine was activated, he was able to rise up in the seat without any binding. The seat had been adjusted to half-up position prior to flight.

Trimming the aircraft for a gentle left turn, he put his left foot in the seat frame and his right foot on the instrument console. Raising up into the slipstream on the left side above the refueling probe, out he went. He was lifted out by the airstream, with no bumping, and cleared the aircraft. Estimated airspeed at the time was 220 knots and altitude at least 5000 ft. The flight was some 690 miles out at sea.

As the pilot left the aircraft, he concentrated on his D-ring, knowing that he must pull it for parachute action in a manual bailout. He vaguely recalls an approximate two-second period of silence before the D-ring was pulled. During this time he loosened his oxygen mask and flipped it to the left because the bailout bottle was not activated. Immediately he found he was unable to breathe.

To his surprise he had to reach above his left shoulder to grasp the D-ring. Aerodynamic forces operating during free fall had forced his horseshoe chute pack to a position 2 to 3 feet above and behind his head. He pulled the D-ring but felt no opening shock.

Looking up, he saw the chute pack about two feet above his head—the pilot chute half-in, half-out. He describes it as looking like a "mass of junk up there . . . like a bunch of dirty clothes sticking out of the parachute pack." He pulled the chute packing container to him by hauling on the risers and tried to tear the pack open. He did not grasp the canopy or shrouds. Suddenly the pack was jerked from his hands with a loud pop. The deceleration snapped him back down to the end of the chute risers. Looking up he saw the pilot chute open and the main canopy partially stream. Chute pack and backpad were gone. The tangled gores of the partially-open personnel chute were scalloped out, catching air with multiple loose and whipping shroudlines. About 12 tight shroudlines led approximately six feet down to his risers. His attempts to shake the main parachute canopy open with the shroudlines failed. The canopy looked to him like a "long pastry twist." It did not blossom out. Again he reached up and manipulated the taut shroudlines two or three times, but they snapped back when released.

The pilot was now below the cloud cover. He could see a large circle of calm water where his aircraft had gone in. His seat pack containing the PK–2 pararaft and survival equipment was still attached to him by the rocket jet attachment on the right. Down he rode his crippled, streaming chute to a point in the water about 200 feet from the plane splash.

He does not remember striking the water. His first recollection is that of hearing his Mk3–C life preserver inflate with a hissing sound and he realized he was still alive.

Pieces of aircraft floated about him and he saw his APH–5 helmet bobbing about 10 feet away. He thinks he retained the helmet during bailout and took it off just after surfacing but he is not sure. He believes he saw his PK–2 seat pack floating just under the surface of the water somewhat further away, but this memory is vague. His immediate feeling was that he was like a mass of jelly . . . detached and unreal. The impact had knocked out one of his lower molar fillings and loosened two others which later fell out.

Still feeling detached and unreal, he watched as his shroudlines gradually entangled him by sea action, but finally he released his upper rocket jet fasteners without difficulty. He cut away the shrouds with his survival knife; it did the job easily though he had considered it dull. He did not deploy dye marker but did attempt to ignite a distress signal. Both daysmoke and night ends fizzled briefly and then failed. At this point he discarded his gloves which had become slippery in the water. He had lost his service revolver and tracer ammunition on impact.

Water temperature in the area was about 65° F. and sea state was Four during the 2¼ hour period before rescue. An orbiting KC–130 dropped dye marker in the water and a raft which was lost because of apparent failure to inflate. An *Albatross* arrived after 45 minutes and dropped two rafts. The first landed and inflated 100 yards from the survivor. The second, dropped 30 minutes later, trailed its lanyard 20 feet from him and he was able to draw it to him. During the remaining hour that he was in the water, he hung on to the side of the raft. He tried to board it numerous times but failed.

The first vessel at the scene was a minesweeper which dispatched a diver in a wet suit to his assistance. He was pulled aboard by means of a rope looped under his arms.

Recuperating in the hospital from injuries which medical personnel believe occurred as he struck the water—a fractured vertebra, broken ankles and a broken pelvis—the pilot was quoted by a reporter, "This business of your whole life flashing before you is baloney, at least in my case, I was too busy for that."

Pucker Factor

April 1965

I had just waved off from a night practice CCA and was headed back to marshal. At angels 10 my mental composure was rudely shaken by a fire warning light plus a muffled explosion. Immediately I turned the *Crusader* towards USS *Boat* and gave the instruments a quick check. No abnormalities—just a very bright fire warning light and a dark, dark night.

A quick call to *Boat* Approach gave a very abbreviated account of what had happened plus a "pull forward, I'm landing now or ASAP!'" Then I lowered the seat just in case.

As radio transmissions were exchanged to establish radar contact, the engine oil/hydraulic pressure light came ON! My first thought was, "Oh hell! I'm losing my oil now!" A quick glance at the oil gage showed that it was holding a steady 43 psi. However, the PC–1 was fluctuating between 0–3500 psi. At least things still appeared to be operating normally in the J–57 department.

As I approached the ship they told me to expect a 5–minute delay. I "rogered" and put out the RAT [ram air turbine] and proceeded down the starboard side. Turning downwind, the pitch control started getting sloppy so I transmitted, "You'd better hurry with the deck—things are turning to worms fast!" I was still in a clean configuration in order to zoom and eject—if necessary.

As I turned to the final bearing, the aircraft kept rolling past the desired 30 degrees angle of bank. Full top rudder and opposite aileron were required to stop the roll. During these efforts, my intentions were to get out and swim if the roll continued through 90 degrees of bank. But the bird slowly responded and rolled back level and within 5 degrees of the final bearing! Control effectiveness was marginal although there was still enough left to get aboard.

At two miles I dirtied up. When the wing came up the nose pitched over to 25 degrees nose down, then to 20 degrees nose up (on the VGI [vertical gyro indicator]). As the SPN–10 glide slope was approached everything was fairly stable again. Nearing the ramp the meatball went a little low and I applied back stick to correct. After pulling the stick all the way back and applying 15 units nose up trim, the ball finally began moving up. The nose pitched up momentarily and then fell through, causing me to lose the ball off the bottom of the Fresnel lens.

The landing that followed resulted in hook marks six inches from the rounddown and a real scared fighter pilot on the end of the No. 1 wire.

As the aircraft came to a welcome stop, a yellow shirt came out to taxi me out of the arresting gear. My thought at that moment was, "#$%¢, did they think I was holding a drill?" As I started taxiing out, paddles called "208 you are on fire!" I shut down and exited the F–8 in record time.

A post-mortem of the incident revealed two items of interest. First, the fire was caused by a fuel manifold failure. Fire had burned through the diffuser section and the PC–1 hydraulic breather lines. The cooling duct down the inside of the fuselage had carried heat and flames down to the Unit Horizontal Tail controls. About the time I landed, the fire had started burning through the fuselage at the amber formation light—two inches above a fuel cell!

The second item of interest is a post-mortem of my actions. I had enough indications in the cockpit to assume serious trouble was going on inside my machine. I had two choices.

If you want to land immediately never underestimate the power of the declared emergency. Use it wisely of course. With so much against me I think I was lucky to have made it aboard. Ejection might have been best.

Bad Day at Black Rock

May 1965

A *Crusader* had diverted from the ship to NAS Black Rock due to a utility hydraulic failure. Upon his arrival, the pilot advised the tower of his difficulties and requested the midfield arresting gear. Since an A–4 had just taken the gear, he was given a 12–minute delay while it could be re-rigged and an F–8 qualified LSO could be dispatched to assist.

When clearance was received, the pilot lowered the landing gear handle.

The wheels did not go down. To pneumatically lower the landing gear, the wheel handle was then rotated and pulled. After a short delay, a down-and-locked indication was received.

When the pilot grasped the wing incidence lock handle, he found that it wouldn't move more than ¼ to ½ inch. Both hands and considerable force were used in an attempt to actuate the wing lock handle.

No luck! The wing wouldn't unlock!

After consultation with the LSO, the decision was made to land the aircraft with the wing down. A straight-in approach was commenced—gear DOWN, wing DOWN, droop UP, tailhook DOWN and with about 1800 lbs of fuel. Airspeed during the approach was 158 to 160 kts.

Touchdown was 500 ft short of the arresting gear at about 160 kts. Throttle was decreased a few percent upon touchdown and the aircraft maintained a nose-high attitude until engagement. Although the hook contacted the No. 1 pendant on centerline, it didn't engage it. The No. 2 pendant was engaged about two feet left of centerline. Initial arresting force was fairly strong until the pendant broke. The broken pendant, which had parted at the port swage fitting, whipped forward from the port side; wrapping itself around both main landing gear, severing large parts of the lower wheel well doors, and damaging or rupturing both main landing gear shock struts.

Immediately after the pendant broke, the pilot noted a vibration similar to that of a blown tire as the aircraft continued rolling down the runway.

Military power was added and back pressure applied. The aircraft would not rotate sufficiently to take off! Afterburner!

As the aircraft rotated, the arresting hook linkage was jammed into the pavement. Amid a trail of sparks, smoke and flame, the *Crusader* became airborne. As the plane lifted the tailhook dropped free from the airplane and fell to the runway.

Climbing straight ahead, the pilot deselected the burner at 1500 ft and took stock of his predicament.

Immediately the yaw stab warning light illuminated. A quick check revealed that PC–2 pressure was at or near ZERO; however, the PC–1 pressure remained steady at 3000 psi.

An A–4 joined the *Crusader* and provided a damage report. About five minutes later, another RF–8A from the ship joined up and gave a more accurate assessment and evaluation. The arresting hook was missing from the aircraft; port main landing gear shock strut was broken but still attached to the plane; a rupture in the starboard shock strut, large portions of both main landing gear wheel well doors were missing and considerable skagging damage was evident in the tail cone area. The inspecting RF–8A pilot did not believe the aircraft could be landed successfully and he therefore recommended ejection.

Another attempt by the pilot was made to unlock the wing. He found that the wing incidence lock handle could now be moved to the *unlocked* position. He then raised his pneumatic landing droop guard and attempted to actuate the landing condition droop.

No change in droop position was noted and no further attempt was made to raise the wing.

The situation was further discussed with the pilot of the other RF–8A, the LSO, and the Commander of the Fleet Air Detachment in the tower. Since time and fuel considerations prohibited an alternative of foaming a runway for landing, the pilot made the decision to eject.

Enroute to an unpopulated area, the other RF–8A photographed the damaged part of the aircraft and positioned his plane to photograph the ejection.

With a fuel state of 800 lbs, the aircraft arrived at the ejection area—just below the overcast at 7000 ft, 175 kts and on a heading toward the sea. The pilot transmitted his position, trimmed the aircraft nosedown, secured the engine and ejected.

All escape equipment functioned normally, including the PRT–3 radio.

After landing uninjured in a farmer's field, the pilot was immediately picked up by a rescue helicopter that had been dispatched from Black Rock.

Return to the air station was uneventful until about three miles out.

The helicopter had an engine failure and crashed into the trees! Although the chopper received strike damage, there were no injuries.

Reluctantly, the *Crusader* pilot climbed aboard another helicopter for his second rescue of the day. . . .

Will to Survive

Cmdr. Wynn F. Foster, commanding officer, VA–163; December 1966

As commanding officer of an attack squadron, I led a routine mission against a suspected target in North Viet-

nam. My wingman and I launched about 0750 and rendezvoused overhead of the carrier. We departed on top at 0810 and headed for our planned coast-in point. We began our descent from altitude.

"Shortly after the coast-in point, we began picking up flak bursts to our starboard side, just north of our track. I called the flak to my wingman's attention and told him to keep jinking. A few seconds later I heard a loud 'bang' followed by a 'whoosh' and I felt a stinging sensation in my right elbow. I realized I had been hit and looked down at my right arm. The arm was missing from the elbow down and half of my right forearm was lying on the starboard console.

"During the first few seconds I had a hard time convincing myself that most of my right arm was missing, but when I tried to move the stick, I was convinced. I took the stick with my left hand and started to head the aircraft back out to sea. I radioed my wingman that I had been hit, then broadcast 'Mayday,' giving my side number and general position. I told my wingman to keep jinking and to get clear of the area. My airspeed was dropping so I eased the nose down and tried to hold about 220 kts. The shell frag (I estimate it was at least a 57mm because of my altitude at the time I was hit) had blown out most of the canopy and it was very noisy in the cockpit. The cockpit was quite a mess with flesh and blood splattered over the windscreen and instrument panel. I made a couple of radio transmissions to my wingman to see if he was OK but the wind noise was such that all I could hear was garble. Shortly thereafter I looked in my mirror and saw my wingman was still with me.

"My arm didn't hurt but I was bleeding quite badly. I momentarily considered trying to make it back to the ship but realized I would probably pass out before I got there. The nearest 'friendly' was the SAR DD [destroyer] stationed about 30 miles to seaward of the coast-in point. I thought I had been hit in the engine as well as the cockpit since I was still descending while holding 220 kts. I thrashed around the cockpit, making radio transmissions, flying the bird, changing tacan channels, and trying to arrest the bleeding by squeezing my right upper arm.

"About the time I descended through 2500 ft, I looked at my RPM and realized I had only 70% power. Things had been pretty confusing, and it was the first time I had looked at the RPM since getting hit. I advanced the throttle and the RPM began to build up. The engine seemed to be working properly, and I climbed back to 4000 ft. I heard a garbled radio transmission and recognized the words 'your posit.' I replied that I was 240/15 from the SAR DD, that I had been hit in the cockpit, that I was bleeding badly and intended to eject as close to the SAR DD as possible. I then called my wingman and told him to tell the SAR DD that I would need medical attention immediately.

"There were several subsequent radio transmissions by other stations, but they were all too garbled for me to understand. I was beginning to feel weak and decided I'd have to eject and get my flotation gear inflated before I passed out. As I neared the SAR DD, there was a broken undercast. For some reason I decided I wanted to see the SAR DD before I ejected.

"The undercast wasn't very thick and I descended through it, leveling about 3000 ft. As I broke out, I saw the SAR DD below, churning white water and heading directly for me. I glanced at the DME, which read three miles. Since I was feeling quite woozy, and beginning to experience tunnel vision, I decided to eject. I made sure

my heels were on the deck, sat up straight, and pulled the curtain with my left hand. The next thing I knew I was tumbling or spinning. I heard a sequence of several snaps and pops, then felt the bladders toss me out of the seat. Shortly thereafter the chute opened and I seemingly was suspended in midair.

"My oxygen mask was still on, and my visor was down. I removed the oxygen mask and dropped it. I looked around. The view was beautiful—blue ocean, white clouds above, and the DD steaming down below. The war seemed a million miles away.

"I was feeling pretty woozy and couldn't concentrate on any one thing for very long. I held tight on the stump for a few seconds and then remembered to inflate my C-3 life vest. I inflated the left side first, then couldn't find the right toggle with my left hand. I groped around for a few seconds, then forgot about the right toggle.

"I unfastened the left rocket jet fitting and let the seat pack fall to the right. Actually, it seemed to hang between my legs. I attempted to get at the lanyard to the life raft but with my left hand, all I could reach was the D-ring for the bailout bottle so I forgot about that too. I went back to squeezing my stump and noticed I was still wearing my left glove. I pulled off the glove with my teeth, let it drop, and went back to squeezing the stump. I watched the glove falling lazily a few feet away from me for a while, then shifted my gaze to the DD. I didn't have any vertical reference points, and for a while it seemed I was not falling. I noticed the DD had a boat rigged out and suspended a few feet above the water.

"I couldn't think of anything else to do so I just kept applying pressure to the stump and watched my wingman flying in a tight circle around my position. I recognized relative movement when I was just a few feet above the water. I crossed my legs, held my breath, and almost immediately hit the water.

"When I bobbed back to the surface, I floated for a few seconds before I remembered to disconnect myself from the chute. The water was warm, with a gentle swell, and there was no discernible wind. The chute had collapsed behind me and all I could see were some shroud lines over my shoulder. I unlocked both Koch fittings and the risers fell away behind me.

"The SAR DD was about a half mile away and the whaleboat was already in the water. I saw someone in khaki point in my direction. I muttered a few encouraging curses to speed them on.

"I had lost the sense of time passage but it seemed that the whaleboat got to my vicinity quite rapidly. As the whaleboat neared me the coxswain throttled back and turned away. Apparently he was concerned about running over me. I yelled to the boat that I was bleeding badly, and to drive right in, which the coxswain did.

"When the boat was alongside, numerous hands reached out to grab me. I told them to be careful of my right side. After I was resting safely in the whaleboat, my right arm became painful for the first time. Up to that point, I had had just a mild stinging sensation. Someone removed my helmet and cradled my head in his lap.

There was a corpsman in the boat and, although I didn't feel him puncture my arm, I was receiving Dextran from a bottle within seconds.

"The pain was severe, so I asked the sailor holding my head to break out the morphine syrettes I carried in my left sleeve pocket. He said he had never given morphine so I mumbled step by step instructions. I told him to unscrew the plastic cap and throw it away, push the wire plunger all the way into the syrette, then pull it out and throw it away. The sailor was obviously shook because he pulled out the plunger and threw the syrete over the side. We went through the whole thing again with the second syrette, this time successfully, and the sailor got the morphine into my arm. I thought I was going to pass out so I told the sailor to remember to tell the doctor that I had been given morphine.

"Shortly thereafter, we came alongside the SAR DD. The bow and stern hooks were sharp, we latched on smoothly, and almost in one motion, were hoisted to deck level. I was taken down to sick bay where the ship's doctor began working on me. After a few minutes, another doctor from another carrier arrived and introduced himself. In my drowsy state that confused me somewhat. After pondering the thought, I announced that my carrier was closer than his and that I wanted to be returned to *my* ship.

"I have no idea how long I was aboard the DD, but recall someone saying 'about an hour ago,' apparently in reference to my accident. That would have made the time about 0930. Shortly thereafter, I was placed in a stretcher, taken on deck and hoisted into a helicopter. Just before I left the DD sick bay, I insisted that my flight boots go along with me. A couple of officers had dyed the boots bright blue . . . the squadron color . . . a few days previously as a joke. This was the first mission I'd flown wearing my blue boots and I didn't want to lose them. The carrier surgeon assured me that all my gear would accompany me.

"I don't recall how long the helo trip back to my carrier took. I was pretty well doped up on morphine and quite weak. When we set down on the flight deck I recall two things distinctly: the air boss announced on the 5MC '163 returning,' which made me feel better and our flight surgeon spoke to me. Hearing a familiar voice also made me feel better. His comment was, 'Boy! Some people will do anything to get out of a little combat!' With friends like that, who needs enemies? I was taken below and into surgery, where among other valiant efforts (eight units of blood) what was left of my right arm was surgically amputated, leaving me with about a six-inch stump.

"In retrospect, I can think of some survival procedures I could have followed to more closely coincide with 'the book.' But it is encouraging to note that the essential things worked. The A–4 Rapec seat, which is famous for its simplicity and reliability, worked as advertised. My wingman stated that, in addition to the frag that went through the cockpit, my aircraft was 'full of holes' and streaming fuel from several places. It is logical to assume that frags could have penetrated the fuselage and damaged the seat mechanism, since my wingman stated the AAA burst was 'close aboard' my aircraft. However, it never crossed my mind that the seat would function other than as advertised when the time came to use it.

"One half of the C–3 life vest is sufficient to keep afloat a pilot with full combat gear (.38 revolver, ammo, survival vest, RT–10 radio, etc.). The Koch fittings worked correctly after water entry. I merely unlocked them and the riser straps fell away. My .38 revolver and pencil flares, carried in a front pocket of my survival vest, were readily accessible although in the circumstances of my rescue they were not used.

"I retained my helmet with visor down throughout the incident until I was in the whaleboat. With the visor down, oxygen mask on, and chin strap cinched, I experienced no facial injuries or discomfort from wind blast, even though the canopy and part of the windscreen had been carried away by the frag. I experienced no difficulties in doing essential things with only one arm, except for access to my morphine syrettes. I carried them in the left sleeve pocket of my flight suit and could not get at them. I recommend that morphine syrettes be carried in a more accessible one-handed location, possibly in a front pocket of the survival vest.

"I could not reach the life raft lanyard with my left hand after releasing the left rocket jet fitting and letting the seat pack fall to my right side. During my flight from the beach to the SAR DD, I thought of applying a tourniquet to my right arm stump. I had the nylon cord lanyard attached to my .38 revolver handy, but reasoned that the effort to untie it, get it around the stump, and secured (with one hand and my teeth, no doubt), coupled with flying the aircraft was a tenuous prospect at best. Some thought might be given to a simple, one-hand operable tourniquet as an addition to combat survival gear. Not everyone will have his arm blown off, but there have been several pilot injuries in the Vietnam war where such a tourniquet would have been handy."

In Extremis

March 1967

There was a loud and distinctive explosion in the cockpit. I don't really remember any sensation of pain but I knew that something had gone wrong—I knew we had been hit. I pulled back on the stick to climb out of the area and the next thing I recall is that my bombardier/navigator came up and said, "You're climbing too high." I opened my eyes and sure enough I was climbing a little too high. I grabbed the stick, rolled the plane off to the right, got the nose over to the right, got the nose to go back down and headed for the coastline.

My bombardier/navigator was apparently unaware at this time that anything was wrong. I kept trying to talk to him on the ICS [intercockpit communication system] but I couldn't talk. I tore my oxygen mask off and told him I had been hit. He looked at me and as soon as he realized what had happened, he immediately took charge, so to speak.

Keying the UHF, the bombardier/navigator said, "This is so-and-so. My pilot's been hit. The airplane is still flying. I'll keep you advised." He came right back to me on the ICS and asked, "How do you feel?" I said, "I'm doing fine. I don't feel too hot—there's something wrong. I've been hit but I don't know where."

I realized that the sensation was somewhere in my left arm but I was almost afraid to look down as I was afraid my arm was gone. But I did look down and I saw that my hand was intact. It was just draped over the throttle and I had no use of it at all.

As I've said, my bombardier/navigator sort of took command. He said to go ahead and take a heading of 100–degrees, I believe, and just hang on and let him know how I felt.

As we got out past the coast, I remember being somewhat nauseated and started getting that flushed feeling as if I were going to pass out. I told him, "I'm not feeling very good. I don't think I'm going to get much

further," whereupon he produced a bottle of medicinal brandy that he carries for just such an occasion. I tossed that thing down and it cleared my head up right away and I felt a lot better.

I remember I said then, "We've got a problem here. What are we going to do?" I realized, of course, that without the use of my left hand we couldn't land back aboard the ship. However, I considered the possibility that with the two of us flying the airplane—the bombardier/navigator using the stick and me reaching with my right hand across to the throttle—we might be able to land at ——. So I asked him how far it was to —— and he told me. I didn't think I could make it that far as I was beginning to feel pretty bad again. We concurred that the best thing to do was to try to get back to the ship.

The ship was in a southerly direction. If we got there we would be doing real well. If we couldn't make that we still could have gone to —— without going too much further, so we agreed to head out straight for the ship and try to get as close as we could in case we had to eject immediately. The alternative was if we got that far and were still doing well we could proceed on to ——. We flew for what seemed like about two or three minutes, (it probably wasn't that long) when I started feeling a little weak again. I said, "I don't think I'm going to make it to the ship. We better slow down and set ourselves up for an ejection." My bombardier/navigator agreed.

I told him to take the stick and that I would reach over and grab hold of the throttle. He took the stick and held the wings level. I reached over with my right hand, retarded the throttle to about 80% and put the wing tip speed brakes out. I then came back and continued to fly the airplane. As we slowed down, I began to feel weak and nauseated again and realized I couldn't go on too much longer. I didn't want to wait too long to eject as I was afraid of losing consciousness and I was sure that if I did that, I would drown. I definitely wanted to get out of the aircraft with a little bit of consciousness left so that I could set myself up as soon as I was in the water. At the time I still hadn't seen any blood and I didn't know specifically where I was hit, but I was sure I couldn't stay up for a heck of a lot longer.

We got down to about 225 kts and I told my bombardier/navigator I was feeling pretty bad and he'd better stand by for ejection. I asked him if he remembered ejection procedures and he said yes. One thing we should've done but we didn't because of the heat of the moment was to have gone over the ejection procedures together but it didn't occur to us at the time as we were pretty pressed as it was. I told him I was going to jettison the canopy.

At about 220 kts I gave him the signal that I was going to jettison the canopy. Jettisoning was normal and uneventful. With the onrush of air into the cockpit, I sort of revived again and told the bombardier/navigator that I thought I could hang on for a little bit longer. By this time the wind was screaming in the cockpit and causing a lot of confusion.

We pressed on for another 5 or 10 miles. It couldn't have been much more than a minute or so when I felt myself really slipping. I knew I was on the way out and I yelled over at the bombardier/navigator and said, "I'm going to pass out. Eject!" He looked at me and gave me a thumbs-up and pointed at me. About this time my vision started to spin and the whole cockpit started to spin on me and I knew that I had better get out then or I wasn't going to have a chance.

(Just prior to this I had reached over with my right hand and picked up my left hand and wrapped it around my lap belt and tucked it between my legs so I wouldn't injure my arm on the way out.)

As I said, my vision started to spin. I reached up and grabbed the face curtain with my right hand and gave it a tug. Unfortunately, I don't remember anything else until I got in the water. I think I must have felt my parachute open because some time before I got in the water I inflated my Mk–3C. I sort of remember pulling the CO_2 actuating lanyards in my semi-consciousness on the way down. I came right to the surface as soon as I hit the water and I was immediately revived.

My first concern, of course, was whether my bombardier/navigator had gotten out and I looked around trying to find the aircraft. I saw neither the aircraft nor his chute but I surmised that he must have made it. Either he had gone down a good way from me or he had entered the water about the same time as I had but I just hadn't seen him coming down.

I was very concerned about sharks as we had been briefed about a number of sharks in this area. I think this is everybody's big fear about going down at sea. I was particularly concerned as I knew I was bleeding though I still didn't know where my wound was. My first thought was to get into my life raft. It caused me quite a bit of concern when I reached down between my legs and found that *I didn't have a life raft.*

Some time during ejection, my whole seat pan had left me. I really don't know why. The only thing I can think of was that I hadn't hooked my Harley buckle to my seat belt. I think this is unlikely, however, because whenever I have strapped in without having hooked up, it has been immediately apparent to me that something was wrong. It is just second nature to you—when you strap the seat belt down and the Harley buckle isn't in there, it just doesn't feel right so you fix it.

The other reason I think I didn't forget to buckle it up was that if the seat pan went off, it had to slide off my legs and past my feet, and I'm sure that with the body position I must have been in on ejection, I surely would have had scratch marks on my boots or a bruise someplace. I didn't so I think probably what happened is that my left hand which I had tucked under the lap belt must have pulled up the lap belt when the parachute opened and just released the whole lap belt assembly.

So there I was in the water—bleeding, with no life raft. I looked over and saw my parachute floating about four or five inches below the surface. Contrary to everything we've ever been taught about getting away from your parachute to avoid getting tangled up, in my concern about sharks I thought if I could just get on top of the chute, since it was already under water, and pull it up

approach

MARCH 1967   THE NAVAL AVIATION SAFETY REVIEW

around me, I could keep the blood contained in the chute itself and it wouldn't attract any sharks. I got over on top the parachute and immediately saw the water turn crimson against the white background. Almost as soon as I got there I began to get tangled in the shroudlines. It wasn't 10 or 15 sec before I realized that this was a real poor idea. I started swimming away from the parachute and started looking for my shark chaser.

I had been the safety officer in the A–6 RAG and in this particular squadron. I think I know survival equipment in the A–6 and ejection and survival procedures as well as anybody. Nevertheless as many times as I had been through it with two hands, I couldn't for the life of me find my flares or my shark chaser with my one good hand. One hand or two hands makes a big difference in this game. I had a terrible time trying to pull the shark chaser out. Fortunately, after about five minutes of playing around and trying to feel my way around under the Mk–3C, I finally found a bag of shark chaser. I opened it with my teeth and started putting it around me and felt a little more secure.

All this time, by the way, I wasn't the least bit concerned about being rescued because from the time I went in the water until about halfway through the episode, the squadron CO [commanding officer] was holding directly over my head at about 1000 ft in a very tight orbit. I knew he had me in sight so I didn't get out my signal devices. I was only concerned about staying alive in the water until the rescue aircraft got there.

I swam away, kicking moderately and thinking if I could let the blood stream out behind me instead of letting it pool around me in one place, I would probably be a lot better off. My whole logic about the sharks and what to do and what not to do down there probably doesn't make much sense, but you just do it instinctively when you're in a situation like this.

About this time two A-1s came over and I saw an Air Force *Albatross*, which they use over there for rescue. I estimate I had been in the water about 15 or 20 min at the time I saw it come up on the horizon. Unfortunately, as the *Albatross* got closer to us, our commanding officer rolled out of his tight orbit around me to give this fellow instructions for my best interest and when he rolled in again, he reassumed his orbit about 3 miles away from me.

What happened was that they had seen me eject and the airplane crash and had heard the B/N talking to them on the air. They assumed that only the bombardier/navigator had gotten out and that I, being injured, had gone down with the airplane. What had, in fact, happened was that we had both gotten out fairly close together but the bombardier/navigator had caught them on their blind side and they never saw him going down. They were only concerned with looking for one person in the water, so they thought. When they rolled out and rolled back up, they acquired the bombardier/navigator not me. They set up the orbit around him, thinking we were one and the same.

All of a sudden, aircraft started coming from every which way. There were A-1s and helicopters and another *Albatross*. I think I counted about 12 airplanes all around me about 3 miles away, and here I was, all by my lonesome, feeling pretty bad about the whole thing. About this time sharks were my second consideration—I had to start thinking about how to let somebody know where I was.

The first thing I looked for was the Mk-13 Mod 0 day/night signal flare. I pulled one out and realized right away that I was going to have a hard time igniting it with only one hand. I thought of trying to do it with my teeth and immediately dismissed that idea. I thought of putting the flare under my dead arm next to the Mk-3C and pulling it with my right hand, but I was afraid to do that for fear it would burn a hole in my life preserver which was the only thing keeping me alive. So finally I decided to put it between my knees under water and pull the cap off, then try and hold it up above the surface. I pulled both ends—the ring on one end just snapped off and the other end peeled off the way it's supposed to but it didn't ignite. I was very disappointed that I couldn't get either end to work. Then I went to my PRC-49 radio which was rigged in a shoulder strap arrangement in a canvas bag that we carry with us on our person. Unfortunately it sits right in front of you at stomach level and it blocks your access to most of the other things in your Mk-3C and your survival bag if you don't have a good arm to push it out of the way to get what you want.

I wrestled with the radio for about 5 min to get it out of the pack and turn it on. I was very disappointed not to hear the beep signal which would have indicated that the radio was working. I went to "transmit" position and tried to call and tell the rescue aircraft that I was in a straight line south of their position and please acknowledge. I

didn't hear a thing so I finally gave that up and went to the beeper transmitter position. I tucked my PRC-49 under my right arm trying to hold it on top of the Mk-3C.

About this time, two A-1s came directly over my head, heading for the big group of circling rescue aircraft which was still about 3 miles away. I pulled out my .38 caliber pistol loaded with ball ammunition. (I had thought that if I ever needed it right away, it was going to be in a situation where I had to shoot somebody and that if I ever needed it in a survival situation I would have time to reload with tracers which I also carried.) Even though it was loaded with ball, not tracer ammo, I thought at least the A-1s could hear me firing. They were about 700 ft and right over my head. When I fired the first four rounds and got no acknowledgement, I was pretty desperate. I damn near took a pot shot at one of the A-1s to get their attention. But I thought, that wouldn't solve any of my problems so I shot off the last rounds under the A-1s right wing and that didn't do any good either.

I tried to reload with tracer ammunition but found I couldn't do it with one hand, so I set it under my right arm and it immediately fell into the water and I lost it. I had had it tied with nylon lanyard but the lanyard was cut or undone because I lost the pistol.

I had taken my hard hat off prior to this and waved it at the A-1s when they approached me. I knew they couldn't see me so I tied my hard hat to my Mk-3C life preserver but it broke loose and also floated away. *I was slowly losing every bit of survival equipment and signaling equipment I had.*

I wanted to get into my survival vest where I carry some extra flares, a compass and a few other things, but I really had a problem getting all my survival equipment with one arm because of the arrangement of the Mk-3C up around me. I had done this in practice but this was a different situation using one hand because you have to push things out of the way.

Then I decided I had to fire my pencil flare gun. I should have tried this initially, but when I looked down to try to decide what to pull out, it was down underneath a bunch of stuff. I had to unhook the Mk-3C life preserver and dig around and finally I came up with the good old pencil flare gun. I screwed it onto the first cartridge and waited until the two airplanes which had just been overhead turned. When they were headed right for me, I fired a flare off and they leveled their wings and proceeded to me. When they arrived I fired another flare. By the time I got the third in the gun, a helicopter was approaching. I fired the flare and he had me in sight and was hovering overhead in a matter of minutes.

I had, as I said, lost my hard hat and was very disappointed to find I couldn't watch the helicopter because of the spray kicking up. Without something protecting your eyes, you just can't look at the helo. I looked up to see what he was going to lower—either a horse collar or a pronged seat. I thought, "If he lowers the seat, I can probably get myself up with one hand, but I don't think I can hook myself up with a horse collar."

The first thing I saw coming down was a horse collar. I remember looking at the helo behind me—I had to keep my face away from the rotor wash. My bombardier/navigator, who had already been picked up, apparently told the helo crewman to hook him up and he came down into the water (after being rescued himself!) and hooked me up by my torso harness. They hauled me up into the helo and then lowered the horse collar again to pick up my bombardier/navigator. He waved them away and was hoisted by another helicopter. We were both taken to the cruiser where our wounds were treated and the next day I got back to the ship. . . .

Over and Out

January 1968

A flight of seven students briefed to fly solo in TF–9Js out to the carrier for initial qualifications. Takeoff, rendezvous, enroute, and carrier breakup proceeded normally.

Student Doaker made two uneventful touch-and-go landings followed by a fouled-deck waveoff. On the fourth pass, his aircraft touched down well to the left of the angledeck centerline (about 10′), moving right to left, and engaged No. 4 crossdeck pendant. Rollout continued to the left with the port main mount dropping into the catwalk. At this point the aircraft came to a stop just forward of the fresnel lens. Although forward motion had been checked, the aircraft slowly eased over the side in a sideslipping manner. It then rolled inverted and continued to stretch out the No. 4 pendant while hanging suspended by its tailhook.

During its slide over the side, the engine was observed to be running at full power. When movement on the No. 4 pendant ceased, the nose section was submerged up to the cockpit. The pilot secured the engine, blew the canopy, manually unstrapped himself and stepped into the sea. His pickup by helicopter was almost casual.

This accident was caused by improper pilot technique in correcting for a right-of-centerline lineup on a normal day carrier landing approach. A right-to-left drift developed and was further aggravated by the pilot making a last minute correction to the left. Moreover, the pilot seemed to be oblivious to good lineup, later attributed to overconcentration on the meatball.

A Night in the Jungle

Evading would-be captors, hiding in the jungle throughout the night and trying to attract the attention of rescuers and, at the same time, elude the enemy the next morning . . . 17½ hours which ended in helicopter pick up at noon.

Fire following the explosion of one of the A–6's bombs under its starboard wing on a mission necessitated the ejection. In the story which follows we will call the pilot "Bill" and the bombardier navigator, "Joe." Joe ejected first so we will begin with his experiences.

February 1968

"Halfway through my wingman's Mayday call, I positioned myself and ejected," the bombardier-navigator recalls. "I cleared the aircraft and the entire automatic sequence happened long before I could do anything myself. Shortly thereafter I noticed that I was still holding on to the ejection D-ring face curtain."

When he let go of the D-ring and tried to hook up the Harley buckle fitting on his torso harness to connect it to the survival pack, Joe found that both of his hands were severely bruised. This, he thought, must have been from

ejecting through the canopy. Giving up his attempt to fasten the Harley buckle, he turned his parachute and saw the pilot below. Both men were headed toward a ridge line. He watched as the pilot touched down in a marshy area.

Thinking he was going to land in deep trees, Joe crossed his arms in front of his face. At that instant he hit the ground smartly in savannah type growth and brush, hurting his back in the process. His pistol, though strapped under his survival pack and lashed to his Mk-3C, broke loose striking him first in the stomach, then under the chin.

"I opened my rocket jet fittings with great difficulty, because my hands were hurting so badly," he recalls. "I then removed my hard hat because I couldn't hear as well as I wanted to and also because it was white and highly visible with orange and white luminous tape on it.

"I opened my raft, disconnected my seat pack, removed the PRC-49 and immediately vacated the area. At first I proceeded towards Bill's chute which I could see because we were only about 300 yards apart and I was on higher terrain. Then I thought, 'This is a bad idea.' (Bill and I had agreed previously not to join up unless it was going to be a long haul.) I doubled back on my tracks and headed east, travelling hard for about 15 or 20 minutes. All this time I heard numerous people yelling loudly back and forth as if they were trying to make us panic and expose ourselves.

"After about 20 minutes of running, I stopped and took off my anti-G suit. I took the little name tag off and put it in my pocket; then I hid the suit as best I could and buried my Martin-Baker garters under the leaves and mud.

"I could hear a stream and I proceeded down an embankment towards it. Checking for possible followers and seeing none, I walked into the stream and traveled upstream to break my trail and scent. I crossed to the other side and climbed up the steepest part of the embankment. I figured, 'The harder it is for me, the harder it is going to be for them also.'

"Completely exhausted, I got to the top of the hill and found a point that would hide me. I rested there for about 15 minutes before I started moving again, following game trails as much as possible so I wouldn't leave any new trails. My terrain was a lot easier to travel than Bill's because it was 7' to 8' tall grass with moderately dense underbrush. I picked up another ravine and found another stream to travel. In this way, as I said before, my scent would be broken. I could travel faster and my noise would be covered.

"Dusk was coming on at this time. I was anticipating sunset somewhere around 1930 but there was still a good amount of light. I rested in the dense undergrowth by the side of the stream for another 15 or 20 minutes as close to the ground as possible with the reeds and weeds pushed up around me so they would look normal.

"My whole philosophy at the time I landed was to put as much distance between myself and my chute as quickly as possible and then work from there. I was also attempt-ing to go for the highest ground. In this way I could survey everything, keep my sense of direction and also make it difficult for them to pursue me. After departing the stream area, I started up an embankment, deliberately doubled back twice trying to throw off my track, and headed for the top of another ridge line about two ridges from where I had landed.

"I reached the top of the second ridge just at moon-rise. The moon was real bright and would show my position if I profiled myself on top of a hill so I avoided the crest. Again I found game trails; the ground was real firm and I didn't leave any footprints. I could see a light below me and occasionally I could hear voices."

After resting a short time, Joe proceeded down the game trail, followed it along a ridge line and then turned off onto a smaller trail.

"By this time I was about a mile from where I had landed. I traveled through some more reeds and brush and got to an area on the lee side of the hill. I decided that this would be a good pick-up spot because I could survey the general area. Now I could see that we had gone down in a bowl-shaped area with a ridge separating two smaller bowls.

"I stayed in this area from approximately midnight until 1100 the next day. I buried myself right down close to the ground, took off all of my survival gear and put it underneath me or covered it so that it wouldn't be seen easily, pushed up all the grass around me as best I could to cover myself, and tried to get some rest. At times during the night I could hear footsteps. I remember thinking 'It might be large game but game is usually quieter.' The next day I saw small shallow bootprints, about size five.

"Like Bill, I had absolute faith that when the sun came up the next day, I was going to see helicopters. I knew that the time we went down was bad for rescue because there was only an hour and a half to two hours until sunset. However, the sight of our orbiting wingman was reassuring. He orbited for about two hours but I had no real opportunity to make radio contact with him.

"The next day, at about 0600, I heard an aircraft but I couldn't see it. It sounded very distant and I thought I was just hearing things in my anxiety. However, at about 0615, I not only heard but saw a C-54 at about 11,000' heading due north directly overhead. I immediately got out my PRC-49 and started talking but received no reply. My transmitter was intermittent and probably down 90 percent of the time but I didn't realize it then so I just kept talking. Shortly afterwards, at about 0630 or 0700, several A-1s arrived and commenced orbiting the area at various altitudes following the terrain.

"I could now hear voices quite heavily around the area. It sounded like they were actively searching for us again. Since my PRC-49 receiver was working, I could hear Bill talking to the A-1's on the radio. I heard the A-1s say that they thought they saw both of us and that they were going to send for choppers. Two of them left the area to escort the helicopters.

"At about 0815, two UH-34s arrived. I started talking to them; however, they probably weren't receiving me.

They started searching Bill's area. They proceeded to a ridge very far north and I quickly realized that the clothing we were wearing was good camouflage and that it would be very difficult for them to spot us. *For this reason, I think the PRC-49 is the single most important item that we could have in the survival kit. You can give your position to your rescuer without revealing it to the enemy and you can be more explicit on rescue directions.* I feel that it is extremely dangerous to use anything else because of the possibility of compromising your position to the enemy.

"As one helicopter attempted to locate Bill, I talked with the other, giving him instructions for locating me. I believe that it was just coincidental that he was doing what I was asking on the radio. I asked him to proceed over to the eastern portion directly across from the area opposite the pilot. He came over to me and I moved a few feet out of my hiding place so that I would be more visible. The copter came around right behind me and passed directly overhead. I waved to the crewman and he waved back at me and they just kept going. Apparently he didn't tell the helo pilot that I was there. At this time, I really felt like I had had the course as the helo went back toward Bill. (*This was, perhaps, the same helo from which the crewman waved to the downed pilot but could not communicate to the gunner.—Ed.*)

"To go back a minute, just before this, I heard a single shot right close to me. Apparently it was someone firing at an A-1. I heard Bill warn one copter that he was streaming fuel and had been hit. The stricken helicopter left escorted by the second helo and two A-1s.

"I felt extremely depressed at this point and I thought the best the helicopter could do in a turnaround was to get back to us in about another hour or two. Since there were troops all around us, I felt that every minute was precious because they were getting closer to us. However, it did occur to me that they didn't know where I was but they knew where Bill was because most of the shooting was coming from his area. In addition, the helicopters were concentrated in his vicinity so I figured they thought that both of us were on that ridge.

"Approximately two hours after the last chopper left, I thought that it was a good time to make my play for better terrain. While I had been waiting, I had thought about making the long walk to the higher terrain and how I was going to go about it. I surveyed all of my survival gear and my personal survival kit pack and took out the signal flares from my Mk-3C. It was my intention to use the daysmoke signal should the helicopters return. I had determined my radio to be down by a radio check.

"I got out of the area and proceeded again on the ridge line just below the top, breaking my way through the reeds and looking for some low cover that I could travel through unhindered. I wanted to get to an area that was relatively clear so that a helicopter could land with a hill to shield it from ground fire and so that I wouldn't be seen using the daysmoke signal. If a chopper should come, I would be in a good position for rescue and, if it didn't come, I could continue on the perimeter of the ridge line and circle my way around, eventually working my way west.

"I noticed as I was walking along a game trail that there were fairly fresh boot prints as close as 20' from where I had hidden during the night.

"I walked as far as I could but tired quickly so I dropped down to rest and analyze the situation. At about 1145 I heard aircraft returning. I immediately ran to the top of the hill from my position 30' below the crest and activated a daysmoke signal which I arced above my head. Apparently they didn't see the first one so I lit off a second and saw a T-28 break and dive for me. Thinking he was going to strafe me, I hit the deck and stayed pinned down. The T-28 climbed, made a tight turn and flew back over my position. I waved at him and he waved back in acknowledgment and I assumed that he was spotting me for the chopper. Shortly thereafter, the chopper came right in over me and touched down. I ran to it, jumped aboard and it quickly took off.

"We then proceeded over to the area where Bill was and circled for about 20 minutes. We were being shot at and an Air Force chopper located about 50 yards south of Bill was drawing fire from the troops. We orbited Bill's area three times before we spotted him and went in. The hoist kept tangling in trees but after numerous attempts, it looked as if we finally had succeeded in getting the sling to him. The cable came up and then the top of the horse collar with nothing on it. I was shaken by the apparent empty sling but then saw Bill's arm lashed through it and here he came with half the jungle tangled around him. We were like two kids with new toys as we shouted greetings to each other above the engine noise.

"In retrospect, I attribute my confidence in the jungle to survival school, hunting experience and the survival trek in the Philippines. I feel that it is good policy to think about what you have for cover and then utilize it to the best of your ability and imagination. I avoided the area where Bill was because I thought it would make it difficult for a helicopter pick-up with two survivors in one place and because I felt that the enemy would be forced to divide its forces for the search.

"Bill and I are avid physical fitness advocates, working out every night as a regular routine. I'm sure that this helped us out a great deal and that we had a lot of staying power that we might not have had otherwise."

The bombardier navigator's philosophy of remaining free in this instance was, as he stated above, to put as much distance as possible between himself and his chute as quickly as possible. The pilot's situation was somewhat different—searchers were in his vicinity within minutes after he landed. His strategy was to hole up until the middle of the night, then move to a better hiding place which would be suitable for a helo pickup. Now we turn the clock back to the cockpit emergency and follow the pilot until rescue . . .

"I slapped the bombardier-navigator's leg and said 'Eject!'" the pilot begins. "I watched him go out and a second or two later pulled my ejection handle and went. Everything happened faster than I could imagine.

"I looked up and Joe was about 1000' above me although he had ejected first; he seemed to be hanging there in space. Prior to hitting the ground, I watched the aircraft fly into the side of a mountain and explode. A secondary explosion after it hit totally destroyed it.

"Upon reaching the ground, I had a good landing in a marshy area with big rushes about 10' high. The parachute caught in a tree about 20' above me, but I landed on the ground, released my rocket jet fittings and took my helmet off.

"While I was descending in my parachute, I had seen people pointing at me so I knew they would be out there immediately. I couldn't wait around and didn't know where Joe had gone. I had last seen him drifting toward a big grassy hill south of where I had landed. I couldn't go that way because it would take me more than 5 minutes to climb this hill and I knew people would be out there shortly. I looked to the northwest and there was a big hill of dense thick jungle undergrowth so I crossed a small stream and proceeded in that direction. I had already removed my survival equipment container with the PRC–49 radio from my seat pan and left the raft behind. I took the pack with me, crossed the little stream and entered a rice paddy. I went about 10' into the rice paddy but the mud was so thick I couldn't run through it. I came back to the edge and ran around the dike area on the side and crossed a little foot path. There were no vehicle tracks on it but there were donkey, horse or oxen tracks.

"I proceeded up the hill and into the undergrowth. I found an area with nice thick overhanging brush and vines which I hid beneath. Within five minutes after I landed, I heard 10, 15 or even 20 voices. I couldn't tell just how many but there were definitely men out there searching the area and yelling and beating the brush and undergrowth trying to find me.

"We had ejected about 1830 local time. I knew sunset would be around 1930 but it seemed as if the sun was never going down. It didn't actually get dark until around 2000. All during this time, people were out hunting for us. I hid in the same location until almost 2200. During the time I was hiding, the voices sounded like the searchers had joined hands and were covering the creek area thoroughly. At 2200 the voices faded off. I waited another hour, then took off my torso harness and anti-G suit. After taking everything off the torso harness, I buried it and the anti-G suit under a leaf pile.

"At this time I no longer heard any voices but there was a strange mechanical sounding noise like crickets chirping in the little valley area in which I had landed. Joe said later he heard the same noises from his position on the other side of the grassy hill. The sound stopped after 30 minutes. (*This may have been some kind of irrigation apparatus.—Ed.*)

"About 2300 I left my hiding place and proceeded northwest up the hill, finally reaching the top at 0200 after stopping every 15 minutes or so for a rest. The vines and undergrowth were so thick that I had to crawl on my hands and knees in some places and on my stomach in others to get through. For protection I tried to get to the thickest, densest places I could find and that is where I got because I could barely make any progress.

"I got to the top of the hill around 0200, as I said, and found the trees were still too high for a helicopter type rescue the next morning. The trees were so tall that I decided to go 20 yards back down the hill and stay in some thick undergrowth. Around 0230 I found a real good hiding place and stayed there the remainder of the time. I put a mosquito net hood over my head and stretched out and tried to get some sleep. Mosquitoes don't usually bother me but they were quite bothersome that evening. I zipped up my flight suit and tried to doze off but never did actually sleep. I was too excited and just lay there with my eyes wide open.

"The next morning around 0500, just before sunrise, I heard an airplane. After daybreak around 0630 I could see a four-engined aircraft circling overhead. The previous evening, I had checked my PRC–49 out thoroughly, pulling the aerial up and making sure the battery was connected. When I saw the aircraft, I pulled the radio out and called them but I didn't receive anything so I figured my receiver was bad (which it was). I called the pilot to rock his wings if he heard me. He slowly rocked his wings for acknowledgment. I told him I was not receiving.

"Along about 0715, four A–1s came over and I radioed to them and told them to rock their wings for acknowledgment if they heard me and they each rocked their wings. Around 0730 or so when the sun got up over the mountain, I was able to give them my location by using a signal mirror. I shined the signal mirror in their direction and told them I was using it. They rocked their wings, signifying they could see my position or my approximate location.

"At about 0815, two helicopters arrived in the area but they couldn't find me. The A–1s could see me and I am sure they were passing the word on to the helicopters but the helicopters couldn't locate me.

"One of the helicopters was searching the area right around me. At this time a man walked within 10 to 15' of me. When I heard him approaching I was standing up transmitting to the helicopter. I immediately got down on my stomach and hid in the undergrowth. I am sure he walked right up near me, then proceeded back off through the jungle. The jungle was so thick he couldn't see me from 5' away.

"The helo was proceeding toward me when the men on the ground started shooting. I heard ground fire below us and sat up and transmitted for the helo to get out of the area. At this time it got hit. This was about 0830.

"Two of our A–6s flew over about this time and I transmitted, 'Hello, A–6. I am at your 6 o'clock position.' I still couldn't receive. Joe had a functioning PRC–49 receiver but no transmitter. He could hear the A–6s talking back to me but I couldn't hear them.

"The A–1s were joined by two T–28s which remained the entire morning and at 1130 three helicopters returned. *Waiting for the helicopters to get back was about the longest three hours of my life.* I knew I should move to a more open area but because of the people around me I couldn't. Every once in a while I could hear them in the bushes so I decided to stay put. I decided if the helicopters couldn't rescue me that day I would move that night to an open area and I would probably be rescued the next day.

"At 1130 the helicopters returned and all this time aircraft continued to circle overhead at around 10 to 12,000'. The helicopters were having a difficult time trying to locate me because I was in 30' high undergrowth. There were two trees almost 50' high next to me. Earlier, I had told the helicopters that they would need about an 80 to 100' cable in order to reach me and that I would direct them overhead with my radio but I could never get them to the right area.

"Along about noon, I decided to do a last ditch type maneuver by using a day-smoke signal. I transmitted to the helos that I would use one the next time a helo was directly over me and they could spot me. A helo came over and I lit a smoke and held it up. The crew member in the helicopter saw me and waved to me and I waved back, giving him the roger signal, but the helo kept going. Later, I found out the man who saw me didn't have a headset on so he couldn't pass my position to the pilot. He punched the gunner and pointed to me but the gunner couldn't understand so they missed me with that helicopter. And there I was standing like the Statue of Liberty with that daysmoke signal!

"At this time, I decided to start moving to the northeast along the ridge. I went about 20 yards through the jungle—physically crashing through it like I was running with a football. I got over to this big canopy tree and I radioed to the helicopter that I was directly to the north of the big canopy tree or umbrella tree. This was an ideal location. They spotted the tree immediately and came right overhead.

"The helo was about 80' above me; it couldn't get any lower because of the tree and the 30' undergrowth. It seemed like it took an hour for the sling to get to me. The down wash of the rotor blades was terrific; it bent the brush down towards the ground and blew the sling all around. The sling had a weight on it but it got caught in the top of the tree; luckily, they were able to maneuver the helicopter over a little bit to free the sling. The sling came down almost to me, 10' away downhill. I had to jump for it and dropped my survival kit and radio which I wanted to bring back. It was either not jump for the sling or leave the radio there, so I dropped the radio and jumped and caught the sling in one arm.

"The helo immediately took off swinging me around the tree and out over the valley in the direction from which it had approached. All this time I was hanging there with one arm in the sling while the helicopter was flying 1000' above the valley floor. It seemed like 30 seconds and about 1500' altitude before I actually climbed into the helicopter. While I was being hoisted up to the helicopter as it was flying down the valley, the A-1s and T-28s made strafing runs under me to keep the ground fire down. When I got in the helicopter there was Joe sitting on the floor in back. Seeing him in there and being free again was the happiest feeling I've ever had."

Wind, Waves and CVs

This article contained a series of narratives about carrier-landing mishaps that were caused by a combination of high winds and waves, and pitching and rolling flight decks. The following story was the fourth story.

March 1968

Elusive Wind and Ship

Rain squalls and erratic winds caused the CV to make many course alterations in between intermittent recoveries. One steady course period was long enough for the ship to safely recover, via CCA, two of three A-4Bs returning from a CAP mission. Unfortunately, the third *Skyhawk* had to be waved off on final so that the ship could avoid a rain squall.

The second pass was VFR under tower control but the ship could not get a steady wind across the deck due to close proximity to the rain mantle. Consequently, a second waveoff was executed.

The pilot was able to remain VFR but when the ship got an acceptable wind direction, its course led into another squall. A third waveoff was given.

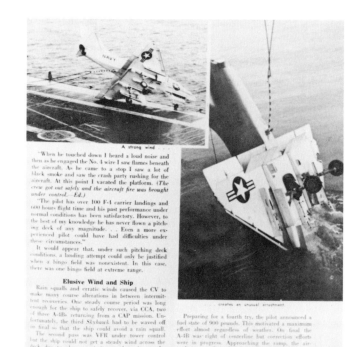

Preparing for a fourth try, the pilot announced a fuel state of 900 pounds. This motivated a maximum effort almost regardless of weather. On final the A–4B was right of centerline but correction efforts were in progress. Approaching the ramp, the aircraft was angling slightly, right to left. The ship again entered a rain area but it was decided to hold course because the wind appeared to be directly down the angle and the precipitation was light. VFR conditions were thereby retained. Crossing the ramp, the pilot banked right trying to stop his right to left drift. Simultaneously, he induced a skid with right rudder. Touchdown was slightly left of center in a left skid and the hook caught the number 2 wire.

During the runout, the *Skyhawk* slewed left on the wet, slippery deck and came to rest 4' short of the port deck edge, angled 12 degrees left of deck centerline. The shifting wind skidded the aircraft's nose further to the left as the plane eased backwards and cocked the nose gear to the left. Then the strong starboard wind tilted the A–4B over onto its port wing and blew it over the side. As it fell abruptly toward the ocean it remained suspended by the still engaged hook. The pilot got out and was quickly picked up from the water unharmed.

The pilot and the LSO each received some criticism for the accident but the real culprit was the wind whipped sea.

Chasing a Pitching Deck

Upon approaching the carrier in an F–8E, the pilot was told to make a CCA because of bad weather. The story of his subsequent difficulties is best told in his own words.

"The LSO informed the aircraft in the pattern that the deck was pitching quite a bit. On my first pass, which was in APC [approach power compensator], I boltered.

The LSO informed me that my bolter was due to the pitching deck. On downwind from the bolter, I informed the controller that I had the ship visually. He rogered and cleared me to final inbound bearing. I picked up the ball and gave my call with a fuel state of 2600 pounds. This pass was in APC also. I noticed the deck was pitching quite a bit. The ball was moving from about one ball low to just off the top of the lens during the approach. As I got in close I had a high ball. I eased my attitude slightly to ensure keeping the ball on the lens. I readjusted the landing attitude and had a ball in the center, wide section of the lens. I sensed an excessive sink rate and added power. However, as I broke out of APC and went to full power, the plane contacted the deck. The landing felt hard. Toward the end of the runout the plane tilted down. I realized the port MLG [main landing gear] must have been broken. I shut down and exited the plane.

"I think this accident might have been prevented, or at least the damage lessened, had I flown a manual throttle vice an APC carrier approach. I also believe that recoveries on a pitching deck should be minimized during the carrier refresher training stage." . . .

Suffice it to say that this incident was a tough one on everybody involved and the pilot's closing paragraph seems apropos.

The pilot of an A–3B was more fortunate than the other pilots mentioned in this article. A rolling/pitching deck almost got the best of him during day carquals. The landing was excessively hard and superficial damage was done to the aircraft. Fortunately, however, the touchdown resulted in a bolter and he got safely airborne. Again, fortunately, a bingo field was within range and a wise decision was made to send him ashore. . . .

A Collection of Midairs

Col. J. H. Reinburg, USMCR; June 1968

Flying high speed military jet aircraft is no small job. Pilots must divide their attention between cockpit duties and constant scanning of the skies for other aircraft. Cockpit manipulations and instrument observations require precise attention particularly during the takeoff and landing phases. But even then, scanning outside the cockpit can not be neglected.

On deck and taxiing back to the line, or once cleaned up and comfortably airborne after liftoff, the cockpit duties slack off. But all too often in the air, a tendency arises on the part of some pilots to assume that the sky is theirs alone. Here are some condensed versions of midair mishaps that demonstrate that such is not always the case.

Internal Noise Distraction

A T–2A was on a basic instrument training flight. While climbing through 15,000', the instructor pilot noticed a noise that seemed to come from the after fuselage. Its intensity increased in the climb, so at 16,500' the instructor took the controls from the student, turned toward home base and commenced a shallow descent. Almost immediately, the noise quit. All instrument readings remained normal so the crew decided that the annoyance had come from the non-critical air conditioning system. The instructor decided to continue the hop so he turned the controls back to the student.

The Big but Not So Empty Sky

Meanwhile a section of T–33s were in the area practicing combat tactics. The *Buckeye* instructor suddenly observed two *Shooting Stars* very close above and converging at right angles just as he made the decision to continue the flight. Realizing that the proximity of the T–33s was dangerous, the instructor took the controls from the student, pushed the throttle up to 100 percent and rolled hard left.

This action was not quick enough and the underside portion of the second T–33s empennage smashed into the underside of the *Buckeye's* port wing. The T–2A immediately became uncontrollable and the instructor initiated dual ejection. The instructor ejected successfully but his student was struck and fatally injured by the falling *Buckeye* before his chute deployed.

The T–33 initially became uncontrollable but the pilot was able to level it off after losing quite a bit of altitude. He ultimately determined that a safe landing could not be accomplished, however, and both occupants ejected successfully.

This very unfortunate accident is another case of complacency in the big and "empty" sky. The weather and visibility were good so it is just a pure case of lax visual observation on everybody's part. The T–2A crew was naturally distracted while they investigated a strange noise. But the student failed to keep up a proper scan while the instructor flew the aircraft. If he had followed the proper lookout policy, the section would have been detected sooner. The T–33 pilots must also share the blame.

Twenty Eyeballs Failed

After finding their primary ground target in a joint service exercise saturated, the leader of a flight of six A–4Cs decided to proceed to their secondary target. The change of plans was coordinated with and approved by their assigned GCI [ground control intercept] station. At the same time, another GCI station was controlling a division of four F–86 aircraft in an overlapping area. Unfortunately, however, the two ground stations were not coordinating with each other.

The *Skyhawk* leader led his flight, in loose column formation, over the secondary target for identification and traffic purposes. No other aircraft were observed in the area. The four *Sabres* were nearby at a higher altitude and were the first to sight the *Skyhawks*. Feeling the spirit of the joint maneuvers would condone a simulated aerial engagement, the *Sabre* leader set his sights for an attack on the number 4 *Skyhawk*. He thought he was picking on "Tailend Charlie" because he had failed to see numbers 5 and 6 in the extended and staggered column.

In his diving attack the lead *Sabre* pilot had to pull 8G in order to hold the pipper on the number 4 *Skyhawk*. Obviously, this was not conducive to good vision and he didn't even see his starboard wing gouge the port side of the Number 5 *Skyhawk*. Fortunately, both aircraft were

able to maintain level flight and both later made safe landings.

Three-dimensional Search Responsibil[i]ty

Even though joint maneuvers such as this are often conducted under GCI control, there is no substitute for continuous personal vigilance in the cockpit. Combat maneuvers are designed to simulate hostile conditions, and for his own protection every pilot's head should be on a swivel. Obviously, the *Skyhawks* were in a poorly deployed position to be on the lookout for "enemy" air attacks because at least one of the six pilots should have spotted the 86s. The *Sabres* had the altitude, and therefore, every advantage. Regardless, they were too quick to assume that only four planes were below. Collision avoidance in VFR conditions is dependent upon heads-up flying for all crews in all situations.

Head-on at 1200–Plus Knots

Three F–4Bs were on an air combat maneuvering mission under the watchdog eye of a GCI station. The purpose of the flight was to introduce the three *Phantom II* replacement pilots to offensive section tactics against a single bogey.

One of the F–4s was assigned the bogey role and the other two took their turns on the offensive. With GCI assistance, the two attackers, in loose section, were lined up for a head-on attack on the bogey. At about 20 miles, lead broadcast his "Judy" and, according to plan, continued to close in order to identify the bogey as an "enemy" target. The "Judy was also a signal for the wingman to barrel-roll in order to let the lead get three miles ahead.

As briefed, when lead got his identifying visual on the bogey he transmitted, "Bandit, bandit, bandit. Cleared to fire." This was the signal for the wingman to simulate a *Sparrow* shot at the bogey. Then lead was to safely get out of the way as quickly as possible and protect the wingman while he fired the missile.

The exercise called for the missile to miss, then the bogey pilot to try for a tail shot at either of his attackers. After identifying and passing the bogey, lead turned hard starboard. A few seconds later, the wingman passed close aboard the bogey then wrapped it up into a high-G port turn. The bogey pilot, meanwhile, strained himself into a starboard reversal. One can quickly visualize that the wingman and the bogey had set themselves up on the same race track going in opposite directions and the high-G turns did not help them maintain visual contact....

Fire Flight

June 1968

Pulling up in a hard climbing turn after rolling in on a railroad siding, an A–4E pilot heard and felt a loud bump which bounced the aircraft up and down. Seconds later the fire warning light came ON and the controls started to get stiff. The pilot reported on the radio that he'd been hit and was heading toward the coast.

"I don't know how many miles it was to the coast but it seemed like it took years," he recalls. "Things started to get progressively worse—I was losing this and losing that. The controls started to stiffen. It took quite a bit of right aileron to keep the wings up. I was still at 100 percent and climbing, still doing 350 kts. I was starting to get wisps of smoke in the cockpit. I began shutting off my electrical equipment—as much as I could remember. I was kind of busy watching what was going on and I might have missed some of it. Then I thought I would try to get the radio back on so I put the emergency generator out; it worked all right. I just kept heading toward the coast.

"About this time I started to get some engine explosions, quite a few of them, 10 or more in rapid succession. I thought the engine was going to blow up, but I still wasn't going to get out of it. I thought 'if I can just stick it out to the coast . . .' and then the coast went under my nose.

"At this point the engine flamed out and the RPM started unwinding all the way down to zero. There was complete silence; I could hear a crackling which sounded like fire and I was still getting explosions.

"About this time the smoke started getting pretty heavy in the cockpit. I cinched my mask up real tight and then the smoke got so thick I couldn't see out. I couldn't even see the instrument panel—it was like somebody had painted brown paint on my visor. I didn't smell the smoke because I had my oxygen mask on. I reached for the ram air switch but I thought the ram air would hardly help this so I reached for the canopy ring and pulled that off and then it really hit the fan—the heat and flames. I just had to get out of it; I couldn't stand it.

"I don't know why I decided I had to get the face curtain instead of the alternate handle. I think if I had gotten the alternate handle I would have burned my hands. *(There is no mention of gloves.—Ed.)* The wind got under my helmet visor and forced my head back; my mask was floating up my face. The wind must have sucked the flames through the vents. I reached up for the face curtain and got my hands in the slipstream; that's how my shoulder was dislocated. I got my hands back in and tried again—kind of crept them up along my face. I couldn't see anything; the smoke was too thick.

"The plane felt like it was rolling and falling off on the right wing. I knew I was going very fast but all I could think about was getting out of the airplane. I had it so fixed in my mind that I had to get the face curtain that I didn't even think of the alternate handle. As I said before,

now that I look back I am glad I didn't think of the alternate handle because I believe I would have burned my hands.

"Finally I got hold of the face curtain and then pulled. Before I punched out, I pulled the lanyard on my survival radio on the front of my vest. I was aware of the seat going out but the opening shock of the parachute just seemed like a little tug.

"I looked over to my right and saw my wingman circling level with me. Below me I could see boats all over the place. I looked up and four or five gores were gone from my parachute. Then I looked down at my feet and that was a great shock. My right boot and sock were gone completely although my left boot was still there. I had zippers in the sides of my boots. The zipper in the left boot was a strong zipper but the zipper in the right boot was one a cobbler had put in and it probably couldn't stand the strain.

"I couldn't see either of the leggings from my anti-G suit, just a couple of burnt tatters, and the legs were gone from my suit. I could see that my legs were burned pretty badly.

"I tore my oxygen mask off. My watch was gone, my arm was burned and everything was twisted around in a state of disarray. I kept trying to remember which seat pan fitting I was supposed to release and finally I remembered, 'left for release and right for retain.' I let the left side go and I found the lanyard and hooked it onto the torso harnass buckle. I started looking around trying to figure out how to get the raft out. I couldn't make head or tail out of the thing; it was just a big mess of cloth and foam rubber. I could see where the lanyard went into the seat and I jerked on it but I couldn't get it out.

"My examination was very cursory. My state of mind was such that I didn't spend a lot of time on it. I thought about pulling the Mk–3C toggles but I saw all those boats down there and thought I might have to do some swimming so I didn't inflate it. I looked down and I had lost one radio, the one on the outside of my survival vest. I took the radio off my torso chest strap and I said something to my wingman—I don't remember what. About this time I hit the water.

"I reached up and released the left shoulder Koch fitting and it snapped right out. Then on the right shoulder fitting I reached up and lifted the safety latch but for some reason I forgot to pull down on the bottom of the buckle and it wouldn't open. Finally it dawned on me and I pulled down on it and it released.

"The swells looked like they were 3 or 4'. My hard hat felt very heavy on me and although I remembered they said hang on to it so when you go into the helicopter you don't hit your head, I said to myself, 'I'll sweat the contusions later; I've just got to get this thing off.' About 15 minutes later I saw it was still afloat.

"I didn't have any trouble with the shroud lines; the parachute was floating next to me. I was treading water and trying to stay as low in the water as I could so the junks wouldn't see me. The seat pack had a little bit of buoyancy; I held on to that for a little while. At this point I got rid of my left boot.

"I kept trying to figure out how to get the raft out. It was just a big wad of stuff. I suppose if I had been able to sit down and fiddle with it, I would have been able to get it out but I was treading water and ingesting a lot of water. Occasionally I would sink beneath the surface and I couldn't concentrate long enough to work on the raft. I'm sure I could have gotten it eventually, though. I think if I had inflated my Mk–3C I could have spent the time dragging the raft out of the pack, but, as I said, I was afraid of the boats and thought at the time that I could get along without it.

"About this time the seat pack started to lose its buoyancy. It was holding about 2 or 3′ under water and then it started to settle further. I would take a good gulp of air and open my eyes underwater. I could see what my hands were doing but I really couldn't see what was going on. I kept doing this and made a last effort to get the raft out this time—get it out or get rid of it. I held my breath and started working on it. When I stuck my head up to breathe I could see the surface shimmering above me. I kicked back to the surface and got a breath of fresh air. Then I took my knife out and cut the raft away. I was treading water but I was having trouble keeping my head up above water.

"I saw my wingman fire his rockets. A *Spad* made a couple of strafing runs. By now I was really starting to hurt. I needed something to hold me up or I was going to drown. I decided to inflate the Mk–3C in spite of the boats. I reached down to pull the toggles and *there weren't any toggles.* I guess they had been burned off. I couldn't

get the thing to inflate. I was starting to get worried; by now I was taking a couple of gulps of water every few seconds.

"I tore the flap off the Mk–3C and pulled the pin out to fire the cartridge. I found the end that had the trigger on it. At first I couldn't get it to go but then I popped it and it floated me right up to the surface. Prior to this I had dumped my survival vest trying to get as light as I could. I was sorry that I had done this because if I had blown the Mk–3C before this I could have saved the survival vest. I was so concerned about remaining free that I was going to do everything to stay out of sight.

"I called the *Spad* and asked him about the helo. He called me back and asked me about smoke flares so I dug one out and lit it off. I saw the helo coming. I told him that he was abeam of me at 9 o'clock and he turned toward me. I told him I was at his 12 o'clock. He was dumping fuel because he was too heavy to pick me up. He got over me and dropped the sling into the water and I swam over to it. I got in and just closed my eyes and held on for dear life. I felt them raising me up and I felt some hands on me and then I was back in the water.

"Apparently the helo had gotten into some kind of power stall because of its weight and the temperature. He settled into the water. Just that little rest on the water was enough for him to build his rpm back up. He bounced back into the air and headed for the tin can. While I was in the helo they cut away a lot of the straps that were really starting to irritate my legs. A doctor was waiting on the fantail when the helo landed." . . .

Crusader Crisis

August 1970

Ever so often in the aviation safety business you run across an aircraft accident that appears to be the culmination of a series of events, failures, circumstances and errors which just couldn't happen—but did. This is the story of one such happening which began innocently enough but terminated in a manner that suggested the pilot of the DF–8F had the proverbial black cloud hovering just above him during most of the latter portion of his flight.

On climbout from a Far East air base, the pilot learned that his IFF/SIF [information friend or foe; selective identification feature] was not being received by Departure Control. This fact, if discovered prior to launch, would have been reason enough not to take off but not sufficient reason to terminate the flight once airborne. Until the pilot arrived at his initial approach fix the flight was quite routine. Sometime before arriving at

the fix he had discovered that his ARA–25 (UHF/ADF [automatic direction finder]) was inoperative. It was noted in the analysis of the accident that by not checking the UHF/ADF on the ground the pilot had deviated from F–8 NATOPS. However, the Board felt that if the pilot had found it to be inoperative on the ground, he still would not have aborted the flight. In the NATOPS manual there is no prohibitive go-no-go criteria pertaining to the ARA–25.

The flight was strictly routine until shortly after the pilot commenced a tacan approach at homeplate. He departed 16,000 feet at 1152 with 2400 pounds of fuel remaining. Approach Control advised that radar contact was established. After reaching 10,000 feet the pilot was advised to hold at 12,000 feet as the field was temporarily closed because of a field barrier engagement. He was advised that the field would be open in about 15 minutes. After this transmission the F–8 pilot told Approach Control that he would be "minimum fuel" in 15 minutes and if the field was not open at that time he would request a radar vectored enroute descent to another nearby airfield. At 1154 Approach Control cleared the F–8 to return to 16,000 feet and hold at his original approach fix. The pilot rogered, broke off his approach and commenced a climbing right turn indicating 2000 feet per minute rate of climb at 250 kias [knots indicated air speed].

At this time the "black cloud" must have been hovering just above the cockpit because the situation started to tighten up. The pilot stated: ". . . I noticed my airspeed was about 300 kias, my VSI [vertical speed indicator] was about 3000 fpm down, with a constant angle of bank on my VGI. At this time the OFF flag in the VGI appeared and I realized that I had lost that instrument." (At this point our pilot was without a transponder, had an inoperative UHF/ADF, no VGI, was not in radar contact— and also was getting a chance to practice his partial panel unusual attitude recovery technique under full instrument conditions!)

We continue. ". . . I slowly leveled my wings using the RMI [radio magnetic indicator] and needle/ball and climbed on partial panel to VFR on top. I also gave Approach a call and told them I had lost my main gyro, *was declaring an emergency and requested they get someone up to bring me down . . .*" (His exact words taken from the Approach Control tape were, ". . . I'm declaring an emergency. I've lost my main gyro and I do not have a backup. Can you get someone up here to bring me down?"[)]

The pilot continued: "Approach came up and asked if I wanted them to launch the F-102s and told me he could give me a straight-in-no-gyro approach to (the nearby airfield). Figuring he thought I had lost my RMI, knowing what an absolutely rotten partial panel aircraft the F-8 is and realizing that when the visibility at homeplate was reported as three miles in rain showers, it is only one mile in our F-8s because of a poor rain removal system, I keyed the mike to tell him that I would take the F-102s. *It was then that I found my transmitter had gone out.*" (Exit another important piece of communications equipment at a rather inopportune time. Black cloud still appears to be hovering above.) The time of this occurrence was 1155—less than four minutes from the time the initial approach began.

Approach Control made numerous additional attempts on the last frequency used, in addition to guard, in an effort to reestablish contact with the F-8. This consisted of 18 transmissions during the next 17 minutes until at 1212 Approach Control made the last attempt at a radio check on guard and from that time on conducted routine control of other traffic only.

Meanwhile, our pilot, who had heard all of Approach Control's transmissions but could not answer, was attempting to get his RT-60 radio out of his survival vest in a last-ditch effort to communicate with someone—anyone! He stated, ". . . My fuel at that time was around 2300 pounds and I started looking around for holes and *waiting for Approach to realize I was a NORDO* [no radio] and request I turn to such and such heading, if I read them, for positive radar contact. I remained up on Approach frequency while looking for some holes to let down through and also tried to troubleshoot my radio by bypassing the seat pan and using my lip mike. Needless to say these attempts proved futile. I then switched to (the adjacent airfield) tacan because I was toying with the idea of heading straight in to that field. I had just heard a radio

report that their weather was six miles with about 3500 foot ceiling. While waiting for the tacan to lock on, I finally succeeded in pulling out my survival radio, took off my helmet and attempted to contact someone on guard. The cockpit noise was bad and I couldn't tell for sure if the radio was working or not. I went ahead and transmitted a 'Mayday' in the blind, informed them *that my receiver was still operating* and requested a straight-in to the field.

"I then put my helmet back on and put my survival radio back in my vest. My fuel was now down to 2000 pounds and the situation was looking bleaker by the minute (no doubt influenced by the proverbial black cloud). By this time I surmised that Approach had forgotten about me because they hadn't tried to contact me for some time. My tacan had locked on (the nearby airfield) bearing 300 degrees with intermittent DME. Because of the driving around I had done looking for holes and all the troubleshooting in the cockpit, I didn't question the bearing. There were two big reasons that prompted me to consider shooting a partial panel approach to the field. One was that Approach Control always seemed to handle Navy tactical aircraft in a rather cavalier fashion. Even though we have the least fuel on hand and the least navigation equipment, we can usually count on getting cut out of an approach pattern by a civil carrier or some other heavy. This method of handling us had already contributed to the loss of one of our F-8s last year. The second was my lack of faith in the F-102s['] ability to find me. This I felt was supported by the fact that last year they were sent out to get one of our F-8 pilots in a situation similar to mine. He picked them (F-102s) up visually as they flashed by him with what he described as 'heads in the cockpit.' He turned, in hope that he would see them turning back to him, but they just kept on going. He was more fortunate than I; he later found a hole and got back VFR with little fuel to spare. With these thoughts in mind I elected to penetrate." . . .

. . . "I crosschecked my RMI and wet compass, turned to a heading of 300 degrees, set the power at 80 percent, tickled the boards out and started a 250 kias, 2000 to 3000 fpm descent. The VSI and RMI proved to be the best instruments in the descent. I broke out VFR underneath about 500 feet AGL [above ground level] and drove along for about five minutes. The island I was looking for was nowhere to be seen and I then noticed the bar in the window of the DME. A quick check of the tacan established it was now inoperative and I had no idea how long it had been. (The black cloud was still with him.) Again checking my RMI and magnetic compass, I reversed course and drove for about five minutes at 500 feet in hope of picking up the island or any of the surrounding islands. This proved to be futile and I decided to climb back to VFR on top in hopes that I would be picked up on radar and possibly be intercepted. *Interceptors were now my only hope!* By the time I reached VFR conditions on-top I had about 1100 pounds of fuel. Because of the way my gear failed and the fact that I still had some a.c. and d.c. equipment left, I elected not to drop the RAT. I already had that tow reel costing me extra fuel and my concern now was to stay aloft as long as possible in hopes that someone would see me prior to flameout and report my position.

"During this time I flew left hand triangles and went through rechecking all my equipment, including extra mikes, headsets and RT–60." The Board noted that he could have flown right triangles indicating he had a receiver only but by flying left triangles he indicated he desired intercept, which he desperately did! "I also switched back and forth on various channels to see if anyone was looking for me.

"At about 600 pounds of fuel remaining I started to prepare for ejection. This simply consisted of body positioning, strap tightening, knee-board removal and helmet and O₂ mask security. By this time my throat was really dry. I was thinking, there was no sun down there—I was thirsty, I would not be able to deploy and use the solar stills, it was cold and it was going to get colder that night and nastier and I was already trying to work all this out of my mind. By this time I had reached a euphoric state. But I had to eject so I was no longer in a panic, I was actually relaxed and I did everything in preparation. At 300 pounds I dropped the RAT to insure control of the aircraft after flameout. I did not energize the emergency generator because I did not have an overall electric failure. At about 100 pounds of fuel, I spotted an F–102 below me at about my 10 o'clock. I added full power and pushed the nose over and dived after him. He started a right turn and I turned to cut him off in standard CV rendezvous fashion. About halfway through, the engine flamed out but I continued to press the rendezvous because I wanted to make sure he saw me prior to my ejection. I pushed my nose over more to keep my speed up and just as he was about 2000 feet ahead of me, I noticed another 102 had pulled alongside of me. I then leveled the wings and pulled the nose up, motioned the 102 to move away, assumed the best body position I could (because of my sitting height I have to slouch to allow clearance for the curtain in the DF–8s, even with the seat full down), slowed to about 150 kias and ejected."

Survival Aspects

The pilot stated that after his ejection the opening shock was like nothing he had ever experienced before and was the worst part of the escape sequence. During parachute descent he removed his oxygen mask, inflated his LPUs [life preserver units] (water wings) and deployed his raft. He felt that deploying the raft when he did was a mistake because of the extreme chute oscillation it set up. He removed his gloves and located the release fitting in preparation for water entry. Impact with the water was exceptionally hard. After releasing the fittings he was free of the chute except for one shroud line which he cut with his shroud cutter.

He got into his raft, removed his helmet and took his survival radio out once more. At this time he discovered the battery was loose. Everything came in loud and clear if he held the battery against the contacts with one hand and pushed the transmitter button with the other. He was then able to communicate with the orbiting F–102s. They informed him the rescue helo was on the way and was able to home in on his radio beacon. To further aid the helo, the pilot lit a smoke flare and verbally vectored the SAR pilot to his position.

The SAR pilot stated, "LT . . . did an outstanding job during the rescue operation. He followed established rescue procedures by jettisoning his parachute canopy to avoid entanglement, using his radio judiciously in not cluttering the frequency with useless chatter, turning on his emergency beeper when requested and igniting a smoke flare at the best time to effect his pickup. He left his raft just prior to the helicopter's coming to a hover over him and entered the rescue device and helicopter in the proper manner. We must stress that his proper use of emergency radios and smoke flares were the two factors which contributed most to his speedy and safe recovery."

Thus ended this soggy saga of an almost unbelievable series of material failures of navigational and communications equipment. Fortunately the pilot was rescued uninjured—the influence of the black cloud apparently left him once he ejected. . . .

Monday, Monday

Lt. W. J. Mooberry, RVAW–120; December 1970

It all started normally enough. It was early morning and I was struggling to work, fighting my way through the high speed gauntlet of freeway traffic, oblivious to most everything but the clatter of my beetle's engine and the chatter of the rock-and-roll show on the radio.

No doubt I would never have left the house had I bothered to read my horoscope. Ferment was in the firmament. Mars was nuzzling Virgo (much to the cha-grin of Mr. Virgo); while Castor, Pollux and Aquarius were off somewhere cavorting with the Pleiades (those seven sisters always were a little loose with their affections). It was, further, the thirteenth of the month and most disastrous of all . . . a Monday.

"What's the matter, Albert?"
"Bad news, Pogo, Friday the Thirteenth comes on a Monday this month."

Knowing all this, no doubt I would have stayed snugly sequestered in the feathers that day; but I didn't and as I blithely rattled up to Gate Four, received a cursory wave from the sentry and turned towards the hangar, the radio person was babbling merrily along.

"From the early sixties, children, a Golden Oldie from Uncle Jack's stacks of dusty wax!"

"All radio people must be a little weird," I thought as I slowed for the policeman directing traffic on the corner, "talking that way . . ."

The fuzz gave me the come ahead.

"The Mommas and the Poppas' Big Big! Smasheroo, 'Monday, Monday'!"

My ears perked up. John Phillips' music has always been my favorite. And that song, mmmmm . . . great!

Second gear.

"Ba da, ba da da da . . ."

"Monday, Monday

"So good to me . . ."

The song was ending as I pulled into super-big-wheel-reserved-parking-space-number-thirty-four. Humming away, I bounded up the stairs, drew a cup of brew and walked into my tiny cell to do a little paper shuffling prior to briefing for a Fam–3 I was scheduled to give that morning. All the while that song kept playing over and over in the back of my head.

Psychiatrists call that sort of thing a compulsion. A normal enough aberration which all of us have experienced at one time or another. It becomes serious only when it reaches a point where the compulsion becomes the driving factor in our daily lives. Like Lady Macbeth. I mean she tried Lava, Lysol, enzyme pre-soaks and a wire brush . . . nothing would get that old gal's hands clean. Now *that's* a compulsion. But I digress.

By nine o'clock I had generated half a wastebasket full of paperwork and still my incoming box was overflowing.

"What ever happened to the SCRAP program?" I wondered as I pulled my slightly rancid nomex flight suit from my locker.

Torso harness on and zipped.

Survival vest. Check radio and strobe.

Boots on and tied.

Quickly I ran through my flight gear checklist, picked up my hardhat bag and swaggered down to the briefing room. I don't swagger as a rule but lately my torso harness has been getting a little snug and I have the option of swaggering or experiencing a rather painful sensation when I walk. So I swagger.

Fam–3 is no big problem for a Frisbee driver. A little high work, some trim emergencies, a couple of single-engines at altitude and you eat up the rest of the time in the touch-and-go pattern trying to familiarize the student with landings at various flap settings and single-engine landings. On this day my student was a sharp young JayGee whose performance on previous hops had been well above average. We briefed it all, going over the various maneuvers and emergencies as I outlined just what he might expect on the hop. No sweat.

"Monday morning.

"It was all I hoped it would be."

We checked the yellow sheets and swaggered out to the E–2 we had been assigned.

"Harness a little tight, kid?"

"I beg your pardon, sir?"

"Never mind . . . just talking to myself."

It was a beautiful morning, really; the gentle rains of the night before had scrubbed the air clean and, except for a thin line of towering cumulus barely visible in the east, the sky was a deep blue.

We ran through the trim emergencies during climbout, discussed them and by the time we were at 15,500 feet it was single-engine time.

"Oh, Monday morning, Monday morning couldn't guarantee

"That Monday evening you would still be here with me."

The student went into slow flight and made a couple of turns just to get the feel of the machine at altitude. When we were straight and level again I pulled the starboard power lever back to flight idle, simulating an engine failure.

Things got wormy fast. He failed to call for the inflight secure checklist, left his gear down, two-blocked the port engine and raised his flaps. My stomach sank; so did the airplane. As we mushed through 14,000 feet I took it, raised the gear, accelerated, turned off the max rudder switch, climbed back up to 15,500, told him what he had done wrong, slowed the aircraft, dropped the flaps and passed control back to him.

"Let's try that again."

"Oh Monday morning

"You gave me no warning

"Of what was to be . . ."

Down came the gear.

Blap! Starboard engine out. (Gotcha)

Two-block! Went the port engine.

Again . . . no checklist.

"Oh boy, I may be up here all day."

This time, however, forgetting the checklist caused even greater problems. Without the max rudder switch on (allowing an extra 14 degrees of rudder throw) the aircraft went into a severe swerve to the right. Standing on the left rudder (as he was) with the starboard engine at flight idle is of little help and we were losing altitude fast.

To stop the altitude loss and to give himself more leverage on the pedal, he was pulling back on the yoke and we got slower and slower and more and more out of balanced flight.

"Enough's enough," I thought.

"What's wrong?" I asked.

"I don't know."

(You in a *heap* 'a trouble, boy.)

I was about to mention that turning the max rudder switch on and simulating feather on the starboard engine would probably help a lot when suddenly and without warning (to recoin a well worn cliché) there I was flat on my back at 15,000 feet! A classic skidded turn stall.

No rudder shaker. No prestall buffet. Nothing. Just suddenly that big, 49,000–pound airplane (which isn't supposed to do that sort of thing *clean* let alone with gear and flaps down) flipped upsidedown and I, both surprised and amazed, found myself gazing down on the farms below through the overhead hatch.

Reveille!

It was at this moment that I uttered a classic exclamation which doubtless will be recorded by historians alongside, "One small step . . ." and "I have returned." for [its] poetic simplicity. Mustering all my mental faculties I grabbed the yoke, sang in a sort of falsetto soprano, "Crimenettey, I've got it."

And closed the throttle on the port engine so as not to overstress anything and to return us to balanced flight.

It was truly a miracle I was able to speak at all as my heart, having gone to GQ, was lodged tightly behind that little dingly-dangly thing in my throat and was pumping one-hundred proof adrenalin allll-ooverrr my bodddy.

It took exactly three microseconds* for me to apply every spin correction I'd ever heard of to that airplane. As the roll continued I tried to fly it out with ailerons and rudders as we passed through the wings level position. No joy. Over again. Hands and feet working like mad. The one-armed paperhanger and the one-legged man all rolled into one. Trying everything. Nothing worked. Mentally picturing myself crawling back through the passageway trying to bail out as we spiraled down. Finally, I neutralized the controls, said a quick prayer and held on tight. Waiting. Not wanting to die.

It stopped! We had stabilized in a nose-down attitude.

> *Easy now.*
> *Gear up.*
> *Flaps up.*
> *Power on—both engines.*
> Raise the nose . . . easy.
> "We made it. We're OK."
> *"Monday, Monday*
> *"Can't Trust that Day."*

Carefully, I turned for home and checked in the overhead mirror to see if we were missing anything serious like the dome or a piece of rudder. Convinced everything was still intact, I made an uneventful right seat landing, taxied in and shut it down back in the line. After kissing the ground affectionately, I bowed three times in the direction of the Hampton Roads Bridge-Tunnel, arose, wiped the grease from my forehead, waddled into material control, got a survey chit for my flight suit, bummed nine cigarettes from the chief and smoked them all at once.

It was close, believe me. I still get the willies when I think of 16 million dollars worth of scrap aluminum and transistors all rolled up in a ball at the bottom of a smokey hole in some bean field. Nobody wants to get it on a Fam–3. Personally, I plan to go at the age of 96 at the hands of a jealous Ensign.

So let me say this about that:

In an instructional situation one must allow the student to make mistakes because trial and error is the name of the game. Conversely, screaming and jumping on the controls each time the student dips a wing is a sure sign you're in the wrong business. The difficulty arises in attempting to determine just how far you will allow him to stray before you grab the reins, pull him up short and say, "Whoa, Snerdly, one more (degree, unit, knot) and you're gonna kill us both."

Sometimes you get lucky, like me. You let him go too far and live to tell about it. Sometimes not.

So, in order to stay lucky (read: *alive*), I have evolved the following set of rules to insure that my logbook will continue to reflect an equal number of safe takeoffs and landings:

1. *Be vigilant.* An instructor cannot afford to relax for a moment.

Sunbathing and sightseeing are great pastimes but *not* to be engaged in while airborne.

2. *Be prepared.* I've yet to meet a student who would admit he can't hack it. He'll keep struggling with the aircraft until it falls out of the sky if you let him.

3. *Be firm.* Like the farmer's mule, getting a student's attention is at times difficult. Luckily, all Grumman aircraft come equipped with a hydraulic pump handle which, when applied smartly to the starboard visor button of the student's hardhat, will often break his fixation on the deicing suction gage and get him flying the aircraft again. Should your aircraft lack a pump handle, I've found sticking the pink end of a pencil in his eye will produce equally admirable results.

4. *Communicate.* Don't do things for the student without telling him about it. Indeed, had I not innocently turned off the max rudder switch that day (confirming my reputation as a nice guy) and then *neglected* to tell him about it (confirming my reputation as a dummy), I doubt the incident ever would have happened.

5. Finally, *Read the skies.* There are signs given us by the stars which we completely fail to understand. If your horoscope looks bad for a given day, be extra alert for catastrophic situations and plan ahead to avoid them. And music. Yes, music too is prophetic. Listen to it and heed its message. Like this morning, as I came through the gate, the radio nut was playing a delightful little ditty called, *"Suicide is Painless."* I turned it off.

*A microsecond is the smallest measurement of time known to mankind and has been defined as that span between the time a traffic light turns green and the lady behind you starts honking her horn.

A Most Regrettable Decision

Lt. Cmdr. C. Thomas Steckler; January 1971

It was early March 1962 when I had the most anxiety-filled flight of my career. I shall never forget that flight and I shall never forget the chain of events which caused it.

I was a member of a utility helicopter detachment on board USS *Lake Champlain.* The detachment consisted of two officers, seven enlisted men and one venerable HUP–2. Our vintage machine (circa 1953) was powered by a Patton tank engine. The tandem rotor configuration made it ideally suited for utility work and plane guard duties but it was grossly underpowered, extremely short-ranged and was not equipped for instrument flight. We did have a compass and one UHF radio. The HUP was truly one of the Navy's last seat-of-the-pants aircraft.

Our detachment's mission was typical of that which utility helicopter detachments perform today, i.e. plane guard, mail runs, personnel transfers, cargo runs and taking the chaplain or doctor to the destroyers or submarines operating with us. In the utility helicopter business there was never a dull moment. The flight which caused such personal concern involved more sweat than I had encountered previously in 1000 hours of flying.

We were conducting coordinated ASWEX [antisubmarine warfare exercise] with our task unit and I had just landed after a brief plane guard flight. The Air Boss called on the radio: "Angel, go out 230, 30 miles and pick up two passengers from a submarine. What is your fuel state and do you desire more fuel?" I had aboard 325 pounds which was sufficient for an hour and forty minutes. The bearing of 230 would be a downwind leg and the wind was about 15 knots. Quickly calculating the time to get to the submarine (25 minutes), the time to hover and pick up the passengers (10 minutes) and the headwind back to the ship, which would be closing the submarine while I was gone, (another 25 minutes) I allotted one hour for the flight. This gave me 40 minutes reserve; so, I replied, "Negative fuel required." Anyway, if I filled up that would just be added weight which might restrict me from being able to take on two passengers. This hop would be routine all the way. Little did I realize how I would regret not taking some extra fuel. Up, up and away we went. After about 15 minutes it occurred to me that the sea had considerably more white caps than when I started out. However, no sweat. I'd just get to the sub quicker. The increase in white caps would make the submarine more difficult to spot so I brought my crewman up front to help as a lookout. *(The normal configuration for plane guard work and personnel transfers in the single-pilot HUP was to remove the right seat and place the crewman behind the pilot.—Ed.)* The bearing of the sub from the ship was accurate but as it turned out the distance was a good 30 miles.

The submarine was not ready to make the transfers when I arrived so I wasted about five minutes in orbit overhead. The sub turned into the wind and the two passengers prepared for hoisting. My crewman was well qualified and quickly hoisted them aboard but again we had a slight delay in returning our passengers' lifejackets to the sub. I departed on heading 050 with the passengers settled into the troop seats and cigarettes were passed around for a smoke as we relaxed to enjoy the return to the birdfarm. After about 15 minutes I began to scan the horizon for some sign of the carrier's mast, wake or smoke. Nothing. After another 10 minutes there was still no sign of our home-away-from-home. About this time an H–34 helicopter joined on my port side and the pilot checked in on the radio to advise he was my escort. He had been vectored by the carrier to join up. I asked if he had a fix on the carrier and he replied, "Affirmative, 23 miles dead ahead." TWENTY-THREE miles! I couldn't believe it. I had been inbound for 25 minutes and that meant another 25 minutes to go. The catch was that I only had 30 minutes fuel left. Suddenly the routine flight had an additional factor—large size pucker—to be considered. Now it was a race to get the helo and its occupants safely aboard. If I didn't make it at least I wanted to get as close as possible. Several thoughts flashed through my mind. I thought of a controlled ditching, but only momentarily as I relived one successful ditching I had made after an engine failure. I thought about unloading the passengers to lighten the load and reduce fuel consumption. After all, the other helicopter could pick them up, but I did not like that idea for many reasons. So I continued grinding along, told my crewman to brief the passengers and prayed the carrier would soon appear. I thought about the irony of the situation that this actually was happening to me. I had been flying identical missions for two and a half years. These bizarre events always happened to the other guy. I had considered all aspects of this mission carefully. My experience would not allow this to happen. But it was happening and I was experiencing a feeling of helplessness which was entirely new to me. I thought, "Where is that ship?"

My escort advised that our ground speed was 60 knots. That was considerably less than it should have been. We were indicating 86 knots. Something else was occurring that was not apparent at the time. It was quite obvious what it was when the ship finally came into view. *It was steaming away from us*—not closing as I had been advised—and if it kept on running away I wouldn't catch it. At the rate of fuel consumption and with the remaining distance it looked as if I might reach the ship about the same time the fuel supply was exhausted. I could not risk an engine failure at the same time I was landing. I didn't like the idea of my rotor blades clawing away on the side of the ship because we *almost* made it. I spelled out our predicament to the Air Boss in a normal voice (two octaves higher). Funny how the word emergency galvanizes people into action. It took no more than five minutes for the C.O. who was "unrepping" with an oiler to break away and turn toward me. Now I realized why the carrier had not been closing the submarine. An oiler, a broken chain of communications, bum word, a few minutes extra delays, not taking on some more fuel had caused this fiasco.

I made it! The landing was the most welcomed of the thousands I've made aboard ship. The fuel gage had stopped recording five minutes before I landed. There was no way to determine the amount of fuel remaining in the tank but I know I never want to get that low again. Later, after I had written the account of the mission, everyone agreed with me. It was a needless predicament—one that could have been avoided easily.

Need we say more about runways behind you, altitude above you, fuel in somebody else's tank, etc., etc?

Carnival Ride

February 1971

"A wild carnival ride."

That's how an A–7 pilot describes his ejection as the aircraft went off the angle deck after engaging, then releasing the No. 2 wire.

Returning to the ship from a daytime combat mission, he led the four-plane formation into the break but had to wave off due to a fouled deck. On his second pass he arrested on the No. 2 wire and advanced power to MRT [military-rated thrust]. As the *Corsair II* decelerated in its rollout he retarded the throttle to idle and raised the hook handle. Anticipating the end of the rollout, he began to advance the throttle and reached for the wingfold lever with his right hand. The aircraft lurched "almost like a rubber band snapping" he recalls.

"My first thought was that the arresting gear had parted so I reduced throttle to idle and clamped hard on both brakes, feeling that I had enough flight deck to stop the aircraft. The aircraft continued up the angle. I could hear someone yelling 'Brakes! Brakes!' on the UHF. (*This was the LSO.—Ed.*) I felt the brakes getting softer under my foot pressure and realized they were heating up so I engaged nosewheel steering in an attempt to steer the aircraft to the right, up toward the bow. But with both legs locked firmly out in front of me holding the brakes I never did get my pedal throw to turn the aircraft. As the aircraft approached the deck edge I still felt I would stop but then all I could see ahead of me was water and I knew I was going over the side.

"As my mind considered the question of which handle to pull, my hands moved and instinctively reached for the face curtain, grasped it and pulled firmly forward."

The pilot was not in the best position for ejection. Both his feet were firmly on the brakes with his legs straight out in front of him. His torso was pushed well back against the seat but his head was bent slightly forward as he looked at the water.

"First I saw darkness as the face curtain blotted out the bright sun, then I heard a loud bang and felt a jolt. From then on it was exactly like a wild carnival ride. I felt as if I somersaulted three or four times and was going in six different directions at once. I distinctly remember seeing the ship upside down, then the sea, the sky and the ship all whirling past me in a hectic but clear pattern."

He doesn't remember releasing the face curtain.

"I felt as if I was cartwheeling through space—my arms and legs flailing. As I felt the jolt of the ejection seat starting to move, I thought, 'I'll make it. This is the best seat in the fleet.' But I remember thinking after gyrating like a human cannonball, 'Well, this isn't right. I've only got 60 feet. Am I connected to the chute?'

"Just then the chute opened with what I would describe as a mild shock and I swung through the vertical, looking at the ship, feeling relief and searching frantically for my LPA–1 [life preserver assembly] toggles. I found the left toggle but didn't pull it because I knew I should pull the right one first (or preferably, both simultaneously).

"My feet hit the water. Still no right toggle. So I pulled the left one.

"Water entry was mild. I went under only a foot or two at the most—the water stayed bright above me. I then found myself floating tilted to the right side with my feet up and my face in the water. Breathing was difficult and I realized I still had my oxygen mask on. I pushed the mask firmly against my face with my right hand and took two deep breaths of oxygen. Then holding my breath, I unhooked the mask from the left side and began the fight to keep my head above water. My attempts to get my feet vertically below me, which I felt would help keep my head above the swells, were frustratingly unsuccessful. This was partly because my left foot had became entangled in parachute shroudlines. My chute was floating on the surface beyond my boots.

"I remember thinking, 'I've *got* to get rid of the chute' and at the same time being thankful it was floating because my left foot was entangled."

The pilot describes his efforts to untangle himself as "pitiful."

"The large bulk of my survival vest was up under my arms and greatly restricted my reach. When I drew my feet up I could grasp the shroudlines but I could not reach far enough to loop them over my feet to free myself. During this effort I would go under water about every third swell. This complicated my problems drastically since each time I had to stop trying to untangle the shroudlines and fight to get my head back above water.

"It seemed to me as if all my buoyancy was up under my left arm and my feet. I was floating bent in a U-shape, my mouth and my shoelaces at water level. I terminated the untangling effort and set some priorities: *first,* release the chute and *second,* release the seat pan.

"With increasing panic I found that with my soggy flight gloves on I could not locate either the koch fittings or the rocket jet fittings. At this point the possibility of drowning seemed very real so I decided to try to relax and float by lying back and taking some slack out of the 'U' while awaiting the helo. This maneuver promptly submerged my head as my body rolled to the right. Now I was scared!

"I forced my head out of the water and saw the helo above me to my right. 'Oh, God,' I thought, 'please put someone down here to help me.' Immediately I felt a hand on my left shoulder—that's fast service! Crazy as it may sound under the circumstances, my first impulse was to shake the swimmer's hand and thank him. He told me to relax and inflate my LPA. Only then did I realize that I had never pulled that right toggle. I found it and pulled. This promptly cured my list and seemed to buoy my head up, too."

The pilot told the swimmer that his left foot was caught. The swimmer submerged and started working to free it. Feeling much better now, the pilot leaned back and meticulously pulled off his nomex flight gloves and threw them away. Then he reached down and unbuckled his seat pan on the first attempt. With his foot now freed, he found himself floating upright.

The swimmer released the pilot's koch fittings, untangled a shroudline from his right foot and pushed him away from the floating chute. The helo, dragging a horsecollar through the water, was now almost overhead. The pilot's helmet visor protected his eyes from the stinging spray. Remembering his deep water survival training, he turned his back to the spray and push-paddled toward the horsecollar. The swimmer got to the collar first and towed it to the pilot.

"In my eagerness to be saved," the pilot reports, "I attempted to get into the collar, thereby succeeding in entangling my legs in the wire hoisting cable. The swimmer shouted, 'No, no, use your D-ring.' Since he was doing a magnificent job of keeping me out of trouble I complied. Once hooked up, I grasped the fitting at the top of the collar, being especially sure not to put my hands on the wire itself. The only problem this presented was that my death grip prevented the swimmer from hooking up his own D-ring. Again his good judgment prevailed and I let go so he could attach himself to the hoist.

"We were then both hoisted aboard the helo and flown back to the CVA. Inside the helo the swimmer's attempts to have me lie still so he could undo my survival vest were nullified by my attempts to shake his hand and thank him. In retrospect I can only conclude that if the swimmer had not performed in such a cool, professionally outstanding manner, I probably would not be here writing this narrative." . . .

Can of Worms

March 1971

Lieutenant Junior Grade Blank was scheduled for a night photo mission originating from the deck of USS *Slingshot.* He thoroughly prepared for his flight which included the briefing of his assigned fighter escort. He was well rested, had eaten a proper dinner and was in all respects ready for his 1800 launch.

He launched in his RF–8G on time and headed for a rendezvous with his F–4 escort overhead the ship. The two aircraft joined and then proceeded to the target area. Upon arrival Blank flew the *Crusader* through two photo runs and then, as briefed, passed the lead to the F–4. With the mission completed the two aircraft headed back to the carrier. At 1920 Blank received his marshall instructions for an approach to commence at 1944. At 1930 approach control changed marshall time to 1945 and at the same time the DME (distance measuring equipment) in the F–8 became intermittent causing the pilot to commence his descent at 40 nm vice the assigned 37 nm. Blank started the approach on time with a fuel state of 3300 pounds. He called the ball with a fuel state of about 3000 pounds and the F–8 in a good final approach attitude but was waved off by the LSO for not having a visible approach light.

From this point on things began to get real hairy for this young pilot. In his own words, here is what happened:

"After waveoff I checked inside and found the doughnut indexer light was also inoperative, however, the fast and slow chevrons were on the line. The angle-of-attack indicator was working normally and the APC (approach power compensator) was good. On the second approach with 2600 pounds of fuel remaining I became rough on the controls, went low in the middle, corrected for it and then went over the top and boltered. At touchdown on this pass the RMI (radio magnetic indicator) froze. I attempted to reset it in both the slaved and free position after becoming airborne but it wouldn't move. Realigning the RMI was impossible so I informed approach control that I had no directional gyro and would need called turns. I arrived on the ball for the third approach with 2200 pounds of fuel on board. Again I was rough and overcontrolled all the way down the glide-slope. The LSO waved me off for poor technique. Remaining in the bolter pattern for a fourth approach I called the ball with a fuel state of 1800 pounds. This pass felt a little better but I went high in close and boltered. I then raised the gear, lowered the wing and broadcast to approach control that I was going to bingo to the divert field; my reasoning here being that another approach would take me below my bingo weight of 1600 pounds coupled with the fact that earlier in the flight approach control had stated that there was no tanker available in the area for practice plugs. Approach told me to stay at the ship and remain in the bolter pattern, that a tanker would be available in two minutes. Here I decided to make another attempt to get aboard the carrier thinking that if I boltered again I would still be close enough to bingo weight to get to the divert field and with a tanker enroute it should be no problem. I dirtied up the aircraft once again and commenced my fifth approach. Shortly after turning off the 180–degree position but prior to reaching the 90–degree position, aircraft electrical power was lost and the cockpit went dark. I added 100 percent power and looked outside to see if I could determine my attitude. There was no moon at this time but there was a faint horizon. Holding my altitude I reached for the RAT (ram air turbine) extension handle and deployed it. With my right hand I turned the emergency electrical power switch ON. The instrument lights came on and I went back on instruments, maintaining the F–8 in a shallow left turn at 600 feet altitude. There was a short delay before the radio came back on the line, after which I

called and told approach control that I had a generator failure. Due to the generator failure my approach scan had broken down and I found myself high and overshooting on final. Approach control asked if I was going to continue the approach and I replied "Negative." I told them I was below bingo weight and would require tanking. At this point I tried to raise the gear but the handle wouldn't budge. I then thought that the probe would not extend with emergency electrical power on but hit the probe switch anyway and the probe extended. I tried the landing gear switch again with no success. I called approach and told them my gear would not retract, the RMI was inoperative and that I would need a steer to the tanker. They then switched me to departure control for the rendezvous with the tanker. I departed the ship gear down, probe out, RAT out and wing down with 1300 pounds of fuel remaining. Enroute to the A–4E tanker my fuel boost pump light came on. It lit full bright and I tried to dim it with the instrument and console light rheostats but to no avail. *(The brightness of the yellow warning light cannot be dimmed when operating on emergency electrical power.—Ed.)* This bright light annoyed me and reduced my visibility outside the cockpit. I attempted to remove the bulb but it wouldn't turn.

"The *Crusader* had a fuel state of 800 pounds when rendezvous was effected with the tanker. The first few attempts to make a plug were commenced from directly aft of the A–4 but on each approach to the basket the turbulence of jet wash created by the tanker threw my aircraft around quite violently. I informed the tanker pilot of my predicament and he tried different flap settings but there was no noticeable reduction in the A–4 jet wash. The tanking was being attempted at airspeed between 190 and 195 kias in order to give me a power range to maneuver the aircraft. After several straight-in attempts to plug were unsuccessful the tanker pilot changed configuration to three-quarters flaps and I approached the basket from the starboard side in an effort to keep my aircraft out of the A–4's turbulence. However, in approaching the basket the vertical stabilizer of my airplane was caught in the A–4's jet wash causing the F–8 to yaw and roll violently. My plane was repeatedly rolled to the right reaching banked attitudes of 90 degrees and occasionally the rolling motion was severe enough to force my aircraft above the tanker. Shortly after the pilot of the F–4 escort flying with us had called out my distance from the divert field to be 40 nm, the main fuel gage read zero and the engine flamed out. I was still trying to plug the tanker at this time. As my aircraft moved aft of the A–4 I lowered my nose attitude slightly and told the tanker and escort pilots that I was going to eject." . . .

The Case for More and Better Hangar Flying

March 1971

Half a dozen pilots lounged around the carrier ready-room. Over in the corner, two of them were occupied with a gin rummy game and up front, three or four more young pilots were discussing the recovery which had taken place an hour or so earlier.

Bob Smith, a nugget, was bemoaning the fact that he had boltered twice during the recovery before trapping on the third pass. "If I had played it cool," he noted with mock seriousness, "and made one more bolter, I would have been sent to the beach. I could be sitting in the club at Barbers' Point this minute having a cool one instead of being here with you guys."

Al McCloy, another nugget, spoke up: "Sorry you missed out on the drink. I can't help you there but if you want to cut out the unneccessary bolters, maybe I can help you. Why don't you do what I do . . . when you're on short final, put in a little nose-down trim. This makes the nose a little heavy and keeps you from floating over the top to a bolter. That what I do and I haven't had but one bolter during the last six months."

This is an entirely fictitious story up to this point. There is no Al McCloy but there *is* a naval aviator somewhere who once held the mistaken belief that the way to prevent bolters was to trim his A–4E nose-down during the final approach. It's too bad that he never ran this theory up the flagpole to see who would salute it. Had he done so, there is a good chance that his contemporaries would have pointed out some of the potential hazards in this procedure. As it was, he kept this bit of personal expertise to himself and as a result, got educated the hard way.

This pilot launched from a CVA in an A–4E one morning for an air combat maneuvering hop and upon completion of the mission returned to the ship for a VFR recovery. During the approach, he touched down past the No. 4 crossdeck pendant and boltered. The aircraft continued rolling down the angle deck in a left to right drift. The aircraft left the flight deck at the intersection of the angle and axial deck in a nose-down attitude. It then settled well below the flight deck level and about three seconds passed before a climbout was initiated. Power and rotation calls were transmitted by both the LSO and the Air Boss as the aircraft first began to settle. The situation looked so critical that a "plane in the water" distress signal was initiated as the aircraft disappeared below the flight deck level. This alarm was "belayed," however, as the aircraft quickly reappeared in a climbing attitude.

As the pilot commenced a turn downwind, the Assistant Air Boss came up on the radio and asked him if he was okay. The pilot replied that he was fine. The Air Boss then instructed the pilot to make a low pass by the ship for a visual check of the aircraft. This was considered necessary because of the possibility that the aircraft had contacted the catwalk and/or the water during the bolter. During the first pass, the aircraft was too high for an adequate visual check so the pilot was instructed to make another observation pass. During these two passes there was no visual evidence of any aircraft damage. The pilot was then cleared for another approach.

On the second landing approach the aircraft again touched down slightly past the No. 4 wire and boltered. As it rolled down the angle deck the LSO immediately began "power" calls. The aircraft was on centerline and as it left the angle deck, it once again began to settle and the right wing dropped about 10 degrees, followed by a left wing drop of about five degrees. As the aircraft reached a near wings-level, slightly nose-up attitude, the pilot ejected. The ejection was successful and the pilot was quickly rescued from the water by a helicopter. The aircraft nosed down and impacted the water about two seconds after the ejection.

During the investigation of this accident, the pilot informed the Board on several occasions that over a period of time it had become his practice to trim the aircraft to a "slightly nose heavy" condition to preclude the possibility of "floating over the top" to a bolter. In describing his thoughts and observations during the two bolters the pilot repeatedly commented on the "nose heavy" condition of the aircraft and the fact that full back stick pressure was applied. Significantly, the pilot stated that even though he required a "little back stick pressure" on the second landing approach, he still added a "click of down trim" while on the glide slope.

The Board compared photographs of the aircraft's horizontal stabilizer (taken during the bolter) with photographs of static aircraft at various trim settings and concluded that the aircraft had been trimmed for only two to three degrees of nose-up trim instead of the six to seven degrees of nose-up trim which would normally be required for that configuration.

The LSO, when interviewed, stated that there was a "cut on touchdown" on both passes, even though the pilot felt that he had added full power immediately after each touchdown. In this connection, an endorser to the AAR commented:

"The aircraft accident board concluded that trim was the primary cause of the accident. Poor power management, however, is an equally important consideration. Witnesses in a position to judge power on the aircraft stated they observed little or no initial power application on either bolter. Yet, as observed by witnesses and recorded on PLAT [pilot landing assistance television] tape, there was sufficient power applied to 'climb out of the hole' after the first bolter and to maintain flight deck level after an initial settle off the second bolter. Had it been only trim which caused the aircraft to settle, it is doubtful that recovery could have been effected with stick movement alone. Therefore, it is considered that the primary cause of this accident was poor power management in combination with insufficient trim rather than insufficient trim alone."

Regardless, the pilot's ill-advised habit of making his final approaches with excessive nose-down trim in order to preclude bolters appears to have been a critical factor in this accident. It's too bad that someone didn't point out the hazards inherent in this procedure. But, how could they? He never let anyone know what he was doing.

This brings up an important point—the need for communication. Actually, that is what NATOPS is all about—communicating the body of naval aviation knowledge and experience among professional naval aviators. But, NATOPS will never pre-empt other forms of communication. The situation may be likened to that of a young lady reading *Glamour Girl* magazine. The magazine can give her a lot of tried and true tips on how to be glamorous but many of the finer points will come from some other source, e.g. the girls in the sorority or mother at home. Likewise, NATOPS can be used to communicate a lot of valuable information but there are some things which can only be learned in the real life atmosphere of an operating unit—in the fraternity. . . .

. . . In any given group of pilots there will always be some who are more knowledgeable tha[n] others on any specific subject. The point is that flight safety will be enhanced if the level of understanding of all pilots is brought up to that of the most experienced and knowledgeable pilots in the squadron. The importance of rank and experience in developing this professional know-how among pilots should not be underestimated and neither should the potential contribution of the less experienced pilots be discounted. It's quite conceivable that a recent flight school graduate (with a recent course in aerodynamics) has a better technical understanding of the forces at play in a crosswind landing than does a veteran of 10 years in the fleet who has not cracked a basic aerodynamics book since preflight. Likewise, a nugget who has just completed two weeks at an instrument school may have the straight skinny on some new instrument flight rule which has not yet percolated down to the operating level.

So there is definite benefit to be realized in improving communication among pilots in a squadron. Without doubt, the least experienced pilots will be the primary beneficiaries but not the only ones. The more experienced pilots also stand to benefit.

How can communication be improved? In many ways; but it seems that a giant step can be taken by assigning increased importance to the ancient art of hangar flying. Any pilot who has spent an evening at the O'Club listening to a series of "There I was, flat on my back, at 40,000 feet" stories, as told by several of his buddies, may think there is enough "hangar flying" going on already. And maybe there is—of that kind. But in this business, there can never be too much of the honest straight-from-the-shoulder discussion of flying. The suggestion is that hangar flying be dressed up and endowed with a new importance and a definite objective—enhancing the professional development of naval aviators.

Now don't rush down to the readyroom and grab the first pilot you see who is junior to you and announce, "I'm going to give you a private course in ACM [air combat maneuvering], or ordnance delivery or carrier landing technique, or whatever." This is much too obvious. Instead, why not first take a personal inventory by asking yourself some questions like these:

● Is there any procedure or technique connected with flying that I would like to know more about? To understand better?

● Am I employing any personal flight technique or procedure which would be beneficial if passed on to my fellow pilots? How about my practice of making a modified barrel-roll entry into the dive bombing pattern instead of the standard entry? Should I pass this on to my fellow pilots?

● Is there any piece of equipment in the aircraft I fly which I would like to know more about?

● Do I understand the operation of some system or piece of equipment better than some of my fellow pilots? Shouldn't I let them know what I know?

An[d] so forth. It won't take much time at all before you will be armed with all sorts of conversational ammunition. And getting a conversation started about flying is no trouble at all. But, if you do have trouble, just walk into the ready room and announce:

"An aircraft stalls at the same indicated airspeed at 40,000 feet as it does at sea level," or if you prefer, "An aircraft does *not* stall at the same indicated airspeed at 40,000 feet as it does at sea level." Either way, the bull session will be off and running. Another tried and true conversation starter is to state: "An aircraft is on short final, 10 knots above stall speed, with a 20-knot headwind. What would happen if the wind were to instantaneously cease?" Actually, the only thing that might come of these discussions is a little intellectual stimulation. The practical benefit is questionable. But . . . consider the following statements and see if you don't think the authors would receive some *practical* benefit by expressing them to fellow pilots:

● "I always land on the downwind side of the runway in a crosswind. That way I won't run off the upwind side of the runway when the aircraft tends to weathercock."

● "When I go off the cat, I always have my right hand on the stick and my left hand on the alternate ejection handle."

● "I'm going to follow the leader at close interval on takeoff so I can take movies of his takeoff."

● "I always fly with my wings slightly overlapping the leader's wings. I think it makes a better looking formation that way."

● "I leave my master arming switch on throughout the bombing pattern. That way I have one less thing to worry about when I roll in."

● "I've flown my aircraft straight up to zero airspeed many times. There's nothing to worry about as long as you take it easy on the controls."

● "Doing a 300–knot loop in a TA–4J is no sweat. I've frequently demonstrated it to my students."

● "What's wrong with making a 500–knot pass close aboard a mountian as long as you maintain adequate terrain clearance?"

These statements have all been suggested by reports received at the Naval Safety Center. Some of them involve obvious violations of NATOPS; some of them do not, but they all imply errors in judgment and/or knowledge on the part of the authors. If the authors had submitted these views to the scrutiny of their fellow pilots before adopting them it is just possible that a number of accidents could have been prevented.

If your usual way of flying cannot stand the close scrutiny of a cross-section of your fellow pilots, then there is an excellent chance that you should consider mending your ways. However, if you think you are right and others are wrong, then fight for your baby. See that your idea or procedure is bucked up the chain of command for consideration. This is particularly important when the matter involves an established NATOPS procedure. There is always the danger that we will accept a procedure without giving it much thought just because it is written in NATOPS or even because "we've always done it that way." This is not in keeping with the spirit of the NATOPS program. NATOPS *is* meant to be complied with but no procedure is sacrosanct if a better way can be developed—and proven. Proving it, that's the crux of the matter. Whether you are presenting an idea or procedure to your roommate, your fellow pilots or to NAVAIRSYSCOM, you must be prepared to support it with facts and informa-tion if it is to receive the consideration it deserves. You should also require that others present sufficient supporting facts and information to prove the point before you buy their idea or procedure. And it goes without saying that neither you nor your fellow pilots should adopt any procedure or practice which is in conflict with NATOPS or other standard operating procedures without first being cleared to do so by competent authority.

To sum up, every effort should be made to make full use of the knowledge and expertise which exists in every squadron in the Navy. This should not be viewed as any attempt to downgrade the importance of instructional procedures established by the chain of command. Rather, it should be viewed as a stimulus for *refining* standard procedures and, perhaps more importantly, as a conscious effort to substantially raise the level of naval aviation expertise throughout the squadron. This requires the utmost in communication and one of the best ways we can think of to effect this communication is to talk it up at every opportunity. The art of hangar flying can be developed and used for purposes other than telling sea stories—and it should be.

Think about it. You may hold the key to successful completion of your buddy's next flight. Doesn't it make sense to pass on this important information?

A Wing and a Prayer

June 1971

It was a beautiful day at an air base in RVN [Republic of Vietnam] when two F–4B crews assembled to commence briefing for a combat mission. A thin layer of clouds was discernible at 25,000 feet and visibility was in excess of seven miles. A thorough briefing was conducted by the flight leader, a young but highly capable pilot. He informed the crews that when over the target area they would be controlled by a FACA (forward air controller, airborne). He then described the bomb load each aircraft would carry. The lead aircraft was configured with MERs [multiple ejector rack] mounted on the centerline and both outboard wing stations and a TER [triple ejector rack] mounted on both inboard wing stations. The aircraft would carry 18 Mk–82 LDGP [laser designated guidance projectile] bombs; six on each of the wing-mounted MERs and three on each TER. The centerline MER was left empty due to maximum gross weight considerations. Because the aircraft had to rely solely on internal fuel in this high drag configuration it was assigned only to qualified section leaders. The wingman's aircraft was configured with a 370–gallon external fuel tank mounted on each of the outboard wing stations, a TER mounted on each of the inboard wing stations and a MER mounted on the centerline. It was loaded with 12 Mk-82 LDGP bombs; three on each TER and six on the MER.

Preflight, start, taxi, takeoff and rendezvous went smoothly and the flight to the target area was routine. The flight checked in with the airborne FAC who gave a target brief and requested that each aircraft drop two bombs on the first run. The flight leader stated that he would rather drop 12 bombs on his first run and have his wingman drop six on his first pass. The airborne controller did not consider this to be an emergency or a high priority target so the suggested drop sequence was accepted. As briefed the flight leader commenced a 30-degree dive, 500 knots, 4000 feet AGL attack run on the target. He selected the ripple/outboard mode for the drop, expecting to release the six bombs from each of his wing-mounted MERs. At release point it became obvious to the pilot that only the left outboard MER had released its bombs when his aircraft entered a sharp right wing down attitude. Even though pulloff from the target was executed to the left, recovery from the unusual attack run was made without incident. The wingman then went in on his first attack run and dropped six bombs on the target. The flight leader decided to make a second attack run and attempt to release the remaining bombs from the aircraft. To prevent an excessive G load and another unusual recovery he planned to make this run at a more shallow dive angle. The airborne controller was notified of the pilot's intentions and clearance was given. The run was made in a 10-degree dive at 500 knots with release to begin at 2400 feet AGL. Ripple/all was selected as the release mode. When the pilot pickled, only the bombs on the left inboard TER dropped from the *Phantom*. The wingman made his second run and dropped his remaining six bombs on target. The flight leader then decided to make one last attempt to drop as many bombs from the aircraft as possible. Clearance was obtained from the airborne FAC and the pairs/outboard mode of release was selected. The run was fruitless; no bombs left the aircraft.

The flight leader felt he'd had it over the target area so he bade farewell to the contoller and he and his wingman departed for the jettison area. Enroute the wingman confirmed the suspicion that nine bombs remained attached to the right wing, six on the outboard MER and three on the inboard TER. Using various modes during several release attempts resulted in the release of the MER and TER on the left wing and the MER on the centerline. The right wing MER and TER and their bombs remained attached to the aircraft.

The flight leader and his wingman began a return to home base. He tried to contact his squadron on UHF base frequency to request possible suggestions for proper approach and landing procedures, but was unable to raise anyone. He made no attempt to contact the group ODO [operational duty officer] on base frequency for suggestions, primarily because of the pressure placed on him by the aircraft asymmetrical condition now complicated by a relatively low fuel state. As has been stated earlier, he had received a very thorough briefing the day before on an asymmetrical condition when in a landing configuration. This briefing no doubt created a feeling of confidence that the situation could be salvaged without incident.

Approximately 20 miles from the base, the flight leader sent his wingman ahead for landing. At the same time he notified the base tower that he would be making a straight-in approach with hung ordnance to the duty runway which was 14. Some confusion existed, but apparently the tower called the winds from 120 degrees at six knots. (Actually the wind was from 070 degrees at nine knots.) The flight leader requested the tower to have a crash crew standing by just in case something went wrong. He slowed the aircraft, lowered the landing gear and extended full flaps. He then maneuvered the aircraft to try and determine the minimum controllable airspeed for the approach. The pilot found that the right wing would begin to drop below 176 knots and set this as his minimum. He started a shallow, low rate of descent approach at 180 knots. When five miles from the approach end of runway 14, he called the tower and reported his landing gear and flaps down and his landing light on. The entire approach was flown with full left wing down trim, nearly full stick displacement to the left and almost full left rudder displacement. The pilot also used about 10 to 25 percent more RPM on the right engine than the left during the approach to take advantage of the asymmetrical thrust. As the F-4 crossed the runway threshold, full left rudder and stick were required to keep the wings level. At between 10 and 30 feet of altitude the aircraft commenced to roll to the right. Full military power from the right engine and a positive forward stick movement failed to correct the roll, in fact it became more rapid. This did it for the pilot. He immediately told the RIO [radio intercept officer] to eject and at the same time used his left hand to pull the alternate ejection handle. The RIO had not selected command eject prior to initiating his own ejection using the alternate ejection handle. Both crewmembers left the aircraft safely with the *Phantom* in a 30 to 45 degree right bank. . . .

"I've Got Trouble"

November 1971

Winter weather is once again approaching. This means an increasing number of flights will be either penetrating or operating within the freezing level. Icing, therefore, becomes a potential inflight problem of great magnitude when the right set of atmospheric conditions prevails. While we will not attempt to review those conditions which *cause* icing, we will recount some of the details of an aircraft accident which is believed to have occurred as a *result* of icing. This case involved a T–2A aircraft but the lessons learned apply to all types of aircraft, particularly those not having deicing equipment.

In this case, an experienced instructor pilot and a student pilot manned the aircraft for a special check flight as part of the instrument training syllabus. The observed weather at this time was 900 feet scattered, measured 1200 feet overcast, three miles visibility and very light ice pellets (rime ice) in fog. The top of the overcast was undetermined.

Poststart checks were normal and the student later recalled that the only discrepancy noted prior to taxi was that both altimeters read approximately 100 feet high. The instructor taxied the aircraft while the student completed the instrument checklist. During taxi, the instructor inquired about the student's airspeed indicator. The student's indicator read zero, but the instructor's indica-

tor was showing some undetermined airspeed. The instructor remarked that he would turn the pitot heat on to melt the ice or water in the pitot-static system, and before takeoff mentioned that the pitot heat must have worked since his airspeed indicated zero. (Note: As the aircraft accident board later noted, turning the pitot-static heat on during ground operation normally has no effect as the heater will not work until weight is removed from the landing gear struts.)

The aircraft taxied into position and the engine checked good with an acceleration time of 11 seconds. Both the pitot heat and canopy defrost were on.

The instructor made a normal takeoff, and shortly after takeoff (with gear and flaps still down) passed control of the aircraft to the student pilot. At the time, defrost air was causing the side panels of the instrument hood to flap back and forth and distract the student. This, combined with the transition from contact to instrument flight caused the rear seat pilot's performance to deteriorate to the point that the instructor had to assume control of the aircraft again. However, when they leveled at 2000 feet the student was again given control of the aircraft. He then completed the climb to on top (tops were about 7000 feet) and leveled off at FL [flight level] 230 [23,000 feet]. Just prior to leveling, both pilots heard a loud "clunk." The instructor remarked that the noise was probably caused by loss of a chunk of ice accumulated during climbout. A check of the engine instruments in both cockpits revealed nothing out of the ordinary.

Thereafter, the flight at altitude consisted of a series of basic instrument maneuvers, e.g. S-patterns. At the completion of the basic instrument work, the instructor assumed control and commenced a descent to arrive at Nearhome intersection for a GCA pickup.

Ten miles northeast of Nearhome intersection initial contact was made with approach control and the T–2A pilots were advised to report Nearhome intersection. Radar contact was confirmed at the intersection and altitude verified to be 9000 feet. To avoid icing, the instructor requested clearance to remain high but was cleared to descend to 5000 feet and given a change of frequency. A level report was made at 5000 feet with an accompanying request for a lower altitude. At this time the student lifted the instrument hood and noted an accumulation of ice on the wings.

Approach control "Rogered" the request for lower altitude but did not grant clearance. About 30 seconds later the instructor made a second request for a lower altitude and remarked that he was encountering ice. The controller "Rogered" the request and issued a frequency change. In his first transmission on the new frequency, the instructor again requested a lower altitude due to rime icing. Clearance was given to descend to 2000 feet and to perform the cockpit landing checklist. The instructor reported leaving 5000 feet for 2000 feet and, when level at 2000 feet, 160 kias, heading 170 degrees, returned control of the aircraft to the student.

The rear seat pilot transitioned to the basic approach configuration of gear down, one-half flaps and 130 kias. This particular maneuver had always proved difficult for the student so he made a special effort to make a smooth transition. He lowered the gear handle and then lowered the flaps to the one-half position. Apparently he did not move the gear handle downward far enough. The instructor noted this and remarked that the next time the student should ensure that the gear handle was down.

In effecting the landing configuration transition, the student had gained about 400 feet. The instructor, noting this, took control of the aircraft and remarked that the flight would be incompleted because of ice buildup, and the fact that the weather precluded completing all the required instrument patterns. The student was anxious about his performance during the hop and was relieved when the instructor stated that the hop would be incompleted.

The approach controller issued missed approach procedures and the instructor acknowledged. To facilitate traffic spacing the aircraft was vectored through the final approach course. The aircraft was then directed to turn right to 320 degrees and 35 seconds later directed to continue the turn to 350 degrees. Fifty seconds later the aircraft was vectored left to 290 degrees. Forty-five seconds into the turn the aircraft was turned over to the final controller. Initial contact between the instructor and the final controller confirmed satisfactory communications. The final controller then requested a wheels report but received no reply to this or subsequent transmissions. Shortly thereafter it was determined that the aircraft had crashed. Both the instructor and student pilot ejected prior to the crash, but the instructor's ejection apparently took place outside the safe ejection envelope since he was fatally injured. The student escaped without injury.

The pilot-under-instruction later recalled that, shortly before the ejection, the aircraft entered a pronounced buffet and then stabilized momentarily. The instructor made an exclamation to the effect that, "I've got trouble." At the first buffet, the student reached up to unsnap the instrument hood but had removed only two snaps when he heard the instructor's exclamation. He reached for the face curtain but his hands became entangled in the instrument hood. The aircraft then departed controlled flight and entered a clockwise rotation. Before he could make a second attempt for the curtain, the student heard a loud bang (the ejection seat firing) and found himself free of the aircraft. . . .

Bronco Bustin'

July 1972

A section of OV–10A *Broncos* departed at night on an IFR flight from one air station to another several hundred miles away. Twenty-five miles from destination the flight was cleared for a TACAN penetration to 5000 feet.

Shortly after reporting "leaving 9000 feet," all communication with the flight was lost. It was later determined that the two planes had collided. Both crews successfully ejected over water and were picked up by fishermen several hours later.

The flight leader described the events leading up to the collision:

" . . . finally contacted approach control, received clearance for a TACAN approach, and was told to report passing the 200 degree radial for descent. I told them I was past the 200 degree radial, and (I believe it was at this time) they cleared me for a TACAN 1 approach and descent to 5000 feet. At that time I was at the initial approach fix and reported 'commencing approach, leaving 9000 feet.'

"I took control of the aircraft from my copilot and reduced power to about 800 lbs of torque. Realizing I hadn't put the condition levers up, I pushed them very slowly watching the temperatures. Everything was normal. We overshot the assigned radial due to the delay in getting clearance. I tracked back onto the radial and at approximately 20 miles passed 6000 feet. This was the last altitude I saw.

"The DME had unlocked, so I'm not sure of my exact distance from the station. About this time the aircraft nosed down and I felt less than one G. I didn't really rise out of the seat but my body got light. Then I heard a bang. The aircraft pitched up violently and rolled to the right. It continued in a hard right turn. I was being thrown around in the cockpit. I put the controls to neutral and tried left rudder with no effect. It felt as if the rudder pedals and control stick weren't doing anything, as if the control surfaces weren't there or were damaged, and my inputs useless.

"Coming around after the first turn, I saw my wingman's airplane. I thought it was on fire but now think I saw him eject. There were a lot of sparks and some were actually passing over our aircraft. I continued turning to the right and into a tighter turn. As the nose went down I looked at the VGI. It was completely in the black telling me that the nose was straight down and we were still in a right turn. There wasn't anything I could do to regain control. I keyed the ICS and said, 'Get out, Jack,' and pulled the ejection handle."

The wingman saw things from a slightly different, but equally interesting, viewpoint. He stated:

"I knew we were overshooting the 179 degree radial and that it would take a left turn to get on the inbound of the approach requested by the flight leader. A rather abrupt left turn was made. I didn't have any trouble staying in position since I was still pretty far out when he leveled his wings and started to descend. I didn't hear what altitude we were cleared to. I heard him call, 'Leaving niner thousand' as cleared, but can't remember what altitude.

"Flight clearance had predicted some light turbulence in the area. I was in a very loose cruise position, so it didn't bother me. There was some turbulence just before we went into the clouds. At that time I moved in a little closer. Looking forward, I saw we had to penetrate a cloud layer of unknown thickness. My altitude seemed to be about 6000 feet.

"I can't really say how close I was at that point. I tucked in to a normal bearing for IFR parade position. I didn't really notice. I was looking at him expecting signals for level off, or whatever. We continued and I tucked in a little bit closer, to about 5 feet overlap and 5 feet stepdown. I was using him as my reference at all times because we were getting ready to go into the goo. We went through a few puffy clouds and came out. It was clear. Then we were back in again, apparently for a good while. I don't have any idea at what altitude this was. This is where it gets sketchy, because this is where it happened.

"I looked around and all of a sudden it was dark. I looked over at my left wing and it was on fire. It seemed that the leading edge was being peeled back with sparks flying from it. The outboard two-thirds of the wing was on fire. Needless to say I was somewhat startled. I moved the stick to the right and looked down at the lead aircraft. His aircraft was engulfed in flames and spewing. It looked like the 4th of July down there with pieces of metal flying everywhere. It must have been metal. It was pieces flying through the air on fire.

"I was so shook up by now that I don't really know what was going on. I saw the leader go into uncontrolled flight. There were more pieces of metal flying and yellow flames shooting out of his plane. I realized that he was in uncontrolled flight. The minute I saw my plane on fire, his plane on fire, and half my wing gone, I knew it was time to get out. It all happened instantaneously, and I wasn't about to mess with a wing that was half gone.

"Without thinking about another thing, I pulled back the stick, reached down between my legs, and pulled the handle. 'Bam!' I was gone. I guess I went into a state of shock. When I pulled up and started to eject, I remember looking at the instrument panel. Everything was on. All I could see was a big bunch of red.

"I don't know what warning lights were on. I saw a whole bunch of them. I don't believe the engine was on fire. At the time of ejection my aircraft was 15–30 degrees nose up, wings level. I estimate my airspeed to be 150–160 knots. There was nothing that indicated that I had made contact with the other aircraft, although I assumed that was what happened. I had the other aircraft in sight at all times and was able to see his wing and my wing throughout the entire sequence." . . .

Eject! Eject!

September 1972

The air boss transmitted, "Off the bow, off the bow, you're on fire. Eject! Eject!" . . . and the crews of *two* F–4s ejected. Only one crew was in trouble—the other crew abandoned a perfectly good aircraft.

Four aircraft had been launched within a 30–second period preceding the accident. The catapult sequence was: an F–4J on No 1, an A–7E on No. 3, an F–4J on No. 2, and an A–7E on No. 4. The air officer, concerned with launches off both the bow and waist cats, had only a short time to observe each aircraft as it was launched.

As the second F–4 cleared the bow, flames were observed trailing the aircraft. On departure frequency the air boss transmitted, "Off the bow, off the bow, you're on fire. Eject! Eject!" The pilot scanned the engine instruments and firewarning lights. All looked normal.

He then looked at the rear view mirrors and saw his tail section engulfed in flames. He gave the command to eject over the ICS and the RIO initiated sequenced ejection. Both ejections were successful and the crewmembers were subsequently picked up by the plane guard helo.

Meanwhile, the crew of the first F–4, which had launched seconds earlier off the No. 1 cat, was having communication problems. During the cat stroke the pilot had lost both ICS and UHF. Once airborne, he regained ICS momentarily and heard his RIO make some comment about the shot, then lost ICS again. Regaining ICS a second time, he heard the RIO request he come up hot mike. He attempted unsuccessfully to let the RIO know he *was* on hot mike.

The next thing he heard was the broken radio transmission from the air boss instructing, " . . . you're on fire. Eject! Eject!" Thinking the transmission was meant for him, the pilot immediately initiated sequenced ejection—with no attempt to verify the fire by reference to engine instruments or firewarning lights. Both crewmembers were picked up by the plane guard helo. . . .

Home Free

December 1982

Big Mother scooped the two-man F–4 crew out of the Tonkin Gulf to fly another day. Investigators of the material failure-caused aircraft loss said the pilot's and RIO's (radar intercept officer's) attention to survival procedures during training "without a doubt contributed immeasurably to their successful rescue."

"The entire SAR operation," an endorser to the investigation report commented, "could not have been executed more smoothly if it had been a planned exercise."

The *Phantom* had been on station during a routine BARCAP [barrier combat air patrol] mission for 1.5 hours. While turning, the aircraft entered a flat right spin. Spin recovery techniques were unsuccessful. At 10,000 feet, the crew made one last assessment of the situation and decided it was time to go.

The RIO ejected at 7000 feet. Starting at 5200 feet, the pilot pulled the seatpan handle three times without success, then went to the face curtain and ejected at 4000 feet—still well within the seat's envelope.

Here are the RIO's and the pilot's accounts of events from ejection to rescue:

"Although 10,000 feet is a standard altitude to eject from when in a spin," the RIO writes, "I was still having a hard time convincing myself that we were in a spin. I thought I felt the yaw rate slow down for a second, and I hesitated. It's hard to tell if anything really was happening to bring us out of the spin, because as quickly as I thought something might happen, we were back to the same yaw rate.

"After this, I knew it was hopeless. I told the pilot I couldn't stay with it any longer. I grabbed the seatpan ejection handle and pulled."

The RIO had always considered the seatpan handle as his primary means of ejection. Normally, he rides with his seat high so that his helmet is 1 or 2 inches from the canopy.

"As soon as I told myself I had to eject, my hands were right on the handle and pulling," he continues. "The first sensation I had was one of tumbling. For a split second, I worried about seat separation. Just as quickly, I was separated—there was no real jerk.

"As I became stabilized in the chute, I disconnected one side of my oxygen mask. Then I reached for the seatpan handle, found it immediately, and pulled."

Both the pilot and the RIO had removed their oxygen masks on station at FL 200—a NATOPS violation. (Cabin altitude was 8000 feet. Hypoxia is not considered a factor contributing to the accident.) The RIO replaced his mask before ejecting, but the pilot did not.

"I looked down and saw that everything came out all right and that the raft was inflated. While I was looking at my gear, I saw the pilot's chute about 3000 to 4000 feet below me. I also saw the aircraft next to him in a nearly flat attitude and barely spinning with the drag chute streaming behind."

Resting for a second, the RIO started to break out his radio, then thought he'd better not take a chance on losing it when he hit the water.

"I reviewed everything I had left to do and figured I'd better inflate my Mk–3C. It worked perfectly.

"As I got closer to the water, I looked down and saw that it was 'coming up' pretty quickly. I fixed my eyes on the horizon and put my fingers under the koch fittings."

When his feet hit the water, he released his parachute and submerged 3 or 4 feet. Surfacing, he saw his raft off to the side. His parachute was not in sight.

"The water was very cold," he recalls. "I went over to my raft and was about to get in when I remembered I still had my seatpan on. I got rid of the seatpan, climbed into the raft, and just sat there for a second or two.

"By this time, I heard our flight leader overhead. I took out my PRC–90 to attempt contact but received no reply. I just sat there and watched him orbit my position. He was relieved shortly by an F–8. I then heard someone say over the radio, 'You have strangers inbound. You better arm up.' I assumed this was for the F–8 and thought they meant the junks which we had seen earlier in the flight."

Eventually the RIO contacted the F–8 pilot.

"My pilot then came up on his radio and said he was okay. It was obvious no one but the F–8 was reading us, so we talked freely over our radios. Although I didn't see him, he said he had me in sight. I didn't tell him about the junks which I thought would be coming in, but I kept a lookout for them.

"Eventually, the helo came in. At the time, I was talking to my pilot on the PRC–90. I could have jumped into the water away from my raft right then, but I wanted to take my time and put my radio away and get set up. The helo continued past me to pick up the pilot.

"By this time, I had my radio packed, and I jumped into the water. The water was so cold I got back into the raft. I figured I'd wait until the helo picked up the pilot.

"When the helo had him aboard, I again jumped into the water, put my helmet back on, and swam away from the raft. As the helo approached, I pulled the day end of the flare and put my visor down. Much to my dismay, the visor was badly cracked, so I put it back up. The water/wind blast didn't bother me, however."

The RIO was hoisted to the helo in the horse collar.

Now, let's back up in time and see what the pilot has to say . . .

"The spin continued and continued. The only change was lessening of nose excursions above and below the horizon," he begins.

"At 10,000 feet, the RIO called the altitude, and I knew I had to get out. For a moment, I tried every conceivable stick and rudder position. No effect. The RIO ejected."

The pilot looked in the mirrors and saw the RIO was gone. He noted that the drag chute was streamed and sticking straight up behind the aircraft.

"I remember the altimeter going through 5200 feet. I pulled the seatpan firing handle three times—hard. It had come out of its seating, and I could feel it on the cable—it didn't work. Scared, I went for the curtain.

"Ejection was smooth. I tumbled, then the chute opened with a jerk. I looked up and checked the chute. It was okay. Then I looked down and saw the aircraft right below me. I hoped I wouldn't land in it. I also saw some debris and realized I would soon be in the water.

"I felt around for the risers and fittings, then remembered the raft. I had to fumble around awhile to find the right handle to get the raft out."

The pilot remembered the Mk–3C. He found a toggle with his right hand just as he entered the water and pulled it.

"It worked, and I popped to the surface. I was facing the chute which was still inflated but not pulling on me. It was easy to get rid of.

"I then inflated the left side of the Mk–3C. My raft was inflated and floating nearby. This surprised me, because I thought I had released it too late. I pulled it over to me, remembering to get rid of the top of the seatpan, and climbed in. This was not difficult at all."

Once inside the raft, he took his helmet off, had a drink of water, and began to inventory his survival gear.

"I noted that my keen watch was screwed up. Then I remembered my radio and got it out. I managed contact with my RIO. I could see him about 200 yards away.

"Both of us agreed not to shoot smoke flares because of the fishing fleet we'd seen earlier. The lead F–4 was overhead at about 2000 feet, but neither of us could contact him. Later, an F–8 relieved him, and we managed a few words with the pilot. He gave us little satisfaction as to how the SAR effort was progressing. Mostly, I just waited.

"The water was cold, and I was shaking hard before too long. I got quite cold before I was picked up."

To pass the time, the pilot looked for sharks and sea snakes and deployed some dye marker. After about 35 or 40 minutes, he saw *Big Mother* approaching.

"When *Big Mother* was about a mile away, I shot off a smoke signal. I did it too early, because it went out long before they arrived. Their course was downwind from me. They overflew my RIO and came to me first.

"I decided to forget a second smoke. I put on my helmet, jumped out of my raft, untied the connecting lanyard, and paddled about 10 feet to the waiting horse collar. I decided to use my snap ring, as it was an easy device. Attaching it was super-quick.

"They hoisted me aboard with no problem. About 2 minutes later, they had my RIO. I couldn't have asked more of *Big Mother*. We were home free."

Out of Control

January 1973

Immediately after being catapulted, the *Intruder's* nose pitched up, and the aircraft entered a steep climb. Nose-down correction by the pilot brought the nose back to the horizon, but was only momentarily effective. The aircraft immediately began another nose-high climb.

The pilot, using both hands to hold the stick, applied nose-down trim, but was unable to halt the movement. At about 200 feet, with the angle-of-attack passing through 23 units and increasing, the pilot dropped left wing and kicked full left rudder.

The nose eventually fell through the horizon, and the incipient stall was prevented. At this time, the air boss

transmitted, "123, what's your problem?" The B/N (bombardier-navigator) replied, "We have control problems, stand by."

With an angle-of-attack of approximately 24 units, the A–6 was turning port, toward the ship. Primary requested that the aircraft remain astern the ship. The pilot established an orbit aft of the ship approximately 3 to 4 minutes after launch maintaining about 45 degrees angle-of-bank in his turns. The general consensus of the flight crew was that, since full nose-down trim was not alleviating the situation, the problem might have its origin in the pitch-trim circuitry.

The B/N pulled the trim circuit breaker. It had no effect. The breaker was pulled and reset several times with negative results.

On the second orbit, with about 45 degrees angle-of-bank, the pilot jettisoned his external drop tanks and raised the gear. Jettisoning the drop tanks had no effect whatsoever on the bird's flight characteristics.

Another A–6 joined on the troubled aircraft for a visual check and to escort him to an air station (about 65 miles away). The escort joined up in the steep port turn at approximately 1500 feet. Both aircraft made two more orbits at angles-of-bank varying from 20 to 90 degrees and indicated airspeed of about 170 knots. The tower gave the bearing and distance to the bingo field and requested they switch to GCI.

During this time frame, both engines were operating at 100 percent with all cockpit indications normal. The gear was up, the flaps down, and there were no *visual* signs of problems. The pitch trim indicator was reading full nose-down, but the aircraft was still trying to pitch nose-up. The escort requested the A–6B to roll out on the base course for the air station, but the pilot replied, "Every time I try to roll wings level, the nose pitches up."

The escort noted that the stabilizer appeared to be in the vicinity of six units nose-up.

The aircraft in trouble reversed to a heading near that of the base course. A visible pitchup occurred as the aircraft passed wings-level on the reversal. The pilot stated that he felt as though he had more "control problems than what might be attributed to trim alone." He also stated that he would attempt to make continuous "S" turns until reaching the air station.

The escort aircraft returned to tower control to receive guidance from the squadron CO. The CO suggested that the pilot attempt to slow flight the aircraft. The escort switched back to GCI frequency and passed this word to the pilot. He also asked the pilot if he had attempted to raise the slats/flaps. The pilot replied that he had and that he had also experienced a severe pitchup each time he tried it. The pilot then lowered the gear, and the aircraft started to decelerate. At the same time, the angle-of-bank began to decrease from 45 degrees in the "S" turns to about 15 degrees. Airspeed was about 150 KIAS.

At this time (about 20 minutes after takeoff), the aircraft appeared to be in controlled flight at an altitude of 2900 feet, slowing to 135 knots, with gear down. Shortly thereafter, it pitched up violently and fell off on the port wing, with about 90 degrees angle-of-bank, 23 units angle-of-attack, and 130 knots. The aircraft then completed four to six turns, losing about 400 feet per turn.

The escort asked the pilot if he could reduce the angle-of-bank, to which the pilot replied, "Any attempt to level the wings causes me to pitch up . . . and I will lose it." About 5 minutes later, the pilot told the escort he didn't think he could regain control. He also told his B/N, "We're going to have to get out soon if things don't change."

Passing 1000 feet with angle-of-attack between 23–26 units and 70–90 degrees angle-of-bank, the pilot told the B/N, "We're going to have to get out. I want to get the wings level and count to three, and we'll eject."

Twenty-six minutes after takeoff, with wings level and 10 degrees nose-up, the crew ejected. At about 800 feet and 160 knots airspeed, both the pilot and B/N ejected through the canopy using the face curtain ejection handles. Both ejections were successful. The pilot, however, suffered a back injury because of poor body position. Both were picked up by ship's helo shortly after entering the water. . . .

Nightmare

April 1973

A TA–4 instructor and student were planning their return from a weekend cross-country early on Sunday evening. The flight was an easy one-point-five back to Homebase. Weather offered no enroute problems, and the forecast for NAS Homebase was typical late summer: 3500 scattered, 25,000 broken, 5 miles in haze, rainshowers and thunderstorms in the vicinity. The syllabus called for the student to fly front seat and terminate with an instrument approach plus some VFR night landings if possible.

It was quiet at FL 310 for Navy 2345, with good vis and very little traffic. Twenty minutes from the 1AF, the student attempted to contact NAS Metro. No joy. He finally raised an AFB Metro 60 miles away that reported NAS to be 7000 broken, 25,000 scattered, 5–6 miles vis, with no change expected for the next hour. When asked for a PIREP [pilot report], the TA–4 reported a slight haze layer, but nothing significant.

It was common practice on Sunday nights for returning cross-countries to request a TACAN approach with a missed approach and GCA pickup followed by VFR touch-and-gos, traffic and weather permitting. After acknowledging Navy 345's request for a TACAN 18 approach, Center cleared the *Skyhawk* to 15,000 feet. Thereafter—apparently not understanding the penetration request—Center cleared the aircraft to 8000 feet at pilot's discretion. The pilots repeated their request. They needed the TACAN penetration to fulfill syllabus requirements.

After handoff to approach control, Navy 345 was cleared for the TACAN approach and was given a new altimeter setting. The student completed the penetration checklist, noting 1000 lbs of fuel above landing weight. He reported leaving 15,000 and commencing approach and received a new altimeter setting. The pilot was told to report the final approach fix with gear.

As 345 turned from the arc onto final approach course, the tower (which had been monitoring approach control) was discussing the *2-mile* visibility and the intensity of the *"heavy, heavy rain"* with the duty forecaster. Passing 1600 feet, the student reported the final approach fix with gear. Tower cleared them for a low approach, requesting they report missed approach. Tower asked if they had the field in sight, and 345 replied, "Affirmative" (meaning they had the approach lights, not the runway or the ball).

Meanwhile, on the landline, Approach asked Tower:

"Why'd you clear him for a low approach?"

"That's what he wanted, wasn't it?"

"Not that I know of . . . He was cleared for a penetration and approach."

Just prior to this exchange, the NAS ODO, who had been checking the weather radar, noted an area of precipitation from 5 miles east to 10 miles southeast, pushed by a southeast surface wind. Knowing a TA–4 was inbound, the ODO went to RATCC [air traffic terminal control center]. On learning of 345's intentions for a low approach/missed approach/GCA, he called the tower on intercom and instructed them to advise the pilots of the rainshowers and to recommend a full stop. This call coincided with the discussion between Tower and Approach on just what 345 wanted.

Meanwhile, the student pilot was late in commencing his landing checklist. They were at or near MDA (minimum descent altitude), 350 feet AGL, when an inadvertent transmission was heard:

" . . . have spoilers . . . (garble) . . . my harness is locked, hook is up, gear and flaps . . . "

"You're cleared to land, cleared to land runway 18." The tower controller was responding to the ODO's instructions by encouraging a full stop, but without mentioning either the deteriorating visibility or the rain.

Twenty seconds later, assuming their intentions were again misunderstood, the instructor transmitted:

"Approach, 345, we'll be requesting a missed approach to runway 18."

To the pilots, the only real problem seemed to be making Approach and Tower understand that this training flight could only be completed with a GCA and some touch-and-gos.

The student had not completed his checklist until past the approach fix. But the approach lights could be seen, and the pilots had no reason to believe they were not VFR. No doubt they were looking for the runway, and no doubt they were asking each other about runway or ball acquisition. The area around the approach path is largely uninhabited and notoriously black at night.

Tower answered the request for a missed approach by saying, "Are you sure you want a low approach with this rain coming in like this? Go ahead and full-stop if you like. It's getting pretty bad."

Thus, less than a minute from the threshold, the pilots were given a late weather warning which required an instantaneous decision, i.e., wave off into possible severe weather, or land a *heavy Skyhawk* on a wet runway, which was not yet visible. There was no time to ask for further details. They had to find the runway if they were going to use it. They were actually IFR, but still believed the field to be VFR. Several seconds after the tower's "rain" transmission, 345 replied:

"Uh, 345, we'll take a full stop."

"Roger, cleared to land."

"I got it," 345 transmitted unintentionally 12 seconds later.

The next transmission received by the tower was from the field.

"Tower, Crash Truck 14, we've got a crash on the North. We're rolling."

The crashcrew was moving 5 seconds after impact.

The crash circuit was activated. The duty forecaster made his crash circuit observation: "1000 scattered, estimated 7000 broken, 25,000 over, 2 miles in rainshowers, wind 140 at 4 gusting to 13. Reason for the observation: TA–4 has flown into the trees 1 mile short of the duty."

The aircraft impacted slightly right of the extended centerline and slid over 200 feet through "moderately dense forest" shedding landing gear and airframe parts all the way. Fuel was strewn throughout the impact area and ignited. The left wing was severed between the wing droptank and the fuselage.

On investigation, both altimeters were found with the last setting given. Both read –30 feet . . . most likely due to a static line being crushed on impact giving a decrease in indicated altitude. The radar altimeter had been secured due to a malfunction. Full power had been added prior to impact, and the fuel control was set at military. No engine malfunction was indicated. Both pilots had been trained and were properly qualified. No material factor, no supervisory factor, no NATOPS factor. Evidently, the casual factors rested with the pilots. Speculation need go no further, however, because the ambulance crew, arriving at the edge of the trees for their grim task, were met by two sober, slightly-burned pilots, walking out of the woods.

With no specifics as to extent or intensity of the rain and feeling they were still VFR with the runway environment in sight, the *Skyhawk* pilots felt it imperative that they acquire a ball and get on deck—taking the A-gear if necessary. An overweight aircraft on a wet runway at night with an inexperienced man in the front seat is a rough combination. Being on final with only seconds to touchdown and still looking for the ball, you realize your predicament is spelled S-T-R-E-S-S. Rapidly closing the runway, both pilots were looking for either the ball or the runway lights when the instructor said, "I got it," meaning he had the runway in sight. The instructor looked back into the cockpit, saw the angle-of-attack passing 20 units, and called for "Power!"

Both pilots saw the tree line as a shadow between them and the approach lights. *Both knew they were dead.* They felt contact with the trees, followed by a feeling "like a violent trap." Realizing they were still alive, each pilot pulled his alternate ejection handle. Neither seat fired because the gas lines had been severed on impact. Neither pilot questioned the absence of the canopy, although neither had jettisoned it.

The right side of the instructor's flight suit was aflame. Pulling his harness release handle, he stood up and dove head-first over the right side. Still on fire, he rolled on the ground until the fire was out. The student caught fire while exiting the aircraft. He also rolled on the ground to put out the fire. As the two moved away from the burning wreckage toward lights near the edge of the forest, the instructor broke out his PRC–63 and called the tower. They met a very surprised crashcrew.

Sure, the pilots were "set up" by the communication foul-ups and bum dope on the weather, but if you don't brief crew coordination and make some "who does what, when" decisions ahead of time, it's like the poet says:

"Of all sad words of tongue and pen, the saddest these: 'It might have been.'"

Sixty Seconds to Doomsday

R. T. Forbush; October 1973

What happened on that beautiful day in May still makes my blood run hot and cold. Hot, because I was boiling mad at a fellow aviator for not doing what he should have done. And cold, because I watched this same fellow naval aviator lose his life. You can dub me a no good SOB for feeling the way I do, but after you hear the details, maybe you'll be a little more tolerant.

First of all, let me give you the setting. I was O–in–C of a helo det based aboard a heavy cruiser. On the afternoon of this particular day, the ship was maintaining station about a mile east of the coastline, and some 40 miles southeast of an area where carrier air strikes were being conducted against the enemy.

Because of the strikes, we were in Readiness Condition I, which meant that my crewman and I were to be strapped in the chopper standing by for a possible rescue mission.

A call for help wasn't long in coming. A jet in company with two squadron aircraft was on its way towards our ship. The aircraft had taken a hit in the port wing, and fuel was pouring out of the fragmented hole.

While starting, engaging, and taking off, I was briefed that the pilot of the crippled aircraft would get as close to our position as possible, then eject. There was no chance of his returning to the carrier.

The ship gave me a steer in the direction from which the three jets were approaching. Less than 10 miles from the cruiser, I was able to establish radio contact with the pilot of the stricken aircraft. He was at 10,000 feet, and we were closing rapidly.

When the pilot was directly overhead, he told me he'd head his bird seaward and punch out. Shortly there-

after, he did just that. His chute opened nicely as he began his descent.

While I waited for him to splash down, I couldn't help but think how lucky this guy was. The weather conditions couldn't have been more favorable. Ceiling and visibility were unlimited, the wind was next to nothing, the sea calm, and the water temperature was in the high sixties. I was standing by to pick him up, two of his squadron buddies were overhead, and the cruiser was ready to assist if needed. Talk about holding a pat hand.

I kept the helo far enough away so that rotor wash wouldn't influence his water entry or separation from the chute.

At about 100 feet above the water, he looked to be in great position for splashdown. He entered the water smoothly, and because there was no wind, his chute quickly collapsed.

I started to move slowly toward the pilot who had not yet appeared on the surface. Thirty seconds passed, and he was not up; then, as his time in the water neared 1 minute, I suddenly felt apprehensive.

"Come up, damn it, come up," I yelled out. "What are you doing, man? We're ready to help you."

Now there was no time to waste. I had my crewman don the sling, and when we were over the chute, I lowered him into the water. While this was going on, I called the ship and apprised the CO of the situation. The captain immediately launched a whaleboat for the area.

My crewman did his best to locate the pilot, but it was to no avail. I gave him the signal and hauled him back up into the helo. By now, about 7 minutes had elapsed since the pilot entered the water, and that sick feeling one gets when he realizes a tragedy has occurred overtook me.

This emotion was quickly followed by that one of boiling madness I talked about earlier. Why had this pilot fouled up? Was it complacency—the feeling that all was in his favor and he needn't worry? Or was it a case of fear? Or did he forget everything he had learned (or quite

98

possibly never learned) about parachuting into the water?

The whaleboat arrived on the scene, and it took those aboard almost an hour to extricate the pilot from his chute. His body was finally hauled aboard, and the boat returned to the cruiser.

Later that day, I talked with the doctor to find out exactly how this pilot had died. The cause of death was drowning, and there wasn't a mark on his body. What a waste of life—a completely unnecessary waste. A wife and two kids in California were in for some bad news.

This tragedy happened in May, 1953. The cruiser involved was *Saint Paul* (CA–73). The helo was an H03S. The jet pilot was from *Boxer* (CV–21), and he was flying an F–9 *Panther*. It occurred south of the bombline, in friendly waters, just off the South Korean coastline.

I've long since retired from the Navy, but I'll never forget that day. The thought keeps entering my mind—I wonder how many similar mishaps have happened to other pilots since that time *(164 through 30 June 1973— Ed.)* and how many more will happen in the future? . . .

We Just Spun It

Imagine the consternation that would arise if the PPC [patrol plane commander] of a P–3 crew walked up to the maintenance officer and announced . . .

February 1974

Approach writers (mostly gray-haired old fudds), have become pretty calloused over the years. Whatever unusual tricks that can be done in aircraft, they have either done themselves, know someone who has, or have read about it in an incident report or AAR.

Every now and then, the quiet in the writer's room is blasted by someone who scans a message and announces to all, "Listen! You'll never believe this!" What follows depends on the absurdity of the communique. Naturally, not all mishaps are absurd. Some are sad. Some are stupid. Others, unbelievable.

It happened on a beautiful spring day. The weather was great—temperature warm, skies cloudless, visibility 15 plus. A P–3 was airborne on a PUI (pilot under instruction) training flight. A ditching drill initiated by a simulated uncontrollable fire in the No. 1 engine had been conducted (No. 1 engine was actually feathered.)—using 4500 feet as simulated sea level.

Upon completion of the drill, the PUI added power on 3 engines and climbed to 4800 feet. The IP (instructor pilot) told the trainee to execute a 2–engine approach and wave off at 4500 feet. Power was reduced to flight idle on No. 2, with No. 1 still feathered, to simulate the 2–engine out condition.

The PUI eased the aircraft down to 4500 feet, dropping gear and full flaps. As he reached base altitude, he asked for full power on No. 3 and No. 4 to wave off. His airspeed was 125 knots. The aircraft began a left turn that could not be stopped with aileron and rudder.

The IP pointed out that the aircraft was below V_{mc} [velocity, minimum control] air. To demonstrate recovery, he reduced power on No. 4, and the P–3 returned to a wings-level attitude. (Naturally, the airspeed bled off to 115–120 knots.) The pilot under instruction called for gear up and approach flaps. (Airspeed 110 KIAS.) The IP

then took over to lower the nose, but not before the aircraft slowed to 105 knots, at which time a moderate airframe buffet began. The *Orion* "departed"—100,000 pounds of patrol plane! The aircraft steadily and rapidly rolled left to a 90–degree bank, and the nose fell through in an almost vertical, nosedown attitude—still rolling left. Wow!

The IP pulled power back, levelled the wings after about 360 degrees of roll, and completed his pullout at 1500 feet. He added power, brought No. 1 back on the line, and scooted for Homeplate.

Postflight inspection disclosed a +2.6G and a –.8G reading on the flight station accelerometer. A thorough inspection of the aircraft revealed only a slight buckle on the starboard forward wing fuselage fillet at station 534. Also, there was a slight wave-type buckle in the leading edge fillet, inboard side of No. 4 engine. There was no popped rivets, and no other structural damage was discovered. The inspectors could not determine if the buckles were caused by this incident.

The PUI's failure to maintain sufficient airspeed resulted in the stall and subsequent departure from controlled flight. Contributing to the unusual sequence of events was dropping below V_{mc} air with an engine feathered.

This incident did not end in disaster because the IP properly executed unusual-attitude recovery techniques. Further, he had the foresight to have performed the instruction at an altitude twice the "legal" limit. The "legal" limit now, as promulgated in a recent P–3 NATOPS change, is a 4000–foot altitude for 2–engine out practice (except in the landing pattern) and for ditching drills. Engines will not be feathered during these maneuvers.

(The most important aspect of this incident is the fact that it was reported. It takes a big man to tell the world "I goofed."—Ed.)

Let's see what a similar situation looked like. This flight was to be a combination post-maintenance check (after a prop valve housing change) and a PP2P NATOPS check flight. One hour after departure, P–3 debris was sighted floating offshore by another crew.

Underwater television revealed the tail was intact, with most control surfaces undamaged. Numerous major components were recovered such as engines, props, flaps, copilot's overhead instrument panel, and landing gear.

Careful examination disclosed 3 engines had been operating normally, but No. 4 had been feathered. Further, flaps were down and the gear was up. Indications were that the *Orion* hit the water hard, relatively slow, and in a right-wing down, nose-low attitude. The mishap board concluded that the most probable cause was loss of control or stall while conducting a low-altitude, slow-speed ditching drill.

The similarity between the two instances is marked. Once again in multiengine aircraft, the question of caliber of instruction and instruction technique arises. In the September '72 *Approach,* the article "What, Why, and How" addressed the problem of instruction in operating squadrons. One of the main points in any kind of aircraft instruction is reiteration of a basic aerodynamic principle—*maintain airspeed. The instructor pilot must not relax his guard for a second.*

Routine Cross Country

Lt. B. L. Palmer, Naval Air Reserve Detachment NARDET, Pax River; May 1974

It was going to be a pleasant weekend. Our coast-to-coast cross country was approved with CAVU [ceiling and visibility unlimited] weather forecast and only 40 knots on the nose going west. Perfect. Even maintenance got into the act by providing us with a 4.0 aircraft.

Well, I won't try to kid you. This was too smooth. Just overhead Mile High City, the flight engineer announced, "Gen No. 3 OFF light."

Wait one. Did this bird have AYC–314 installed? Our squadron had three aircraft with, and six without. Which did we have? The discrepancy book had no notation, the generators weren't labeled, and I hadn't asked. Too bad. Also, too late to ask. So, we initiated generator reset procedures, but no luck. OK, Flight, feather No. 3.

Our original destination had no P-3 support, so we diverted to P-3 West. After landing, postflight troubleshooting revealed a bad supervisory panel—and no AYC–314 installed. By the time the panel was repaired, we had already decided to RON and go forth the next day.

Early next morning, we continued to our original destination—an uneventful flight with that evening centered around solving all the world's problems.

The next day and time to go home. Weather wasn't quite as good. For example, we had lost our 40–knot tailwind going back, but we still could make it in 7.5 hours.

Start, taxi, and takeoff were normal, and we were on top at FL180. Just as we were passing Tall Mountain AFB, things began to deteriorate.

"Firewarning on No. 2."

"Roger, feather No. 2, HRD [high rate discharge] No. 2."

"Prop feathered, feather button light out, checklist."

"Northwest center, Sickbird 23, we are declaring an emergency."

"Sickbird 23, repeat, unable to copy because of loud horn in . . ."

"This is Sickbird 23, request vectors to Tall Mountain AFB."

"Flight, give me alternate HRD No. 2."

"Pilot from afterstation, no smoke or flames visible back here."

We made our routine landing followed by a parade of little red trucks.

"Hey! What's happened to the 'pleasant' weekend?" The rest of the day we spend scrounging parts. The HRDs were replaced, but the cause of the firewarning light couldn't be located. We called home to explain the situation and requested permission to make a three-engine ferry back to P-3 West.

We were granted permission and then conducted a thorough review of NATOPS. When ready for takeoff, with the prop on No. 2 at attention, the Air Force tower called and wanted to know, in a strange-sounding voice, if we wanted to notify anyone along the way. (I swear he was thinking of NOK [next of kin].) We said negative and let him know that Center was aware of our problem.

The flight to P-3 West was routine until we asked Approach for a GCA pickup. As we turned GCA final, the flight engineer said, "Generator No. 3 OFF light." Wasn't that great?

"Sickbird 23, you're above glide slope."

"Start the APU [auxiliary power unit]."

The copilot chimed in, "You're 5 knots fast."

"When we touch down, secure No. 3."

"You're below glidepath . . ."

Various other conversations continued on and on until landing. (Someone called it a touch-and-go.) Oh, well, no sense dragging this out any more. After 5 days, we made it home.

One thing is evident on reviewing the week. The days spent in the books and simulators and the hours in flight spent practicing emergencies all allowed this to be a routine . . . cross country and not something else.

Putting Yourself on Report

Cmdr. J. D. "Bear" Taylor, CO VA-46; June 1974

Experience is still the best teacher, but in naval aviation we have learned that it is also the most expensive method of getting the lesson across. Elaborate reporting systems with widely distributed reports have been developed in an effort to ensure that the problems of one unit are quickly and completely made known to others even as the search for a solution begins.

A good reporting system is essential for the conservation of our critical aircraft and people assets. Included in this comprehensive reporting system are eight kinds of mishap reports. Additionally, the UR (Unsatisfactory Material/Condition Report) is a prime communications vehicle used to keep other units within an aircraft community informed of incidents and material problems common to all. These reports provide an exchange of experience and eliminate the need for all to endure or suffer many of the problems which individual units incur. They enable early corrective action and are effective in saving aircraft and people.

There are extensions to the formal reporting systems which are equally vital in achieving this goal. *Approach* and the Safety Center always highlight the anonymous "Anymouse" reports wherein individuals relate experiences from which others can learn valuable lessons. The shared experience of one becomes a lesson for all. It has also been SOP in many squadrons to have the pilot of an attention-getting flight or hair-raising experience stand before his mates at an AOM [all officers meeting] and give all the details.

The *Clansmen* of Attack Squadron FORTY-SIX have extended this reporting system one step further. The Clan maintains a Martini Log wherein the unseen, as well as the seen, errors of the pilots are voluntarily logged and explained. The log provides a running source of information for all pilots on the kinds of errors that can be and have been made and should be avoided.

There are never any adverse repercussions (other than a little readyroom chain pulling) from these confessions. Though each pilot in the squadron constantly strives for errorless, water-walking perfection, he is ready and willing to confess an error if it will help someone else avoid the same mistake in the future. The log and the list of errors also provide the Commanding, Safety, Operations, Weapons Training, and NATOPS Officers with additional indications of weak spots in their respective training programs.

The price for logging an error is a quarter. Measured against the needless loss of human life or loss of a valuable aircraft, the cost is minimal, and the procedure unquestionably cost-effective. The willingness of each squadron pilot to "put himself on report" for each procedural or switchology error has enabled the squadron to profit from a free, untainted flow of experience and information.

Placing oneself on report is never easy, but continued progress in making naval aviation accident-free requires that each of us be willing to share his experiences. Each must be willing to put himself on report for the good of all.

The "Scapegoat"

November 1974

I just couldn't hold onto it. I suspect there was some kind of control failure, or else the downwind oleo collapsed just as I approached flying speed. Maybe a tire blew, but then I didn't touch the brakes during the roll. I had done everything right—complied with NATOPS all the way—but just couldn't hold onto it.

As soon as I saw we were going off the edge, I told my rear seat stick to stand by. I punched us both out as the bird homed in on the arresting gear enclosure.

Funny thing. As the canopy blew and the rear seat exploded, I thought—perhaps I'd forgotten something. Was there anything else I could have done to save the bird? No! Nothing! I had tried my level best. I was in the clear. ("In the clear?" Where did that thought come from?)

After a quick checkup for me and my back-seater at sickbay, and treatment for a skinned elbow, I went back to the scene where the one winged, seatless *Skyhawk* perched on its one remaining gear.

The skipper, there with the ASO and Ops, wanted to know how I was and did I feel like talking right then.

"Sure, skipper, I'm OK." Wish I could have said the same for 307. She was a strike for sure.

The safety officer had his duty tape recorder, so we moved away from the immediate site so I could give him my side of the story. (There it goes again! "*My* side of the story?" What other side was there?)

The ASO [aviation safety officer] started asking a few questions, and I wondered if the mike would pick up our words because of the wind. (Wind? My God! What did the tower say the wind was when they cleared me to roll? It was nearly 90 degrees from the right, but not bad enough to push me off the runway. No. No sweat in that area.)

ASO: You say after Tower cleared you for takeoff you lined it up in the middle of 28?

Me: Right down the centerline.

ASO: What winds did the tower give you?

Me: Uh . . . let me see. Something like, variable 360 to 010 at around 12 to 15. I remember it was a little gusty. Up to 25 knots or so. But I've never had any problems with crosswinds—especially on takeoff. Hell, I've got close to 2000 hours in the A-4. That should count for something.

ASO: Yeah, you oughta know what the bird can do and can't do by now. Uh, Bob, did you think about aborting when your port tire failed?

Me: What port tire? I mean, I didn't have a blowout—did I?

ASO: Sure did. Take a look at what's left of your port tire. Nothing but threads; the rim's all chewed up.

Me: (That tire had a bunch of plys showing when I preflighted. The troubleshooter wanted to change it, but I told him not to sweat it—that I was only going to make one landing.)

ASO: Another thing. Neither droptank ruptured, and from what I can tell, it looks like your right drop was only half-filled. Didn't you check them visually?

Me: (Half-filled! Hell, they both sounded full when I tapped them on preflight. Damn plane captain didn't have the caps open—and I was in a hurry.)

ASO: Tell you what, Bob—why don't you go ahead and knock off the rest of the day? When you feel up to coming in tomorrow, we'll talk about it. Right now, relax. OK?

Me: (Relax? That's easy for him to say. It's not all hanging out for him. Have one little accident and they twist things around to make you the scapegoat. Why don't they pin it on Mother Nature? The crosswind was her idea. I was just doing my job.)

Well, the CO didn't want me to drive home, so I called my wife to pick me up.

Leaning against the hangar, waiting, I decided that I was a victim of circumstances. This day, this one lousy day, all the odds were stacked against me. I was handling the situation no sweat, 'til my luck ran out. Should have checked my Bio-Rhythm chart this morning—it's probably a critical day.

If it hadn't been for that complacent plane captain or that idiot who fueled the bird—or if the troubleshooter had gone ahead and changed that weak tire despite my objections—I wouldn't be in the AAR limelight now.

Another thing. Tower should have been more explicit in their wind information. Hell, I was busy briefing that nugget rear-seater on how to contact Departure.

Oh, well, I still think the oleo bottomed out, and I couldn't get full throw on my ailerons into the wind. They'll more than likely find something jammed in the aileron power package—or whatever.

Here she comes. Wonder if she's speaking to me yet after my Happy Hour scene last night?

Midair

L. K. Reed, VF-11; December 1974

It was a beautiful Friday afternoon with clear weather and unlimited visibility. I was inbound from the warning area at 14,000, using the newly instituted positive control procedures. Only a few minutes stood between touchdown, a quick beer at the club, and home to the family for a weekend of leisure. My machine was responding perfectly, and with radar separation provided, this would be a piece of cake, right? Wrong!

I had just completed an IFF change and a quick instrument check when a flight of three A–7s first became visible at my 8:30 o'clock position, slightly low on a climbing course and very close aboard. Instinctively, I rolled hard starboard, but the sickening shudder immediately dashed all hope for avoiding a midair. My now crippled *Skyhawk* began rolling and tumbling uncontrollably, and the probability of ejection appeared imminent. Surprisingly, however, the aircraft stabilized itself, and my attention was then directed to countering the numerous warnings vividly displayed on my telelight panel.

It was subsequently determined that I had been in a collision with the lead A–7. One of the other two *Corsairs* passed forward and below, while the other A–7 passed aft and below. Neither sustained any damage, but the lead aircraft went out of control and crashed. Apparently, the pilot was incapacitated on impact as there was no ejection attempt observed.

In the tense moments after the collision, I completed the emergency procedures for fire in flight and loss of all hydraulic systems. The possibility of saving my wounded bird began to dominate my thoughts. This "can do" attitude, coupled with a lack of external A–4 knowledge, subsequently placed me in a nearly unrecoverable position. (Normally available A–4 expertise was not forthcoming since local units were secured at the time of the collision.)

I switched to guard and transmitted a "Mayday," but was cut out by one of the downed *Corsair's* wingmen. After several unsuccessful attempts to broadcast, I switched to tower frequency and asked for a visual inspection.

Another flight of A–7s in the area joined on me and reported the following damage: the entire port slab and elevator were missing, the rudder was half torn off and jammed hard over to the right, and a quarter to half of the port droptank was gone.

A contollability check showed that I could maintain wings level by cross-controlling with aileron, but I could only make gentle turns to the right. There was no response to elevator inputs, but by varying power settings, I could establish various nose attitudes, thus enabling shallow climbs and descents. Minimum controllable airspeed appeared to be 220 knots.

At this point, I requested advice as to the feasibility of making an approach under these conditions, but the A–7s and tower personnel were unfamilar with the A–4. The requested assistance was not forthcoming, so the "can do" spirit prevailed. I decided to try a gear-up, no-flap arrested landing. I think I can categorically state that it was the worst operational decision I have ever made since the necessary high approach speed exceeded arresting gear limitations and the lack of elevator effectiveness made glide slope extremely difficult, if not impossible, to control. Nevertheless, the approach went fairly well until I went high and pulled power for the necessary correction—the nose fell through more rapidly than anticipated. From there, it was 100 percent power and full backstick in what was then a desperate attempt to wave off.

The lowest point of the approach was approximately 4 feet—with the tailhook dragging on the runway. An eternity later, a steady climbout was established, and the LSO advised me to find a clear area and eject. Heart in mouth, I readily concurred. The subsequent ejection and recovery were normal in all respects, making the final chapter of the episode nearly anticlimactic.

After extended debriefings on the accident, I was finally released for the beer which I had envisioned hours earlier. . . .

King of the Road

August 1975

A West Coast F–4 squadron was returning its nine *Phantoms* to homebase from an East Coast deployment. The first day of the transcontinental flight proceeded without incident. All nine aircraft launched from USS *Boat* and flew to NAS East Coast. After a quick turn-around, they continued on in flights of three to NAS Inland for RON.

The plan for the second day called for the flights of three to continue on to Southwest AFB, where they would refuel and join for a nine-plane flight into NAS West Coast. However, one aircraft was having fuel quantity indicator problems, so the plan was changed to fly the faulty bird two legs to Southwest AFB with one aircraft to accompany it. The remaining seven aircraft were split into flights of four and three.

At Base Ops, the flight planners for the squadron called Southwest AFB and found that not only had Southwest not received the squadron's message stating its intention to stop there, but also that the AFB was PPR and would not be able to accommodate nine F–4s. The flight plan was changed to stop over at Nearby International. Weather there was forecast as 5000 broken, 9000 overcast, with 7 miles visibility. Southwest AFB was also reporting VFR and expected to remain that way, so it was chosen as a possible alternate. The individual flight leaders briefed their flights.

The two-plane flight was the first to launch—no problems.

The four-plane flight followed 30 minutes later. Their launch was delayed for 10 minutes on the ground because of a bad starting unit, but was otherwise without incident. The division joined and climbed to altitude. The

lead aircraft was lowest state in the flight by several hundred pounds.

As the flight of four progressed beyond the halfway point, No. 2 switched to Metro. His report to the flight leader was the first warning of impending trouble.

Nearby International was reporting 800 scattered, 1400 overcast, 1½ miles visibility in rain and fog, and expecting to get worse. Southwest was in a similar condition with 300 overcast, 1⅛ miles visibility in rain and fog. The flight had passed Big State Air Terminal just a few minutes prior, at 35,000 feet, and had been able to see the ground at that point. The flight leader requested and was granted clearance to double back and land at Big State. Weather at the field was given by Center as 700 variable overcast with 3 miles visibility. At this time the squadron's two-plane flight checked in on the same center frequency, enroute to Nearby International. They decided to continue on because of their higher fuel state, and better chances if an alternate was needed.

As the flight of four descended, the leader requested breakup into sections for two-plane GCAs and section landings. Center acknowledged the request. At 12,000 feet the flight was switched to Big State Approach. Low state was 4.2.

On Big State frequency, the flight leader again requested section GCAs and landings. Approach rogered the flight now at 6000 feet and asked if the flight had the current weather. The weather given to the leader at that time was 200 obscured, ¼ mile visibility in fog. Well into the approach and with intermittent ground contact through a broken cloud layer, the decision was made to continue the approach, but in single-plane elements. Low state was 2.8, well below the 3.0 VFR or 4.0 IFR bingo to the nearest alternate, Southwest AFB.

The flight leader, a commander with 1300 hours in the F-4, had as his crewmember a maintenance chief petty officer to ensure proper servicing of the flight and to correct maintenance difficulties encountered enroute. As he turned final in section with No. 2 at 18 miles, Approach advised that the RVR [runway visual range] was 1800 feet. After splitting the section, Approach notified No. 1 to continue the ILS [instrument landing system] approach and contact tower. Number 1 immediately replied, *"Hey, babes, I said GCA. We're not ILS equipped,"* to which Approach replied, "Roger, we do not have precision radar, sir. Stand by for a surveillance approach." Number 1 descended to ASR [approach surveillance radar] minimums of 500 feet until called over the runway, then descended further to 200 feet on his radar altimeter. He spotted the runway to his right, did a modified wingover, and landed on the 13,500-foot runway with 9000 feet remaining. His rollout was uneventful, compared to the approach, and he waited after clearing the runway, monitoring the other approaches. One down, three to go.

The wingman of the first section (No. 2) was new to the squadron, with 140 hours in the *Phantom* and 1700 total hours, mostly as a primary flight instructor. His RIO was a senior lieutenant on his second F-4 sea tour with 1500 hours of F-4 experience. Their surveillance approach to published minimums was unsuccessful and they were vectored downwind for a second attempt. Their state at waveoff was 3.2.

Leader of the second section (No. 3) was a junior lieutenant on his first tour with 400 *Phantom* and 700 total hours. His crewman was a second class petty officer from

the line division, also along for maintenance purposes. This was his first flight in an F-4. Their approach was equally unsuccessful, and a missed approach to downwind was taken.

Tail end Charlie (No. 4) was a foreign exchange pilot who had been with the squadron 2 months and had accumulated 130 hours of F-4 time. His crewmember was also a second class petty officer from the line division, but with 2000 hours in F-4s as a crew chief for the Blue Angels. Through a misunderstanding of minimum descent altitude, No. 4 ended up over the field 2000 feet higher than the MDA—clean. As he turned downwind, the flight leader came up on common approach frequency and told No. 4, "Go to East AFB. It's your only chance—fly a bingo profile—go!" *Number 3 heard the transmission and asked for an initial vector. Number 1 responded "Zero niner zero."*

A short recap at this point: No. 1 is on deck; No. 2 is on final for his second attempt; No. 3 is on a bingo for East AFB; with No. 4 ahead at some undetermined distance. Number 2 saw the ground on his second approach, but was unable to locate the runway. He asked for a vector for East AFB and quickly figured the fuel required. Fuel required for 130 miles—3.3 VFR, fuel onboard 2.2. Number 2 then requested vectors for one final approach at Big State and if unsuccessful, a vector to a clear area for ejection. The crew of No. 2 planned for a TACAN approach with gear held until the last portion of the approach. When asked if there were any holes in the clouds near the field through which No. 2 might break out, *Approach responded, assuring the crew that the runway was 300 feet wide with no holes in it!* The crew requested flares if possible, but none were available. At ⅛ of a mile they spotted the field, eased over some powerlines, and landed with 800 pounds of fuel remaining. Two down, two to go.

As No. 4 climbed, he gained a TACAN lock on East AFB of 105 miles with 1800 pounds of fuel remaining. He continued to fly the prescribed bingo profile, leveling at 36,000 feet. At 55 miles he started an idle descent with 900 pounds remaining. Flying mostly from TACAN information, No. 4 spotted the airfield at 7 miles. (Weather: 3000 scattered, 7 miles visibility.) He held gear and flaps until on final and landed with 400 pounds on the counter and zero on the tape. Three down, one to go.

The section leader (No. 3) had not been so lucky. As No. 1 transmitted for everyone to bingo, No. 3 was 10–15 miles *west* of the field, in the opposite direction from East AFB. Turning to follow No. 4, he asked approach for a heading and range to the alternate. Approach came back with a Center frequency. Again he asked for a vector, got no response, and switched to Center.

Declaring an emergency, he asked for vectors to any suitable airfield in the vicinity. Center never gave a radar vector to No. 3, although one controller was painting his IFF squawk until he descended out of radar coverage. Center estimated him at 20 miles from Small Town Municipal Airport on its 330 radial, and instructed him to turn to 120 and switch to Small Town radio. Hearing No. 4 ahead of him call 85 miles to East AFB and reading 1600 pounds of fuel remaining, plus not knowing his position nor having the range to any field, the pilot of No. 3 began an idle descent through the broken layer below. He spotted a small town, and hoping for an airfield, turned in that direction. The town was not equipped with an airfield. His narrative follows:

"We turned to look for an airfield but realized that with 500 pounds, time was growing short. I spotted a highway with a long straight stretch. I could hear Small Town radio calling on Guard and attempted a transmission back, but got no answer. I lowered the gear and flaps and made an approach to the highway. My main concern was traffic. As we dropped to about 100 feet AGL I saw some cars down the highway, which was only two lanes wide. I couldn't tell which direction they were going and I thought there was a chance of hitting them, so I waved off. As I turned downwind, I raised the gear and flaps. I had instructed my crewman during the idle descent how we would eject, so while downwind I told him if the engines started to unwind, we would get out. As we turned through the 90, I could see the highway was clear.

"I dropped gear and flaps, lined up on the highway centerline, and descended through the powerlines on both sides of the right-of-way. We touched down close to onspeed. My main concerns were traffic interference and staying in the middle of the 42-foot-wide roadway. I saw no cars coming, so I deployed the drag chute and rolled. As we reached taxi speed, we rolled by a U.S. highway sign.

"I transmitted on Guard that I was on the highway and that the plane was OK. I taxied to the right side of the highway, folded the wings, and shut down with 200 pounds showing on the counter, and zero on the tape. We chocked the aircraft with boards and secured the drag chute. Four down—safely—none to go."

Local authorities quickly arrived and provided traffic control and security until personnel from East AFB arrived. The next day, fuel was brought to the scene along with starting units. After a FOD [foreign object damage] walkdown of the highway, the plane was started, traffic halted, and personnel cleared away. The squadron commander flew the light-loaded *Phantom* off the highway and to the AFB, 50 miles distant. No damage was done to the highway or surrounding property. At East AFB, the remaining aircraft were refueled and flown to Homebase.

Low, Low Approach

August 1975

Two hours and 30 minutes after takeoff for a night instrument training flight, the IP (instructor pilot) took control of the P-3C to demonstrate an ILS approach to the two PUIs (pilots under instruction) aboard. Approach control cleared the aircraft to return to the outer compass locator and commence the approach. The second pilot under instruction was asked to read the abbreviated landing checklist while the aircraft was enroute to the outer compass locator. The checklist was completed down to "landing gear" and held at that point.

Upon passing the outer compass locator outbound for a teardrop approach, approach control had the aircraft extend its outbound leg to provide traffic separation from a helicopter and three other aircraft shooting instrument approaches to the same airport. During this time, the instructor pilot was attempting to obtain visual contact with other traffic, fly the aircraft, and discuss flight director instrument indications and ILS intercept procedures. Upon intercepting the final course inbound, the instructor pilot was told to contact Tower at the outer compass locator. A descent was commenced on the ILS glide slope at the outer compass locator, and the instructor pilot switched to Tower.

While waiting for the tower controller to complete landing instructions for another aircraft, the IP continued to discuss proper ILS technique. Up to this point, the flight engineer under instruction and his instructor were engaged in a discussion about a previous pressurization problem. On short final, the P-3 received landing clearance. The instructor pilot switched to an outside scan, extended land flaps, and commenced a transition to the landing attitude. He experienced, however, an uneasy feeling of being too low, as the aircraft appeared to sink below touchdown altitude.

A waveoff was initiated and full power was applied, but as the aircraft accelerated, cockpit personnel observed a flash to the starboard of the aircraft. Realizing some part of the aircraft had probably contacted the runway, the instructor requested clearance to homefield. During the return, a check of aircraft handling characteristics indicated the aircraft flew correctly and that the 41-degree coordinator switch and wheels light worked correctly. The flight terminated with a normal landing.

Postflight investigation revealed that the aircraft had contacted the runway on the ECM [electronic counter measures] and LLLTV [low light level television] pods— *the wheels had never left the wheelwells!* . . .

Phantom Phlameout

January 1976

An F–4J met an F–14 adversary aircraft over an offshore range for scheduled dissimilar ACM training. The first engagement commenced with a 25 nm separation. The F–4, which was at 27,000 feet and descending to 21,000 feet on the run-in, attained a speed of Mach 1.2. The first pass was port-to-port with approximately 1500 feet lateral separation. Both aircraft turned into each other to decrease lateral separation.

After the port-to-port pass, the F–4 pilot leveled the wings and pulled up to a 60–70–degree nose-high attitude to gain separation and execute a left oblique maneuver. The RIO maintained visual contact (padlock) on the F–14 which was low at his 8 o'clock position in a port turn.

While in the inverted position, the pilot commenced a starboard turn but was called to reverse port by the RIO as he was losing sight of the adversary. The pilot utilized coordinated rudder and aileron to maneuver the aircraft to port and commenced a pull of 2–4Gs that would bring the aircraft from a 50–degree nose-high inverted position down through the horizon.

Full afterburner had been selected at 15 nm separation from the F–14 on the head-on pass and was deselected as the aircraft was coming over the top in the oblique maneuver. The throttles were then retarded to a position somewhat less than full military. Passing approximately 40 degrees nose high above the horizon, inverted, approximately four loud thumps and vibrations in the airframe were heard and felt by the aircrew. Just prior

to experiencing the vibrations, the RIO had transitioned from his visual of the F–14 to the cockpit mirrors to maintain padlock. At that time, the RIO noted a white vapor appearing in the engine vortices which he thought to be contrails.

Hearing the thumps, the pilot asked, "What was that?" Experiencing the airframe vibrations and seeing the white vapor prompted the RIO to call for the pilot to check for compressor stalls. Altitude at this point was approximately 30,000 feet. The pilot noted engine RPM decreasing from approximately 70 to 65 percent on both engines. The pilot immediately attempted an abbreviated airstart by pressing the engine igniters, but the airstart was unsuccessful before the generators dropped off the line. During this sequence of events, the pilot was rolling the aircraft upright, wings level.

The pilot placed the emergency RAT (ram air turbine) control handle to DOWN (RAT out) position and the port engine throttle to OFF as he commenced emergency procedures for a double engine flameout in flight. The RIO did not observe the deployed RAT and told the pilot to get the RAT out.

When the generators dropped off the line, all power was lost, but the aircrew was able to communicate by removing oxygen masks and shouting. The pilot again physically rechecked the RAT control handle DOWN, at which time the RAT control handle separated from the RAT level arm shaft. (The most likely cause of this failure was later determined to be metal fatigue caused by corrosion and stress.)

The pilot established a 250–knot glide while attempting to deploy the RAT by replacing the RAT control handle on the broken shaft. This was unsuccessful. The pilot then displayed the RAT control handle to the RIO by holding the item over his left shoulder. The pilot and RIO discussed ejection and determined it would be necessary. The aircraft was then headed toward land in a 250–knot glide.

At approximately 10,000 feet, 220 knots, entering the overcast, the aircrew ejected. The pilot signaled for ejection by activating the eject light. The RIO initiated the command ejection sequence by pulling the face curtain. Ejection was normal, but both the pilot and RIO felt that the opening shocks were severe. After the chute deployment, the pilot noticed a tear approximately 3 feet long near the apex of his chute.

During the descent, the pilot and RIO drifted very close together. Each had deployed his raft and inflated his LPA–2. The RIO's raft became partially entangled in the pilot's shroudlines, creating grave concern for both airmen. Fortunately, pulling on the risers of their respective chutes freed the raft. The pilot then drifted down and away because of the hole in his chute. The aircrew broke out of the overcast at about 4000 feet.

During the descent, the pilot removed his gloves and oxygen mask and discarded both. Upon entering the water, he immediately released both Koch fittings, and the chute drifted clear. The LPA kept his head completely out of the water. The pilot experienced some difficulty during raft entry due to the seat pan still being attached to his torso harness (lapbelts). He solved the problem by releasing his lapbelt fittings and letting the seat pan fall into the water. The pan was still attached by the lanyard to the raft.

After entering the water, the RIO attempted to release his Koch fittings but only the right side disconnected. He removed his left glove and successfully released the left Koch fitting. The RIO entered his raft and experienced the same problem with his seat pan that the pilot had encountered. The same solution was used to rectify the situation.

The aircrew rafts were approximately 100 yards apart, enabling both visual and verbal contact. The pilot fired two pen flares to signify he was OK. The pilot deployed one dye marker and tried his survival radio. It was inoperative. The RIO's survival radio receiver was operative, but his transmissions were garbled and unreadable. The RIO, however, was able to monitor voice communications during the entire rescue.

Meanwhile, the F–14 descended below the overcast, spotted the survivors, alerted SAR, and remained on scene as SAR commander until fuel requirements forced him to pass command to a C–9. The C–9 remained on the scene until the survivors were rescued, uninjured, by a Coast Guard helo a short time later. . . .

The Night the World Died

October 1976

Every pilot who has flown on an instrument flight plan has had problems, at one time or another, involving lost communications, navaid outage, change of frequencies, etc. This is a story of a P–3 crew who were airborne the night *everything* went off the line.

The weather wasn't great: 1200 broken, 2500 broken, 4000 overcast with visibility varying from 1 to 3 miles as rain showers moved through the area. A P–3 crew deployed to Cubi Point was "taking advantage" of the IMC [instrument meteorological conditions] weather to log the kind of time you can't buy and to brush up on their instrument proficiency. They had filed a flight plan to Clark AFB where they planned to shoot a variety of instrument approaches.

Six GCAs had been completed and the seventh was well underway. The *Orion* was on a 4–mile final when the reassuring voice of the PAR [precision approach radar] controller stopped abruptly, and the silence became deafening. In accordance with the lost comm procedures given them earlier, the crew quickly switched from a precision approach to a VORTAC [very high frequency omnidirectional range combined with TACAN facilities] approach and checked their new minimums. Their initial optimism over seeing the HSI [horizontal situation indicator] course bar dead-centered was shortlived when they observed the OFF flag accompanying the course bar.

Taking advantage of the many nav systems available in the P–3, the crew went to their TACAN in an attempt to complete the approach. It was a good idea except the TACAN wouldn't lock on either. At this point they had run out of approach options and had no choice but to execute a missed approach.

Their missed approach procedure was to climb out the 020 radial to 15 DME and hold. Ordinarily this would be strictly routine, but how do you hold at a fix when there are no navaids whatsoever?

During the waveoff they passed right through a hole in the clouds over a point where they estimated the field to be. Hoping to acquire the field visually and perhaps make a VFR entry, the crew searched the ground for evidence of the airfield. Nothing. It was absolutely pitch black. Not a light was shining anywhere on the airport.

Correctly assessing the problem as an airfield power outage, the P–3 crew climbed to 4500 feet to ensure terrain clearance above a nearby 3300–foot volcano. Clark AFB has the only navaids in central Luzon that could be received at 400 feet and since they were kaput, the crew could do little but attempt to maintain VFR by flying in tight circles in a hole in the clouds. They tried to raise Manila Control but were unable.

The pilots held a conference to discuss the options available to them at this point. They agreed that they had conformed to all established lost comm procedures, and there was no set procedure for the situation they now faced. Since the problem was a power outage at the field, they elected to bide their time, hoping the airfield could regain power shortly, and then handle them.

They didn't have to wait long. Clark came up on emergency power, gave them one vector to depart the restricted area they were in, and promptly went silent again.

Clark was able to transmit in segments only, but eventually the crew pieced a clearance together back to Cubi Point. The pilots and crew agreed it had been an interesting time, cruising around with no navaids, on airways, while the whole world kept silent.

Clark AFB had had a complete, massive power failure; everything had quit at once—all radars, radios, navaids, lights, and electric guitars. Strangely enough, Cubi Point also had a 20–minute outage about the same time.

Recounting the episode in the secure surroundings of the readyroom, the crew advised that if Clark AFB had not been able to give them a clearance, they would have proceeded to Cubi Point, off airways, at a VFR altitude in IMC conditions. Not an ideal solution, but what else could they have done? When you have lost communications, in IMC, and have no clearance, you have to do something! What would *you* have done! . . .

Nugget Nightmare

November 1976

Ramp strike! Oil starvation! Barricade engagement! Nosewheel-first landing! Sheared mainmount! What is this—a list of naval aviators' worst dreams? Probably, yes. But definitely, when this happened to an inexperienced pilot all on the same night, you know it was a real nightmare.

The young JG had been in the A–7 squadron only 2 months and had but 442 total hours the night he was scheduled for a surface and air surveillance hop. Nevertheless, he had been brought along carefully and was showing normal progress as his experience built. He had had eight day and four night landings in the past 30 days.

The flight and initial portion of the approach was normal except for a slightly late commencement at a fast airspeed. The pilot corrected his speed during the approach, however, and was on speed by platform. CATCC [carrier air traffic control center] instructed the pilot to dirty up at 8 nm and proceeded with an ACL [automatic carrier landing] lock-on. When the needles failed to check OK, the approach was downgraded to a Mode III.

Watching the approach from the platform was the CVW [carrier air wing] LSO, a qualified LSO, and an LSO trainee who was manning the pickle. The approach was slightly underpowered and low, but the aircraft arrived at the waveoff point in an acceptable position. Unexpectedly, the pilot reduced power further at this point. Four power calls, with more volume and urgency, caused the pilot to go to military power. In an effort to clear the ramp, he also rotated noseup. But the ramp strike occurred.

The *Corsair* impacted the ramp with the hook and the lower portion of the aircraft, approximately 9 feet from the trailing edge of the tail cone. The aircraft skipped all the wires and boltered.

The LSO called the air boss and reported the ramp strike. Meanwhile, the CO of the ship directed another aircraft to get an inflight inspection of the A–7 to determine the extent of the damage. The airborne tanker rendezvoused on the damaged *Corsair* and noted a dented tail cone and partially extended tailhook. To add to this damage, the A–7 pilot noticed the MASTER CAUTION light on and saw oil pressure decaying to 15 psi. Following emergency procedures, he extended the EPP [emergency power package] and set the power at 84 percent. Meanwhile, the oil pressure had dropped to zero.

Based on the oil pressure loss and damage to the tailhook, the decision to barricade the aircraft immediately was made. CATCC gave inbound vectors to the A–7 and passed control to the final controller. Since rigging the barricade was not complete at this time, the controller gave a downwind heading and intended to turn the aircraft in at about 5 miles. As the aircraft passed 2.5 miles downwind, the LSO transmitted, "306, Paddles, we have contact with you; you're in a left turn; is that affirmative?" The aircraft rogered this transmission, setting up a communications misunderstanding back on the ship.

CATCC and the pilot assumed the LSO had taken control of the approach by virtue of this transmission. The LSO assumed the aircraft was turning inbound on a radar vector and was thus 5 miles or so from the ship. Air ops assumed LSO had control. The end result was that the crippled *Corsair* arrived at the ramp before the deck was clear and had to execute a waveoff.

Fortunately, engine response was normal on the waveoff. The aircraft turned downwind and the LSO took control of the approach. By this time the barricade had been rigged and the landing area cleared, so the LSO talked the aircraft around to a 1.5-mile final. As the pilot reported the ball, the air wing LSO, who had taken over on the platform, started talking.

"OK, now fly that ball right in the center for me. When you cross the ramp, I'm going to ask you to pull the power to IDLE. No higher, now. No higher! Let it down now. LET IT DOWN! NOSE IT DOWN! POWER BACK, POWER BACK!"

The pilot had arrived on the ball with zero oil pressure, fast, and slightly high. The power was set at 84 percent and only one power reduction was made on the ball. As a result, the aircraft was high and fast on the glide slope, and when urged by the LSO to "get it down," the pilot dropped his nose and went to IDLE. The result was a nosewheel-first landing at an estimated 1600 fpm rate of descent. The aircraft bounced once, engaged a wire, and was then enmeshed by the barricade, 25 feet right of centerline. The starboard mainmount sheared, and the aircraft sustained CHARLIE damage. A parked A–3 sustained damage from flying debris, and two flight deck personnel were injured. [The pilot survived.] . . .

Nighttime Eye-Opener

Lt. Bob Knapp, VF-191; March 1977

Two F–4s were launched off USS *Boat* for a 2-hour air intercept hop. The mission was uneventful, and both aircraft returned overhead for a Case III night recovery.

Weather was good, but there was no visible horizon. After check-in, both aircraft were assigned Marshal instructions and told to use the plane guard's TACAN, since the carrier's TACAN was inop. Though the plane guard's TACAN was intermittent in azimuth and DME, both aircraft were able to proceed to their respective Marshal positions. Neither aircraft had an operative nav computer or ADF.

The lead aircraft pushed over on time with a fuel state of 5.3. Bingo fuel for F–4s was 3.7. Although the lead experienced directional gyro problems at this point, with the assistance of Approach he was able to get lined up on final and achieve SPN–42 Mode II lock-on at 6 miles. The approach was continued on the needles, but the LSO gave the *Phantom* a technique waveoff. Fuel state on the go-around was 4.7.

The wingman, meanwhile, had commenced a minute behind lead, dirtied up at 8 miles on final, but had unsafe gear and flap indications. The pilot requested a fly-by near the LSO platform for a visual gear check. This was approved by Approach, and they cleared him to continue the CCA. Simultaneously, the CATCC officer passed word of the *Phantom's* gear malfunction to "paddles," but the LSOs were unaware that the wingman was going to make a low pass for a visual check. To complicate things, the F–4 pilot, preoccupied with his emergency, did not fly the CCA profile. Instead, he recycled his gear and flaps in an attempt to get a down indication while maintaining his altitude. As a result, the wingman accelerated and arrived at the ramp simultaneously with the lead *Phantom*. In concentrating on the lead aircraft, none of the LSOs noticed the wingman approaching the port side of the ship at 1000 feet. The end result was that both aircrews ended up approximately one-half mile ahead of the ship, on the gages, attempting transition to the night bolter pattern.

The lead aircraft was cleared downwind by the CATCC supervisor. Turning downwind at 1200 feet, the lead saw his wingman flash by underneath his aircraft at an estimated clearance of less than 20 feet. Simultaneously, the wingman caught sight of his lead as he was closing on his tailpipe, and pushed over excitely to avoid a collision. The wingman recovered at 400 feet, but, somewhat flustered, elected to bingo. His subsequent field landing, after a visual gear check, was uneventful.

Exciting times were not over for the lead F–4, however. He entered downwind and reported abeam with a 4.1 fuel state. Approach control issued the F–4 vectors for base leg and turned him inbound to final bearing at 6 miles astern. The F–4's interval was an EA–6 on final, 2 miles ahead.

Somewhere between base and final, communications from the ship ceased. With no navaids or traffic advisories from CATCC, the *Phantom* crew commenced a self-contained radar approach. Approximately 3 miles aft of the ship, the pilot started down from 1200 feet. By now the EA–6 was receiving final control 1½ miles ahead of the F–4 on the alternate approach frequency. Unnoticed by the final controller, aircraft separation was rapidly decreasing due to the F–4's higher approach speed. The approach controller, monitoring his search radarscope, recognized closure and told the EA–6 twice to elevate to 2000 feet. The final controller (a trainee) did not hear these calls since the intercom with the approach controller was inop and under repair during the recovery. He proceeded with glide slope directives to the EA–6 pilot, who continued the approach.

At 1 mile aft of the ship and approximately ¼ to ½ mile behind the EA–6 (which the *Phantom* pilot could not see due to its position below his nose), the pilot of the F–4 requested glide slope assistance from paddles since neither SPN–42 or –41 information was available. The LSO told him to "start it down, you're high," and the EA–6 pilot, now on the ball, was waved off. Almost immediately, the *Phantom* pilot saw the EA–6 pull up into his view. Confused, he continued his approach—until he hit the jetwash from the waved-off EA–6.

The turbulence threw the F–4 into a 60–degree right wing down attitude and caused the *Phantom* to settle below the flight deck before the pilot regained control. Selecting afterburners, the F–4 wallowed over the ship's island structure. His state was now 2.4, 1300 pounds below bingo!

The F–4 aircrew immediately switched to departure frequency and requested an expeditious tanker rendezvous. Though some confusion ensued as to the tanker's exact location, the F–4 ultimately plugged (with 1700 pounds remaining) and took on 2000 pounds of fuel enroute to the divert field. . . .

Not Just Another Sea Story

Lt. C. M. Drake and Lt. G. W. Brown, VF–194; April 1978

The flight was scheduled as a normal intercept training sortie. The aircrews watched the air wing intelligence brief over the readyroom TV, making note of the primary divert field: Kunsan, South Korea. After the common portion of the brief, the flight leader went into the specific flight and mission details. He ended his portion of the brief by pointing out the existence of Kwang-Ju, an F–4 suitable field in line with Kunsan, but closer. All flight members studied both fields from their IFR Supplements and approach plates.

The launch was normal. Aircraft 213 tanked off the cat, and 210 was informed that he would be mission tanked. The flight ran a few intercepts until 210's tanker was available, at which time 213 went into an orbit. While in this orbit, 213 lost its starboard generator with the bus tie closing. Efforts made to reset the generator were unsuccessful. Little did either crewmember know that this relatively minor malfunction was just the beginning of what would turn out to be a real nightmare!

Although the pilot's telelight panel indicated a good bus tie, the RIO began to have indications of bus tie difficulties. The TAKE-COMMAND lights on the UHF/NAV panel began to blink intermittently in conjunction with the UTILITY light. A squadron representative on the ship was called to CATCC and apprised of the circumstances. The pilot of 213 was informed that the recovery had been completed and he was to remain airborne until the next scheduled recovery time.

As 213 joined with 210, other problems began appearing. The RIO's UHF/ICS transmitter began to degenerate to the point that about 30 percent of his transmissions were not going out, although he still had a side tone on all transmission attempts. This problem was not resolved by reseating the upper block, which was a repeat gripe on 213. Next, the TACAN lost DME and started to wander in azimuth. Because of 213's deteriorating situation, 210 was asked to lead a section approach when the recovery commenced.

After about an hour of flying loose formation in the horizonless night, the pilot of 213 deployed the RAT, and the section approach commenced. The account of the events that followed is narrated by the pilot and RIO of 213.

Pilot: CATCC held the gear until 8 miles. As the gear was lowered at 1200 feet, the port generator went off the line. The RAT picked up the load after about a second's delay. I became extremely disoriented; it was pitch black, with no visible horizon, and the stab augs had kicked off just as the gear configuration changed.

RIO: In fact, we lost about 200 feet. The pilot informed me that he had a bad case of vertigo. Two Ten gave a call to "Keep her flying" and informed us that the nose gear was trailing, which concurred with our unsafe indication.

Pilot: I had my hands full flying the aircraft. I finally got comfortable enough to think to cycle the port generator, which reset. The nose then indicated safe, which was confirmed by 210. We decided to commence another approach immediately while the port generator was still functioning.

RIO: The lead realized that my pilot was extremely taxed, and called for wide, easy turns from CATCC. We received excellent control—except the controller was also controlling another aircraft on the same frequency, leading to some confusion.

As we approached about 2 miles from the ship, I noticed two lights forward of the ship on the right side of the canopy. These lights split about 30 degrees of arc and were in line with where the horizon should have been. I didn't realize at the time how valuable these lights would prove to be.

Pilot: I took over the lead after getting good needles and visual contact with the ship. The LSO called for a gear check, which we answered. This approach ended with the aircraft being high/flat at the ramp and boltering. As the gear hit the deck, the port generator kicked off the line. The RAT again took some time to pick up the load, meaning we left the angle with a completely black cockpit! The stab augs were off, the flaps were coming up, and my attitude gyros were tumbling when the lights came back on. I felt the aircraft rolling right. I reacted by putting in left stick but felt no response. At 75 feet, I thought we had reached 60 degrees right wing down, and called for the RIO to initiate dual ejection.

RIO: When the aircraft left the deck, I knew that the pilot would have to be on his instruments. I checked for the two lights to the right and estimated that we were about 10–20 degrees right wing down. I went back to the instruments, saw a good angle-of-attack, and read 50 feet on the altimeter, going up. I then transitioned back outside the cockpit.

I then heard the pilot calling, "Eject! Eject! Eject!" At the first eject call, I started yelling, "No! No! Don't!" I made this call after rapid consideration of the following factors: the pilot was disoriented and experiencing vertigo; the level of engine noise assured me we had adequate thrust; and even though my gyros were tumbling, my outside light reference convinced me we were basically wings level and our aircraft was recoverable.

I did have some bad thoughts running through my mind, though. I was not sure that the pilot was receiving my ICS transmissions. As an aircrew, we had discussed low-altitude ejection situations in quite some detail. Our basic assumption had been that he would probably make the eject call due to his superior instrumentation and forward visibility, but that I would be the one to physically pull the handle as he strove to maintain a level attitude. On the third eject call, the plan was for the pilot to pull the handle.

Pilot: As I called for ejection, the RIO said, "No! No! Don't!" I shut up and let him talk me back to wings level. The aircraft remained in a good rate of climb, but I still had vertigo and was leary of trusting my gyros when they came back on the line. As soon as I thought we were safely airborne (at about 3000 feet!), I again cycled the port generator, which came back on.

Following the bolter, 213 picked up his lead in the 9 o'clock position and commenced a join-up. With the flight rendezvoused, the section circled back for another approach. At this point, fuel was becoming a factor, 213's UHF/ICS difficulties were getting worse, and the troubled *Phantom* was experiencing a multitude of minor erroneous electrical indications.

Considering the circumstances, the next approach was uneventful. The LSO asked for confirmation of gear down and locked. Both 210 and 213 replied vociferously in the affirmative. The LSO then asked for a fast or slow indication on the approach light, which 213 attempted to give. Although on a rails pass, 213 was waved off because the LSO was not assured that the gear was down and locked.

The squadron CO, in conjunction with Air Operations decided at this point to have 213 clean up and tank. The assigned tanker was A–6E 503, carrying a buddy store. The pilot of 503 told tanker control to remind 213 that he was blinking red vice green, but this word was not passed. This led to a delay in the rendezvous due to the presence of several aircraft in 503's vicinity, one being a dry KA–6D.

When 503 was finally sighted by 213, he streamed his package—but no lights illuminated. The *Phantom* attempted to plug anyway, but received nothing. After 213 backed out, the basket was cycled and the amber light illuminated. With the probe engaged, however, the green light blinked on, then off. By jockeying with the basket,

213 was able to find about a foot and a half of play where fuel transfer could take place if the hose was pushed to the 3 o'clock position in relation to the store. Two Thirteen spent 13 arduous minutes plugged in, burning 100 pounds of fuel for every 200 received.

During the tanking evolution, squadron playmate 206 was launched and vectored toward 213. Before they had a chance to commence an approach, however, the ship decided enough was enough. Rather than risk another blacked-out bolter, 213 and the other 200 series aircraft were all bingoed. An initial vector of 155 at 74 was given.

Each aircraft questioned the vector, as it didn't jibe with their DR plot. Nevertheless, they received two confirmations. The aircrews knew this was wrong, however, and made a right-hand turn to 360 degrees while climbing to the bingo altitude of 40,000 feet.

Two Zero Six attempted contact with several GCI sites in the route of flight. After many attempts, one was contacted. In keeping with the way things were going that night, this GCI informed the flight that Kunsan was closed at night for runway repairs! Fortunately, the flight had briefed the alternate airport. Two Thirteen asked to proceed direct to Kwang-Ju and requested vectors.

The rest of the flight was as normal as any night bingo evolution can be—until touchdown at the divert field. At that point, 213 again lost the port generator. Fortunately, there was a long, lighted airstrip ahead of it, and the *Phantom* was able to roll out safely.

With no maintenance capabilities at Kwang-Ju, the decision was made the next day to fly back to the carrier under VMC [visual meteorological conditions] conditions. But the Gremlins of the previous night were still alive and well and determined to tax the fighter pilots to their fullest. Shortly after takeoff, the RIO lost all his oxygen flow and was forced to fly back to the ship with his mask off. Maybe it was a good thing because as the gear was lowered back at the ship, the RIO detected electrical smoke in the cockpit. As 213 trapped, the generator dropped off the line. The aircrew performed an emergency ground egress after some delay due to the RIO's total loss of ICS on touchdown. . . .

How Not to Do It!

September 1980

After years of living with the memories of my worst night of naval aviation, I guess it's time to write about it so someone else might learn from my experience.

It was the last night of a predeployment workup prior to sailing for the Mediterranean. Our three *Whales* were part of a 25–airplane flyoff to NAS East Coast to reduce the deck loading for a one-night, RAG, carqual period. The ship was scheduled to pull into port the next morning and sail 1 week later. Our early afternoon flyoff was normal in all respects, and the flight lead, our skipper, was happy to learn all our aircraft were up when we got ashore. He emphasized how important it was for the planes to get back to the ship that night. Otherwise, we would have to fly to another base and be craned aboard—"Something we want to avoid at all costs."

The fly aboard was scheduled in two recoveries of 12 and 13 aircraft after the carqual evolution. We had arrived at NAS East Coast at 1500 and were scheduled for the 2100 recovery aboard USS *Ship*. However, we were to wait for a confirmed overhead time via Raspberry before we manned our aircraft.

I went to the BOQ [Bachelor Officers' Quarters], where I got some chow, and then to my room for a 2–hour combat nap (the smartest thing I did all day). Two hours later, my crew and I attended the three-plane *Whale* flight brief. Unfortunately, the brief was rather general, covering not much more than the rendezvous and breakup for individual Marshals; no inflight emergencies were addressed. I reviewed some individual emergencies with my crew, another nugget and an AT3, and returned to the BOQ for word from the boat.

After awhile, it became obvious things weren't going as planned with the RAG carquals. Our original overhead time of 2100 came and went with us still waiting in the BOQ. Around 2300, we got the word to man the aircraft. All 25 aircraft were to return to the ship at once! By this time, we all were tired of waiting and glad to be heading for our aircraft.

Our preflight, start, and taxi were normal, and I was happy to see that we were apparently ahead of everyone else, as none of the other air wing aircraft had taxied yet. Our three *Whales* taxied to the hold-short line with me as number three. I thought it was odd that number one and two had parked in the hold-short area in such a way as to block traffic, but the press of getting the takeoff checklist completed blotted these thoughts from my mind. With our checklists completed, the lead switched us to Tower. It was immediately obvious something was wrong with the lead's radios; both his No. 1 and No. 2 radios (one on Tower and one on Ground) were constantly transmitting static and cockpit conversations. The lead tried several transmissions, requesting takeoff clearance and acknowledgement of the frequency shift from the other aircraft.

Confusion began to reign supreme. NAS East Coast Tower tried calling on Guard, Tower, and Ground frequencies to tell the lead he had a stuck mike. I knew there was more to it than that, so I told my AT3 aircrewman to run over and get in the lead's aircraft through the lower hatch and clarify the situation. By this time, the other air wing aircraft were lining up on the taxiway behind us. I was somewhat surprised to see the lead's aircrewman running over to number two and then back into his aircraft. Suddenly, the radios were clear and I told number two that we should clear the hold-short area so everyone else could take off. He agreed, and as the dance of the *Whales* began in the hold-short area, I very nearly taxied off the taxiway into a big mud puddle. Finally, we were clear and waited while the rest of the aircraft took off.

As we were sitting there, I noticed someone again get out of the lead's aircraft and go over to number two. I gulped as number two, a nugget also, informed me on squadron common that the skipper wanted him to lead the flight back to the ship and that the skipper would fly on number two's wing, **NORDO!** We discussed the wisdom of doing this and decided to send one of the navigators over to talk to the skipper to see if that's really what he wanted to do. The navigator, another nugget, returned with the word we had to get back to the ship and that's what we were going to do. So, we switched to Tower and number two transmitted, "East Coast Tower, AZ 611, flight of three for takeoff. My wingman's NORDO." After a long pause, East Coast Tower said, "Well, we can't really clear an aircraft to take off NORDO, but if he wants to, I guess it's alright with us. You're cleared for takeoff; the wind is calm."

As the new lead took the runway, I noticed the skipper was not taking the runway as number two. Thinking he must have thought better of his plan, I took the runway as number two and rolled down the runway 10 seconds after my new lead. I rendezvoused on the lead, and the two-plane flight headed towards the ship with the skipper nowhere in sight. We motored on for awhile when, suddenly, another set of aircraft lights appeared, closing fast. We soon had the skipper with us and pressed on to USS *Ship*.

At the ship, the carqual period was finally ending, and the recovery was marshaled to await a push time. Number two switched our flight to Marshal, and as he did that, the skipper decided to try his radios again on Marshal frequency and the one approach frequency being used for the recovery.

Pandemonium broke loose on the radios. The ship and everyone concerned tried transmitting to the skipper that he had a stuck transmitter. The confusion forced the ship to bingo the remaining carqual birds on Guard frequency. Finally, the air wing aircraft got switched to a new Marshal frequency. Unfortunately, in the ensuing confusion, I lost radio contact with the lead. Now we had three *Whales* flying formation at night, none of whom had communications with one another.

Frankly, I was scared by now. I tried to transmit my situation to the ship and get an individual Marshal. I tried

every frequency on the card that should have worked, and all I got was static or silence. In the midst of these radio changes, I suddenly noticed the lead was descending, and without warning, he put his speedbrakes out. I just barely avoided a midair by pulling up and to the right. As I pulled up, I was shocked to see the complete underside of the skipper's aircraft on the left, in a 90 bank to avoid the lead. That was the end of formation flying that night. I cobbed the power and climbed as fast as I could. Finally, I was able to get through to the ship on Guard, and they switched me to a clear frequency.

The skipper, now on his own, decided to make his own approach to the ship. We had no emergency Marshal information to fall back on, so he circled the ship and, when he saw a hole develop in the pattern, descended, jumped into the night recovery pattern, and flew a night, visual approach. No one knew for sure who (or what) he was, so he was waved off on the first approach. He flew a normal NORDO bolter pattern and recovered aboard on the second pass.

By this time I was feeling better. Approach gave me individual vectors, and I flew one of the nicest three-wire passes of my life. As it happened, I landed just behind the skipper. As I got out of the aircraft, I saw the skipper walking down the deck and somehow suppressed my urge to kill. The remaining *Whale* was having his problems. Just after he had put out his speedbrakes for his approach, he had a utility hydraulic failure. This was complicated by the fact he was now below dirty bingo fuel requirements. He had been given instructions to tank, and had rendezvoused and tanked dirty. In the process, his flaps had bled up. He didn't notice his increased approach speed on his first approach after tanking. He floated high over the top and nearly flew into the water on a long bolter, which I witnessed as I cleared the flight deck. The LSO recommended a bingo and the ship directed the same, even though he was 1000 pounds below dirty bingo fuel requirements. Fortunately, he flew a good profile, received good handling by Approach Control, and landed with 10 minutes of fuel remaining.

Well, that was it. As I look back at all the mistakes we made, it's a wonder we weren't all killed in one big midair. All of us had the opportunity, but refused to break the chain of errors that precedes most accidents. Get-home-itis (our floating home, that is), inexperience, and complacency all reared their ugly heads. I only hope that this article has given you a good example of **how not to do it,** and that you won't let yourself be led down the garden path by an overzealous skipper, as I did.

Touch-and-Go with the Grim Reaper

**Lt. Gordon Heyworth, VF-171 Det Key West;
December 1980**

The stench of jet exhaust and scorched tires and the deafening roar of a *Phantom,* just snatched out of the blackness, drift down the flightdeck. Four sets of eyeballs return seaward, scanning the glide slope for the next triangle of lights above an unseen horizon. "Geez, he's below the..." LSO–1 stopped short and keyed the UHF, "201, watch your altitude!"

The lights continue to settle slowly below the plane-guard's masthead light.

"201, watch your altitude! ... Don't go lower! ... CLIMB!" pleaded LSO–1. Frustration, horror, and grief pervade the platform as the *Phantom's* lights are snuffed out 1½ miles behind the carrier; with them go the lives of its crew.

Setting—The office of the Grim Reaper—two aviators in wet flight gear.

Reaper: Holy meatball, line-up, angle-of-attack! Let me guess... night CCA... yep. Been gettin' a lot of you guys over the years. Can spot 'em a mile away. No pun intended!

Pilot: I hardly think...

Reaper: Yeah, yeah. Don't like me making light of your misfortune? Tell me, Sport, anything mechanically wrong with that airplane you flew into the drink?

Pilot: Why, no, but...

Reaper *(to RIO):* And you, young fella, I suppose you were just along for the ride?

RIO *(protesting):* No, sir... my instrument lights didn't...

Reaper: Lights, schmights! That doesn't change a thing, does it? You two flew into the water. Look, I've been at this business a long time and I've seen more young, capable guys in front of me because of a moment's breakdown in instrument scan or just plain poor flight discipline. After witnessing so many ramp strikes and other senseless fatalities like your own, one just stops feeling sorry for the victims. You guys are responsible for your demise.

Pilot: Well, I had a lot of help.

Reaper: All right, self-righteous one, let's hear your story. *(Aside—You can always tell a fighter pilot, but you can't tell him much.)*

Pilot: In retrospect, I suppose the deck was stacked against us. But if I thought it would come to this, I'd have blown the whistle. The ol' can-do spirit got us, I guess.

Reaper: How so?

Pilot: Well, we started bouncing for this REFTRA [refresher training] 26 nights ago, my last three double FCLP [field carrier landing practice] periods having been the 7th, 9th, and 10th nights.

Reaper: I'm confused. Get to the point.

Pilot: What it boils down to is that I haven't had a night bounce period or a night hop in the past 17 days. I did all right at the boat yesterday and this morning, getting my one touch-and-go and 5 day traps, but that 17–day layoff sure caught up with me tonight. It wasn't like we weren't scheduled during that 17 days. In fact, we briefed five of the nine preceding nights. Briefs started anywhere between midnight and 0200. Problem was, maintenance was strapped for parts. We were low supply-priority 4 months prior to deployment. No jets—no fly.

Reaper: Sounds grim...

Pilot: ... to the tune of having only one or two "up" aircraft a night after a full day's schedule.

Reaper: Did you bring this to anybody's attention?

Pilot: Yeah... I talked to the Ops officer, but I was preaching to the choir. No one was getting his periods flown, and there were more junior pilots than I who were understandably higher priority. 'You can hack it,' the Ops boss said. Of course, I agreed. Boy, were we wrong.

Reaper: The record is written in blood.

Pilot: That's not all. The clincher was that the bird we launched in had no instrument lights in the rear cockpit.

Reaper: Bad idea. So the young RIO here *was* along just for the ride.

Pilot: Well, we didn't want to miss our overhead and have to come out to the ship again tomorrow night. I like being home at night as much as the next guy. At least I *used* to.

Reaper: Instrument lights ... I don't understand how that alone...

Pilot: It wasn't just that. It was, typically, 'all the wrong things happening at the right time.'

Reaper: How so?

Pilot: Off of a bolter, I established a good rate of climb toward 1200 feet and then commenced my down-wind turn shifting attention to roll-out heading, abeam position, etc., anticipating our next approach. Noticing that I had ballooned up to 1800 feet, I eased it down to 1400 (my usual 1200+200 gravy). On base leg, the ship called for a descent to 600 feet for a surveillance approach, at which time the TACAN started spinning. The final bearing also was changing, so here we were in a rate of descent, turning inbound, looking outside for the ship and lineup lights. If that wasn't enough, remember ballooning to 1800 feet? Make that *800*. Yep, I misread the altimeter by 1000 feet in my haste to turn downwind and preoccupation with everything else. My descent out of 1400 for 600 was actually out of 400 for ... well, you know the rest. If only *Paddles* could have called a few seconds earlier.

Reaper: Famous last words. You know ... [phone rings] ... excuse me ... Reaper here ... yes sir ... yes sir, they're right here in front of me ... I see ... right away, sir. [Hangs up phone.] You guys are in luck. I have it from higher up that you're going back and recover your aircraft at 200 feet when the LSO first called you. This is extraordinary, but it happens on occasion ...

Pilot: You mean? ...

Reaper: I mean get your butt on the gages, wave off, and take that aircraft home. You get a good night's rest 'cause you've got to finish quals tomorrow night. Oh, and while you're at it, why not share this experience with your cohorts.

Pilot: Roger that!

Back on the platform

LSO 1: ... Wave it off, 201 ... What's the problem?

CATTC: 201, climb and maintain 1200. Upon reaching, turn left 270.

201: 201 is RTB for cockpit lighting failure.

CATTC: Roger, 201. Signal Bingo; gear up; hook up; steer 282 for 78.

201: 201, Wilco.

The story above is fictitious where obvious. All other details are true. In fact, the LSO calls were received in time to avoid needless catastrophe. The author will be forever grateful for this service from the platform.

Oh What a Night!

Lt. D. J. Franken, VA-85; February 1981

It was a routine hop during night carrier operations in the month of March in the Mediterranean. The mission was straightforward enough—a single A-6 was to conduct a low altitude raid against the carrier about 1 hour after takeoff. The weather was forecast to be 2,000 scattered, 4,000 broken, with good visibility outside the scattered rain showers throughout the operating area. No problem. It was an easy hop for two aircrewmen with thousands of hours and nearly 1,700 carrier landings between them.

The crew briefed and planned a short overwater navigation route including several practice system attacks to be conducted prior to the primary raid mission. The takeoff and climbout were uneventful, except that the actual weather was considerably wetter than forecast. The A-6 was in and out of rainstorms and the crew noted an exceptional amount of static electricity buildup. At frequent intervals, the cockpit canopy was literally aglow with fingers of St. Elmo's fire.

The crew completed the navigation route, making several practice weapon releases, and proceeded to the designated starting point for the raid (50nm from the CV). The attack on the CV was performed at high speed. 1,000 feet AGL, and went like clockwork. Again, even at low altitude during the raid, the A-6 was engulfed in a heavy buildup of static electricity. Following the ship strike, the aircraft switched to Marshal and proceeded to holding.

In and out of the weather in Marshal, the A-6 pushed on time with a fuel state of 7.5. The B/N followed his routine procedures by setting up the computer for an *Intruder* approach and placing the radar cursors on the ship—a backup for the ship controlled TACAN/CCA. Significant turbulence was encountered throughout the descent.

Inbound at 250 KIAS, at about 12nm and level at 1,200 feet, the A-6 canopy area, radome, and refueling probe became covered with tongues of static electricity. Large streaks of blue fire were observed reaching out from and extending forward of the refueling probe. The pilot and B/N could not help but exclaim to each other that what they were witnessing was incredible! Blue slivers of electricity were extending 6–8 feet forward from the refueling probe! Suddenly, there was a loud, cracking boom and an intense flash of light followed by silence. Both men were blinded. Neither said a word at first, but each was wondering how long this temporary state of blindness would continue. Within the initial 10 seconds, the B/N extracted his flashlight, but with the red lens attached, the light was useless and neither pilot nor B/N could see anything. Meanwhile, the pilot held the controls as they were.

Nearly 15 seconds had now elapsed and the B/N rapidly began a fingerwalk along the center canopy bow, his hands tearing for the location of the thunderstorm lights switch. The pilot, meanwhile, applied a small amount of back stick. About 20 seconds after the flash, the thunderstorm lights were switched on and the crew recovered enough vision to interpret essential instrument readings. Happily, the A-6 was climbing through 1,800 feet, a little right wing down. Still extremely disoriented and experiencing blurred vision, the crew called CATCC and advised the controllers of their difficulties. The A–6 climbed to 2,000 feet and leveled off so the crew could get ready for the night approach that still had to be completed.

Several minutes in holding elapsed, and the crew agreed that it was time to continue for the landing. Other aircraft had been recovered, fuel state was becoming a definite consideration, and as always in the Med, a night-time divert was a less than desirable option. Accordingly, the crew called CATCC and informed them that the aircraft was ready to come aboard.

The A–6 received a vector inbound at 13nm, intercepted the final bearing, and dirtied up at 9nm. The pilot was concentrating on the instruments. The B/N was both monitoring instruments and looking outside the cockpit. Neither crewmember knew exactly how good or bad his vision was at this point. The A–6 commenced a Mode III approach. The B/N acquired the ship visually at about 2½ miles and realized that things didn't look normal—in fact, his vision was still somewhat fuzzy and blurred. At about a mile and a half, the B/N saw what he perceived to be a centered ball and notified the pilot on the ICS. The

pilot rogered the B/N's observation. With the A–6 at 1 mile, CATCC advised, "You're on centerline, below glidepath, call the ball." The B/N received an acknowledgement from the pilot that he also had a ball, advised the pilot that they were low, then called the ball over the UHF. At this point, both pilot and B/N saw a low, blurred ball. Seconds later the LSO called "You're low, work it up," soon followed by several emphatic LSO calls that the A–6 was low. Simultaneously, the B/N made several ICS transmissions stating "We're working a low ball." At less than ⅛ mile from touchdown, the crew still felt things just didn't look normal, and at about the same time full power was added, the A–6 was given a waveoff. It was then that both pilot and B/N realized just how low they had been as they chillingly noted that the low, blurred image of a ball they had been flying was in fact a low, "phantom" ball (ball actually off the mirror). The real ball appeared from the bottom of the lens as the aircraft waved off!

The A–6 turned downwind, set up for its next CCA, and trapped aboard with a "fair" pass. The crew retired to the readyroom and sank into their chairs to recount and debrief the previous half-hour . . .

A Terrible Trip

Lt. Cmdr. Ralph E. Arnott, VA–27; April 1981

It's been about 5 years, the shakes have stopped, and most of the guilty parties are in other occupations, so it's probably safe to tell the story of how many errors of judgment four experienced naval aviators can total up and still be lucky enough to walk away.

The Setting—NAS Southville

The Weather—Bad

The Training Aids—Two TA–4Js

The Players—Two experienced pilot flight instructors and two experienced pilots undergoing refresher training.

The Mission—Head west to greener pastures and clearer skies chasing the almighty "X" for fam, form, instrument, and tactical formation.

The Brief—

Ops Officer: You need to complete at least three 2–hour hops a day, including a night form hop, and have them back here in 3 days. Get them enough hours so they can bounce for the boat next week.

Maintenance Officer: That aircraft had some bad power applied to it at an AFB last weekend. We haven't been able to find anything wrong with it, but try to stay VFR the first couple of hops.

Skipper: Don't screw it up.

And so the odyssey was launched through a break in the overcast, between the thunderheads, to a standard rendezvous in a fair-sized sucker hole. As an "experienced" instructor, arms on the canopy rails, O_2 mask at half-mast, and enjoying the scenery, I noted we were closing the lead a bit fast. "He can hack it. He's an experienced refresher pilot," were my final thoughts. A brief scan of the horizon with thoughts of nachos and pitchers of margaritas and... "Oh no!!" With a fist full of forward stick, a handful of idle and boards, and a hearty "I've got it!" we executed the time honored slashing attack underrun.

After regaining composure and returning control of the aircraft to the student, we pressed on to AFB Halfway. About 15 miles out, I again took the aircraft so we could execute our prebriefed section landing. Shortly after dirty-up, my fearless front-seat veteran piped up, "Hey Ace, this is really neat. I've never done a section landing before." My reply was, "That's OK, neither have I!" The landing went well in spite of the front-seat occupant's constant calls to watch lineup, altitude, etc.

On the section takeoff for the next leg, our nose gear indicated unsafe, but a visual check by the wingman indicated the doors were flush. The obvious decision was ... press on for the almighty "X." Transient maintenance was unable to fix the faulty microswitch but assured us that the switch was the only problem, so we manned our *Skyhawks* for our night formation/NATOPS check. When the student complained that the light in the gear handle indicating the unsafe nose gear was distracting him, I informed him that if he'd take out the bulb and put it in his pocket, like I had in the back, it would solve the problem.

The next day proved even more interesting, as we started the tactical formation hops. Our comprehensive 30–minute brief (which also counted as the ground school brief) had to be a little rushed to make our restricted area time, but we were six wheels in the well shortly. Starting with mild maneuvering and gradually increasing the gyrations, we quickly reached our front-seat pilots' upchuck level and had to knock it off occasionally for the necessary cockpit cleanup. The other refresher pilot was doing quite well in his yo-yo maneuver, so I showed him my best last ditch maneuver. Out of the second reversal, the two droptanks of the other TA–4 passed close enough to our cockpit for us to count the missing fasteners on the hell hole door. That it was an excellent last ditch maneuver there was no doubt; whether or not it was prudent or instructional was open to some question.

The next day presented immediate problems since the available restricted areas were all booked up. Not to worry! A quick check of the chart showed a reasonably close area relatively free of airways. Quickly designating it the "Agony 69" area, we were off in section (with two sets of well-trained eyes on my nose gear) on a VFR flight plan.

As God takes care of idiots and drunks (we qualified on both account), we completed the hops and captured four more "Xs." It was time to head home. The two legs back would fill out the hours needed and we'd have the students in before midnight so they could start FCLP the next morning.

We made a short stop at Midwest AFB for gas. "You guys go on to the gedunk and order me a cheeseburger. I'll be right there after I get a quick weather brief." Twenty minutes later, they returned with a soggy burger, and I was still listening to this weather guesser who insisted on telling me about this wall of thunderstorms across our path. The buildups were in excess of 60,000 feet, with hail, rain, lightning, etc., but there was, or at least there might be, a narrow gap. Of course, we could hack it! He further delayed us by providing weather at several alternates, all of which were well short of where we were going to land. After finally appeasing this over-conscientious second lieutenant, we were back in our aircraft when the ODO's truck, complete with flashing lights, arrived. It was that pesky weather guesser coming all the way out and delaying our launch just to tell us there were funnel clouds sighted in the wall of thunderstorms. "Thank you, but we're experienced naval aviators. We can hack it. Besides, it's time to get home."

"Let's get moving. I'll do all the checks and the takeoff and copy clearance taxiing out. Oops, I almost ran off the taxiway. They don't make 'em as wide as they used to, but could be I'm a little tired. Cleared for takeoff, 85 percent check, what's that, Dash Two? Fuel venting out of my droptank? There's a little fuel venting, but we've got to make the gap in the storm, so let's press. And give me a thumbs-up for that nose gear."

Well, so far so good, but that line of thunderstorms didn't look all that inviting. I really wasn't sure yet, but I thought my right drop might not be transferring. We kept climbing and looking for a bright spot in the frontal wall. We were in it solid then, but it wasn't too rough. The droptank wasn't transferring yet, but I cycled the switch and got out the book for any other ideas. It was getting rougher. Boy, was it dark! We couldn't climb any higher yet because we had to drop the RAT for a last ditch attempt to transfer that droptank. We did some quick figuring and decided we just might be able to make Homeplate without that 2,000 pounds. We checked weather at Shortstop AFB just in case.

We finally found the thunder cell! The front-seat pilot couldn't maintain altitude within ± 1,000 feet! Dash Two was hanging on, but he looked scared.

"Center, Smoke 01 checking in Flight Level 290."

"Roger, Smoke 01. Do you have weather radar onboard?"

"Ahhhhhh, negative."

"Vector heading 100 to clear the worst of the storm."

Having taken control of the aircraft and completed the turn, I found that even I couldn't control the altitude within ± 1,000 feet! It was now becoming obvious there wasn't enough fuel to make Homeplate.

"Center, Smoke 01 requests destination change to Shortstop AFB."

"Understand; vector heading 100," was the controller's answer.

"Center, Smoke 01 declaring minimum fuel."

"Understand," said the controller.

"Wow! What a flash of lightning! What's that, Dash Two? My exterior lights are out? The switch is on, it looks like that A799 electrical problem wasn't A799 after all."

Meanwhile, the number two instructor, keying UHF instead of the ICS, stated in a loud and clear voice, "We're s——d." The controller replied, "Understand."

Number two had lost sight of us, so now we were bouncing 1,000 feet either side of assigned altitude in the thunder and lightning. Shortly afterwards, the exceptionally sharp Center controller had us on separate vectors. On the descent to Shortstop AFB, we broke out a little below 4,000 feet over a big southern city, with lights from horizon to horizon and lightning bolts to match. Things were looking up! It was only a few minutes to the AFB. As I breathed a huge sigh of relief, my ICS crackled with, "Hey Ace, what's that low oil light?" My reply was, "Hey Jay, that's a low oil light!" "Hey Ace, why don't we declare an emergency?" "Hey Jay, that's a good idea!"

"Hello, Center, Smoke 01 declaring an emergency with possible pending engine failure!"

After a short discussion concerning duty runway, gear available, etc., we found ourselves abeam the runway at 2,000 feet. I had never shot a night VFR precautionary approach, but it was time to land. A short while later, we were, believe it or not, safely on deck with Number Two right behind.

Later, four shaken pilots with libations in hand were trying to piece together how four experienced aviators could make so many mistakes in such a short time and escape relatively unscathed.

The next day, the oil level checked satisfactory and the lights worked fine. External lights on the lead aircraft worked as advertised. We had a droptank failure due to a missing gasket on the cap because of an improper pre-flight. A short, uneventful flight finally returned us to Homeplate.

Nothing wrong could be found with either aircraft, with the exception of the bad microswitch on the nose gear door. A few weeks later, the same aircraft threw a turbine blade, however, with the engine seizing on touchdown after an emergency landing. The overall reaction of the operations officer, OINC [officer in charge], etc., was "Nice job, you got them qualified for the bounce!" Well and good, but I just wonder what they would have said if any one of a number of things had gone wrong and we had dinged an aircraft, or worse. The almighty "Xs" weren't really worth it.

Experience by Proxy

My pilot was dead.
Cause: drowning.
Reason: unknown

Lt. Cmdr. Ted E. "Stump" Dewald, Phantom *RIO*, NAS Chase Field; October 1981

An autopsy showed no incapacitating injuries. Nonetheless, his life preserver was not inflated, his chute was still attached. He was observed in the water upon entry but never moved, apparently unconscious. In the chop and swells of the Pacific, the rescue swimmer could not save him. My fear was that I'd ejected him when he was not ready and stunned him into a deadly daze. This was proven false when the engineering investigation studying the recovered seat found he'd initiated his own ejection. What killed him?

He was a good student with only the normal growing pains coming through the RAG, but on one February night in 1978, we both took the final exam. We'd trapped aboard a pitching carrier deck when I fully expected a bolter. We'd been high when in-close, but he wisely left the power on and, thankfully, did not execute the standard student "go for it." The deck came up just as we cleared the ramp, resulting in a hard landing—but by no one's estimation hard enough to cause total failure of the centerline splice plates to which the wing spars were

attached. Still, that's exactly what happened! This was borne out when an engineering investigation uncovered massive corrosion and a crack in the splice plate.

The impact was unexpected and very hard, since all of the shock was taken by the fuselage and not one foot-pound was absorbed by the landing gear. The break was immediate, and my head fell forward harder than usual. When it came up again, all I saw was flames. I knew instantly that ejection was in order. The LSO, being of quick mind, pointed that out to us in case we had doubts. Finally, I found my handle and yanked. After several eternities, I "slipped the surly bonds" of the fireball below, followed closely by my pilot.

Everything tumbled, and though completely unhurt, I could not "cage" my conscious mind. I knew there was something I had better be doing, but I felt as if I were awakening from a deep sleep and struggled to find reality. By the time I managed to wake up, I was quite amazed. I had already inflated my life preserver and was preparing to detach my parachute! **I had already done these things**—uncommanded by my conscious mind.

Regaining the "present tense," I continued with my water entry procedures, and the rest of my story reads like an excerpt from NATOPS or a rescue manual. The ejection-to-rescue time was 2 minutes, but the critical first few seconds were carried out virtually unconsciously. But again, why was my pilot dead?

I asked myself that question over and over for months as I relived the incident repeatedly. Then, as suddenly and unexpectedly as the accident itself, a theory appeared on the horizon.

The very night of my ejection, I had listened to a fellow RIO describe his own carrier accident and ejection in great detail. I remembered that, as he talked, I could picture the crash, smell the air, feel the wind, and sense some of his sensations. I was almost living it! I was gaining "experience" in this emergency situation without having to be there. Of course it was not as vivid, but it was not as hazardous either. And it was vivid and real enough to my senses to firmly implant the event into the emotional and instinctive part of my mind. My nervous system had somehow been educated into "remembering" something I'd never experienced.

When it suddenly happened to me, just a few hours later, my conscious mind was jarred loose and became confused, unable to process the data and recall the procedure. The instinctive part of me took over while my reasoning part tried just to find "up."

At that time I had 1,100 hours, had heard about innumerable emergencies, and had known some of the participants involved. Every time I read about a friend or listened to a sea story, I was unknowingly receiving emotional preparedness training or *experience by proxy*. My pilot in that mishap had spent 2 years learning only NATOPS, raw facts, procedures, and whatever emotional training the stresses applied by the training command instructors could provide, which is considerable but not exhaustive. He had very little practical knowledge of "how he would feel in the event of . . ." He had never before ejected. I had. Only by "proxy" perhaps, but my

mind was familiar with the experience, and it was programmed with a backup system.

Theory? Maybe, and I treated it that way, too. But just in case, for the next year, I related the incident to every RAG class. I saw some of their eyes widen as I spoke, and I felt it was helping. Then, less than 1 year later, I got another piece of supporting evidence—firsthand—to substantiate my theory.

As if once in a career is not enough, I suddenly found myself looking down at the cold Pacific. I was again without my trusty *Phantom*, but this time it was from 24,000 feet. This ought to be a cinch for a veteran like me, right? Not quite.

Upon ejection at negative G, the 350-knot wind blast forceably removed my helmet and oxygen mask, which were both cinched tightly for ACM. The blast, or something else, knocked me unconscious momentarily. When the lights came on, I was again in a daze and operating at a reduced mental capacity (nothing close to the cool, collected state in which I studied the procedures for a high-altitude ejection). I noticed the ocean and realized I was quite high, but I was still concerned because I felt I was tumbling end over end. That perception, for starters, was wrong. I was merely spinning upright under my stabilizer drogue (just as stated in NATOPS). If I had remembered that, I probably would have realized the seat was working as advertised. Instead, I concluded that I did not have a parachute over me (correct) and that it must have malfunctioned (incorrect). I then pulled my D-ring, which was also wrong, since I had not released my seat pan first (NATOPS is quite clear on that). In my dazed condition, I did not know I was under a drogue, I did not know I had lost my helmet, I did not even feel the seat pan firmly attached to my rear or have a sense of being in it at all!

So I pulled the D-ring. Nothing happened. I considered the situation rather unexcitedly, I must say, but still did not realize the presence of *Martin-Baker's* finest attached to me. Though I was still muddled, that trusty H–7 ejection system knew its role precisely and performed flawlessly. I then felt a very positive jolt, and shortly thereafter, the bats left the belfry and I realized what had happened. I was in my seat all along and the H–7 was counting off the feet barometrically—from 24,000 feet, where it and I left the F-4 to 13,000 feet ($\pm$ 1,500 feet) MSL [mean sea level]. And when it got there, it deployed my chute and freed itself from me, as a good seat should.

From then on, the events closely followed the DWEST [deep water environment survival training] training, complete with an oscillating chute, parachute drag, partial entanglement, and helicopter pickup.

So where is any evidence of experience by proxy? Well, I'd never mentally put myself in the position of a high-altitude ejection. I'd never heard anyone describe the free fall from high altitude, so I didn't even recognize it, consciously or otherwise. My instinctive backup system was trained for pulling a D-ring but not riding a seat.

"So what? That proves nothing," you say. Maybe, but my pilot, who had never ejected, had heard a vivid description of the free fall, and he remembered. He knew he had to wait out the seat. In fact, he remembered even more! While anxiously awaiting his chute-opening, he saw mine open—well above him. He thought he then had a possible malfunction, but instead of pulling the D-ring, as I had, he remembered to beat the seat first and started with those procedures. His seat had merely been calibrated lower than mine, and his chute opened automatically before he could release himself from the seat. We had similar rescue experiences and are both around to tell the tale.

There are two points I wish to make. I think it would be well worth the effort, in terms of improving aircrew performance under stress and reducing accident and (especially) fatality rates, to devise a way to expose all aircrews to emotional preparedness training in the form of face-to-face briefings on "sea stories" by those involved. We're doing it to some extent in SERE [survival, escape, resistance and evasion] seminars, for instance, when we actually talk to an ex-POW. I get that same feeling of being there when I hear them speak as I did when my RIO friend described his accident. Consequently, I feel I have some idea of how I will feel if that situation ever happens to me.

In *Topgun,* we were exposed to an actual MIG killer and heard him speak. That kind of *war story* training acquaints us with the stresses and sensations of combat. And the biggest single source of this type of training is in readyroom sea stories on everything from combat to emergencies to liberty! (Hey, a good naval aviator has to be emotionally prepared for everything!)

I strongly believe a more organized and complete set of briefings by good storytellers who were actually involved in an aircraft mishap would greatly improve overall fleet preparedness to handle all types of combat, emergency, and survival situations.

My second point is aimed directly at all my colleagues. If you spend your whole career thinking "It'll never happen to me," you are ignorant. (I was told once that of all aviators who spend 20 years in the Navy, 52 percent ejected at least once. That, of course, excludes those who get killed trying to finish one cruise.) You will also be unprepared and cheating yourself out of an extra chance to live if it does happen to you. In terms of combat, you are cheating your boss out of a totally professional person able to perform in all respects. Besides, if you get the bad guy the first time, or blow up the target, or find and destroy the submarine immediately, you might prolong your own life in the process.

So, seek out the guy who has "been there" and ask him what happened and what he did. Above all, have him describe *what it felt like.* If you get enthralled and feel your heart beating harder, you are getting experience that will help keep you alive and effective. That kind of experience is less painful, believe me!

Look Out! Midair Collision in the CV Pattern

Richard A. Eldridge, Reprinted from August 1982; July 1985

"I then told the air boss I was overhead at 21,000 feet, dirty, with only one nosewheel tire. He told me I'd be recovered last. My recovery began at 1530. Taking up a heading of 240 degrees, I flew away from the base recovery course of 060 degrees. At 12 DME, I started a 2,000 to 3,000 fpm rate of descent with 180 knots, gear down, and flaps up. At 15 DME, 16,000 to 17,000 feet, I felt a heavy impact on my port wing and fuselage. I was looking out my starboard canopy at the time of impact. I then looked to port and saw an F-4 trailing a large amount of debris pitch up about 500 to 1,000 feet in front of my aircraft. The planform view that I saw of the F-4 was with the starboard wing slightly down (15 to 20 degrees). Before I could focus to make out any specific features, my aircraft departed to port.

"I seemed to be spinning, airspeed indicator showed zero, and altimeter read 15,000 feet. The controls were still movable, but I felt no reaction from the inputs. I put in antispin controls and then looked to see what the damage was.

"My port wing was badly mangled. At least one-half was completely gone, along with the MER from Station 1. Altitude was 13,000 feet, and at this time I decided to eject if I passed through 10,000 feet. I transmitted a Mayday at approximately 1532. The departure and spin were mild initially. Then, things progressively got tighter, with intermittent negative G and nose tuck. Passing 9,000 feet, using the upper handle, I ejected. I estimated my wing position to be 90 to 120 degrees angle of bank.

"I didn't see the F–4 during any of this evolution. Seat-man separation was normal. I inflated my LPA, took off my mask, deployed my seatpan, and checked for the position of my Koch fittings and the condition of my chute and risers. I released my chute when the raft hit the water. I swam to the raft, disconnected my seatpan, and climbed in."

The A–7 pilot was rescued uninjured and returned to the carrier by a SAR helo. Unfortunately, the pilot and RIO of the F–4 failed to survive this tragic midair collision and were probably killed at the instant of impact.

The A–7 had launched at 1339. Just after being catapulted, the pilot was informed that something had dropped off his aircraft. An airborne inspection by another aircraft revealed that the port nosewheel tire was missing. For the rest of that event, the A–7 was held overhead the carrier in a dirty configuration until its 1530 recovery began.

Air intercept control was the F–4 crew's assigned mission. They were to be controlled by one of the screen destroyers. Following a normal launch at 1525, the F–4 switched to the CAP [Civil Air Patrol] control frequency of a DD. When the RIO checked in, the DD controller did not acquire radar contact with the F–4 due to the large number of aircraft in the VFR pattern near the carrier. A transmission by the F–4 requested a Link–4 check from the controller. The F–4's final transmission acknowledged the DD's Link–4 status. This was 45 seconds before the midair.

In looking at the mishap, the most logical explanation was the failure of the F–4 crew to visually acquire the A–7 while climbing VFR. From what little debris was recovered from the two crash sites, evidence tended to corroborate that the F–4 struck the A–7's port wing from below and behind the A–7.

One factor possibly contributing to the mishap was the elevation of the sun. The A–7 would have remained in the same relative position in the F–4's windscreen all the way to impact, with the sun's position at the same constant bearing, although a number of degrees higher.

There was little likelihood that the A–7 would have observed the F–4 approaching from below and behind. Normal scan pattern in a holding situation would devote a minimum of attention to the rear quadrants.

Lack of significant damage to the A–7's Station 2 and 3 pylon fairings indicated the most probable point of collision was at Station 1. Since the wings of the F–4 presented a normal planform appearance to the A–7 pilot following impact, the point of impact was probably not in the wing area. It was later speculated that the impact occurred near Station 1 (MER and 6 Mk–76s) of the A–7's left wing and the F–4's forward fuselage area. This impact probably resulted in incapacitation or death of the F–4 crew and damage to the cockpit areas, precluding ejection. . . .

Nightmare

Lt. Cmdr. Pete Blackwood, Staff Safety Officer, COMSEABASEDASWWINGSLANT; September 1982

Helicopter search and rescue is defined by some as the only evolution in naval aviation in which we are willing to risk four invaluable crewmen and an extremely expensive aircraft to save a single life. As a professional helicopter pilot, I believe that judicious preparation for a search and rescue mission can alleviate all but the most unpredictable of hazards. However, as a wise man once said, "The best laid plans of mice and men . . ."

1915: Last day of a 3–week at-sea period. Flight ops are over. Preparations are underway for a port visit the next day. Winding down . . .

1930: Notification is received of a fishing vessel sinking 80 nm away.

1945: Experienced SH–3H helo crew is selected and assembled with CV engineers in readyroom. Plan is to lower a P–250 pump and its accessories to the distressed vessel. CV engineer will be lowered if HAC [helicopter aircraft commander] determines such an action is safely feasible.

2000: Weather is CAVU with a full moon, seas 3 to 5 feet with a short-interval swell, and 20 knots of surface wind—almost ideal for a night transfer.

2055: Rescue and escort helos are airborne. Briefing was thorough—crew continues to discuss general conditions and available options while en route. Overhead E–2C is providing comm link from SAR scene. Stricken vessel has an HF [high frequency radio], so helos, CV, E–2C, distant Coast Guard rescue center, and stricken vessel are all able to talk. How could things be better?

2200: Helos are on scene and assessing situation. Second fishing vessel is standing off, ready to assist. Stricken vessel is still high in the water, the ship's captain is calm on the radio. Boat is broadside to the 5–foot swells and DIW [dead in the water]. Antennas and fishing outriggers are everywhere. This isn't going to be easy.

2215: Several low passes have been made, and our helo is now hovering at 60 feet alongside distressed vessel. Bow is the only feasible transfer point. Tending line will be used as a tether on our hoist. We instruct vessel's crew not to fasten hoist hook or tether to anything! Decide it's too dangerous to attempt transfer of CV engineer. Place second fishing vessel off helo's nose to aid in providing visual horizon. Arm cockpit hoist guillotine circuit and brief crew chief to call for hoist guillotine if necessary. Illuminate guillotine switch with map light, just in case. Altitude coupler engaged, cyclic coupler off. "Easy right, easy forward, pump going down . . ."

2245: Sea state makes holding helo over stricken vessel nearly impossible. Back off . . . cyclic coupler and hover trim engaged. This time, pump goes down quickly and is on deck. Hey, that was easy! "MAD TRAIL" capsule illuminates. "What's going on back there?" Violent pitch of vessel causes hoist cable to cut into MAD skirt and become lodged there. Suddenly, helo nose pitchup of 5 degrees and left yaw of 25 degrees occur simultaneously! Pump is lodged against vessel's deck edge combing and a big wave has opened the gap between the helo and the vessel. The hoist is pulling us out of the sky! "Guillotine, guillotine!" BANG!

2300: Steady hover. Pulse gradually residing. Everything is okay. Transition to forward flight. Orbit overhead and explain our situation to everyone. Ask the vessel if he can possibly stay afloat until morning. "Yes, sir, no problem!"

Silence.

(Why are we here?)

Later that night, a very careful readyroom analysis of this incident provides some food for thought. No one ever thought to ask the distressed vessel if he could stay afloat until first light. After all, he was sinking! Our ship had a long overnight transit to its port call and did not wish to remain in the area longer than necessary. Communications were progressively degraded as the distress call went from the "sinking" vessel to the Coast Guard, then to the CV, and then to the helo crew. In our haste to be heroes, we attempted an extremely hazardous hoisting evolution that was unnecessary under the circumstances.

Well, we're older and wiser, and this near-mishap is only a nightmare to us now. However, here's a suggestion for SAR types for future reference. None of us in that four-man crew had ever considered arming the hoist guillotine circuit in our collective 38 years of experience. Why it occurred to us to do so that night is a mystery. However, next time you're out night flying, see how fast you can find the jettison selector, select "hoist" to arm the circuit, and place your finger over the "activate" button—all while in a dark cockpit in a coupled hover. But for that one precaution, there might be a decidedly different ending to this story. As I said in the beginning, "Judicious preparation for a search and rescue mission can alleviate all but the most unpredictable of hazards . . ." . . .

The Disappearance

Lt. Colin Sargent; November 1982

You were downwind in the carrier bounce pattern, flying a deep 90 this time before turning into the groove. During the last approach, you'd run into 48 knots of headwind right here at the 90, and it was funny—as if you were flying backwards for a while.

Everything looked great as you continued your turn. You liked wind adjustments. Wind was one of the variables that kept carrier ops interesting to a third-tour aviator like you. Fine tuning things a tad slower or faster. Working on that elusive 1 percent of finesse that can prevent everyday pilots from becoming . . .

Oh! What's that? Another hydraulic failure? Let's see now. No real problems, said the calm little voice that had pulled you through so many close ones in the past.

"Boss, 204's got fluctuating hydraulic pressure. I want to land."

"204, Roger."

Up ahead, the island's antennas and green eyes stared at you while you found the groove. Adept and calm, you flew a textbook approach to an extremely satisfactory arrested landing. That hit the spot! You felt the reassuring recoil of the No. 3 wire as you decelerated.

"Really nailed that one," you said to yourself, relaxing your inflight concentration a bit as you rolled to a stop. You looked around. A small rainstorm was sweeping across the carrier deck.

Another uneventful Monday.

Your mind took a snapshot of your postflight world. The island, the usual steam from the cats, the yellow shirt signaling for wire retraction and for you to pull your hook up . . . these small events on deck seemed like footnotes compared to the flight adventure you'd just finished writing in the sky.

Following the yellow shirt's signals, you raised your hook, folded your wings, engaged nose gear steering, and used brakes while taxiing clear of the area. Next stop, the dearming platform.

The little rainstorm was heading west now. Watching the storm, it didn't occur to you that you'd forgotten something **big.** Lulled by the familiar hand signals, you taxied to the No. 1 elevator, where the yellow shirt handed you over to the dearm taxi director. Guided by his directions, you continued forward until slowing to a stop 5 to 10 feet inboard of elevator No. 1. Raising your hands, you indicated you were ready for dearming.

Suddenly, the **big something** you'd forgotten about exploded into a fountain of pressurized reality gushing from the skein of aluminum veins beneath your wing. It gushed its way clear into your memory. The hydraulic failure!

It was then that you and your jet started moving again, nudged forward by residual idle thrust toward the edge of the carrier's steel cliff and a vertical drop to green seawater.

No amount of brake stomping could help you. Your hands were still up and visible above the canopy rails while you shook your head vigorously back and forth in answer to the director's signal for brakes.

Exasperated, you jumped on the UHF: "Boss, no brakes on 204!"

Two seconds later, the air boss was on the 5MC, screaming over and over, "Get chocks on that Navy jet—no brakes!"

Everyone froze.

Then, like Lilliputians, a dozen flight deck personnel in muticolored jerseys grabbed your main gear, wings, and control surfaces in an attempt to stop you.

They didn't have a chance. There were 48 knots of wind whipping across the slippery flight deck, and no chocks or obstructions were readily available.

By the way, looking down at you from his 32–foot perch in the island, your tower rep was extremely surprised by these events. In fact, he'd never heard your UHF report of hydraulic problems and was amazed to see you make an arrested landing instead of a touch and go. He'd been distracted by another recovery episode and couldn't even see well, much less hear the radios.

Perhaps you should have made a bigger deal of your hydraulic problem. At the very least, you might have remembered that you had one!

No one should have had to tie a string around your finger to remind you to consult your own pocket checklist. In stark black nouns and verbs, the blue plastic book stated that you were supposed to remain in the arresting gear until you could be pinned and towed away. Now the edge of the carrier deck was moving toward you very quickly. It was time for an instantaneous ejection decision.

Why had you relaxed your concentration once you had the trap in the bag? It was easy. A lot of pilots do it! Some helicopter pilots, for instance, let down quite a bit after they've finished negotiating a landing to the bob-bing spot of a *Spruance*-class destroyer, even though their tip path plane may be only half a rotor diameter away from the superstructure, ripping through the sky nearly as fast as the speed of sound.

Some multiengine pilots relax a little early during GCA rollouts, even though they're still buzzing down active runways.

Maybe quite a few naval aviators are letting their caution drop a bit prematurely—while they're finished with the sky flying but still right in the middle of some critical taxi situations . . .

Your brakes still wouldn't stop you, and surprise still showed on your face. Your silent indecision narrated the next few seconds as you reached immediately for the face curtain, then back into the cockpit, then back to the face curtain, only to remove your hands one last time as your Navy jet started over the side.

You and your aircraft disappeared from view.

That amazed you even more. In your years of flying, you'd developed a false sense of security in believing that the deck edge coaming (not designed to stop aircraft) and the personnel safety nets (also not designed to stop aircraft) would stop you. Those unreinforced steel rumors didn't hold you for an instant. And as far as the history of planes hanging in the catwalks was concerned, well, there aren't any catwalks around a carrier's elevators!

Everyone on the flight deck was watching you disappear.

One observer would later say, "If any man had seen the expression I did, when the pilot knew he was going over with the aircraft . . . it is one expression I'll never forget."

Another saw it this way: "Running toward the area, I heard the air boss say, 'Somebody do something with that airplane.' Then to see the vertical fin rising upward and over the side of the elevator. The flight deck was wet and slippery. I ran toward elevator No. 1, only to see aircraft 204 go over the edge."

Witness No. 3: "Suddenly I heard the boss yell over the 5MC, '204 has no brakes!' I turned to my right and saw the jet approximately 35 to 40 feet from the starboard side of the ship, traveling outboard. His speed was not excessive for taxi. Approximately 5 feet from the outboard edge of elevator No. 1, I saw the pilot's right hand reach for his face curtain. The aircraft proceeded over the side and paused momentarily (a split second) in a see-saw motion. The rest of the aircraft continued overboard and disappeared from my view."

Well, you haven't disappeared entirely, even though you diluted your survival chances by not ejecting. You egress the cockpit and swim to the surface.

Cold water can really douse the warm amnesia you get from overfamiliarity. From now on, your flights won't end until your engines are cold, you've drunk a glass of purple bug juice, and you're resting in your stateroom for the next launch.

The helicopters move in for the pickup.

Your legend may be soaking wet, but it's worth it—you're never going to let your caution roll over the deck edge again!

Real Aviators Don't Read NATOPS

Lt. Cmdr. John G. Holewa, HSL-35; January 1983

REAL AVIATORS

—Never read NATOPS: "Everyone knows NATOPS is for Nurds, Safety is for Sissies."

—Don't believe in briefs, debriefs, or checklists: "Whoever learned about flying by talking about it?"

—Don't believe in preflights (unless someone is watching them): "This aircraft has had its daily, hasn't it? . . . If it flew in, it'll fly out."

Famous **REAL AVIATORS**	Famous **NATOPS Readers**
George Peppard	Jimmy Thach
Waldo Pepper	Alan Shepard (except
Wrong Way Corrigan	when golfing)
Mickey Rooney and	John Glenn
William Holden	Robert Crippen
Humphrey Bogart	Anymouse
Slim Pickens	Grampa Pettibone
Robert Duvall	Every Gray Eagle
John Wayne	
Robert Conrad	
Dilbert	
Jonathan Livingston	
Seagull	
Anybody in *Launch 'Em*	

REAL AVIATORS

—Always have nicknames like Sluggo, Speedy, Ace, Dusty, Ski, or Big (anything).

—Never write "up" gripes: "Leave those for the nuggets."

—Always have personalized flight gear, to include the mandatory helmet lightning bolts and nametags with Sluggo, Speedy, Ace, Dusty, Ski, or Big (anything) on them.

—Always add at least 1,000 hours to their flight time when in a bar (2,000 if females are present).

Recommended REAL AVIATOR Diet

Breakfast

—Bowl of cigarettes

—Gallon of coffee (add sugar if night flying tonight)

—½ dozen donuts (except if flight physical within 2 weeks)

Lunch

—2 or 3 *Hershey* bars (must be consumed during climbout)

—*Diet Pepsi*

Supper

—2 TV dinners

—½ gallon *Baskin-Robbins*

—1 pitcher of margaritas (salt on glass mandatory)

REAL AVIATORS

—Never submit NATOPS changes: "They should have written it right in the first place . . . Why change something I ain't gonna read anyway?"

—Always log all their night time as instrument time: "3710 is all screwed up."

—Never memorize all those niggly limitations: "They wouldn't have painted little white and red stripes on the gauges, right?"

—Think crew rest is when the autopilot is on.

Things You'll Never Find in a REAL AVIATOR'S Flight Suit

1. NATOPS Pocket Checklist
2. TCA [terminal control area], sectional, or any other *current* chart
3. Earplugs
4. Flashlight (**REAL AVIATORS** don't fly at night.)
5. Flight gloves (who wears flight gloves?)

10 Things You'll Always Find in a REAL AVIATOR'S Flight Suit

1. Screwdriver or a "Snoopy" dzus key
2. Twelve-bladed *Swiss Army* knife complete with *Phillips* screwdriver
3. Butane lighter
4. 10-year-old Falcon Code list
5. *Vick's* nasal spray
6. 4 old *Contac* capsules
7. 2 Caesar's Palace poker chips
8. Little black book alphabetized by cities with good country-western bars adjacent to AFBs
9. Program from last year's Tailhook Convention
10. Dicecup

REAL AVIATORS

—Don't believe in DD-175s; they file in flight.

—Don't believe in TCAs and all that other ATC [air traffic control] garbage: "It's my word against some controller, and after all, I'm the **REAL AVIATOR!**"

—Don't study tactics: "Leave that for the eggheads and ground-pounders in Washington."

—Hate helos until it's dark and they're wet and scared.

SQUADRON BILLETS

REAL AVIATOR	**NATOPS READER**
—Functional check pilot ("I can really wring it out . . . Push it to the limits.")	Commanding Officer ("Doesn't fly enough to be a **REAL AVIATOR**.")
—Stan pilot ("He got it started, out and back, and shut down without looking at the book once. He done real good!")	Executive Officer ("Too worried about setting a good example to be a **REAL AVIATOR**.")
—Instrument check pilot ("He remembered it was white on top, black on the bottom for the	Safety Officer ("Real Pansy.")
	NATOPS Officer ("Even bigger Pansy.")
	Maintenance Officer ("Spends far too much

whole hop. He done sorta good.")

time preflighting.")
Administrative Officer ("Ever heard of a **REAL AVIATOR** who pushed paper?")
Operations Officer ("He's too worried about whether he divulged any classified info on his last phone call.")
Flight Surgeon ("You must be kidding!")
LSO ("You must *really* be kidding!!")

What Do They Do when They Get Out?

REAL AVIATORS
Crop duster
Bush pilot
Air America (etc.) pilot
Used car salesman
Bookie
Numbers runner
Stuntman
Get bolder

NATOPS Readers
Airline pilot
FAA consultant
NTSB [National Transportation Safety Board] investigator
Insurance salesman
Stockbroker
Banker
Department-store floor-walker
Get older

REAL AVIATORS

—Never exercise: "You only have X amount of heartbeats . . ."

—Never fool with instrument hoods: "It interferes with my scan."

—Never report overspeeds, overtemps, etc., because **REAL AVIATORS** "Never have overspeeds, overtemps, etc." Besides, "Some four-eyed engineer has added a fudge factor."

REAL AVIATOR Vocabulary and Cliché Guide

"Gizmo(s)"
"Doodad(s)"
"It came off in my hand, Chief."
"Waveoff, hell. I had the ball."
"I swear, it never came close to redline."
"You have to go out, you don't have to come back."
"What do you mean I need an alternate?"
"If he knows so much, how come he's not a flier?"
"Name me someone who doesn't blow a tire now and then."
"Mayday"—A term used by doctors in *Cessnas* and Air Force tansport drivers. Used only once by **REAL AVIATORS** in VT–1.

REAL AVIATORS

—Gaff off NATOPS quizzes: "There goes the NATOPS puke getting his FITREP [fitness report] filler again."

—Don't believe in aerodynamics, they just "cob it."

—Always wear rings while flying (except wedding rings on cross countries).

—Always plan their annual leave during the squadron annual NATOPS evaluation.

REAL AVIATORS

—Never go around.
—Never go around thunderstorms.
—Never go around anything.

FAMOUS LAST WORDS BY REAL AVIATORS

"Just throw it in the back there."
"It's better to die than look bad."
"If it's not leaking a little, this isn't a real (fill in aircraft type)."
"It's probably just the gauge."
"The weather was fine when we took off."
"Let me show you how it's really done!"
"Hugging the ground really develops my flying skills."
"What mountains?"
"I've got this route memorized."
"NOTAMS [Notice to Airmen]?"
"This LSO (LSE) doesn't know his paddles from a hole in the ground."
"We can go a little further if we just (pick one)."
  —Lean out the mixture.
  —Pull one out of FLY.
  —Feather No. 1.
  —Get it down in ground effect.
"If this SOB will hover, it'll fly."
"You've got it!!!"
"OK, No. 3, we're not going to make it. Tuck it in, and let's look good!"

**Commanding Officer's Guide For
Mishap Investigation Report Endorsements
"He was our best pilot .. a REAL AVIATOR."**

Into the Island:
An NFO's Eye View

Lt. Michael C. Wade, Reprinted from March 1983;
March 1985

Windy and choppy seas surrounded us as we walked on elevator No. 2, where our EA–6B *Prowler* was spotted for the 1800 go. The sun had just set, and I knew we were facing a black, moonless night. We were slated for a routine night ECM raid against the USS *Richmond K. Turner* and a dark night would aid us in avoiding fighters. I was flying as ECMO 2 in the right rear seat of the aircraft. Our crew consisted of a nugget ECMO [electronic counter measures officer] 1, experiencing one of his first Case III launches, an experienced pilot and me, a second-cruise Lieutenant.

We'd just returned to sea from a long Christmas stand-down in Naples, Italy, and this was our first night flight in more than three weeks. Our brief was thorough, and we, as a crew, had elected not to wear our wet suits because the air/water temperature was one degree above NATOPS minimums.

Preflight in the gathering darkness was normal. I checked the top of the aircraft, the ECM pods and then strapped in. The engines were started, checklists performed and radio checks completed expediently. While we waited for taxi directions, I noticed that the ship was now rolling and pitching quite heavily and thought to myself that it would be a hell of a night to punch out. Our turn came, and we armed our seats and taxied in line for catapult No. 1. By now the darkness was complete.

Sitting behind the catapult, something came over me and I began to prepare more meticulously than usual for the coming shot. I'd never been unprepared, but I'd become a bit careless. Tonight I arranged my LPA perfectly and positioned my toggles where I could find them quickly. I adjusted my ejection seat, positioned my arms and legs and gave my lapbelts and torso harness an extra tug for snugness. Finally I located the lower ejection handle and locked my harness.

The whoop and an S–3A careening off the cat ahead of us and the bang of the piston hitting the water brake signaled our turn. We taxied forward onto the cat and went into tension. I heard the engines spool up to full power, our ECMO 1 finished the takeoff checklist and the pilot signaled for launch. I braced for the acceleration, but we delayed momentarily while the cat officer waited for the bow to come up in the swells. I felt a bump and momentarily felt acceleration, but as suddenly as it started, the G-forces slacked and we were moving down the catapult track far too slowly for takeoff. My first reaction was disbelief—that I was really having a nightmare. But I came to my senses quickly and realized that the cat had somehow failed and was probably pulling us slowly off the bow.

The rear seat of the EA–6B contains only one instrument, an altimeter, and allows no forward vision. I looked to the right and left and saw only blackness. The aircraft was still moving forward at full power, though, and I figured we had three or four seconds before the bow. I heard the pilot say *get ready* over the ICS, and without hesitation, I pulled my lower ejection handle when four seconds had passed.

The seat went off with a loud bang, and I zoomed into the darkness. During the ascent, I instinctively began performing IRK (Inflate-Release-Koch), my low-altitude version of IRSOK [inflate, release, snap, oxygen, Koch]. I remember feeling my LPA inflate as I neared the silent apex of the ejection arc and then the comforting bang of the chute snapping open in the wind. Hanging in my chute, I turned around and found myself 200 feet above the bow, facing the ship and a flight deck crowded with airplanes. Things began to happen quickly as my chute, buoyed by a 50–knot wind, accelerated me into the island. I dropped my raft and braced for a collision with the superstructure. I saw the yellow deck lights close with a blur just before I felt the sharp jerk of my canopy snagging something above, twisting me around and slamming me into a steel bulkhead. I hung briefly, the wind knocked out of me, then dropped like a stone.

Because it was black below, I knew I was over the water, so I released my chute, crossed my legs, folded my arms tightly over my chest and straightened my body so I'd hopefully hit either feet first or head first. I was concerned about getting knocked out, bursting my LPA or breaking a limb. I entered the water feet first, almost vertically, and in spite of my LPA I stayed under for several seconds. Those moments under that cold black water were chilling to the marrow, and every molecule in my body strained to get me to the surface. When I broke the surface, my raft was floating a foot away and my chute was gone. (Later I learned that I'd collided with the aux conn of the navigation bridge and fallen 100 feet to the water.) I was heartened when I realized I'd ejected safely, survived both a collision with the ship and a 100–foot fall and was now floating with a good LPA/raft, clear of my chute and four feet from steel. I thought I had it licked and would be back in the ready room in a few minutes with a great sea story. So I began to let down. That was a mistake. Fifteen seconds had passed since the catapult had failed.

I swam away from the ship, mindful of the screws and turbulence. When I'd moved far enough away, I attempted to enter my raft but neglected to use the proper technique and tried to pull myself onto the raft without first attaining the proper body position. Finally, after several unsuccessful attempts, I used the proper technique. Again I was thwarted, because I hadn't removed my butt plate. (I'd left it on because I couldn't remember where the retaining lanyard was and was afraid of losing the raft.) I disconnected the butt plate and managed to enter the raft but was constantly turned out since the sea was so rough and the wind was so high. The effort of getting into the raft was tiring, and after about four or five attempts, I was exhausted. Next, my oxygen mask went slack on my face, indicating the bail-out bottle was empty. I discarded my mask and let go of my raft because the sound of an approaching helicopter indicated that my rescue was imminent.

I turned my attention to signaling the helicopter and tried to open my vest and get out my strobe. I had difficulty locating the tab in the darkness, and because I was becoming extremely agitated, I attempted to rip it open with brute force. The ship had disappeared behind the waves, and I was cut off in the towering seas. Without the oxygen mask, I was having trouble breathing in the waves and spray and I was frightened and beginning to panic. My water survival training and discipline came through, however, and I calmed myself, then methodically located my equipment in the darkness. I found my strobe and placed it in my helmet, fetched a day/night flare and set off the night end. By now I could see the helicopter working his way upwind, and my hopes soared. Six minutes had passed.

The helicopter hovered around me for some time without stabilizing, and it was obvious that he was having extreme difficulty maintaining a hover in the 15–foot seas and 50–knot winds (he also had a malfunctioning doppler). For about 15 minutes, he drifted around me erratically. At one point I glimpsed a SAR swimmer arc through the air at the end of the rescue hoist and disappear into a wave. I never saw him again, but he did manage to return safely to his helicopter, stripped of his mask and flippers. Seeing his difficulty, I feared that the water was too rough for the helicopter to effect my rescue. The helicopter began to fly upwind, then drift back, trolling the harness near me. On the third attempt, I saw it about six feet away and managed to lunge out and grab it. Unfortunately, the helicopter couldn't see that I had hold of the harness and continued to circle. I was dragged for several seconds, still clinging desperately to the horse collar with my numb fingers. Finally, during a brief pause in movement, I scrambled to the top of the collar and snapped my "D" ring in. I was now going wherever that helicopter went, but the helicopter continued to fly about, searching for me, and I was dragged helplessly behind. This nightmare continued for about a minute, and all the time I was struggling for air and concerned that I might be rendered unconscious by the beating I was taking. Suddenly the cable went very slack as the helicopter reversed course. Frantically I signaled that I was hooked up, but there was no response, and the helicopter began to move away rapidly, taking up the slack. Soon the cable snapped taught, jerking me out of the water to my knees, at which point my "D" ring merci-fully failed and I fell back into the water, dazed and struggling against a wave of blackness. I knew if I blacked out for even a few moments that I would drown.

My head cleared slowly, and I realized I was alone and concluded that it had been deemed too risky to attempt further rescue. I'd been in cold water for 30 minutes now without a wet suit, and I was feeling signs of hypothermia. I couldn't maintain the huddle to conserve body heat, because I needed my limbs to swim and balance myself in the high seas. The balance was needed to control my breathing between the spray and the waves breaking over my head. I was further demoralized when I found that the violent jerk of the harness had ripped my radio loose and I couldn't even talk to another human being. My hands and lips were numb, my strength was waning and I slipped to the lowest point of my life. My realization that death was near was depressing me, and the isolation was sapping my will to live. I could only see ships and lights occasionally as I crested a wave. I was dying alone in a blackness pierced only by the strobe light marking my position in the night.

After five or 10 minutes of solitude, I heard the comforting sound of an approaching helicopter and came out of my depression. I took steps to beacon my position and popped more night flares. The helicopter soon saw me and hit me with a searchlight from about 60 yards downwind. With the Aldis lamp on me, I popped two of the day-end flares to aid the pilot in determining the wind and watched the pilot creep up slowly until he was 15 yards away. There he lowered a SAR swimmer part-way down so the swimmer could signal my position to the hoist crewman, who relayed it to him. This was very successful, and soon the helicopter harness was within 15 feet of me. At this point, the swimmer leaped off the harness and swam over to me and my spirits soared.

The SAR crewman asked my condition, checked me for injuries and then started towing me back to the harness, which was drifting away. We weren't making progress toward the drifting harness, but the hoist crewman above was alert to this, so he ran out all of the cable to stabilize the horse collar in the water. We reached the harness, and both of us grabbed it and were towed a few feet before it stopped. In an instant, I crawled into the collar, the swimmer snapped us in and we were hoisted into the helicopter. We returned to the ship, and I was treated for exposure and a gash in my arm. I'd been in the water for 45 minutes! . . .

Feast or Famine

Lt. Cmdr. Robert L. Payne, Jr.; September 1983

After all, I've got almost 2,000 hours in these aircraft. (Something's not right.) Wait, I've got over 200 hours just in this helo! Yup. We've been through a lot together. (We shouldn't be settling—why is the noise level changing?) This is a detachment helo—one of the finest you'll find! (I can't believe it—a load on and an engine at ground idle? It won't fly like this! Maybe it's the gauges? Maybe that's why we're settling into these other loads on the deck?!) I've got some *time* in this aircraft—not only flying it—I've watched the crew change the rotor heads—the blades are trimmed to perfection; I've even helped wash the old buzzard! (I have to *do* something—*now!* OK—turns are 88 percent going down—Take control of the aircraft.)

"I've got it!" (Do I really? Or has it got me?) I need power and turns—too much chatter on ICS/UHF/VHF—I can't even hear myself call for load release. (I still don't believe it, but there it is—No. 2 has just let me down.) The Engine Condition Lever is in "fly." Why? No. 1 is at topping power. I've got to get clear of the flight deck. No room to land! OK—Rotor RPM has stabilized—load has been released. (These crewmen are *great!*) I milk the collective—it's a fine line of lift versus drag. (I almost failed that class!) In our case altitude versus "turns." I've got emergency throttle armed—should I use it? No—RPM is stable—worry about missing the loads and then the deck edge nets. We've got to get some airspeed. (My crew seems to be responding faster than I can perceive.) We clear the nets—I push the nose over. (I've practiced it a thousand times. It's worked before, but somehow knowing it's not a self-induced failure makes it all seem unreal.) Ground effect—freeze the collective—a little right yaw. "Fuel dumps on." (That's me? The training is coming back—it *does* work!)

"OK—we've got an engine failure—let me know when you're all ready for possible water entry." (Now where in *** is the carrier? I'll never get it back to home-plate on one engine—deck is prestaged for the day's VERTREP [vertical replenishment] evolution.) The crew reports ready! (Faster than I expected—they are *really* fast!) Copilot has completed the single-engine checklist—APP is started and switched over. Airspeed is coming on—I note No. 1 at topping power, No. 2 still at ground idle—maybe the ECA has failed—try beeping up emergency throttle on No. 2—nothing—no change—I've got 65 knots, still 88 percent rotor RPM, I turn towards the carrier. "Yankee Three Bravo—Hotel Whiskey Fourteen has one engine out requesting immediate landing." "Roger—cleared immediate spot three—uhh—make that green deck on the fantail." (I think for the first time we might make it!)

What the #%&*@! Suddenly we got power—I mean *lots* of power—turns! Too much? RPM goes over 104 percent—pull collective—that engine is back on the line! "Reset No. 1 engine emergency throttle." (I've heard too many stories of eager pilots inadvertently burning up the good engine—besides I sure don't need RPM at the moment.) I roll rotors level with a bead on the carrier about one mile off. We're climbing like bandits—maybe I should pull the ECA circuit breaker? Too late! No. 2 is back to ground idle! Rotor RPM has dropped to 94 percent—I drop collective a little until I see we are stable again and now at least we have airspeed and a little altitude. (Brother, was that fast! Feast or famine! One extreme to the next—come on baby! We're almost there!)

"Hotel Whiskey Fourteen—abeam—fixed gear—four souls onboard." Did he answer? Don't remember. No. 2 is back on again! RPM not too high this time. Turning final, I call for the landing checklist. (I can't believe how calm my crew is!) Copilot goes through every item carefully—reminds me fuel dumps are still on. "Landing check complete, call for fuel dumps." "Roger—secure dumps." (We went from a full bag of fuel to about 500 pounds each side in this short period of time.) "Dump secured." Our landing is uneventful—a no-hover, low-power required landing. As we complete the shutdown checklist, I can't believe what has just transpired! I've got an LSE trying to signal me to fold it up and the crew scrambling to get blade tiedowns. I get out on shaky legs—pat my crew on the back—what a job they did! We done good! Did emergency procedures work? Yup. Did it pay to practice it time and again? Yup. (I've got too many hours in this thing—it wouldn't *dare* quit on me! Would it?)

Yup.

Hard Knocks

Lt. S. D. Hissem, VF-21; December 1983

When my pilot and I settled into our readyroom chairs to listen to the brief for that night's hop, we had little idea that we would not be back for our standard midrats and card game. Instead, we would have been through a hard school and learned lessons which would stay with us for many years to come.

We had been operating off Westpac Divert for some time and had become comfortable with the area. There was no moon but the weather that night was clear with a well defined horizon. The mission was a routine combat air patrol that went as briefed, and we marshaled with only a little trepidation about that night's pass.

Soon, however, it became apparent that this was not going to be an easy night. The first pass was a technique waveoff which was followed by a long bolter. On our trick or treat pass we were again waved off, and we called that we were "bingo."

We turned to our divert heading, accelerated to climb airspeed and began our climb when departure advised us that a tanker was available.

We were soon to learn about hard knocks.

Despite our previous problems, we wanted to come back and get aboard. This time we *knew* we could do it. We knew we could prove ourselves, and this, more than anything else, forced the decision for us.

I told departure, hedging my bets, that we would continue on our bingo heading but that we would hold our altitude to let the tanker catch up. In a climb, he would have had no chance.

With the lights of the coast glowing on our nose, we continued on. After a time I spotted the tanker joining on our left side.

My pilot remained unsure of the tanker's position. I tried to keep him advised by describing the tanker's join-up and crossunder. As the tanker slid in, I advised him that the tanker was "in close, nice and tight. He's real

close, he's . . ." and I realized in that awful second that it was all wrong as the tanker bore in. "Left, left, come left!" I called as I instinctively ducked my head in the cockpit. Too late for action, the tanker struck us and, as I looked up, fell away into the night. Later we learned that they had called for the lead and then assumed they had it even though we had not replied. We had, in fact, heard nothing.

We had been scared, but we were okay. The aircraft was still flying, still pointed towards our divert field. When we heard that the tanker was okay and heading back to the ship, we knew that we had been lucky.

But the night wasn't over and neither were the hard knocks.

We called bingo again and this time meant it as we followed all the procedures and climbed to altitude. Calling divert approach, we advised them that we were emergency fuel and that we had had a midair, though there was no apparent damage.

We earned immediate respect with that call. After clarifying several more times that we were okay, we got vectors to the field.

The divert asked if we wanted to make an approach to the off duty runway, which was more direct. They also asked if we needed an arrestment. Our fuel looked good so we declined the downwind landing and decided that an arrestment was not indicated.

That was true, but that was not why we made the decision. At that time a field arrest required a hook point change that would have kept us on deck and delayed our return to the ship. Once again we felt that we had to get back to the ship as quickly as possible, but this time in order to explain to the skipper what had really happened that night. We "knew" we were being accused of hitting the tanker, rather than the other way around, and before things got blown out of proportion we wanted to tell our story.

We vectored towards final, lowered the gear and flaps and checked controllability, which was normal. On landing we deployed the chute and began a standard rollout. Just as we passed over the approach and arresting gear, the aircraft began a left drift.

I'm not sure why I knew that we had blown a tire; I certainly hadn't heard anything. Perhaps being keyed up, I sensed things more closely, or more likely I had become fatalistic. I know I wondered to myself "What else could possibly go wrong?["] Whatever the case, the immediate action steps come to mind and I called for nosegear steering.

Looking back, there are many things I might have done differently. Had there been time, I might have told the pilot to be sure and center the rudder pedals before selecting nosegear steering, but there really was no time. I might have remained silent and let my pilot work out things for himself. My call may have interrupted him and caused him to skip over that vital step, but I know I could not have remained silent on the hope that the "other guy" would take care of everything.

It remains that upon selecting NGS with the right rudder pedal fully depressed, we swung wildly to the right and ended up staring at the runway down our left shoulders doing over 100 knots.

The aircraft swung back and forth several times as the pilot fought to gain control and get the aircraft at least heading in the same direction that the gear was pointed. She finally steadied out but 30 degrees off runway heading. As we approached the edge of the runway, I told my pilot that I was staying with the aircraft. I thought briefly about the advantages of securing the engines to save a possible FOD, but more important to me was keeping electrical power so I could communicate with my pilot in case anthing *else* happened.

The aircraft rode well through the grass and quickly came to rest. We told the tower where we were, then shut down the engines and egressed.

Now it was over. We wouldn't return to the ship that night or for many more to come.

We were unhurt and the aircraft was only slightly damaged. All four tires were shredded, but, despite going off the runway, we had damaged only one brake line. In the midair, we discovered the tanker had hit our starboard wing pylon which had jettisoned upon impact and fallen into the sea. The tanker itself had been unhurt as the pylon tumbled over its left wing. . . .

Censored-mice Arise!

Lt. John Flynn, editor; February 1984

An Anymouse form was submitted recently, which described an illegal and dangerous action by a pilot airborne. It was one of those judgment errors that many pilots have made and several have died from. In this case, some skillful airmanship and a lot of luck prevented a disaster. The incident was not officially recorded except for the Anymouse. The pilot happened to be the commanding officer. A postscript on the Anymouse read:

"If you print this, please wait until (a later month). I transfer (then) and the CO will recognize this and bury me if you print it before then."

My first reaction was to dismiss this as a crank remark. But after careful reflection, I remembered times when I would have felt just as nervous about submitting an anonymous report. Then, with uncanny timing,

another Anymouse arrived, saying that a squadron CO was requiring Anymouse forms to be chopped through him before being sent to the Safety Center!

Let it be known that you can always submit an Anymouse. You don't need to chop it through anyone, put your name on it, or even have the proper form. You can mention names, dates, squadrons and any other details you feel are necessary. We will pass the information along to those in positions to do something about the problem, where applicable. If we decide to print your Anymouse, we will then "sanitize" it to protect the identities of all concerned. If you want us to delay printing it, we can honor that.

Communication is vital to safety. Personnel must have a means of passing along safety information without getting "put on report" for it. Anymouse is a means to do that for everyone from E–1 on up. Sure, we get "crank" and "poison pen" submissions from time to time that contain no safety information. We put those where they belong—in the wastebasket. But action gets taken on every legitimate safety problem submitted.

A Look Back:
Forty Years of Reminiscing

Richard A. "Chick" Eldridge, Approach writer; February 1984

This article is different from those I have written during the past 21 years. It is a swan song, a way of saying sayonara to my long association with naval aviation.

My first thoughts about naval aviation were generated by an advertisement in men's magazines of the early

'40s showing a newly designated Ensign leaning on the prop of an F4U Corsair. The poster to the right was another effective inducement. Both enticed a lot of aspiring aviators, myself included, to try for those coveted wings of gold.

I was accepted by the Navy in August 1942 for flight training. My original designation of seaman second class was shortly changed to aviation cadet. Although originally ordered to report to preflight school at Chapel Hill, North Carolina in November 1942, I was allowed to finish college and report to Athens, Georgia in April 1943.

In those years the preflight schools were structured into three main areas of concentration—academics, athletics and military aptitude. Like several thousand other cadets, I will carry some memories of those days with me to the grave. Those who spent hundreds of hours marching in the red clay of Georgia under a broiling sun will never forget those hard-bitten Marine drill sergeants fresh back from Guadalcanal. Talk about marching to the tune of a different drummer!

I remember the infamous "pack test" which all cadets had to take upon entering and leaving preflight school. The test must have been the brainchild of some sadist to test the staying power of prospective aviators, when their every instinct was to quit and sit down. It involved toting a pack of sand on your back, the weight of which was based on your weight. You then had to step up and down about two feet, with an iron bar to hold onto for balance. This was kept up for five minutes to a rhythmic beat of about 15 per minute. The purpose of the test was to measure the time it took the heart to return to normal after the five minutes of exertion. I sure hope the medics learned something from this torture.

The athletic instructors at preflight school were naval officers recruited from the ranks of professional and college athletes whose names were well known to sports buffs. There was Dale Burnett, a back from the New York Giants and Billy Patterson, an All American halfback from Southern Methodist. Our hand-to-hand combat instructor was Ed Don George, the former heavyweight wrestling champion of the world. There was no lost motion in the curriculum. It was three months of rugged sports participation, with battalion competition on the weekends, a no-nonsense course of academic instruction, mostly in naval subjects, and the never-ending drudgery of military drill. If the aviation cadet failed to finish preflight a better individual physically, mentally and academically than when he entered, it wasn't the Navy's fault. In retrospect, I feel that preflight was the best organized and well run school I attended in the Navy.

Following preflight, I was introduced to my first taste of hands-on flight training in the venerable N2S—a very forgiving biplane trainer (nicknamed the Yellow Peril). For the most part, primary flight training was a thoroughly enjoyable, most interesting three-month stint of new experiences. One humorous incident of my primary days occurred to a cadet the day after we had received our lecture on the use of the parachute.

When the student reported to the flight line for his first flight in a naval aircraft, he was incorrectly listed on the scheduling board as a C stage (acrobatics) student. No words were spoken as the instructor and student manned the N2S. After takeoff, they climbed to the acrobatic area where the instructor promptly demonstrated a beautiful slow roll. After the slow roll, the instructor attempted to talk to the student via the gosport but got no response. When he turned around and looked into the rear cockpit—the student was gone! The cadet had forgotten one important thing on his first flight—to fasten his safety belt. However, he didn't forget his parachute lecture and was one of a small minority who joined the Caterpillar Club on his first flight.

To my recollection, there was little emphasis on aviation safety. What safety information was imparted to the fledgling aviator came from the primary instructors. Lessons learned usually came in the form of "gems of instructor wisdom." You were simply told to fly certain maneuvers in a specific way or wind up as a statistic. In those days, there was no such thing as NATOPS. What pleased your own instructor might not please a check pilot, who had his own idea how a "slip to a circle" or a "slip to a small field" landing should be flown.

We were all aware, however, that a stupid mistake, or a forgotten procedural step, could cause one to suddenly quit eating potatoes and occasionally it happened. One aspect relating to aviation safety which was drummed into us was keeping our head on a constant swivel to avoid the ever present threat of a midair collision. I've always wondered why more collisions didn't occur, since the number of aircraft returning to the field at the end of a hop was like a swarm of bees buzzing around a honeycomb.

Despite these slight idiosyncrasies, the primary flight instruction was excellent, and the instructors were a very dedicated cadre of professionals. But I believe that after a year's experience in instructing, the majority of them would have sold their soul to get into a combat squadron.

Following primary, I went to Corpus Christi for basic training in the SNV (Vultee Vibrator), a fixed landing gear, 450 HP low-wing monoplane, and instruments and advanced training in the SNJ. At Corpus we were introduced to formation flying, instruments, inverted spins, navigation, gunnery, bombing and night flying to mention most of the phases. In keeping with the rest of the naval air flight training program, the basic, instrument and advanced training squadrons were well organized, provided excellent instruction and thoroughly prepared the soon-to-be naval aviator for his next training—an operational training squadron where he would fly the aircraft that he would fly in a fleet squadron.

Graduation, the awarding of those coveted gold wings, was the culmination of a year's blood, sweat and frustrations. It was the carrot at the end of the stick that kept the adrenaline flowing. My wings were pinned on in April 1944 by Admiral C.P. ("How We Lost a Gallant Lady") Mason, who was the CO of the original carrier *Hornet*, before it was sunk by the Japanese.

After Corpus Christi, it was operational training at Ft. Lauderdale and an introduction to the TBM (Grumman Avenger) torpedo bomber. I will never forget the feeling of awe that I had just before mounting the wing for my first flight in the *Avenger*. Going from an SNJ to the TBM, I suppose could be likened to stepping into a Mack truck after driving nothing but a Volkswag[e]n.

At operational training we met and flew with the crew that would go with us to the fleet. The TBM had a crew of three, and my gunner and radioman stayed with me for the next two and a half years.

In operational we were introduced to FCLP, probably the most important aspect of flight to the carrier pilot—learning how to land aboard a carrier. We were soon to experience our first taste of carrier aviation, of all places on Lake Michigan.

In 1944 the Navy was using two old paddle wheel coal-burning steamers (USS *Sable* [IX–81] and USS *Wolverine* [IX–64]) which had been converted into aircraft carriers of a sort. The *Sable* and *Wolverine* were a far cry from combat carriers but were suitable for accomplishing the Navy's purpose—that of qualifying naval aviators fresh out of operational flight training in carrier landings. The two carriers had certain limitations such as having no elevators or a hangar deck. When barrier crashes or other flight deck crashes used up the alloted spots on the flight deck for parking dud aircraft, the day's operations were over and the carriers headed back to their pier in Chicago.

Another problem they had to contend with was wind over the deck (WOD). Certain WOD minimums were required to land aircraft such as F6Fs, F4Us, TBMs and SBDs. When there was little or no actual wind on Lake Michigan, operations often had to be curtailed because the carriers couldn't generate sufficient speed to meet the WOD minimums. It is doubtful if the two carriers were capable of making more than 20 knots under their own power.

Occasionally, when low wind conditions persisted for several days and the pool of waiting aviators started to bunch up, an alternate system of qualifications was used. The alternate system was to qualify the pilots in SNJs—even though most pilots had not flown the SNJ for four or five months. Can you imagine what kind of an impact that would have on aviation safety today?

My own operational flight was a good case in point. We were sent to NAS Glenview to qualify in the TBM. After several flights of refresher FCLP, we were exposed to our first arrested landing. Unbelievable as it sounds, a one-wire arresting gear had been constructed in what for all practical purposes looked as if it had been a cow pasture. It was not an airfield, but a small landing strip that had been hacked out adjacent to the arresting gear where the LSO was positioned. That was where I made my first arrested landing in a TBM.

Unfortunately for those of us who were awaiting carrier qualification at that time (July '44), it was a period when there was very little true wind on Lake Michigan. Therefore, the powers that be decided that they would get rid of the large pool of aviators by qualifying them in the SNJ rather than the service type aircraft flown in operational training.

On the face of it, that decision seemed to be an expedient way to solve the problem. From the viewpoint of aviation safety, it could have been a disaster. About 40 pilots were assembled for a briefing on how to fly the SNJ in the carrier landing pattern. The briefing was given by an LSO and included such things as flying the pattern, speeds, altitudes and procedures on the flight deck after landing. One incidental point mentioned was that some of the SNJs had airspeed indicators calibrated in knots while others were calibrated in miles per hour. We were advised to be certain which type airspeed indicator we had.

In today's aviation safety conscious environment, what we were about to do would cause Grampaw Petti-

bone to have a heart attack! Our briefing LSO told us that we would get one warmup flight in an SNJ and then load aboard the USS *Sable* the next day, for a three-day excursion on Lake Michigan. As mentioned earlier, it had been about five months since most of us had flown an SNJ, *and not one of us had ever flown it during FCLP.*

Surprisingly, the qualifications went rather well, considering that no one had ever flown an FCLP pass in the J-bird, much less a carrier approach. Flights of SNJs took off from NAS Glenview and came out to the carrier. As these pilots finished their carquals, the 40 or more captive pilots onboard were hot-seated and in three days finished their qualifications.

After the short interlude at Glenview, my operational flight was sent to COMFAIRWESTCOAST where we were split up and assigned to various VC [composite] squadrons. In those days the VC squadrons consisted of 20 fighters (FM–2s) and 20 TBM torpedo bombers. We managed to get our taste of combat at Iwo Jima and Okinawa. For the most part, our TBM missions consisted of flying close air support for the ground troops, dropping bombs and shooting lots of rockets.

It's funny how memories stick with you. I can still remember thinking to myself as we were flying on our first combat mission, "Am I really qualified for this hop?"

Another memory has to do with the intricacies involved in operating with a multicarrier task group. While operating in the Okinawa area, it was not uncommon to find ourselves conducting carrier operations with as many as 12 jeep carriers, all launching and landing aircraft simultaneously. It is a very impressive sight to see 12 carriers swing into the wind on signal and start catapulting aircraft. It was also mighty important to know what your 30-degree landing pattern was and what bearing your own carrier was from the guide, lest one land on the wrong carrier.

Probably the most vivid scenes etched in my memory were the occasions when our jeep carrier task force joined forces with Task Force 58. The night before the rendezvous our task force might consist of 20 to 25 ships. When we arrived on deck the next morning, there was nothing but ships as far as the eye could see. For 20 or 25 miles one could see nothing but carriers, battleships, cruisers, destroyers and auxiliaries. It was indeed an awe-inspiring sight and left no doubt in our mind as to the awesome destructive power assembled at one time. I'm sure there were 100 or more ships rendezvoused on these occasions.

In the post WW II Navy, I completed two more torpedo squadron tours, a year at General Line School and a tour in the Training Command's Carrier Qualification Training Unit where I was trained to be an LSO. Following the Training Command, I arrived at AIRLANT [Naval Air Forces Atlantic] and was promptly assigned to an Air Anti-Submarine Squadron as LSO. I was still flying TBMs, the ASW version, and was back to flying on and off jeep carriers. During the years I spent in torpedo squadrons (1945–1948), my squadrons operated from Essex Class carriers. When a carrier aviator learned his trade flying off Kaiser Class jeep carriers, the transition to an

Essex Classs CV was as the saying goes, "like shooting fish in a rain barrel." It was quite a comedown to go back to a jeep carrier CVS.

In January 1953 I reported to the Naval Aviation Safety Activity and from that day on I became safety oriented. The Safety Activity had been moved from one obscure room in the Pentagon to NAS Norfolk during December 1951. When I reported aboard, there were a total of 27 personnel, about equally divided amongst officers, enlisted and civilians. At about this time the powers that be in Washington determined that there was definite need for an all-out improvement in naval aviation safety. Take a look at some statistics that apply to Fiscal Years '50, '51 and '52.

[Fiscal Year]	Major Accidents	Rate	Destroyed Aircraft	Fatal Accidents	Fatalities
1950	1,488	53.7	481	137	227
1951	1,714	54.0	675	185	391
1952	2,066	54.8	708	224	399
[Calendar Year]					
1982	90	4.42	83	40	74

If you look at these statistics and compare them with those for calendar year 1982 (we changed from fiscal to calendar year statistics beginning in 1975) you can note a tremendous improvement in 32 years. Since 1950 the Navy's mishap rate has been lowered from 53.7 to 4.42—a whopping reduction.

I did two tours of duty at the Safety Center, 1953 to mid-1956 and from June 1960 until I retired in 1964. During most of those years I wrote the *Weekly Summary* and for *Approach Magazine*. In March of 1970 I returned to the Naval Safety Center as a civil servant, and for the past 14 years have written aviation safety material for both *Weekly Summary* and *Approach*. You might say that I found a home away from home at the Naval Safety Center, since I spent nearly 22 years within its confines. I am retiring once again from the Safety Center on 3 February 1984.

In looking back over the 20 plus years at the Safety Center that I have been reading and writing about incidents, accidents, mishaps and other hazardous occurrences, it is obvious that there are rarely any new types of mishaps. Errors of omission and commission which caused accidents 40 years ago still do so today. We still lose aircraft from midair collisions, running out of fuel, hitting the ramp, inadvertently landing wheels-up and stalling from insufficient airspeed to give a few examples. Looking on the positive side, however, is the fact that these type of losses are far less in number today. I believe this can be attributed to the tremendous importance that has been given to aviation safety at all echelons of command. Today's naval aviators are instilled from the beginning of flight training with the philosophy that aviation safety is a personal matter. That this philosophy has paid dividends can easily be understood by comparing the statistics cited previously for the early '50s and those for 1982.

Although it would be difficult to relate a specific instance of mishap prevention to an article written in *Approach* or any other safety publication, nevertheless, that is the ultimate goal of all who write about aviation safety. The idea is to make aircrews aware of what has happened or can happen under certain circumstances and then to react in a positive, safe manner considering all alternatives. Hopefully, I may have been successful in this endeavor.

During my 40 years of association with naval aviation I have noted a number of innovations, improvements in existing equipment, the manufacture of new equipment and the use of new operational concepts, all of which have had a tremendous impact on aviation safety.

Angled Deck: When the Navy started to convert existing aircraft carrier flight decks and to construct new angled deck carriers, the greatest single benefit for aviation safety was acquired. The Navy's first carrier landing on an angled deck was made January 12, 1953 when the CO of the USS *Antietam,* Capt. S.G. Mitchell, landed aboard in an SNJ. The main advantage of the angled deck was that aircraft which did not catch a crossdeck pendant for whatever reason, no longer wound up as a barrier crash accident. As the saying goes, it took most of the "sweat" out of a carrier landing. Except for a very rare and unique set of circumstances, the angled deck eliminated the catastrophic type of accident when an aircraft bounced over the barriers and into the pack of aircraft parked forward of the barriers on axial decks.

It also helped the mental attitude of a pilot making his first carqual landings to know that his initial efforts did not have to be letter perfect. A bolter resulted in just a poor landing grade rather than a barrier crash.

The Mirror and Fresnel Lens: On August 22, 1955 Cdr. R.G. Dose, CO of VX–3, made the first carrier landing using the mirror landing system, when he landed aboard the USS *Bennington* in an FJ–3. The mirror landing system, or OLS (optical landing system) as it later became known, was one giant step forward for aviation safety. If the angled deck took most of the "sweat" out of a carrier landing, the mirror and Fresnel Lens systems took the anxiety out of a carrier approach. Not only did the system allow the pilot to visually note his relative position to the desired altitude, it raised the carrier landing pattern several hundred feet. This aspect alone, in conjunction with a Marshal point aft of the carrier, eliminated the necessity of a formation to break at 300 feet ahead of the carrier and turn to the downwind leg of the old carrier approach. Such a break, particularly when there was no horizon at night, contributed to the deaths of a great many naval aviators when they became disoriented and flew into the water.

Field Arresting Gear: The advent of jet aircraft brought with them the need for a runway system to arrest jets with landing and takeoff emergencies when normal deceleration wasn't possible. Initial trials with such a system began in 1948 at NAS Patuxent River. The original anchor chain type arresting gear has gradually evolved into several very sophisticated arresting gear installations at Naval and Marine Corps air stations and facilities. It would be impossible to state how many arrestments over the years have prevented accidents, but when you consider that the yearly total of field arrestments in 1982 amounted to 4,822, the savings in aircraft, dollars and lives is tremendous.

NATOPS: Another great stride was made in aviation safety when we gave birth to NATOPS in 1961. The essence of the NATOPS program is one word—*standardization*. It certainly makes sense to have all pilots flying the same aircraft in the same manner, following standardized procedures, including emergency procedures. In the more than 20 years that NATOPS has been in existence, it has proven to be an excellent tool to keep pilots and crewmen vitally aware of aviation safety as it applies specifically to their aircraft. It's refreshing to know that a pilot can change from one squadron to another, knowing that as long as he is current in his knowledge of NATOPS, he will make an easy transition.

Ejection Seats: The ejection seat has undoubtedly been the greatest single life-saving device since the parachute. In August of 1948 Lt. J.L. Fruin was the first naval aviator to eject successfully, when he ejected from an F2H–1 Phantom at 597 KIAS. Since that time there have been more than 3,650 successful ejections from naval aircraft. In those 35 years, ejection seats have been modified and improved to the point that under the right set of circumstances, safe, zero altitude/zero airspeed ejections have become a reality. Although successful ejections do not prevent accidents, they do preserve lives, and that's the name of the game.

Naval Safety Center Accident Investigations: In 1953 the Naval Aviation Safety Activity established a division of special aircraft accident investigators. The division is tasked to conduct independent aircraft mishap investigations of selected mishaps, primarily fatal crashes of the Navy's latest model aircraft. The investigators receive intensive training at a variety of locations such as aircraft manufacturers, engine manufacturers, NARFs [Naval aviation repair facilities], ejection seat manufacturers and the Navy's aviation safety officer school at Monterey, California.

In the past 30 years there have been occasions, particularly after a new aircraft has been introduced into the fleet, where a rash of similar mishaps have occurred for unknown reasons. This is the type of mishap investigation which the Safety Center's investigators are tasked to solve. Today, wherever in the world a naval aircraft is lost, if the wreckage is available for investigation and the cause is not readily apparent, the chances are excellent that a Safety Center investigator will soon be on his way to conduct an independent investigation. Safety Center investigators have been eminently successful in determining mishap cause factors in approximately 80 percent of all investigations conducted. Subsequent to such determinations, operators of that model aircraft are alerted to specific cause factors and other possible hazards.

If just one aircraft mishap a year can be prevented as a result of Safety Center investigations, the yearly cost of operating the aircraft mishap investigation division will have been returned a hundredfold.

RAGs (*formerly Replacement Air Groups, now known as FRSs or Fleet Replacement Squadrons*): During World War II whenever a replacement pilot arrived at a squadron in the combat area, it often took three to four months before he was able to pull his own weight under all types of combat conditions. Such is no longer the case today because of RAG training. The RAGs came into being in the 60s. Now when a RAG graduate arrives at a squadron, the CO can expect to receive a fully qualified pilot in the model aircraft, in all phases of its employment including weapons training.

The Barricade: The 22–foot high barricade used aboard carriers during emergency landing situations was an aviation safety feature born of necessity. In the WW II era and for a few years thereafter, the cable type barriers were adequate to stop prop aircraft which for one reason or another were not capable of being arrested normally, e.g. having a tailhook broken off. With jet aircraft and their much higher landing speeds, an improved method was needed to stop them in extremis landing situations. The 22–foot nylon barricade was developed and has saved many aircraft from serious or strike damage. Before the advent of the angled deck, the barricade also stopped jets from plowing into aircraft parked forward on the flight deck. Although not designed to prevent mishaps, the barricade has certainly lessened the damage inflicted on aircraft when it has been necessary to recover them into the barricade.

If the next 40 years brings as many innovations and additions to naval aviation safety as I have seen in my lifetime, we should have nothing to fear about naval aviation's role of prominence in the next several decades. It's been a grand 40 years and if history is any teacher, it should be even greater in the years ahead.

The Marble Theory

Lt. Cmdr. P.S. Mansfield, VA-75; March 1984

As we depart on cruise after an extremely intense workup period, I wonder how we're going to maintain the high motivation found during ORE.* Yes, I know, what else does the safety officer have to do? OK, that's part of the job. I'm just trying to put into perspective the enormity of a seven-month deployment.

My CO put it best: "Accept it, we're out here and our goal is to bring *everybody* back with us!" I liked that—just the sort of thing the safety officer likes to hear. Now, how do we do it? I mean, seven months is a *long* time. How do I keep interest and motivation up? The answer, I think,—I can't. Not by myself anyway. Everyone's got to do his part, from the most junior airman to the skipper. We work as a team, you know. The maintenance guys have to do their job right to keep themselves and the airplanes healthy; the administration and personnel guys have to keep the paperwork going, and the flight crews, upholding their end of the bargain, have to fly the airplanes safely. Sounds simple enough, doesn't it? Everybody just does his job. Easy, no problem here! We've proven time and time again during workups that we can hack it. Routine, that's the word, it's just routine. Or is it?

During my first deployment, I was involved in a "routine" night raid that terminated in tragedy. The mission called for two A-6s to simulate enemy bombers, along with four A-7s which would simulate their cruise missiles. Fighter aircraft would then attempt to intercept these "raiders" in defense of the carrier. It was a bright moonlit night, halfway through a Med deployment. Each raid element was inbound on their respective radial to the point where we launched our A-7s. As I called missiles away, I watched the A-7 on my port wing detach then begin his descending, accelerating profile. Confident that he had cleared my airplane, I went back on the gauges to ensure I didn't leave my assigned altitude of 20,000 feet. Shortly thereafter, we experienced an uninduced, violent wing rock and pitching moment (similar to flying through jet wash) followed immediately by a bright flash. I thought, "My engines have exploded" but a quick glance at the instruments assured me that this was not the case; however, my BN started calling over the UHF, "Mayday, mayday, mayday." Quickly, I wanted to reassure him that even though *something* had happened, we were not in dire straits. Before I had a chance, he continued, "This is 504, we've just had a midair with 302." "We did!!??" I calmly asked. Now, looking outside, I saw the lights of another aircraft rapidly descending below us.

Just that fast, it wasn't routine anymore. The A-7 on the starboard wing had turned back into us and impacted from below. A SAR effort was immediately initiated for the A-7 pilot, but he was never found. Assessing the damage to our own aircraft as we turned toward the ship, a flashing master caution light directed my attention to a rudder throw light. In itself, this was no big deal, but it made me suspect damage to the tail. The airplane was flying fine, though. Next, I noticed the starboard outboard droptank fuel quantity had gone to zero. Telling my BN, he looked out and discovered our droptank and bomb rack on his side were missing. Wow! I wondered what else could be wrong with the wing, damaged flaps/slats? About this time, the other A-6 had joined. His call of "being able to see stars through your airplane" was not encouraging. With our playmate watching, we began a slow flight check at altitude and discovered that everything was in proper working order except the hook, which was jammed in the fuselage. With a suitable divert nearby, we completed our "routine" flight with a night landing at a foreign field.

Routine flights like this one have made me a firm believer in the "marble theory" of flight. You see, there's this big jar full of white, gray and black marbles. There are a lot of white ones, a fair number of gray ones and just a couple of black ones. Each time you go flying, it's like reaching into that jar of marbles and pulling one out. White means a safe flight, no problem. Gray means a close call. These are scary, but quick reactions and a little luck will pull you through unscathed. And then there is the black marble—waiting to bite you if you let it. To survive the black marble flights, you're going to need it all—aircraft knowledge, judgment, alertness, you name it. Oh, I almost forgot: You don't find out the color of your marble until you get back. The only way to beat the marble theory is to assume every one is going to be black.
*Operational Readiness Exercise

Living an *Approach* Article; or, All Is Well and Pressing On

Lt. M. Carriker, VA-27; June-July 1984

Looking down at a low overcast from six miles up, sipping my gin and tonic, I hear the airline captain come up on the intercom. "Folks" he drawls, "we are slowing down and dropping the landing gear to cool off a warm right brake." I hear the gear drop, raise and the engines spool up. The intercom comes on again, "The brake cooled right down, so all is well and we are pressing on."

It then dawned on me that I had said that same line numerous times on my flights the day before. It had also occurred to me that I had lived through an *Approach* article and I know better.

You know *Approach* articles. Somebody telling his mistakes or someone telling how not to be a dummy. I've read *Approach* cover to cover since AOCS [aviation officer candidate school]. Pay attention and learn, I tell myself. It may keep you alive.

The saga started as an incredibly good deal: Ferry a jet bound for overhaul to an East Coast rework facility and bring a completed one home. Twelve hours cross-country, middle of the week and funded orders to top it off. Choose me! The maintenance officer says go on Wednesday and come back on Thursday, nine days before Christmas. Tuesday comes, I call weather, scribble out some fuel figures and a course to NARF EAST. I'd just spent a week proofing a computer program to do just this. I knew I would get there, so no detailed jet log (much less the TACAN identifiers dit-dahs of the training command). Show up on Wednesday; not so fast, the jet is still broken. Thursday it is still broken. It looks like Friday and a weekend visit to NARF EAST—the weekend before the Christmas weekend. I wasn't planning on doing my Christmas shopping 2,500 miles from home. Friday comes: No part and a reprieve from the weekend.

By Tuesday the jet is up but the weather is down, everywhere. I convince the skipper it is too bad to go and I'll try Wednesday. The weather improves slightly Wednesday, and three legs may work. I give NARF a call and uh-oh, the return jet has not even been test flown yet! The maintenance folks from the wing call over and inform me that the jet goes *today* or they lose the rework slot forever. Visions of a NARF Christmas and a disappointed wife dance in my head. I call Ferry Squadron East. "How am I gonna get home??" "No problem," says the chief, "Get a transportation request cut and fly commercial." Oh great, four days before Christmas and try to get airline reservations across the country. I call the local travel section, and they need five days notice. I call NARF transportation, and they come through when the pressure is on.

The skipper comes by. "I want you in there before dark—safely." I call to recheck weather and find out our sister squadron is going to the same place. I ask to join up and give him my SSN [Social Security Number] and aircraft bureau number. Preflight planning completed, I hustle the duty driver to travel for the tickets, hold a hallway brief with my lead and go to man up. I plan enough to get a second hook point (the plane will need two field arrests en route), and a brief on how to change it.

Lighting off my jet I realize that my inflight gouge book is still beside the computer. I call base to deliver it—and a southeast approach plate and a HI [high altitude] East chart. The duty driver runs out with them all—including my airline tickets. Now I'm ready to taxi, but a boarding step door won't stay closed. "Take it off," I advise. Bolts won't come loose. Not knowing the max extend speed of step, I risk it and call up and ready. All is well and pressing on.

One hundred knots on the tail makes the leg to Southwest AFB a short hop. Just having operated out of there for a week, I was familiar with the area. Even the radios were still channelized to their frequencies. We hop out, refile (the ATC computer dumped the first flight plan) and over a coke I brief to lead the next leg. It is a straight shot to NAS Bourbon Street, just past a thunderstorm front. On start, my chart blows out of the plane, goes down the ramp—(not down the intake)—and is gone. A call to my wingman provides another map. I copy down pertinent frequencies and TACAN channels and call the taxi. "All is well and pressing on," I think to myself.

Passing 18,000 feet I can't get my altimeter to go to reset. Leveling off at 37,000 feet, center calls me 500 feet high. Not wanting to guess at an altitude to suit center I relinquish the lead. Arriving at NAS Bourbon Street we break up for individual GCA's (my altimeter error is negligible below FL 240, and field elevation is one foot so the RADALT [radar altimeter] will be helpful). Despite a high cross wind, the landing is OK. Taxiing to the transient line, I get a call of "Dash two, left at the next intersection, follow your lead." Field diagram in hand I look to find my lead who is already on the ramp and parked. Passing a left turn off to the P–3 ramp, I look down the taxiway for an intersection, no taxi light on. Somebody once told me that REAL Navy pilots don't use taxi lights—wrong answer! Suddenly two police barricades with a dim light apiece appear on the taxiway. Firm brake pressure results in two *loud* noises, but I stop short. "Hello Ground, No I won't be able to turn around and exit onto the P–3 ramp." Downlocks on, I shut down and hop out with an indescribable feeling of stupidity, anger with myself and the ground controller and the thought of missing my flight home.

A quick call to Reserve Corsair Bourbon Street results in two new tires and some recalled folks to change them. Two hours later the jet is ready to roll. My lead has pressed on to beat an incoming storm. I plan a route and check the weather. Not too good. Five hundred feet broken, 1 ¼ mile visibility in fog, occasionally 200 overcast ½ mile. A call to NARF East weather says the same. No improvement till late tomorrow—zero-zero till noon. Well it is minimums, so I find a suitable alternate and file (for FL 200 so my altimeter reads OK). Walking to my steed I think of times I've launched in that weather at the ship and if I nail the numbers I will be OK. Again, "all is well and pressing on."

Start, taxi and call for takeoff with lightning close by and the wind picking up.

The flight to NARF East was quiet and peaceful. With "George" flying, I take a good preview of approaches and set up my navaids. A well-called GCA has me seeing the approach lights at 250 feet and half the runway at 200 feet. I take the arresting gear due to water on the runway. Taxiing to the hangar, I receive a query from tower on why I'm taxiing so slow (I didn't remember that I had no anti-skid due to no exciter rings on the wheels replaced by the Reserves). At NARF East they have to tell me to turn off my taxi light. They want to know why an airplane with two new tires is coming to be reworked. I fill out the paperwork and head for the Q.

Sipping my gin and tonic, I think it must be kind of embarrassing to the captain to have to tell 200 people that something is wrong. I think I have a hard time admitting that something is wrong to myself. . . .

My Time

Capt. Bert B. Tussing, USMC, HMH–461; November 1984

We had been flying since 0420 that morning, a part of a rehearsal exercise for one of those huge, interservice efforts. The first shutdown time had been 0751. The CO was occupied with debriefing the powers that be on what should have happened that didn't and what did happen that shouldn't. My copilot and I along with the crews of the other three aircraft in the flight ducked below decks and gratefully consumed the boxed breakfast supplied by the mess decks and returned to the rack. After all, we had briefed at 0200 and even having gotten to bed at 1830 the night before, we figured rest was the next order of the day. Following that would be at least another three-to-five hours of flying.

At 0930 we were up again, getting ready for the 1000 debrief/brief. The skipper had returned with all of the new gouge. The new plan called for an additional fun-filled hour of delta time over our ship after our simulated troop pickup from an LPH [amphibious assault ship]. As per the standard on any shipboard operation, my copilot and I were on the deck a full 30 minutes prior to the time we were supposed to spread the rotor blades, standing by. We took the time to talk a little about how things had run in the early morning launch and to rebrief how we were going to play through the afternoon. For the most part, both of us had been pretty pleased with the way things had run for us and our crew in the wee hours . . . in spite of our initial trepidation with Ol' Number Seven.

Now, Number Seven had not been a bad flying machine for the launch; pretty smooth, in fact. But that isn't to say she didn't give us reason to pause before we left. She had been a perennial "stable queen" among the Sea Stallions. In recent memory, Old Seven had always been the one (or at least one of the ones) we really had to stroke before any major operation. This isn't to say the crew chief was to blame. This particular sergeant was one of that grimy breed who knows the airplane with an intimacy that draws them to a plane until it is either well or K-balled beyond recognition. The sergeant had pleaded Seven's case sufficiently to prevent her from becoming a parts bin and had made the aircraft a reasonably safe, smooth flying creature, but she still had her quirks. . . .

And the quirks bothered me. One had to do with an irritating propensity Seven had for "winking" a flight ready light at you. This is not particularly uncommon for a Stallion with its elastomeric rotorhead[;] on board a radar/radio platform certain HF signals release "gremlins" in the logic unit. Ole Sarge assured me that there was nothing wrong with this part of the helicopter that a new wire bundle (which we didn't have, natch) wouldn't fix. But I've always been less than anxious to fly a bird whose caution lights are waving the not-safe-for-flight banner in my eyes. QA [quality assurance] joined in the

"but it's still safe to fly" chorus, and I finally succumbed. Before you Lazyboy quarterbacks deposit your Delta Sierra ballots for yours truly . . . the call was good. The aircraft, from all that could be determined, was safe for flight, and the rotorhead had nothing to do with our eventual catastrophe.

There was one other "quirk," however, that caused me even more concern. The discrepancy book had warned against it, and preflight bore it out: The copilot's cyclic was out of alignment. When the flight controls were neutralized, the pilot's stick was standing up straight and pretty, just like all good cyclics were raised to do, but the copilot's canted slightly to the left. In my infinite knowledge of the H–53 and its systems, I realized immediately that this was not according to Hoyle and said as much to Ol' Sarge. But, like a protective mother, he plaintively appealed for the bird, explaining that she had been that way for some time now, the whole thing was just a matter of a *slight* mechanical misalignment, and the condition certainly had nothing to do with jeopardizing the safety of flight. QA joined in on the refrain, and I surrendered, satisfied once again with a reasonable explanation.

So, Okay . . . Seven wasn't exactly your premier VIP vehicle, but performance had backed up mother crew chief's faith. The plane had flown like a champ for better than four hours in night carrier operations, and neither the pilot nor the copilot could complain about end results as we prepared for the follow-on launch. I joked with the crew chief about how I'd probably have nightmares about the avionics in Seven's rotorhead, but admitted openly that the plane had been all he had said she would be. Prior to launch, he visually verified that the promising wink of the flight ready light was justified, and at 1120 (right on time) we launched.

The approach to the ship was smooth (I commented to my not-too-modest aviator self). We had been waiting in the delta pattern for a deck spot, second in our section. When the spots cleared, both of our planes landed directly on the spot with no extraneous delay. Such had not been the case a couple of times in the earlier launch. My copilot and I had had to wave off as our wingman had not quite settled on the deck as we were on short final. There's nothing particularly unusual about that, but it can be irritating if your approach to that point had been good. This time, however, everything was fine. We landed behind our wingman, made our simulated pickup and were off of the deck without incident.

From there we proceeded overhead for our sojourn in the delta pattern. The delay for our flight was necessary for staging, but nothing is quite as miserable as doing circles in the sky for an hour, going round and round in a right-hand orbit until one gluteus isn't as maximus as the other. We had already been in that sorry state for 25 minutes when we received a call from center extending the invitation of an LPD [amphibious transport dock ship] for us to shoot some approaches to her deck. Apparently, her deck crew needed some practice with our breed of cat, and it had become obvious that at the moment, we had nothing better to do. So the skipper cut the last two aircraft of his flight of four free, and we were on our way.

As we descended from 1,000 feet Delta, a number of things were running through my mind. First of all, I welcomed the opportunity to escape Delta (that almost goes without saying). I was happy, too, to be going to an LPD because there I would finally have an opportunity to let my copilot shoot a few landings. This operation was the first time he had been exposed to shipboard landings, and although I wanted to give him as much exposure as possible, night operations from the left seat of an H–53 did not seem to me to be the most prudent introduction to carrier approaches. A day-lit LPD, however, was just what the doctor ordered, and I intended to let the copilot take every advantage of i. I was time for his patience to be rewarded.

Our section flew an unusually deep downwind for a port to starboard approach, partially in an effort to lose altitude from 1,000 to 300 feet and partially to ensure the side numbers on the vessel were the one's we sought. As we turned to final, our altitude was still 500 feet, and I told the copilot to keep her going down. As we approached the prescribed altitude of 300 feet, I told him to hold it there for a while, as I judged our distance to be well beyond the glide slope we would want to intercept. He leveled us out at around 275 feet, lined up nicely for an approach to spot 2. Our airspeed was good, at about 50 knots.

Continuing the approach, it appeared to me that our wingman was slowing down a little early in front of us. It appeared to me that we were going to have to take it around again. No sooner had the thought formulated in my mind than the copilot was declaring, "I'm going to wave it off," over the radio. Sensing no particular alarm, I mentally congratulated him for the call and told him that I had the aircraft. Being in the right seat, I was going to do a simple 360 and set him up for another approach. As I took the controls and started my turn, he said it:

"I can't get enough left cyclic!"

For the first time, the alarm was there, and my own matched it. The right roll I had initiated for my turn continued on its own, independent of my inputs. As we rolled to 90 degrees angle-of-bank, and maybe beyond, efforts to bring the stick back to the left were useless; my hand, my shoulder, my leg and the cyclic were all locked to the right side of my seat. As we rolled through 270 degrees of turn, and maybe more, I saw the water coming up to meet us. The cyclic betrayed me again as I tried to bring the nose up to avoid the ocean. No pitch and no roll, with the sea closing. All I had left was the collective, and with our nose heading for the deck, I pulled all that we had . . . maybe to bring the whole front end up to avoid the impact . . . maybe to level it up enough to be survivable. As the crew chief was screaming "What's wrong?," and I was answering in expletives, the plane impacted.

From my perspective, we impacted five to 10 degrees nose down, 60 to 90 degrees angle-of-bank. The motion had barely slowed when I began screaming, "Get out! Get out!" Without thinking . . . totally without thinking . . . I reached for the emergency release handle on my window. As I pulled it, I looked up to see maybe four inches of light between the top of my window and the light brown waterline. Water was rushing in from what had been my lower windshield and the chin bubble as I pushed the pilot's window out. Before I could release my shoulder harness, the plane continued its roll to the right.

Initial exit from the helicopter was mercifully free of entanglements, disorientation and all of the other horrors we sometimes depict in our mind's eye. But because of what I perceived to be the right roll of the craft, I egressed down and out away from the plane. After what seemed to be a long time, I broke the surface.

I came up gasping, disoriented and swallowing saltwater and JP–5. I had only been above the surface for maybe two seconds when I realized I was being pulled back in. The suction of the water filling into the aircraft cabin was pulling me back in! In one horrifying moment, I found myself back in the helicopter, beneath the surface, shut off from the air and the light. And I was scared!

This was the first time that I had really had a moment to be frightened, and the surroundings were perfect for it. I was just struggling, taking in more JP and not having the slightest notion of which way was up or out. After several long moments, I found an opening with a light behind it and went for it. Following a time that seemed far longer than the first, I broke the surface again.

My first sight out of the water was the first mechanic, and in the chaos of the moment, I was somehow *amused.* There he sat, 6 feet 3 inches of drenched humanity, perched atop part of the helicopter like a fisherman whose rowboat had simply overturned. The crew chief was scrambling up the side of the remnants of my right wheel well. The lightness of the moment passed as soon as it appeared as I splashed to get away from the wreckage, terrified that I would be pulled under again. I pulled the right side of my LPA; it inflated as advertised, and I left it there, the upper left and lower right of my life vest buoying me up, apparently content with it, and not even attempting the other toggles. Then I began screaming for my copilot.

It didn't make sense to me. From where I sat, my side of the aircraft was the one that impacted heaviest; the roll was in my direction; where the hell was he? An H–46 was already overhead with the harness in the water right in front of me, but I had to find him. I don't think I intentionally ignored the harness, but I was still swimming around, yelling for a copilot who wasn't answering. When the harness passed in front of me the second time, I reached out and pulled it in. I took the harness under my arms and hooked it to the fastener above me. As they pulled me out of the water, on the way up the hoist I watched as a light blue civilian yacht pulled alongside the wreckage of my helicopter. As I was pulled in by the H–46 crew chief, I saw two of my three crewmen being helped aboard the vessel. I never saw my friend again.

There was no reason for him to have remained in that helicopter. Mine was the side that had impacted. If anyone overhead had wanted to guess whose was the helmet bobbing among the wreckage, the safe bet would have been mine. But only three of four crewmembers escaped from Seven's last ride. More than 24 hours would pass before we would begin to learn why.

The copilot's side had remained intact, with only the chin bubble broken out. Even the notorious H–53 pilot's seat had, for once, held true. His window was still closed; the emergency release handle still shear wired in place, untouched. When the divers found him, he was near the ramp area, with two blade ropes loosely wrapped about one arm and one leg. The flight surgeon's examination would reveal no signs of injury, no marks, no possible indication of unconsciousness as a result of the impact. The findings were clear and painfully simple: Death by saltwater drowning. . . .

A Cold, Rainy December Night

Lt. Cmdr. Tom Massicotte; March 1985

It was still raining while I sipped my Coke outside Base Ops. My trusty A–4M glistened in the night under the bright lights of the transient line. The turnaround would be quick; nothing like a cold, rainy night to get the transient alert crew moving. This would be my third leg of flight, a large weather system over the entire central U.S. forcing a detour. We started out at NAS East as a flight of two, my wingman flying an A–7E. We were split up now, he diverting to a field with a dry runway because the arresting gear here was "not available." Getting in here was no easy task. The weather was solid goo from FL 350 to 1,000 feet AGL. There was lightning and St. Elmo's fire on the descent. Ground control lost me because of heavy rain on final approach course, but I got a good approach on the second try. Only the 8,000 foot runway was open, and I had to use it all to get the Skyhawk stopped. Now it was time to man up again.

The transient folks did a super job, and in no time, I was at the hold short ready to go. There was no doubt in my mind that I would beat my Corsair wingman to NAS Big Valley. On the runway, good run-up, and I was airborne into the rainy night. At 500 feet (AGL), I entered the overcast just as departure control directed "right turn, climb on course." It was then that the fun started. Passing flight level 200, solid IMC in a 30–degree angle of bank right hand turn, all the lights went out. All the lights, that is, except the "GEN" cowl light telling me the obvious: my generator had failed. Trying hard not to move the stick, I quickly pulled out my flashlight and found the ram air turbine (RAT) handle. With the canopy jettison handle so close to the RAT handle, I wanted to be sure I had the right one. I felt a little better when the red lights in the cockpit came back on after RAT deployment. In the few seconds that the lights were out, I was surprised to see I had gone from a climbing right-hand turn to a descending left-hand turn. I checked the pocket checklist, but it was no help. I simultaneously declared an emergency with Center and attempted to reset the generator. Center switched me to Approach Control who gave me a heading to fly and an altitude to descend to for an approach to the field I had just left.

I must have tried to reset the generator at least 20 times a minute for the remainder of the hop without success. I rolled out on heading, leveled off at assigned altitude, still solid IMC since takeoff, and began to take account of my situation. My TACAN DME was not working. I would be heavy upon landing with no spoilers, no speed brakes and no nose gear steering to help me. The weather wasn't the greatest. I was going to have my hands full trying to get the Skyhawk stopped. What did the approach plate have to offer? My assigned altitude is 3,000 feet below the emergency safe altitude. I hope Approach knows what they're doing tonight. Speaking of Approach, I haven't heard from them in a while. Better give them a holler. I keyed the mike once, and nothing. Again. Nothing. And again. And again. In my nearly 2,000 hours of flying mostly single-seat jets, I had never had so much as a hydraulic failure. And here I was, night, IMC, no TACAN DME and operating on the RAT, NORDO.

My heart was pounding in my chest as I contemplated my predicament. Could I find the field in this weather? What was the terrain *really* like around here? Immediately, I climbed to the emergency safe altitude. I turned and put the TACAN needle on the wing and started arcing toward the final approach course. A thousand thoughts raced through my head. I must have scanned the needle a couple of hundred times in the first minute, and I swear, it wasn't moving. *It wasn't moving!*

Night, IFR, no generator, no DME, no radio, and now, no azimuth! My mind continued to race. Where would I go? How would I get there? Should I climb? How high? I knew the weather was better to the west. I began to become very depressed. I had gone beyond panic into depression.

But finally, slowly, the azimuth needle began to move. I felt a rush of optimism come over me. I studied the approach plate like I had never studied an approach plate before. I had not done any ADF work in years, but I had to give it my best shot. I turned in on final approach course. I didn't really know how far away I was, exactly, but I had a pretty good idea.

I timed two minutes inbound, then began a shallow descent to 6,000 feet (the TACAN approach had a 15–DME arc at 6,000 feet). I experienced station passage, then turned outbound and timed for three minutes. I turned inbound and put the flaps down. I had to hold the gear as TACAN is lost with gear down on the RAT. I timed inbound for one minute, then descended to TACAN mins, but I didn't break out.

I went back outbound and tried again. This time, I broke out at 500 feet AGL and spotted the runway. The red lights were flashing from all the crash trucks waiting for me. I lowered the gear, saw three down and locked and noted I was on-speed at 160 KIAS. I touched down on the end of the runway and began a slow deceleration. I started braking at 110 KIAS, and shortly thereafter, the left main tire blew.

The left brake pedal went all the way to the floor, and I had now set up a right drift that full rudder could not correct. The RAT dropped off the line and I shut the engine off, knowing I was going off the side of the runway. With all the rain, I just knew the Skyhawk was going to sink into the mud and flip over when it left the runway. I decided not to eject, but don't ask me why. With my hand on the canopy jettison handle, the Skyhawk left the runway at about 50 to 60 knots, 20 degrees off runway heading. The plane rumbled through the mud and came to rest without flipping over. I opened the canopy, pinned the seat and jumped out. I looked the airplane over and it was OK except for being covered with mud. I had been airborne for 31 minutes, but it had seemed like an eternity. I was physically and mentally drained, but felt enormous relief that my ordeal was over. I had made it. . . .

Squeaking by a Sandstorm

Lt. Nels A. Frostenson; June 1985

The flight briefed at 1445 for a normal late afternoon cycle. It was routine mission of the area for 90 minutes and return to the ship after sunset. Our television brief rambled on: "mission ESM [electronic sensing measures], under E–2 control; monitor button 3; case III night recovery; the weather is layered, 2,000 scattered to 30,000 broken, visibility three miles." Afterward, we discussed emergencies, radio controls and who would carry the camera, authenticator and divert pubs.

In the paraloft, Dan, the pilot, and Bob, another NFO [naval flight officer], and I suited up. With 40 pounds of flight and survival gear, we strolled across a greasy, slick, steel flight deck. The sky was white, hazy and cut at the horizon by a solid, deep, intruding blue ocean. "The wind has died off a bit," Dan commented, as we preflighted 606, "but the visibility is worse." Unknown to us on the night before a North African front had created a sandstorm which would soon engulf the carrier.

Ascending the ladder, stepping on platform, strapping in at six places and setting up the cockpit switches—it was all routine. Not a word was said to anyone. Dan broke the silence, "starting number one." Flipping switches, turning on instruments and reading checklists were all procedures that we could repeat "blindfolded in our sleep."

As the humming engines ran up on the power, the aircraft slowly lurched forward. We taxied to the "yellow shirts" directions. The air boss cut in on the radio, "99 Battle-axe, case III launch, altimeter 29.50." That meant the visibility was getting worse. Dan was right.

Number one, the closest catapult, was ours. Slowly the aircraft moved through the steam and into the shuttle. Tension, full throttles and the thunder of the engines beckoned us to launch into the silent twilight. "Compass, controls and cat-shot to go!" Above the roar of the engines I heard, "Controls are free. I'm ready and saluting." I pressed my head firmly against the upper seat and stared at the instruments. My initial feelings were a tug and a jolt, like being slammed against a wall. My peripheral vision told me we were moving quickly but I kept my eyes caged on the airspeed. The needle moved slowly until, poof, silence and we were off of the end of the ship. The airspeed kicked up to 150 and the pressing force of the shot that held us against the seat magically disappeared.

"Doppin', squawking and talkin', 606 airborne." Priority actions were more checks and a quick glance out of the cockpit. To my surprise, we were only 500 feet above the water and already in a milk bowl. It was not a nightmare, an illusion or a trick. It was the worst visibility I had ever experienced. Any combination of weather with the current visibility would be unflyable.

We continued climbing through the stratus layers and the light cumulus. At 24,000 feet the visibility broke wide-open over an ocean of gentle white puffs. The sun dipped towards the horizon; it was sneaking out the back door.

We found the tanker and joined for "Texaco." Our plane plugged the trailing basket and we continued on our way. Little did we know, the 2,000 pounds of gas that we received would be helpful later. Dan updated the computer navigation using the radar, pinpointing "friendly island airfield." We flew above the ceilings for an hour, proceeding southwest while Bob operated the system in back.

The sun dipped further, creating an orange tint that rested on the horizon. Thirty miles southwest of the ship, the cloud-lined cold front broke into an open sea. A second glance revealed that the open sea was actually a solid haze spread smoothly to the horizon, hovering at 4,000 feet.

At 1800, 15 minutes after sunset, we called "RTB [return to base]." Our initial holding instructions were: hold on the 020 radial, 22 DME at 7,000 feet. Halfway to that point while descending through the milk bowl, 'marshal' called us to descend to 1,200 feet and head two-three-zero degrees vectors to the ship. It alarmed us that we were commencing the approach now, 20 minutes ahead of schedule. Something had gone awry.

The fading light and invading haze were getting worse. Twelve hundred feet above sea level appeared to be no better than the previous 23,000 feet. Our external lights were turned on and what we saw was not encouraging. I could barely discern the green wing tip light.

The plane sank at 650 feet per minute. "On glide slope and on centerline, three-fourths of a mile, call the ball," said the controller. The 'meatball' was not visible. 'Paddles' called, "contact." He saw us first; "left for lineup, easy on the power." Suddenly, at one-half mile, the white mast light of the ship pierced the snowy surroundings. Within one-fourth of a mile, the meatball appeared. It was low, then red, then it dropped off of the lens. We were below the flightdeck! 'Paddles' called for a wave-off and flashed the red 'wave-off' light. Dan added power and raised the gear to fly clear of the deck. We were safe. The controller radioed, "606, climb to 1,200 feet, cleared downwind, report abeam." The end of that pass released adrenalin[e] and eased anxieties. We knew what the vis' was like now. I called, "606 abeam, state 7.5." There was plenty of gas to shoot a couple of approaches or to bingo. The controller set us up immediately on the approach at three miles. No one else was in the landing pattern. The other aircraft were either aboard or had bingoed.

The sight of the same milky goo started our hearts pounding just as fiercely as the first time. At three-fourths of a mile, paddles called "contact" again. The controller dropped us off left of course. As the lights pierced the white haze to the right, Dan dropped the right wing, arriving on centerline. The meatball was high. The plane hung in the air as it floated over the landing area, missing the pendants. "Bolter, bolter, bolter."

Dan flew the plane around the pattern, back into the foggy night, and set up for the next approach. Now we had the reassurance that we could touch the deck.

The third pass was less eventful and the controller guided us to position that would not allow us enough time to make corrections to land. We were waved off by the time the lights came into view.

The fourth pass made me eat my heart. "Paddles contact," rang out at three-fourths of a mile. The gyro had tilted left in the turn while we were setting up for the approach, but my body sensed something different as I leaned to the right. Vertigo had set in; it was time to believe the instruments.

At one-half mile the drop lights appeared left and the mast light was straight ahead. "There are the drop lights, bring it left." Dan rocked the wings, dipping left, adding power and straightening. Our eyes widened. The whole approach was confusing and disorientating as I remember it. The plane swayed and descended over the stern. Then it smashed down and the hook trapped one of the pend[a]nts. We rolled out towards the end of the angle-deck, happy to be survivors. The tug and release of the wire completed our landing and we went back to flipping switches and reading checklists.

Flight 606 ended with a sigh of relief, "That trap felt good, nice to be back aboard." Dan acknowledged with two clicks of his mike.

Lt. Frostenson is an NFO with VAG–137.

Skiing Lessons from an A-4

Lt. John W. Casey; October 1985

During my student tour at NAS Southwest I had the distinct pleasure of joining the Skyhawk ski club. The initiation took place on my second formation flight, which was my third solo flight in the TA–4 Skyhawk. We planned to practice section maneuvering, break ups, rendezvous and section approaches. Once safely airborne, I raised the gear and flaps as usual, checking them up and locked. I heard a "thump" as the gear came up and locked. All engine indications checked normal. Once in the operating area, we did the standard formation basics; practicing maneuvers till I got them right.

Then came time for the practice section approach: Two planes simulating a TACAN approach starting with a descent, dirty up, level off and missed approach.

I was hanging in there pretty well as we started down. We slowed the aircraft to gear speed then the instructor signaled for the gear and flaps. The lead called, "Three down and locked, over to two." When I glanced down to check for the three little wheels on the position indicator, the nose gear indicated unsafe. I reported the problem to my lead and he confirmed that my front "roller" had not come down.

We changed the lead and leveled off at 10,000 feet for a visual inspection. The instructor pilot gave me the bad news: The shrink link, or retracting link of the nose wheel was broken and strut pressure had lodged the nose wheel in the wheel well. We proceeded to contact base and both broke out our pocket checklists. I executed all the "prescribed" procedures for an unsafe nose gear: Positive and negative G s, yawing and recycling, all to no avail. Now my stomach started to churn, realizing that my second formation flight would end with a landing in extremis. As I was mentally preparing myself for a trap with no nose gear, the experts back at home plate came up with a better idea. They said that this particular problem calls for a belly landing with the cross deck pendant removed. Heck, I thought, why do that, when I can snag a wire in-flight and stop quickly? It was explained to me how much safer it would actually be to land on the drop-tanks than attempt an in-flight. Thank goodness I had two tanks! Preparing myself for the worst, I foolishly asked base, "If I go off the runway, should I eject?" I was told it would be a decision I would have to make; in other words, "You're a big boy now . . ."

I proceeded back to the field burning the fuel down to a minimum. The instructor went on ahead to land when he himself started getting low on fuel. I was told to set up for a 10–mile straight-in and that an LSO was on station. Uncomfortable as it was, I checked all gear up and locked flaps full down. I selected tank transfer one more time to ensure the tanks were as empty as possible, reducing the threat of fire. As I intercepted the runway centerline at 10 miles, I did a little praying. At five miles, I slowed the aircraft to optimum angle of attack. At three, I started it down.

I tried to fly the best approach I could, so that lineup and sink rate were well under control early in the approach. After I called the ball, I started to decell and the LSO promptly said, "Fly it on speed." Applying power, the inevitable soon happened. The runway was under me so I started to flair. As I flaired, the aircraft decelerated and became extremely cocked up just before impact. The plane touched down and the nose fell through breaking off the nose cone. The plane started drifting to the right, but a little left rudder helped out as the plane came to rest just right of centerline after 2,000 feet of slideout. Secur-

ing the engine about half way through the landing allowed me to open the canopy normally on engine wind down. All those egress drills really paid off; witnesses said I was practically out of the plane before it stopped. I forgot to safe my seat as I egressed, but fortunately didn't fire the seat by catching my foot in the lower handle. I kissed the ground after I was well clear of the aircraft. (A real crowd pleaser!) . . .

Night Skimmer

November 1985

It was a two-plane A–6E bombing mission to the island target practice range off the coast of NAS Far East. The wingman *was* scheduled to fly with the squadron commanding officer since his regular B/N was medically grounded. However, the CO had a last minute schedule conflict and another B/N was assigned to ride shotgun.

The pilots of both Intruders were on their initial tours, having served on board for less than a year. They were qualified and designated formation leaders. Both B/Ns were nearing completion of their first tours and were qualified mission commanders and section leaders.

During the flight briefing they decided to fly the mission as singles rather than in formation. Although they didn't talk about a specific run-in altitude, the squadron's SOP minimum altitude at night was 500 feet MSL.

Both A–6s went through preflight, man-up, engine start and launched just before sunset. They climbed to 5,000 feet MSL but then descended to 200–400 feet MSL during the remaining daylight en route to the target area, approximately 145 nm away. On the way at this low altitude, chaff/flares were dispensed while they performed mild maneuvering.

Before reaching the target area, they climbed to gain radio contact with NAS Far East range control (a remote facility located at the base and not at the target). Failing to make contact, they continued climbing to 15,000 feet and contacted NAS Far East approach to advise they would be working the range. The current altimeter setting was received and set. They descended to 2,000 feet MSL and approached the target from the northwest, intercepting the 12–mile arc, arcing south to intercept the 070–degree run-in heading. During this run the wing pilot set his radar altimeter at 1,000 feet AGL.

While on the 12–mile arc, the wingman had contact with the first A–6 which had just made a target clearing pass and had reported a small boat in the area about a mile short of the target along the run-in heading.

By the time the Intruder approached the target, it was hazy and dark with no visible horizon. On the run-in heading, several mountain ridgelines were visible against

the night sky. The pilot began his turn into the target. When completed, he descended at 1,500 to 2,000 fpm, resetting the radar altimeter to 450 feet AGL. They leveled off at 500 feet for the approach to the target. The B/N's attention was focused on the radar and position of the target.

Established at 500 feet inbound, the pilot noted aircraft heading to be about 100 degrees. He then turned starboard to intercept the pre-briefed run-in heading of 70 degrees. This initial correction was followed by a port turn to center steering. A computer optical placement (COP) check was performed during the run-in. The B/N identified the target on radar, shifted to an expanded display and continued attempts to locate the small surface contact reported earlier by the lead aircraft.

The A–6 was in its final seconds to the target at 400 KIAS when suddenly the aircrew felt a severe "thump." The pilot instinctively began a shallow climb, retarding the throttles to 90 percent, and remarked "It sure felt like we hit something. Maybe a bird."

"It didn't feel like a bird to me," the B/N responded. "It seemed to slow us up too much. I noticed a strong decelerative-type force at the moment it happened, but I'm not sure what it was. I *am* sure that I'm glad we're still flying."

143

What actually happened was that the A-6 had glanced off the water.

They contacted the other Intruder in the area to come in close to look for any damage. A cursory inspection revealed none so the two aircraft separated for return flights to the carrier.

Performing a slow speed controllability check, though, the pilot learned his landing gear wouldn't lower and gear handle recycling had no effect. Activation of the flaps/slats handle resulted in full down slats but no flaps. The other aircraft returned for a close examination, and the crew spotted damage to the engine bay doors.

At the direction of the carrier air traffic control center, the companion plane was detached to marshal, and another aircraft (with the squadron executive officer) was directed to examine the damaged Intruder. They saw that the centerline drop-tank was missing and that the underside of the aircraft had been damaged.

Both aircraft were diverted to nearby NAS Far East. The XO's plane closely monitored the stricken A-6's landing procedures which included a successful emergency landing gear extension. After some tense moments leading to final approach, the Intruder made a safe "slat/no flap" field arrestment.

"That Was Barbed Wire We Just Flew By!"

Lt. Cmdr. G. R. Murchison; February, 1986

The pilot in command was a very senior naval aviator with thousands of hours in type. The co-pilot was a second tour naval aviator with plenty of experience, but new to the aircraft in question. They departed home plate on a two-leg cross-country to NAS West for two days of conferences with a Friday afternoon return scheduled. The co-pilot, who was in the process of qualifying in the aircraft, got into the NATOPS and did the planning for the whole trip.

The trip to NAS West was uneventful in beautiful weather. The pilot-in-command let the co-pilot do most of the flying from the back seat so he could get a feel for the airplane. The co-pilot made a point of verifying the climb rates, cruising speeds, fuel consumption, descent distances and handling characteristics, etc., that he'd been studying in NATOPS. The fun began on the trip home.

A review of the winds aloft forecast and the very high altitude performance indicated a one-leg flight would be feasible *in good weather,* but the weather forecast for home plate was for 800–foot ceilings with three miles visibility. The co-pilot advised the pilot-in-command that the fuel computations did not meet NATOPS requirements with the existing forecast and that he felt a fuel stop was necessary. The pilot-in-command opined that the weather at home plate would probably get better, good alternate fields were nearby, the winds aloft would probably be at least as high a tailwind as forecast and that he could get better gas mileage out of the airplane than the book indicated. The co-pilot voiced his reservations and again recommended a fuel stop; the pilots finally agreed on a target fuel overhead halfway airport and a minimum acceptable weather at home plate of 500 and 1. If either the target fuel or the minimum weather was not met, a fuel stop short of home plate would be made.

After level off at FL390, the co-pilot was relieved to see that the old hand in front was indeed right. The winds aloft gave them a tailwind of just over 120 knots, and the airplane *could* beat the book a little on gas mileage if handled just right. It would be no problem to be above target fuel at halfway airport. Still, there was the weather to consider.

A check with metro at halfway showed home plate to be 300 overcast, visibility one mile in light rain. The co-pilot recommended to the pilot that even though target fuel had been met, since the agreed upon weather minimums had not, a fuel stop should be made as planned. The pilot in command reminded the co-pilot that there were plenty of other suitable fields available before getting to home plate and made the decision to press on.

The co-pilot was a bit uneasy with this decision but comforted himself that he was flying with one of the most experienced aviators in the Navy; they also had a little more gas than planned and the weather wasn't really all that bad and, of course, he didn't want to look bad in the eyes of the old salt who incidentally wrote his fitrep. After all, if push came to shove, he could make sure of a good approach himself with a little coaching from the front seat, right? And so our heros pressed on for home plate, a hot supper and an early evening with the family.

It's amazing how the powers that govern the laws of aviation always seem to save special surprises for those who dare shave the margin. This crew had given away their options when they left halfway and headed on for home plate. Sure, there were plenty of suitable fields in the area, but it turned out that the best weather was at home plate, and that wasn't overly wonderful. If only they'd known what tricks the gremlins had up their sleeves . . .

About 100 miles from home plate, center advised that radar contact was lost and requested an ident. Several repeated tries and three squawk changes later it was apparent that the transponder had died. Just a minor irritation. A TACAN approach to a GCA final was still a perfectly good option. It would only cost a couple of hundred pounds over an en-route descent, and they'd made that up on the way. They'd still be able to land with planned fuel.

Descending through 20,000 feet for the TACAN initial, the TACAN needle began to spin, followed shortly by the loss of DME. A quick check of local TACANs showed it to be an airplane and not a ground equipment problem. The pilot advised approach control that due to a TACAN failure, he was transitioning to the overhead ADF approach (there goes another 200 pounds) and [advised approach control] of his estimated position. The situation now was beginning to get a little tight. With only an ADF the likelihood of shooting a successful approach in the existing weather was less than optimum. And the weather at *all* fields within range that even had an ADF approach was below ADF minimums, including home plate. The pilot made the decision to stick with home plate and hope for a skin paint radar contact from approach.

On the outbound leg of the approach a most welcome "I have a skin paint heading 150 . . . now in a left turn" came over the radio. "Roger, that's us" from the pilot brought prompt and accurate radar vectors to final from approach followed by a very nice GCA. Breaking out under the overcast with the runway in sight the following call came from approach: "100, tower clearance not received, wave-off straight ahead, stand by for approach this frequency." The co-pilot immediately scanned the runway and adjacent taxiways and said to the pilot "Sir, the runway is clear, I recommend we land now." (Post-flight investigation revealed that the reason landing clearance had not been received on the first approach was that the tower watch had been less than alert and had missed the request for clearance from approach. There was, in fact, no conflict.) The pilot elected to take it around just in case there was some unseen conflict.

Fuel was now becoming a real factor. As the aircraft entered the clouds on missed approach, the pilot advised the controller he wanted an "emergency fuel approach." The controller brought the airplane around the pattern for an abbreviated approach that ended up high, fast and lined up well left of centerline—too high and too fast and too far left to land.

By now the situation was getting tense in the cockpit. The pilot decided to try a circling approach under the overcast, but lost sight of the runway and once again ended up in a position from which a landing could not be made. The pilot elected to try a 90/270 maneuver to make a downwind landing on the duty runway. About 180 degrees through the 270–degree turn the pilot went outside the cockpit to look for the runway, and the co-pilot noticed the aircraft rolling rapidly toward the inverted with the nose falling through. The co-pilot slammed the throttle to MRT [military rated thrust], yelled "I've got it" over the ICS, leveled the wings on the instruments and pulled to just below stall angle of attack. The airplane came out of the clouds in a slight nose-down attitude with a considerable rate of descent, which was arrested just inches above the water! Both pilot and co-pilot distinctly remember being able to see the barbs on a barbed wire fence extending out into the shallow water as the airplane bottomed out.

This brush with death had a marked calming effect in the cockpit. A flawless instrument 360–degree turn was executed just below the overcast and a final landing made downwind (winds were only 3 knots) on the duty runway. The crew shut down in the line with 400 pounds indicated on the fuel gauge and went home a whole lot wiser.

Ledr. Murchison is assigned to VA–27, an A–7 squadron based at NAS Lemoore, Calif.

Somebody Out There
Is Trying to Kill Me

Lt. Cmdr. Jim Barnett; March 1986

The Tomcat I was assigned had been downed on its last flight for a bad front cockpit airspeed indicator. "No problem," the maintenance control chief said, "they put a new indicator in it and it checked good on deck."

I taxied my trusty Tomcat to cat one for launch. It was pretty dark, so I reminded my RIO to give me an airspeed call as we went off. I also wanted a backup if my airspeed indicator didn't work. Sure enough as we became airborne my RIO called 150 knots while my indicator was only showing about 80. The angle of attack (AOA) was working OK so I felt relieved. The hop would not be difficult with an operable AOA system and backup airspeed calls from my RIO.

A 2 + 15 night air intercept flight is not very challenging and fuel considerations require that you be conservative with the throttles. I wanted to be at max trap fuel for my approach because you never know when the recovery will be delayed or if airborne fuel is available.

I was assigned a marshal altitude of 6,000 feet. Oh boy, I thought, I must be the sacrificial lamb. It never seems to fail that the first airplane on the approach gets a foul deck wave-off. After checking my fuel state I felt good because I would be a couple of hundred pounds above max trap at my ramp time.

I was established in the marshal stack in plenty of time to relax and think about the upcoming approach and trap. The airspeed indicator problem seemed to be more of a nuisance than anything else, and I was adjusted to using the AOA indicator as my airspeed reference. Wouldn't you know it, marshal said the launch was running late and assigned new approach times. No problem though, I had planned ahead. I'd still have enough gas for a possible foul deck wave-off and other approaches.

I commenced on time (as usual) and felt confident I could get an OK three wire as I came down the chute. Leveling off at 1,200 feet, without my airspeed indicator, I began to feel a bit uncomfortable. Fortunately, that didn't last long, since I could use my AOA indexers after lowering the landing gear. I slowed to 15 units AOA and compared that to the RIO's airspeed and my computed airspeed for current landing weight. Everything was working as advertised. At three NM I prepared to start my descent using the ACLS [automatic carrier landing system] needles. It sure seemed awful dark in front of my airplane. Oh well, I consoled myself with the knowledge that I would see the boat in a mile or two. At one mile, I finally realized that it wasn't going to happen. The FLOLS [Fresnel lens optical landing system] and landing area lights were still not on and at three-quarters of a mile, approach control directed a wave-off due to the launch still in progress.

I established myself on the downwind leg of the wave-off/bolter pattern and waited for approach to turn me back in. They finally called my interval but I was 12 NM downwind before I was directed to turn in for another approach. No sweat, I had plenty of time to get established on the approach, but I was using a lot of extra gas on that "cross-country" downwind.

A quick calculation of my fuel revealed I would have only 3,600 pounds of fuel when I called the ball. My RIO called the ball but forgot to tell Paddles that I did not have an airspeed indicator. Oh well, he was backing me up with calls off his indicator. He kept calling me fast, with a fast chevron in the AOA indexer. The meatball was showing me a little low, so a little attitude would fix the fast and low conditions. Then the LSO said I was *slow*. Well, every naval aviator will tell you low and slow is not a good place to be, when you're behind the boat at night. I applied power, but too much of it, and proceeded to bolter.

I really blew that one. Now it was time to prepare to do the next approach right. I got turned in at seven miles and as I came out of the turn, I saw an F/A–18 turning in front of me. Well, the approach controller really screwed that one up. My radar showed the Hornet 1.7 miles in front of me. Fortunately, the 18 got a foul deck wave-off. I was all set for a "rails" pass and a "slider" in the wardroom, but the wave-off lights came on for me, too! Now I was really hurting. I had 2,600 pounds of fuel, at night, in blue-water ops. Off toward the tanker I went and got a "tally-ho" after passing 2,500 feet. That F/A–18 was already plugged. And my RIO couldn't contact the tanker on the radio.

My RIO finally discovered that his radio had the wrong preset frequency dialed in. A quick check of my fuel state showed 800 pounds in each tank and my personal "fun meter" was already pegged to the left side. I made a quick call to the tanker that "I need to plug ASAP" and he said "hang on for just a minute and we'll be complete with the F/A–18." Great! I told myself to cool down, because I could easily fly around for another 15 to 20 minutes (assuming my fuel quantity indicator was accurate), but a little voice in the back of my mind kept reminding me what would happen after that 15 to 20 minutes were up if I didn't get some fuel *fast*.

Finally the Hornet left, and I set up to plug the tanker. I engaged the refueling drogue and my heart began to slow to a normal pace as my RIO called that we were receiving fuel. Suddenly, the IFR probe just popped out of the refueling drogue. I thought my heart had stopped beating. I backed out and plugged again. The probe popped off again. But each time I was getting 300 to 400 pounds of fuel. I think my fun meter finally broke at that point.

I called the Air Boss and explained my dilemma as I continued to engage and disengage the refueling drogue, getting 300 to 400 pounds each time. I told him I needed a ready-deck because when I got up to 3,500 pounds of fuel in my aircraft, I wanted to commence my approach. He said to "come on down" as soon as I was ready.

I finally left the tanker with 3,700 pounds of fuel, feeling like I was upside down. By now the airspeed indicator problem was **really** getting on my nerves. I told myself not to worry because I was always taught in the training command that the attitude instruments **never lie.** Thank God . . . this time they told me the truth.

At five NM I called Paddles and told him all my problems. He told me not to worry, that they'd catch me this time, but he advised (oh, by the way) that the two and three wires had been pulled. Wonderful! After all this, the pass was almost anticlimactic. My heart finally started beating again after I taxied out of the landing area.

To me, this experience reinforced a well-known philosophy. There are hundreds of people on the carrier directly and indirectly involved in my mission every time I fly my jet on and off the boat. They are doing the best they can to ensure my flight is a safe one. Nonetheless, every tail hook naval aviator knows that he must operate under the philosophy that "Somebody Out There Is Trying To Kill Me."

LCdr. Jim Barnett entered the Navy through the AOCS program and was originally a F–14 RIO. After his first fleet tour with VF–24, he reported to the training command for pilot training. He is currently the aviation safety officer for VF–21 and just recently returned from a [Western Pacific]/Indian Ocean deployment in USS *Constellation.*

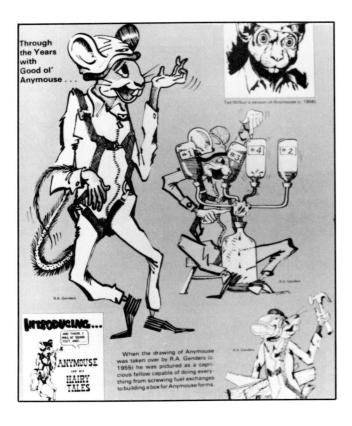

Through the Years with Good ol' Anymouse . . .

When the drawing of Anymouse was taken over by R.A. Genders (c. 1955) he was pictured as a capricious fellow capable of doing everything from screwing fuel exchanges to building a box for Anymouse forms.

Needed: A Bigger and Better Anymouse

Cmdr. Richard Shipman; May 1986

Anymouse is growing old, fat and non-productive. The Anymouse (anonymous reporting) column of *Approach* has been a fixture since the magazine began. It allows people to identify safety hazards in a way that would never have existed within the established Naval safety reporting system. But Anymouse has more than 30 years in, and is ready for retirement.

Since all contributions are submitted anonymously, the information sometimes tends to be of the "sour grapes" variety with little safety relevance. Feedback from the good information is limited to a few pages in *Approach,* and there is no cumulative data base. Neither is the system structured to proide follow-up on safety hazards identified. Finally, there is little official encouragement to submit these reports.

In contrast to the Navy's Anymouse program, the civilian aviation sector has established an informative and well-organized anonymous safety reporting system (ASRS) funded by the FAA and run by NASA [National Aeronautics and Space Administration]. The ASRS has been in existence since 1976 and provides three important functions:

- Gathers candid information on safety hazards from the aviation grass roots: pilots, controllers, dispatchers, mechanics, etc.
- Provides information on safety hazards, gleaned from the reports, to agencies that may be able to take action—FAA, NTSB, specific airports, etc.
- Gives feedback to the aviation community through a monthly publication entitled "Callback" and through computer data established from ASRS reports.

The keynotes to the success of the civilian program are absolute anonymity and immunity from prosecution for the submitter. The reports are handled using security measures that are equivalent to secret. The only record of the identity of the submitter is destroyed shortly after the submission of the report. Immunity from license suspension is guaranteed by federal aviation regulations, provided certain provisions are met.

The safety benefits of an anonymous safety reporting system are immense. Without having to worry about prosecution or personal identification, pilots and controllers are free to "tell it like it is" and "'fess up" on errors or shortcomings in their performance. This type of real-life human factors information is almost impossible to obtain through traditional methods such as mishap investigations. And since human performance is the most common cause of aircraft mishaps, this is the kind of information that is most useful in any accident prevention program.

The Navy, through the Naval Safety Center and its safety publications department, is well-suited to establish an improved anonymous reporting system—hereafter referred to as the NAASREP (Naval Aviation Anymouse Safety Reporting Program). Details of the program could be laid down in OPNAVINST 3750.6 with a concurrent written guarantee of immunity from prosecution leading from submission of the report. As with the ASRS program, immunity would not be granted for reports of aircraft accidents, deliberate misconduct or criminal offenses. The system would in no way supercede any existing reporting requirements. Instead, the program would tap a resource that is generally unavailable now: insights into individual errors which probably didn't lead to an accident but could very well in the future.

All reports would be submitted to the editor of *Approach* magazine. The submitter would need to identify himself on the report for two reasons. First, to avoid the sour grapes "my boss is a loser" type of submission that is really not productive. Second, identification is necessary to gain additional information, if necessary. After a maximum of 10 days, the originator's identification would be removed and destroyed with no further method of recall available. The report would be sanitized and entered into the computer bank for future reference. Those reports that provide good safety information would be sanitized and published in *Approach* magazine. Follow-up action on anonymous submissions would often be necessary. Reports that appear to warrant further action would be routed in their anonymous versions to the appropriate department at the Naval Safety Center. If they determine that a bona fide problem exists, they could then forward recommendations to the air wing, air station, squadron or staff for action. The Safety Center has never had nor does it want punitive authority. NAVSAFECEN's role would be limited to recommendations to those staffs or officers who do.

A hypothetical example of a NAASREP might help bring the process into focus. A tactical jet lands by mistake at the wrong airport while on a visual approach at night. The civilian field is uncontrolled and no traffic conflict exists. The crew realizes the mistake immediately on touchdown and does a touch and go. An uneventful landing is completed at the nearby intended point of landing.

Under the present reporting system, no report is required. The crew could submit a hazard report since a safety hazard did exist, but the chances are slim that they will confess their error to their squadron superiors who will then submit an official non-privileged report. Most likely, the story will go untold except perhaps in the bar late one night.

With the NAASREP program in place, however, the crew could submit the report with no one else in the squadron being the wiser. The crew might provide some insight into why they made the error: distraction in the cockpit, unfamiliarity with the area, reluctance to ask for vectors due to pride, etc. An insightful piece of information would then be fed into the computer pertaining to visual approaches and mistaken landings. An interesting article could appear in *Approach,* with all details sanitized except the two airports involved. And, if this was the fifth NAASREP received by ATC specialists at the Naval Safety Center relating to these two airports, they might recommend that a warning be printed on Approach Plates about possible confusion between the two airports. Finally, safety experts looking into problems related to visual approaches could get a printout on all reports related to visual approaches submitted to NAASREP.

The Navy would not have the "carrot" of immunity from FAA license suspension to stimulate report submission, as does the civilian ASRS program. Why then would the naval aviation community submit these reports? Because they care about safety. Ask a pilot how to improve safety and he will tell you, and tell you and tell you. If the submitter is guaranteed that no negative repercussions will result from his report, there will be plenty of submissions.

The ASRS program was spurred by the TWA crash near Dulles Airport in the mid–1970s, which was caused by confusion over the meaning of "cleared for the approach." Investigators learned later that an identical situation had happened to United Airlines several months earlier, but visual weather conditions enabled the crew to avoid the hills prior to impact. United internally shared its lessons learned, but there was no vehicle available to share the information with the rest of the flying commun-

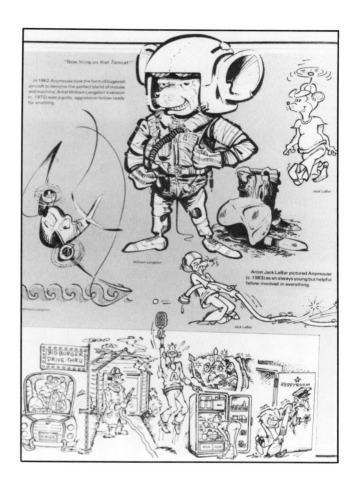

ity. The Navy has a similar situation within its squadrons, and it needs a way to share its lessons learned—be they embarrassing or not—with the entire naval aviation community. The NAASREP could be that vehicle.

Anymouse ain't dead yet. It's still available for your use if you want to report on a naval aviation safety hazard anonymously. But we're not getting nearly as many as we used to. Anymouse is 33 years old this year, and it was very popular in the fleet during its early years. Even today we receive some very important letters addressed to Anymouse. Some appear in the magazine. Others are implemented and responded to without publication which still serves a purpose in enhancing safety. In such instances, we don't have to publish them and the system still works. Until such time that Anymouse would be superseded by another system, be it the NAASREP or some other program, keep using Anymouse, Approach Magazine, Naval Safety Center, NAS Norfolk, VA 23511-5796.—Ed.

Cdr. Shipman, a naval reservist with Volunteer Training Unit 8686 at NAS Norfolk, Va., is currently on special assignment to *Approach.* He was editor of *Approach* from January 1975 to January 1977. When on active duty, he flew A–4s and A–7s and now is a 727 pilot for People Express Airlines.

Fuelishness

Lt. Bud Bishop; June 1986

USS *Boat* had just returned from 100 days on Gonzo Station in the Indian Ocean. It had been a successful line period, challenging our aircrews time and again. On this particular day, the weather was not looking good, with towering cumulus and stratus layers to 35,000 feet. A few squalls were in the area, and it looked like the weather was starting to deteriorate.

I was crewed with an experienced pilot for a routine tanker flight. We had 26,000 pounds of fuel, with only 4,000 pounds scheduled to give away. I briefed a secondary mission of flying a simulated FCF [functional check flight] profile so that I could get my qual. We discussed the flight in depth, concentrating on some of the weather aspects. The aircraft we were assigned had just landed on the previous recovery. While maintenance personnel turned it around, we obtained a brief from the last aircrew on its status.

We were told that the selectable fuel quantity needle was intermittent whenever the wings or drop-tanks were selected, but it worked fine when the fuselage tanks were selected. The main fuel quantity gauge seemed to work well, but they said that it had stuck momentarily at 4,000 pounds during their approach. However, they selected "main" on the selectable needle, and it matched the indication on the main quantity needle.

We discussed as a crew whether we should down the aircraft but decided to go ahead, man it up and check the gauges during turnup. Fuel was sorely needed airborne with the weather deteriorating, and there wasn't another tanker available to replace ours. We rationalized that we had 26K, a give of only 4.0 and would never be far from the carrier even if we did have fuel quantity indicator

problems. We were forging that well-known chain that leads to mishaps.

We manned up, started the engines, checked the fuel quantity indicating system and found that the selectable needle was "out to lunch" as advertised. The main needle (registering the tank that directly feeds the engines) indicated a good quantity, though. Our crew decision was to go with it. The system looked adequate for the intended flight profile, even though we were uneasy about the stray trons in our fuel quantity gauge. We forged another link when we heard that the *one* aircraft we were scheduled to tank was having mechanical problems, and was not going to launch. That fact simply cemented our decision to launch; now we were really fat.

We launched for a practice FCF profile, in a tanker with no scheduled give, in less than optimum weather. No problem—usually. We launched Case II, but the ceiling shortly dropped to 1,800. It was going to be a *colorful* recovery with all the squalls around!

We climbed to 20,000 feet, trying to complete the items on the FCF profile sheet. Due to our gross weight, we could not climb to the required 40,000 feet. Besides, we wanted to stay lower in case any of the recovering aircraft needed some fuel. We noted cloud layers at 13,000, 15,000 and a solid block from 17,000 to 19,000 feet. We found a hole abeam the ship at eight miles that seemed suitable for refueling, and informed tanker control that we would amend our tanking altitude from 10,000 to 14,000 due to weather. We had a layer below us at 13,000 and one above us at 17,000. We were all set.

Just then tanker control called us back. An A–7 tanker needed a package check. Great! He could check ours at the same time. We gave the A–7 our position and waited. Glancing down at the fuel needles, we noticed that the selectable needle was not functioning even when the main tanks were selected. We now had all of our chips riding on that main indicating needle.

Suddenly, the A–7 appeared in front of us, coming out of a cloud and crossing right to left. Initiating a rendezvous maneuver, we worked to keep him in sight. My pilot placed the fuel ready switch in "Flt."

It has happened before, and will probably happen again . . . while reaching for the fuel ready switch, the pilot **inadvertently actuated the fuselage fuel dump switch.** We spent the next 8 to 10 minutes dodging clouds as we completed the join-up. I noticed during this time that our main fuel needle was stuck on 4.0, when it should normally be reading 8.0. I told the pilot that I thought our main needle was "outta there." He acknowledged it, but was concentrating on the A–7. As we got closer, the A–7 pilot transmitted "DUMPS." *That* was when it hit us. We had dumped the fuselage tanks down to the standpipe and were transferring all of our fuel remaining from the wings and drop-tanks directly out the back end. The chain continued to grow.

The pilot secured the dumps and switched to "Flt," checking his switchology this time. When the checkout was complete, we returned to our holding position and attempted to determine our fuel state. We decided on the worst case, arriving at a figure of 15,000 pounds. We estimated we had dumped 7,000 pounds of fuel. But we didn't *know,* and the only way to find out was to keep transferring the wing fuel into our main tanks, then either dump the wings or pass fuel to other aircraft until our main bag started to empty. We accepted the latter plan and determined to accomplish this right before the recovery. We called other squadron aircraft and asked them to join for tanking.

It was a difficult rendezvous but was accomplished without incident. We gave away as much gas as we could to each aircraft. One asked us what our state was and how much we had to give. We replied, "We're not sure." Finally, as we tanked the last aircraft, our main needle started to fall again, dropping to 7.0. We secured the tanker package and reported ourselves as a "dry tanker" to departure. It looked like the main needle was working. However, we didn't know that another link had just been added to the chain.

We were given radar vectors to the 10 DME fix on a Case III approach. As we descended, our main needle was still indicating 7.0. "Hey, we have more gas than we thought!" We figured, and were feeling a lot better.

We commenced a normal approach, then watched in dismay as our main needle dropped to 4.0 when we dirtied up. Maybe we *didn't* have as much as we thought. Although 4.0 was still enough at this point, we were 3,000 pounds below what we planned for, due to delays in the recovery. Flying in and out of rain squalls, we struggled to stay lined up, and worked hard to see the boat. At the ball call, I glanced down to read our fuel state, and was shocked to see the needle at 2.0! A–6s have flamed out with as much as 700 pounds remaining on the indicator, and with each Case III approach we knew we would use around 800–1,000 pounds of gas.

As the pilot struggled to keep the aircraft lined up, I held windshield air on so he could see through his windscreen. We were in a violent squall that substantially reduced visibility. Murphy's Law just added another link to the chain—we boltered. The moment we touched down the main needle went to *zero,* and the master caution light came on as the left generator warning light illuminated. As we passed 800 feet on climbout, the main needle went to 2.0, then to 4.0, then back to 2.0, then fluctuated in little increments in the 2.0 area. I didn't have any idea how much fuel we **really** had.

CATCC knew we were low state from our ball call, so they readied another tanker in case we boltered again.

On the next approach we caught the three-wire, and rolled out of the wires indicating 1,300 pounds remaining. The selectable needle was still dead. As I reflected on all of the decisions during the brief and the flight, I realized that we were taking small chances here and there that, combined with one switchology error and two applications of Murphy's Law endangered us and our aircraft. A *minor* fuel indicator problem wasn't so minor after all.

Lt. Bishop flies A–6Es with VA 52 based at NAS Whidbey Island, Wash., on deployment in USS *Carl Vinson* (CVN 70). He is the squadron schedules officer.

A Night to Remember

Lt. Dave Parsons; June 1986

Ninety-nine tarbox, rigging MOVLAS [manually operated visual landing aid system] Station 3 . . . "

"Station 3 . . . where the hell is that?" I wondered. Wherever it was, it was beginning to look as if tonight was not going to be a normal CASE III recovery. We had already been waved off once, following our flight lead, two other F–14s from our sister squadron, and a pair of

A–7s, into the "penalty box." It wasn't unusual for the first two A–7s to get waved off. But now there were six of us at 1,200 feet, dirty and burning gas.

Something was definitely wrong with the ball; we'd gone CLARA [which means the pilot doesn't see the ball on the lens] in the middle and only half the datums were visible in close. Since no one else had trapped, I assumed it wasn't my pilot's fault. He was a nugget, but the pass wasn't that bad. As we soared by the ship on the wave-off, it was too dark to make out any details that might explain the mysterious disappearing ball.

I couldn't imagine CATCC letting this many aircraft push if the delay was merely a slow launch. Perhaps we had caught a taxiing jet in front of the lens as they wrapped up the launch. But the Station 3 call? Was the Whale parked too far forward? Was the deck really moving big time? It wasn't adding up.

"Uh . . . Do you know where station 3 is?" my pilot asked. "Never heard of it, but something's screwy down there," I replied.

Station 3, Station 3—I racked my memory and came up blank. Two cruises, more than 1,000 Tomcat hours and that was a new one on me. I had a hunch that I wasn't alone. I was willing to bet most of our partners in the bolter pattern didn't know where it was either. Paddles would have more information shortly. As if on cue, Paddles asked us where we lost the ball and whether we had regained it in close. Something was definitely wrong and it didn't appear the solution was soon coming.

What we didn't know was that an A–7 on Cat 4 from the preceding launch had wedged its launch bar firmly in the dustpan—the assembly that was supposed to guide the launch bar into the box. A pitching deck combined with a wet surface had caused the nosewheel to cock just as the launch bar entered the narrow throat of the assembly. With wings folded, the A–7 did not foul the landing area and the ball was still visible from the fantail at deck level. However, as the first aircraft called the ball, it was obvious that the folded starboard wing was obscuring the lens in close.

While the first aircraft were making their approaches, human and mechanical muscle were trying to free the troublesome launch bar. Despite the help of a tractor and every able-bodied man available, the launch bar refused to budge. The comm circuits between the LSO platform, tower, CATCC and the bridge were alive with discussion of the alternatives. While it was becoming obvious that the standard lens would not hack it with the A–7 parked on Cat 4, one of the A–7s suffered a PC–2 hydraulic failure, necessitating an immediate landing. The Boss conferred with the Captain and the LSO and decided to rig the MOVLAS on Station 3, the starboard side.

Meanwhile, every two minutes, aircraft were making stabs at the deck. As flight deck personnel were rigging the MOVLAS, and the emergency A–7 was working his way around the pattern, our flight lead *landed his F–14 without a ball of any kind.* That really bolstered the Boss's confidence in the LSOs. However, the LSOs knew better—the timing had been just right on that one. The pilot was one of the best F–14 drivers in the air wing. He'd had the pass wired with good calls from the LSOs and a momentarily steady deck.

As the MOVLAS was being rigged for the A–7, we waved off a second time, tank-plus-one on the ball. In the cockpit we concentrated on turning downwind and assessing the situation. I asked my pilot for confirmation of fuel state off the tapes. My gut feeling told me we'd really need to hawk the gas tonight. Paddles now began the Station 3 brief. "Ninety-nine, MOVLAS Station 3, starboard side, fly a normal ball, but watch out for the tendency to drift right, especially in close. Your scan won't feel natural."

"Holy Cow!" *Starboard side!* I wasn't looking forward to the next pass; night, pitching deck, no needles and MOVLAS on the starboard side. I could imagine what my nugget pilot must be thinking.

I heard the voice of the seasoned A–7 driver with the hydraulic problem call the ball and watched his lights approach the dark shape of the ship. They stopped abruptly, showing it could be done. The A–7 driver's problems were ended. Ours were about to start.

I called our state (now down to 3.4) and was directed to tank. Good call, since there were still four of us in the bolter pattern and the rest of the marshal stack could show up at anytime. We might as well get our gas while the tanker had plenty to give. Besides, maybe the problem A–7 could be moved and the normal lens cleared. In any case, we welcomed the chance to get off the merry-go-round. CATCC directed us to "clean up, take angels three, texaco twelve o'clock, five miles, cleared to switch button fourteen."

Great! Only now we had a problem: we couldn't clean up. The gear retracted but not the flaps. Whipping my PCL [pocket checklist] out, we went through the appropriate steps but nothing in or out of the book worked. That would really make the night interesting, I thought. I hadn't seen anything yet!

I informed both CATCC and the tanker of our problem, also letting the A–6 know we'd be at 225 knots to avoid overspeeding the flaps. Talking to our squadron representative in CATCC yielded no further answers. We reviewed our situation while executing the rendezvous with the tanker. I knew we'd covered everything, and felt reasonably confident that we were still one step ahead of the game.

The rendezvous was uneventful, although it seemed to take an eternity to complete at 225 knots. Our fuel had decreased to 3.0. As the basket came into view, it seemed to be moving a bit more than normal. We moved in and stabilized a few feet from the basket. It was well lit, for which I gave silent thanks. The first try didn't make it, but no sweat—it had been a while. I wasn't too concerned as I used my most confident and coaxing calls on my nugget pilot. After the fifth or sixth try, though, I allowed a little concern to creep into my mind.

It was painfully obvious that tanking with the flaps down was not easy. The slower speed was causing the basket to move more than usual. Any power application in the flaps down configuration caused us to balloon and produced excessive nose movement.

We seemed to get tantalizingly close each time, only to lose it at the last moment due to the bow wave or the pitching moment as power was applied to make the connection. I knew my pilot wanted to get into that basket just as badly as I did. His breathing was getting heavier with each attempt. The last power application seemed to be causing us to tap the rim each time despite a good approach. Eight, nine, ten, eleven tries . . . no luck. Finally a wobbly stab and a boot of rudder on try No. 12 and we were in!

The green light came on as we drove the hose into the takeup reel. Relief! I relaxed in my straps and waited for the totalizer to show an increase. "106, you'll have to back out while we recycle our package." Stunned, I rogered the call while wondering what could possibly be next. Monitoring the transmissions, CATCC requested our state to which I replied 2.4. I knew they couldn't be any more pleased than we were at the prospect of chasing that elusive basket again. I soberly watched the swaying basket fade away as it journeyed back into its berth inside the buddy store and began to back out again. "106, cleared in."

I prayed for a less painful bout with the basket this time. Our prior experience revealed no secrets-to-success in plugging with flaps down. I silently kicked myself for not practicing full-flap tanking in the past. So much for hindsight.

We moved back into position and began our first approach. The first few tries weren't as bad as before, but we still weren't in. Each time we backed out for another try, I looked at the totalizer as it counted down 2.3, 2.2, 2.1. CATCC was silent, but I knew they were listening intently as I updated the state every 200 pounds. Try No. 6 and still no dice. The low-fuel light was glowing now. I didn't want to consider how long we should keep at this before calling it quits and making a play for the deck. We didn't know it, but our squadron had sent the squadron expert on barricades to CATCC.

The sweat that was trickling down my back under my wet suit suddenly began to feel very cold as I considered the option of ejection. The thought of losing a mega-buck F–14 and then swimming in the cold, black North Atlantic did not appeal to me in the least. I asked for a readout of the tapes from my pilot: 1,000 on the left, 900 on the right. We had to get in, now! Time was running out. Trying to

exude the utmost confidence in my pilot, I kept my comments as positive as possible.

The last stab seemed to be doing us in each time. At my suggestion, we tried setting up a constant rate approach, trying to avoid any rapid addition of power. On the first try, it almost worked. So close! The second try looked good all the way in. I think perhaps we both willed it in. It was a good plug—green light and golden flow. The right tape had gone as low as 800 pounds. The dark thoughts of ejection left my mind and I no longer cared which side of the deck the lens was mounted on.

During our time on the tanker the troublesome launch bar yielded to the Crash and Salvage crew's electric saw, which allowed the stuck A–7 to be moved well away from Cat 4. Normal landings were now being made although that didn't end the problems Murphy had sprinkled throughout the air wing.

When Murphy strikes, he strikes big. An F–14 from our sister squadron experienced a combined hydraulic failure and an A–7 blew a tire upon touchdown. The latter required a FOD walkdown, which caused more wave-offs. A KA–6D was unable to retract his basket and then an EA–6B with no external lights had to take a gear check wave-off. No single aircraft made it aboard on the first try; *one F–14 made seven passes*. Paddles was really earning his money.

And us? A hook-skip bolter due to pitching deck on the first try. We snagged the three wire the next time around. That familiar deceleration never felt so good. After the last aircraft hit the deck, the CAG LSOs began looking over the passbook. One remarked, "You know, we saw just about everything tonight . . . except a barricade." He wrote the following words in the margin: "A night to remember."

Lt. Parsons, formerly a RIO with VF 102, has just checked aboard to be the next editor of *Approach*.

More than Just a Single-Engine Landing!

Lt. D. C. "Rip" Dykhoff; August 1986

Gotta keep these Tomcats tight on this section go. I'm sure some of these Air Force types here at Nellis are watching. Off come the brakes and we're lookin' good on the roll as we thunder down the runway. With "Nevada" (our flight leader) being smooth as usual we rotate and are airborne. There's the signal to raise the gear, now the signal to come out of afterburner—hey, I can't get the right one out of burner! Yahoo, here we go, spitting out in front of our leader; he probably wonders what the heck I'm doing. Got the throttle back to military now and it seems to be working ok. I must have just ham-fisted it.

"Had a little problem there Nevada, but got it squared away now. You still have the lead, I'll rejoin."

Damn sticky throttle. How embarrassing, and at an Air Force base no less. Well, this sortie can only get better.

"Black Knight Three, your bogeys bear 060 at 22 miles." All right, I smell F-15 meat. My trusty RIO, "Kid," has the knobs spinning in the back. We'll probably have a contact any second. Getting closer to the action; better use a little burner and get some smack on these jets. What the—not again! What's the deal with this right throttle? Stuck in burner again. Maybe there really is something wrong with it. I'll just cycle it up to zone 5 and back. Nope. How about manual throttle mode or the throttle friction? No joy again. I suppose deadly force is authorized here; maybe I can bust it loose—still no luck. I guess the right throttle is going to stay right where it is.

"Kid, there isn't anything in the book about this, is there?"

"I'll check, Rip, but I don't think so."

Hmm . . . guess we'll head home, shut the right one down with the emergency handle and land single-engine. Not a fun situation, but it could be worse. Sure glad I've got 11,000 feet to land on instead of USS *Boat*.

"Rip, Nevada will follow you back. You've got the lead."

"Let's run through the single-engine landing checklist, Kid. We'll do it again after we shut the engine down."

Everything's looking normal except for the stuck throttle. Flying the arrival route with the right engine in minimum afterburner and the left one at idle is giving us about 520 knots indicated—sure wish I could get the speed brakes out to slow down, but the military throttle interlock is working as advertised, keeping the boards retracted.

"Nevada, I think I'm going to go ahead and shut it down so I don't burn all my gas."

"I think I'd wait until we get a little closer to the field, Rip," lead replied.

I guess he's right. Might as well keep it running as long as possible. I'll just have to dump gas anyway since we've still got plenty.

Got the field in sight now and we're going to run over these two F–5s in front of us if we don't slow down; looks like a good time to shut it down and get set up to land. Better start dumping, too. We don't need this 6,500 pounds of JP–4.

"I'll let Approach know we're shutting down the right engine, Rip."

"Ok. Thanks Kid." Emergencies sure make you appreciate two-seat airplanes.

It didn't take much time to starve the engine after I pulled the shutoff. I guess it burns the last few drops in a hurry when you're in afterburner. Better bring the power up on the left engine; we sure don't need a compressor stall now that only one engine is running. I'll just push the left throttle smoothly up to military. Hey, that doesn't feel like military—and it's only reading about 90 percent! I'll bring it back and then advance it again. Now it's only reading 88 percent. Holy smokes, that's not enough to fly

a Turkey with the gear and flaps down! And I don't even know if it's enough to fly it clean.

What now? Should I try to restart the right engine? Let's see, airstart procedure: throttle—off, airstart switch—on, throttle—idle. Definitely can't do that with the right throttle stuck in burner. Maybe if I just pushed the shutoff back in and turned the airstart switch on. I really don't think this thing will restart anyway; I must have cavitated the heck out of the fuel lines when I pulled the shutoff with the engine in burner. I can't land in burner anyway. I would just be buying some time and if it doesn't start I'd be wasting time—I think I better concentrate on using what altitude and speed I have to make this approach work the first time.

Let's see—I know from single-engine landing practice that 88 percent isn't enough to fly level with the gear and flaps down, and I know I don't have any wave-off capability. Salvaging a high rate of descent often requires military power when you're single-engine; we sure don't want to get into that situation. This one approach looks like my only chance to land this jet. We're only eight miles from the field and it looks like a glide slope I can make even with the power I have. I've got to make it happen now; once this altitude is gone that's all she wrote. I wish I had some time to think about this, but it looks like this is my only chance.

We're still really fast. I should have figured that since we shut the engine down indicating 500 plus. That's ok, I can get rid of the extra speed. I just don't want to get caught slow. I think if I get to landing speed I'll have no chance to climb or even fly level. I could raise the gear, but with this much power available I doubt that we could fly with the flaps down and we sure couldn't accelerate to raise them. I guess I better have the runway made and be positive that I can land before I dare let the airplane slow down to landing speed. Oops, forgot to start dumping with all the excitement.

"Dump's coming on, Kid. I don't know how much we'll get rid of with this nose-down attitude."

"Roger that, Rip, I've got my finger on the gage."

Let's see, how did that PEL [precautionary emergency landing] profile go that we used to fly in A–4s? I wish I knew what kind of glide slope to expect but we never practiced anything like this. I've got to get slowed down here. I'll sideslip and bleed some speed. Geez, this isn't working! With the aircraft clean it's just not slowing down at all on this space shuttle approach I'm flying.

"We're cleared to land on the right, Rip."

"Roger that, Kid."

Only a couple miles out now, and we're still at 400 knots. What do I do? I don't know if I can go around.

"The gear is coming, Kid; the heck with the gear doors!"

That still isn't going to do it. I don't believe it, we're going to cross the threshold at 360 knots! There's no way I can land this thing—but with this much speed I certainly have plenty of energy to get back away from the ground.

"We're going around."

"Roger that, Rip, I'm right behind you."

OK, gear up and we'll zoom-climb to a low key position if we can get there.

"I think a left turn is our best bet, Kid. After we're through the turn, there's not much below us in case we have to get out."

"Concur, Rip."

Looks like one of the main mounts didn't come up; no wonder after using them for a speed brake at 400 knots. I hope the gear will come back down after all that! Oh good, now all three are up and locked. Better get the dump going again. I sure don't need this 5,500 pounds of fuel.

"We're doing ok, Kid, the airspeed is bleeding fast, but I think we'll make it around."

"Roger that, Rip, we're cleared for either runway."

Abeam the landing area we're about 700 feet AGL and the airspeed is decaying through 250—we should make it, no problem. I'll just hold the gear and flaps. I can still see us settling into the ground with a single TF–30 at 88 percent. We could be stars in the next film about the backside of the power curve.

Coming through the ninety, we've definitely got it made. The gear is coming, now the flaps. Boy, we're not bleeding as fast as I thought. Don't tell me I'm going to do it again! I am, we're fast again! Crossing the threshold at 230 knots this time. I just can't believe we're this damned hot! We don't have max knots to zoom with this time. I'm almost sure we don't have go-around capability on this one. I'm going to have to land.

Here goes my first 220–knot landing—oh geez, two big bounces—this is not any fun at all. We're halfway down the runway now, still airborne (after two "touch and goes") and we've still got 190 knots. Even a long field arrestment would be a crash here and if we miss the gear I don't even want to think of what would happen.

"We're going around again, Kid. Gear's coming up."

"What about the flaps? I've still got about 175 knots. I know it will fly flaps up at that speed and I've got to minimize my drag.

"Flaps are coming up, Kid. We can fly in ground effect for a while. I'm going to try to restart the right."

But how can I restart the right? It's a long shot that it would work given the state of the right engine. Besides, my only option at this speed is a crossbleed start and that would suck power from the working engine, something I don't have enough of anyway. I better try to fly with what I have. We've done all we can do to minimize the thrust required to fly; thank God we're not any slower. We may be accelerating a little—the airspeed seems to be creeping up towards 180. This ground effect may be helping; we're sure low enough to get it. Our altitude was later estimated by an observer at 10 feet above the runway.

Some small obstacles appear at the end of the runway. I guess this is it—we'll see if we can get this hog away

from the ground. Gently now, if we start bleeding our speed badly this jet's on its way into a smoking hole. We're doing ok. Now a very gentle left turn, we might just make it. Definitely real low through the turn, maybe it will climb a little on downwind.

"Dump's back on, Kid, we may just make it around again."

Uh oh, the flight controls are shaking now; hydraulics seem to be holding up though, not much we can do besides press on.

We're awfully wide abeam after that easy downwind turn. I'll angle back toward the abeam position. Finally made it to 300 feet AGL and 175 knots (clean, of course). I can't get another knot or another foot to save my life. I don't want to pull the nose up. We're just barely hanging on with this airspeed and slowing down will surely increase our drag. If I can just get it through the approach turn, I think we'll make it.

"Tower says we can have a three mile straight-in if we want it, Rip." I guess they think that might help after watching my last landing attempt.

"No, Kid, when we start the approach turn we'll be coming down. Let's plan on turning just past abeam."

"Roger that, Rip." Kid's got about 65 hours in this airplane; at least he's getting a good sea story early in his aviation career.

Time to start the approach turn. Come on, trusty Turkey, hang in there. Bleeding speed a little in the turn but I think we'll make it. Don't have much altitude to play with so I'll have to give away a little speed here. I think we're going to make it! On short final now. "Gear's coming, Kid, and the flaps." Little balloon from the flaps will help us. Now if the wheels just make it down before touchdown—there's the nose, and now both mains! Whew! Now this is a much nicer speed to land at.

"Without the speed brakes and spoilers, we may be a little long on the rollout if we don't catch the gear, Kid."

"I'll read you the airspeeds, you just watch the runway and slow us down, Rip."

Sounds like a plan. It looks like we did miss the short-field gear. Maybe I floated over it as the flaps finished coming down.

"We'll try for the long-field gear but I think we'll be slow by then, Kid."

Coming to a stop now, I think I'll get out and kiss the ground.

"Left engine's coming off, parking brake is set. I'm clear on the canopy. Safeing my seat, Kid."

"I'm safe top and bottom, Rip, the canopy is coming up. . . . "

Lt. Dykhoff flies the F–14 Tomcat with VF 154. He recently completed a seven-month cruise with CVW 14 on board USS *Constellation* (CV 64).

Gold 11 stopped refueling . . . left two crewmen in Base Ops, didn't pay for the gas, didn't have a clearance, didn't align his INS and made an intersection takeoff . . . in near zero-zero weather

Transoceanic Ordeal

Capt. Rob Coopman, USMC; Winter 1986

Our squadron was planning a TRANSLANT [trans-Atlantic] to Bodo, Norway, via Lajes, Azores, to participate in the Anchor Express Exercise. The original plan was to send 15 A-4s split into five plane cells; each cell paired with one KC-135 tanker. The A-4 cells would launch one hour apart from Cherry Point and join the KC-135s near Long Island, entering the first air refueling track. The KC-135, with five A-4s in tow, would then follow the northern route, tank a second and final time south of Newfoundland, then continue to Lajes.

Fuel planning played a key role. Lajes is one of only five locations in the world designated an "Island Destination," which qualifies it for special weather and fuel planning criteria under Air Force Regulations. These regulations allow a TRANSLANT flight to launch with destination and divert weather forecasts at or above 1,000/2. In effect, your destination is also your alternate, so you don't need the standard 3,000/3. Additionally, the aircraft being tanked must arrive over the island destination with one hour of holding fuel, and the tankers must arrive with two hours of holding fuel. Extra fuel to make the continent would not be available.

Our first TRANSLANT attempt ended with our 15 A-4s diverting off the first air refueling track into Pease AFB in New Hampshire. Eleven of the 15 A-4s were unable to receive fuel due to excessive spray around the probe during linkup with the basket; the reason for the spray was not apparent, and the problem is still being studied. We flew back to Cherry Point to regroup and try again a week later with SAC KC-10s.

The day prior to the new TRANSLANT, a KC-10 instructor pilot from Seymour Johnson AFB gave the squadron a rundown on the KC-10's capabilities which included worldwide communications through a command and control center at Langley AFB. He assured us that the KC-10 would always have the latest Lajes weather. Next, the Aerial Delivery Group (ADG), which was responsible for the movement, gave each TRANSLANT pilot his own computer-generated flight log booklet and strip charts. These booklets were beautifully assembled and included divert criteria for each member of the flight. The combination of the KC-10 brief and the fuel log booklets gave me the same "it's too good to be true" feeling I get when I listen to financial planners. We felt we were in good hands. All we had to do was join up, shut up and hang on.

It was tough to get a good night's sleep with all the excitement of the next day's transoceanic flight and our alarms set for 0130, so I doubt many of the A-4 drivers felt well-rested when we met at 0300 for the weather brief. The forecast weather for Lajes was 4,000/7, and the divert fields were also good. "It looks like a go," the ADG rep said.

The first cell of A-4s, Retro 61-65, launched in the dark at 0500. They joined their assigned KC-10, Gold 11; but unfortunately, three of the A-4s had assorted problems, and the Retro 61 flight diverted into Pease AFB.

Gold 11 elected to stay airborne and pick up the second A-4 cell, Retro 71-75, which had launched just prior to daybreak at 0545. One of these A-4s went NORDO, so a section returned to Cherry Point. Now, Retro 71, a flight of three, joined with Gold 11 and proceeded to Lajes with a weather update.

Back at Cherry Point, ADG approved the addition of a sixth A-4 to the third cell, which launched as Retro 81-86 at 0715 and joined with Gold 21 as planned but without the extra on-load for the sixth A-4. All members of the Gold 21 and Retro 81 flight also continued without a weather update.

Question: What happens when one KC-10 crew and six A-4 drivers don't check the latest weather update?

Answer: The Lajes weather office starts sending out special amended weather updates forecasting the sort of weather that, if you knew about it, would convince you to divert.

Gold 11 made radio contact with Lajes ATC approximately 200 NM out. The weather was reported as 500 overcast, one mile in fog. Gold 11 detached Retro 71-73 for individual PAR [precision approach radar] approaches. Gold 11 held 20 NM south of the field while the A-4s attempted their individual approaches.

Gold 11 attempted to contact Gold 21, who was 45 minutes behind with six A-4s, to divert them to Newfoundland. Radio contact was never established. Meanwhile, the Air Wing Movement Control Officer, noting the situation, called a Marine KC-130 crew at the Lajes

BOQ and told them to prepare for an emergency launch to save the A–4s. The KC–130 crew was airborne in 40 minutes. Their biggest obstacle was finding the plane on the ramp in the fog.

Just prior to Retro 71–73's approaches, a civilian Boeing 707 executed a missed approach and reported the field zero-zero. Following the Boeing 707, Retro 71 miraculously landed during a momentary break in the weather. The fog was so thick that Retro 71 had trouble taxiing off the runway. The follow-me truck almost ran into him. After Retro 71 shut down, the ADG rep told him he was sorry, but it looked like his two wingmen were going swimming.

Retro 72 and 73 did not break out at decision height and rejoined with Gold 11 for emergency refueling. The ADG Command Center directed Gold 11 and Retro 72 and 73 to divert to Rota, Spain, and meet a strip alert KC–10 launching from Zaragoza, Spain, for refueling en route.

In the climb, Gold 11 figured his fuel and informed Retro 72 and 73 that he didn't have enough fuel to give them and make it to Rota himself. Gold 11 said he would give each A–4 1,000 pounds at a time to keep the A–4s airborne until joining with the strip alert KC–10. Gold 11 asked for the A–4's optimum cruise altitude and airspeed. This raised an interesting question. If you're 1,200 miles from your divert without enough fuel to make it halfway, and a tanker is launching to meet you, do you fly max range or max endurance? The flight elected max endurance.

Two hundred NM east of Lajes, Gold 11 was informed that there wasn't a strip alert tanker en route and that Santa Maria, located 150 NM southeast of Lajes, was the only place to land. Gold 11 with Retro 72 and 73 turned around, headed to Santa Maria, and discussed the options. Santa Maria has no TACAN or VOR, just a published VHF-ADF approach, and the weather was going down. The A–4s had no compatible NAVAIDS and could not talk with the controller because the A–4s were UHF only and the Santa Maria controllers VHF only. Gold 11 agreed to make one or two approaches with the A–4s on this wing. Retro 72 and 73 decided a section landing was appropriate considering the deteriorating weather.

Just after Gold 11 began the ADF approach, a Navy A–3 pilot who had just diverted into Santa Maria and was listening in, advised Gold 11 of an unpublished ILS approach frequency. On the approach, the flight encountered thick clouds, fog and heavy rain that almost completely obscured the KC–10. Just above decision height the KC–10 broke out with both A–4s in section on the right wing. The KC–10 executed a missed approach. The A–4s called their sides of the runway, but Retro 73 detected a heavy crosswind and also executed a missed approach. He advised Retro 72 to land alone, which he did safely.

Fortunately for Retro 73, Gold 11 had air-to-air TACAN capability that aided in the join-up once on top. The second approach ended with Retro 73 safely on deck, and Gold 11 landed safely on a third approach.

Gold 11 taxied into the line at Santa Maria and immediately started to refuel. He knew Retro 81–86 and Gold 21 were now holding over Lajes in a fuel-critical state.

When Gold 21 came within 170 NM of Lajes, he received the weather as zero-zero and passed that info to the Retro 81 flight, who at first thought Gold 21 was joking. Gold 21 and flight were also informed that Otis 75, a KC–130, was launching from Lajes to drag the six A–4s to Rota, Spain.

Retro 81 entered holding over Lajes at max endurance awaiting Otis 75. When Otis 75 broke out above the cloud deck, the six A–4s joined and began refueling. Gold 21 departed and headed for Rota with just enough fuel to make it.

The pilots of Retro 81 and 82 displayed outstanding airmanship plugging the KC–130 at 160 KIAS in a climb. The other wingmen followed suit as must-plugs. The KC–130 off-loaded its entire 30,000 pounds of give-away fuel but everything was not OK. Otis 75 didn't know about the plan to go to Rota and didn't have the fuel to do it. Fortunately, Gold 21 was still monitoring the frequency, so he turned around and rejoined. As a result, Gold 21 no longer had the fuel to make Rota.

Santa Maria ATC passed to the Gold, Otis and Retro flight that Retro 72 and 73 had landed successfully at Santa Maria, and the weather had improved to 600 overcast, 2.4 miles visibility with a 12–knot crosswind.

At this point, Retro 81 decided to split his flight for approaches into Santa Maria. Retro 83, 85 and 86 went with Otis 75, and Retro 81, 82 and 84 joined with Gold 21 to follow the Otis flight.

In the descent, Retro 85 requested two approaches into Santa Maria. Otis 75, however, said he was now fuel critical and asked that the **three A–4s** land on one approach. For the approach, Retro 83 and 86 were on Otis's left wing, and Retro 85 was on the right. During the approach, the flight encountered the same bad weather that Retro 72 and 73 had experienced. About 100 feet above decision height, the flight broke out, and the A–4 drivers called the runway environment in sight. Otis 75 went missed approach. Retro 83 and 86 were in the lead maneuvering for a section landing. Retro 83, who was leading, felt high and close after breaking out and started a rapid descent. He then realized the runway was on top of the cliff ahead, added a lot of power, flattened out and landed safely, as did his wingman.

Retro 85 had difficulty getting separation behind the section, so he 'S' turned to the left, then turned right to realign with the runway. The overshooting crosswind was not in Retro 85's favor. Despite setting down on the numbers with 20–25 degrees left wingdown, he still had a right drift and landed 15 degrees off runway heading. As a result he veered off the runway, hitting the VASI [visual approach slope indicator] lights which sheared off the right main gear. The pilot stayed with the A–4 until it came to rest on the right drop-tank and then egressed uninjured. However, Santa Maria tower called the runway closed because parts of the landing gear were scattered on the runway. Additionally, the Santa Maria weather had deteriorated to zero-zero.

Otis 75 started its slow flight back to Lajes and managed to break out on approach during a lull in the weather.

Gold 21 and Retro 81, 82 and 84 were becoming dangerously low on fuel. Gold 11, who had been on the deck at Santa Maria, saw the situation clearly: If he didn't launch quickly there would be some A-4s and possibly a KC-10 in the water. So Gold 11 stopped refueling, pulled away the ladders, left two crewmen in Base Ops, didn't pay for the gas, didn't have a clearance, didn't align his INS [inertial navigation system] and made an intersection takeoff in front of the mishap A-4 in near zero-zero weather.

Gold 11 joined and refueled Gold 21 and Retro 81, 82 and 84, saving the day (for the moment). But still, none of the aircraft had the fuel to make Rota. Fortunately, there was now a KC-10 en route from Zaragosa. It was dark by

this time, but the joinup was successful, and both of the KC-10s and the three A-4s successfully tanked. This was especially significant because the Retro 82 and 84 pilots had never refueled at night. They all made safe landings in Rota. Retro 81, 82 and 84 set a new record for the longest flight in an A-4: 10.0 hours—and in a dry suit, no less. The day ended with the A-4s in five different locations, but with everyone thrilled that no one was lost.

The Anchor Express Exercise was subsequently scrubbed for other reasons, and the A-4 crews never flew to Norway. I think the lessons learned were especially valuable at such a small cost. I expect that nine A-4 drivers, the Otis crew and the KC-10 crews will recount the story more than a few times. . . .

Capt. Coopman flew A-4Ms with VMA-223, the last FMFLANT Skyhawk squadron. He is currently attending law school at the University of Florida and flies A-4s with Marine Air Reserve Squadron VMA-142 at NAS Cecil Field.

A Day to Remember

Capt. J. D. Chase, USMC; May 1987

On March 5, 1986, my crew of seven, our KC-130, and I had been waiting at Lajes Field, the Azores, for eight days with an advance maintenance pack-up. We were waiting for A-4s from VMA-223 to arrive so we could continue our mission to Edinburgh, Scotland, thence to Bodo, Norway, to participate in exercise Anchor Express. The A-4s, originally scheduled to arrive at Lajes on Feb. 26, had been delayed by problems with the Air Force tankers and then by the weather.

The morning of the 5th, we received word from the Marine movement control officer that the A-4s with a KC-10 tanker were en route to Lajes from Pease AFB. Later that day, around 1540, my co-pilot received a call that six of the arriving A-4s needed immediate emergency tanking due to low fuel and poor weather conditions at Lajes. He immediately returned to our shared room, donned his flight gear, dispatched our navigator to gather the enlisted crew members, and went to find me at the gym. It was drizzling and the ceiling was right on the deck. It was hard enough to drive, let alone consider flying. The co-pilot and the enlisted crew went to the aircraft. My navigator and I went to base ops to get the brief.

On arrival we were informed by Marine and USAF reps that six A-4s (Retro 81-86) were due in one hour and that they would need fuel to continue on to Rota, Spain. The weather at Lajes was below minimums, intermittent 0/0, which prevented the A-4s from landing. An alternate plan was to launch a strip alert KC-135 out of Lajes

to refuel the KC-10, which would in turn refuel the A-4s. That plan was abandoned when the pilots of that aircraft declined to launch due to the weather. Remembering that sentence in OPNAV [Chief of Naval Operations Instruction] 3710 that says the pilot in command can bend or break weather mins in the event of emergency, I asked, "Is this an emergency situation?" The unanimous response of "Yes!" eased my mind concerning several factors: I was a very junior aircraft commander, I had no special instrument card, I was planning a below mins takeoff and not expecting to have to fly, neither my crew nor I had been observing crew rest requirements.

At 1618, my navigator and I made our way to the aircraft. The flight engineer had already preflighted the airplane and started all four engines. Although we could hear the engines, we couldn't see the aircraft until we were within a wingspan's distance away. We eventually made it to the runway, cautiously groping our way in the poor visibility. Six minutes later, we were airborne, a feat made possible mainly through the flight engineer's professionalism and high degree of technical skill.

Departing Lajes runway 16, with 58,000 pounds of fuel on board and passing through 3,000 feet, we made radio contact with the KC-10 (Gold 21) and Retro 81-86. Gold 21 gave an ETA [estimated time of arrival] overhead Lajes of 1640 at 41,000 feet. Continuing our climb and maintaining radio contact with Gold and Retro, we broke out of the clouds at 22,500 feet and leveled off at 23,500 feet. We gained visual contact on Gold 21 and Retro flight, and gave them vectors to us. At about 1700, they called a tally on us and maneuvered to refuel.

We were then confronted with two new problems. In order to maintain an acceptable refueling speed at that altitude and at our weight, we were forced to set military

158

power and leave it there for a period of time that would well exceed NATOPS limits. We decided the operational necessity dictated doing it. The second problem we faced was our refueling hoses indicated they were "dead" when tested. This meant that there was no indication of hydraulic response to "soften" the hose and that a receiver could possibly set up a sine wave in the hose that could easily rip off his probe. We tried to minimize this possibility by cautioning the A–4s to be smooth and by providing a stable platform from which they could refuel. The problem with the hose turned out to be just a bad test; we did have response in the hose.

At 1707, the refueling began on the Lajes 120 radial at 90 DME with each A–4 taking an initial fuel load of about 2,000 pounds. All six receivers were then cycled through the tanker again to receive a total off-load of about 5,500 pounds each.

During the refueling, Gold 11, who had landed at Santa Maria earlier with the first wave of A–4s, advised Retro flight to attempt a landing there due to slightly better weather. Gold 11, expecting the later wave to need fuel, had been refueling and launched with a partial load, and during his climb discussed with Retro 81 how to recover the A–4s at Santa Maria. The result of the discussion was a request from Retro 81 to allow three A–4s to fly my wing on the ILS runway 19 approach into Santa Maria. The other three A–4s were going to fly the identical approach on the wing of the KC–10.

This request conflicted with our original plan of continuing on to Rota single ship after the refueling was complete. Flying the approach at Santa Maria would mean we wouldn't have the fuel to continue to Rota. On the other hand, if we went to Rota, the A–4s lacked ILS and couldn't get under the weather to land, nor could they continue to Rota by themselves. We elected to stay with the A–4s.

The only other problem with this option was that we did not have the particular approach they wanted to shoot on board the airplane. The navigator started gathering information about the approach from the Portuguese controllers and the IFR Enroute Supplement. This information was then passed to Retro 83, 85 and 86, who

had been assigned to fly our wing on the approach. We weren't sure that one approach would be enough to get all three wingmen safely on deck. Though our own fuel situation was becoming a concern, we again opted to stay with the receivers and fly another approach if required.

So, with 11,000 pounds of fuel, which is getting slim for a KC–130 in this situation, we started our descent for the approach. With Retro 83 and 86 on our left wing and Retro 85 on our right wing, we tried to keep our descent very gradual and our turns very shallow. During the approach, those three pilots demonstrated an outstanding level of airmanship. After descending through 20,000 feet of solid weather and breaking out 100 feet above minimums, they were still tucked in tight. On breakout we called the field in sight, continued the approach to decision height, and then initiated a wave-off to allow the A–4s to land. Turning to a missed approach heading of 280 and beginning our climb, we confirmed with Retro 83 that he and 86 had safely rolled out. The whereabouts of 85 was unknown. We thought he had remained with us, but we were quickly informed by Santa Maria tower that the runway was closed. Retro 85 had veered off the runway and sheared off a landing strut in the process.

Contacting Retro 83 again, we asked if there was anything further we could do to assist. The reply of "I don't know," coupled with a closed runway and a deteriorating fuel situation, dictated that we proceed to Lajes to attempt a landing. With all three A–4s accounted for, we continued climbing and contacted Lajes approach control. Proceeding to Lajes, we flew the ILS runway 16 approach to 100 feet above mins. We landed uneventfully at 1906 with 8,600 pounds of fuel remaining.

Capt. Chase flies a KC–130 tanker with VMGR–253, a Marine aerial refueler transport squadron. At the time of the incident, he was assigned to VMGR–252.

Both the crew of the KC–130 (Otis 75) and the KC–10 (Gold 11) were recognized by *Aviation Week and Space Technology* magazine in their 1986 laurels tribute for outstanding airmanship. The KC–130 crew, Capt. Chase, Capt. Ramonowski, CWO2 Grigalis, M/Sgt. Hunt, S/Sgt. Ceybold, Cpl. Peeper and LCpl. Launkitis were all awarded Air Medals for their actions.

The World's Greatest Attack Pilot

When I was last published in Approach, *it was as an anonymous (thank God!) nugget explaining to the world how one goes about landing at the wrong airport. The wrong airport was Fallon Municipal. It turned out I was one of three fools who had done the same thing, though at three different places, and our written confessions with*

names changed to protect the guilty were published in one article. My skipper told the CAG that a lesser pilot than Coonts would have killed himself landing at Fallon Muni at night, but the CAG shot back that a better pilot wouldn't have landed there at all. I did get a good lesson out of it though, and I'm still alive after 2,000 hours in jets, none of which I ever bent up.

Stephen Coonts; August 1987

"Sam, what do you think of all these accidents lately?" Jake Grafton was lying on his bunk flipping through *Approach*. "We were doing real well on the accident rate, then all at once there's a rash of crashes."

Sammy Lundeen leaned back in his desk chair and dolefully regarded his roommate. "All the nonhackers are paying the price. They just don't have the 'pure, righteous stuff,' like I do."

"Cut me some slack. I'm serious."

Lundeen tilted his chair precariously and propped his feet on his desk. "OK; my humble J.O. opinion. Anyone can have an accident if he gets careless, even if just for a little while. You have to be on top of the game every minute in a cockpit. If you let down for any reason, you're asking for the shaft. It can happen to anybody, any time, any place."

"Is that the voice of experience?"

"Yeah," Sammy said defensively. "Yeah. I've made my share of mistakes and almost cashed out a time or two. I'm big enough to admit it. The first few times in the training command, it was ignorance. I just didn't know enough to realize how thin the ice was. But the scariest mistakes were afterwards, in the fleet, when I knew what to do and still got too engrossed in one task, or was too tired and spaced out to get the big picture."

"What was the worst mistake you ever made?"

Sammy shifted uncomfortably in his chair as he rubbed his jaw. "I guess the closest I ever came to the fiery pit was on a night dive-bombing run on Route One in North Vietnam, south of Vinh. We were looking for movers and couldn't find any. For once no one was shooting. When they don't shoot over the beach you get jumpy, edgy. Then we saw this little light right on the road. It looked like a stopped truck. So I figured what the hey and rolled in with four Rockeye."

"And . . . "

"I was so intent on the pipper, I didn't keep my wings level. By the time I figured that out, I was steep, which I didn't notice. Then after I pickled, I waited too long for all the Rockeyes to go. Training them off a third of a second apart, it's a lifetime from the instant you pickle until the last one goes. So when I finally looked at the altimeter, I was going through a thousand feet, 20 degrees nose down; and I still had 12 Mark 82s under the wings and 10 thousand pounds of fuel." Sammy fell silent and waggled his feet thoughtfully.

"But you managed to pull out," Jake prompted.

Lundeen sighed. "It was too late to eject. I pulled 9½ Gs, bottomed out at 50 feet on the radalt. Thought I was dead then and there and had killed my bombardier." He examined the soles of his shoes. One of them had a hole in it. "Man, I shook for days after that one."

"What went wrong?"

"A combination of things. I didn't set the radar altimeter to my pickle altitude to give me a warning. Then I was jumpy waiting for the guns to open up and didn't concentrate on flying a good run."

"So after an experience like that, how come you're always telling people you're the world's greatest attack pilot?"

Sammy's eyebrows rose toward his hairline. "Because I am! You see, after I about made a spectacular 12 o'clock hit, I decided that accidents could happen to anyone who gets complacent, and I mean anyone. Even me. So I stay in shape, get all the rest I can, and when I get into that cockpit, I work like hell until I get out. I don't take anything for granted."

"The grind can be real tough though," Jake admitted. "Especially when it's your second or third flight of the day."

Lundeen nodded. "Other guys might be better sticks than me, they may occasionally get better hits, and they may even have more talent; but no one works as hard as I do at flying. No one works as hard at mastering his art. So I'm going to be there dropping those bombs until the bad guys get me or my plane comes unglued. But I am not going to kill myself!" He flipped his hand. "That's why I'm the world's greatest. I work harder, every flight, every day."

"That reporter, Rucic? He told me a few days ago that the guys who are going to get ahead in naval aviation are the Mister Peepers, guys with zero aggressiveness who fly like they were driving Air Force One."

"The planes cost too much to let hot dogs crack 'em up," Lundeen grunted. "But I still think you can fly aggressively and not have accidents. The secret is to approach every flight, even the most routine, as if it's your solo check ride in basic. Don't let complacency sneak up on you. 'It' may only come out of the sewers every 28 years, but if 'it' latches onto you, you're going to lose a chunk of hide."

"You should have told Coonts about your dive bomb adventure. Maybe he'd have put it in that book about us."

Sammy levered himself out of his chair and headed for the door. "Yeah, like that little scene on the beach with you and Callie. I wonder who told him about that." He chuckled and darted through the door as Jake groped for a flight boot to throw.

Mr. Coonts served as an A–6A pilot in Vietnam in 1971–3, flying from the USS *Enterprise* (CVN 65). He is the author of the best-selling novel *Flight of the Intruder* (U.S. Naval Institute, 1986) which deals with an A–6 pilot in Vietnam.